Big and Little Poison

ALSO BY CLIFTON BLUE PARKER

Fouled Away: The Baseball Tragedy of Hack Wilson (McFarland, 2000)

Big and Little Poison
Paul and Lloyd Waner, Baseball Brothers

CLIFTON BLUE PARKER

McFarland & Company, Inc., Publishers
Jefferson, North Carolina, and London

Library of Congress Cataloguing-in-Publication Data

Parker, Clifton Blue, 1963–
    Big and little poison : Paul and Lloyd Waner, baseball brothers / Clifton Blue Parker.
        p.   cm.
    Includes bibliographical references and index.

    ISBN-13: 978-0-7864-1400-0
    softcover : 50# alkaline paper) ∞

    1. Baseball players—United States—Biography. I. Title: Paul and Lloyd Waner, baseball brothers. II. Waner, Paul. III. Waner, Loyd. IV. Title.
GV865.A1 P37   2003
796.357'092'2—dc21   2002014638

British Library cataloguing data are available

©2003 Clifton Blue Parker. All rights reserved

No part of this book may be reproduced or transmitted in any form or by any means, electronic or mechanical, including photocopying or recording, or by any information storage and retrieval system, without permission in writing from the publisher.

Cover illustration by Mike Benny. Design by Seraphein Beyn, Inc.

Manufactured in the United States of America

McFarland & Company, Inc., Publishers
  Box 611, Jefferson, North Carolina 28640
    www.mcfarlandpub.com

To Rhiannon,
daughter of the diamond

Acknowledgments

I'd like to thank the following people who helped me with this book and my baseball efforts: Susan Stodden, Kevin Ferenchik, Bill Enfield, Donald Honig, Lawrence S. Ritter, Peter Beagle, Bill Iliff, Greg King, Bill Deane, Steven Gietschier, Royse "Crash" Parr, Bob Beyn, the Pittsburgh Pirates, Lloyd Waner, Jr., Lillian Porter, Beth Noe, Corinne Waner, and the late Tony Salin.

A special thank you is extended to Bob Beyn of Seraphein Beyn Advertising in Sacramento and illustrator Mike Benny who generously donated the magnificent art for this book's front cover, and Jim Knight, who provided wonderful photos of his kin, Paul and Loyd Waner.

Finally, I am forever grateful to my wife, Laura, for welcoming all the baseball that fills the house in one way or another, and for bringing to me the special kind of understanding that reflects true love. To her, and my daughter, Rhiannon, an up-and-coming baseball fan, and our gentle-hearted Cody, a faithful pal, I give all my love, always.

Contents

Acknowledgments vii
Introduction 1

1	Corncob Balls and Branch Bats	7
2	Go West, Young Seal	23
3	Smoky City Blues	37
4	Roaring Baseball	42
5	Big and Little Poison	65
6	Appalachian Stomp	84
7	Rough Seas for the Pirate Ship	103
8	The Cruel Business	113
9	The Exploding Universe	127
10	The Return of the Dead Ball	136
11	Pennant Hopes and Misadventures	145
12	The Curiosity of the League	154
13	Celebrating the Common Man	161
14	The Bambino's Last Hurrah	168
15	Hoisting the Black Flag	180
16	The Last Great One	185
17	Shadow Ball and the Gloamin'	193

18	Requiem for a Lost Season	207
19	Go Gently Into the Night	216
20	Farewell Steel City	227
21	A Hallowed Hitsmith	237
22	Wearying War Years	247
23	End of Encores	257
24	The Professor of Batting	264
25	Little Poison Goes Home	284
26	Without My Spikes	294
27	From Corncobs to Cooperstown	300

Appendix: Career Statistics — 313
Sources — 315
Index — 323

Introduction

Years ago I used to walk past where Paul and Lloyd Waner had played together for so many years in the same Pittsburgh Pirate outfield. Back in the late 1980s, I was attending graduate school at the University of Pittsburgh, and though Forbes Field had long since been demolished, it lingered around like some faint ghost. As if a tribute to some ancient race, the home plate of Forbes Field is gently encased in a sidewalk on campus. Many feet scuffled over the plate without ever noticing it, but I took solace in its presence on the way to my classes in the sprawling postmodern building now sitting on the old Forbes Field site. Off in the distance an ivy-covered portion of the park's famous right field wall remains as another shrine of sorts. Taking a break from class on a sunny afternoon I could almost smell the wafting cigar smoke, hear the cry of the hot dog vendors, the chatter of thousands of fans, and the bark of the umpire, "Batter up," and suddenly a whole new baseball universe would rise up out of the earth.

One could almost see Paul and Lloyd Waner leap from the top steps of the dugout and race like a pair of jackrabbits onto the field, their small horse-leather gloves swinging from their hands.

Their blue eyes are cat-like, their bodies firm and flowing with energy. It is the kind of energy you feel after a night of Midwestern thunderstorms, when suddenly in the morning you hear the shrieks of kids playing stickball outside in the wheat field, and it is a new game, a new day, something to rush out and embrace like mad.

Moving swiftly toward the emerald grass in the outfield, the players look almost identical. One is a little broader in the shoulders, maybe taller, and his smooth face is drawn a bit more tight and fierce. In the outfield, they stoop forward, one grabs some grass and tosses it in the wind to check direction, and they both rest their hands on their knees, ready to glide after their quarry.

◆ ◆ ◆

Growing up in Pittsburgh during the 1970s I had heard about brothers Paul and Lloyd Waner. By their very nicknames, the diminutive Waners conjured up a certain mystique—"Big Poison" and "Little Poison." Arsenic for pitchers. Toxin to fly balls. They sounded exotic and seemed from a faraway time and space.

The Waners were more than just a clever dualistic nickname. And this is more than just a biography of them.

It is the story of two eras—the Roaring Twenties and the Dirty Thirties. It is about America and Pittsburgh in the boisterous, high-living Twenties and the dark days of the Depression. It is about the challenges faced by ballplayers in the best and worst of times in this country's love affair with the game. Strangely, the popularity of baseball did not decline as the economy faltered. People may not have been able to afford to go to the park as often, but they followed the game closely in the newspapers and with that new phenomenon, radio.

Paul and Lloyd Waner created baseball lives for themselves against the odds that typically confront physical underdogs. They understood the American work ethic. As players they worked harder and hustled more than everyone else; they put the team above their own statistics; and they were good listeners to friends and teammates in the clubhouse. Then, baseball held a special place in the hearts of the Depression-era America that the Waners knew, for, in spite of the poverty brought on by the national financial collapse, people still believed in the American Dream. They believed it was possible for the farm boys in Oklahoma to grow up to be president or to play major league baseball. Baseball was one of the few shining stars left in the Depression sky. It was a beacon of hope for an impoverished nation.

The Waners remind us that baseball rewards brains as well as brawn. Even in our ESPN-homer-highlights day and age, the game—on the field— respects precision just as much as power and recognizes speed as it does slugging. Today we see this kind of approach in Ichiro Suzuki of the Seattle Mariners. It is exciting and explosive baseball that puts thinking over thump, and winning teams are built upon it.

The Waners are proof that baseball, unlike the other major sports, is a democracy of talent not physique. Though short in stature, they stand tall on a mountain of hits. More than half a century after retiring, Paul and Lloyd Waner still rank as the greatest-hitting brother duo in major league history with 5,611 hits—517 more than the three Alou brothers, 758 more than the three DiMaggio brothers, and 1,400 more than the five Delahanty brothers. And both Waners are in the Hall of Fame—the only playing brothers so honored.

Almost seemingly joined at the hip, the Waners pop up in baseball stories throughout the 1920s and 1930s, and yet they remain elusive somehow. They played in Pittsburgh for clubs seldom chasing the pennant, far from the limelight of New York and the glory of baseball in that city during the 1920s and 1930s.

The Paul and Lloyd Waner story has a fairy tale quality. They began as turn-of-the-century Oklahoma farm boys with 400 acres of wheat and alfalfa and plenty of room to play ball. Games were played under sparkling blue skies and in glorious sweet-smelling daylight. The boys made equipment out of anything that came to hand—corncobs, rocks and tree limbs. Life on the farm demanded resourcefulness.

That kind of thriftiness reflected the brassy, bare-knuckled America of yesteryear. Coming out of the heartland to industrialized Pittsburgh, the Waners displayed a steely confidence and agrarian-bred decency. From the beginning, they were taught to believe in themselves and respect the game, no matter how small or light they were, no matter what the scouts said, no matter what the bench jockeys chirped. These boys had grit and gumption.

Beyond their hits—and the hits kept coming and coming—the Waners enjoyed one of the rarest opportunities in the history of the game. They played together for 14 seasons in the same Pittsburgh outfield, a duration unmatched in the history of baseball and a poignant reminder of the game's former continuity before free agency. Imagine having your brother at your side while facing the Darwinian grind of baseball—a utilitarian-minded sport favoring the strong and despising the weak. It must have added a sense of solidarity to a game of boyhood dreams.

The Waners' pride in each other defied the norm. Most siblings at one time or another need space from each other. Yet so synonymous were the Waners it seemed their souls could hardly squeeze an inch closer together. When Lloyd was elected to the Hall of Fame in 1967, he broke down and cried, wishing he could have shared the event with his brother Paul. After all, they had each other through almost all of their ups and downs.

They climbed a long way to the summit together. The way baseball works today, Paul and Lloyd might never have gotten a chance to play in the majors. The game has little room for 5-foot 6-inch, 150-pound hitters, even for a guy like Lloyd who once ran 100 yards in 10 seconds flat in his school shoes using a small hole in the earth as a starting block. When Lloyd came to the majors, he weighed 132 pounds. One might think the Waners looked more like horse jockeys than baseball players.

Paul is among the game's elite players with his 3,152 hits, and his .333 lifetime average ranks among the highest ever in the game. Gazelle-like Lloyd was an exceptional center fielder and lead-off hitter, and the second hardest guy in major league history to strike out. Lloyd, a lifetime .316 hitter, collected his share of hits—2,459. Had it not been for health problems, Lloyd might have cleared the 3,000-hit milestone as well. The Waners were not interested in walks or on-base average—alien concepts back then. They slashed away for all the hits they could.

The unpretentious and candid Paul Waner was one of baseball's most colorful figures in the 1920s and 1930s. Once he refused to accept an error-tainted 3,000th hit and waited for his next try—because he wanted to get the hit clean and straight.

Paul was as confident as anyone in the game, but that confidence emanated from a sincere belief in his ability honed on the Oklahoma prairie. Away from the diamond, Big Poison was a fun-loving Rabelaisian character who drank hard at night and played ball just as hard the next day. A writer once noted that Paul "hit doubles and triples during games and drank them after."

Little Poison defended Paul's free-spirited approach. "Paul thought you played better when you were relaxed, and drinking was a good way to relax," Lloyd said. During their careers, Paul was portrayed as the heavy drinker and Lloyd as a teetotaler. Fact was, Lloyd drank, too, just not as much and more quietly.

Indeed, Lloyd was the self-sacrificing sort to all those around him. While Paul was always considered a class act, ballplayers speak reverently of the gentlemanly and kind nature of Lloyd Waner—like a singles-hitting Lou Gehrig. The respect extended beyond Lloyd's character to the hustling way he played the game. For the Waners, playing the game was a family event, and you don't let down family.

◆ ◆ ◆

Brothers in baseball are as old as the game itself. When Harry Wright, the son of a famous English cricket player and one of baseball's earliest converts, formed the first professional team shortly after the Civil War, the first player he recruited was his brother George, a shortstop.

That team, the 1869 Cincinnati Red Stockings, toured the country and won 56 games without a loss. When the National Association was formed in 1871, the Wright brothers came to Boston, where Harry, who also played outfield, managed his team to four pennants in five years. A third brother, Sam, was playing when the Boston Red Caps became a charter member of the new National League. Harry and George Wright are both in baseball's Hall of Fame.

Baseball took place in a different world back then. Look at the hard-lined faces of players in Donald Honig's *Shadows of Summer: Classic Baseball Photographs, 1869–1947*. The young players shown on those pages look more like middle-aged cowboys, mill workers, and farmers than they do ballplayers. Their faces are creased and wrinkled from thousands of hours squinting in the sun on hundreds of ball fields. Some are missing teeth, and some have scars. Compare these weathered mugs with the smooth, well-fed ones of today's professional athletes.

The game's early players did not have the benefit of night ball, air conditioning, batting gloves, elbow guards, batting helmets, agents, nutritionists, or pension plans. Despite the glamour attached to being a big leaguer, most players never saw big money and never really expected to. Many of them had grown up the hard way in farm country or in mill towns. They considered themselves lucky to have a job playing baseball. While they might complain about cheap owners, they knew that many guys had it far worse back on the farm, factory, or in the bread lines of the Great Depression.

Lloyd Waner once admitted the "miracle" of opportunity that baseball had given him. He and his brother could have been eking out their survival back in dust bowl country if it had not been for baseball.

But these underdogs never gave up.

Corncob Balls and Branch Bats

Oklahoma's influence on baseball in America is phenomenal. One of every ten of the 14,000 men who have played major league baseball since 1876 have come through Oklahoma. Some of the names are legendary, Mickey Mantle, Warren Spahn, Carl Hubbell, Lloyd and Paul Waner, and Dizzy and Daffy Dean. Others are more obscure such as Cat Clanton of Antlers who struck out in his only major league at bat. Oklahoma and baseball are inseparable. The players and their stories are woven permanently into the fabric of American life.
— *Parr et al. from* Glory Days of Summer

French historian Jacques Barzun uttered a great many profound things about baseball. One of his more obscure observations was that America's national pastime reflected the Greek spirit of heroism and nationalism, and that the game was broken up into the rivalry of city–states at a time when baseball fever raged.

If this is true, then the state of Oklahoma may have thought of itself as the Athens of baseball around the turn of the century. Players blossomed there like wild hyacinth on the prairies, and even the smallest towns had fiercely competitive baseball clubs. With the nearest major league club 300 miles away in St. Louis, Oklahoma spawned a baseball frenzy from high schools to the minor leagues. Beyond oil, Oklahoma would gush players such as Dizzy Dean, Carl Hubbell, Pepper Martin, Allie Reynolds, Wilcy Moore, Harlond Clift, Marty McManus, and the Johnson brothers,

Bob and Roy. A few decades later, Oklahoma yielded stout native sons in Johnny Bench, Mickey Mantle, and Willie Stargell, all of whom would find their way to immortality in Cooperstown.

In the midst of this Oklahoma baseball universe, Paul and Lloyd Waner were born in a turn-of-the-century farmhouse outside Harrah, Oklahoma. Their upbringing was rustic and simple, the kind of Horatio Alger farmboy narrative that baseball mythologizes. Looking at them, few would have dared bet they would wind up in the Hall of Fame in Cooperstown. They didn't have the muscle of Mantle or Stargell nor the crazy charm of Dizzy Dean or Pepper Martin.

What the Waners did have was a penchant for hits—lots of them. They totaled more hits than any other brother set in baseball.

There was more to their game. They were fast and smart ballplayers, and were supreme defenders in the field. The Waners played the game with purpose and pride and were always honored to have each other on the diamond, from the summer days of childhood to the trials and tribulations of adulthood.

◆ ◆ ◆

As the crow flies, Harrah is about half an hour east of Oklahoma City. There rushing streams and wooded rolling hills make for good farming in the warmer months and plenty of hunting all year round. The bumpy, sprawling land includes an irregular chain of knobs or buttes, entering Oklahoma from Missouri and Arkansas on the east, extending through the southern part of the state to the western boundary, and connecting the Ozark range with the eastern plateau of the Rocky Mountains.

Beyond here, the Great Plains stretch in all their emptiness, the endless horizons broken only by small farm towns. In the 1870s, the wide open range of the prairies, sometimes known as the Great American Desert, inspired General George Custer to call it "the fairest and richest portion of the national domain."

Prior to 1800, the land around what would become Harrah was Osage Indian territory. In the 1820s, the five tribes from the southeastern United States were relocated to Indian Territory over numerous routes, the most famous being the Cherokee "Trail of Tears." Forced off their ancestral lands by state and federal governments, the tribes suffered great hardships during the rigorous trips west. The name "Oklahoma" comes from the Choctaw words "okla" meaning people and "humma" for red, which means "red people." Today, Oklahoma has the largest American Indian population of any state.

1. Corncob Balls and Branch Bats

In 1889, the U.S. bought two million acres of Oklahoma territory from the Indians and threw it open to settlement. The day previous to the opening more than 10,000 people were just over the borders. When the guns sounded, people on foot, horseback, in trains, wagons, and carriages entered the promised land. Oklahoma was the proverbial land of opportunity.

Another land rush in 1891 opened Harrah for development, and thereafter business expansion was rapid. Harrah built a cotton gin, lumber yard, and hardware store. Several other businesses followed quickly. The "New Town on the Canadian River" was advertised as far away as St. Louis. Special excursion trips for immigrants were arranged. Farms, residential lots, business property, and mercantile lines were offered for sale. Public auctions were held in Oklahoma City to encourage people to come to Harrah.

One of those newcomers was Ora or "Oates" Lee Waner. Born in 1876 in Huntsville, Illinois, Ora Waner came to Oklahoma and would marry the proverbial "girl next door," Etta Beavers. She had been born in Iowa. Both the Beaver and Waner clans had come to Oklahoma in the 1889 Land Rush and had staked claims not far apart from each other near Harrah. Both were from Methodist families that had emigrated from Germany to America. The Waners have also been described as "Pennsylvania Dutch," which refers to the descendants of German and Swiss immigrants who settled in Pennsylvania in the seventeenth and eighteenth centuries.

Like his father, Ora was a hard-working farmer. As a young man, he toiled as a day laborer, taking odd jobs around neighboring farms for, as he later put it, "grocery money." He worked so much he got paid sometimes in acreage in the land-rich, cash-poor state. He ended up with 400 acres of land about two miles outside of Harrah. By the time Oklahoma had become a state in 1907, Ora Waner had built a prosperous enterprise from scratching the earth and seeding it.

Farm work, however, did not keep Ora Waner from indulging in baseball, which in those years captured the public's imagination as the country's first truly organized spectator sport. Ora loved the game with its fast, exciting and dramatic action and would one day teach his sons and daughters all about it. Those days would come soon enough.

On April 16, 1903, Etta Waner gave birth to a boy in the Waners' two-story farmhouse. He was named Paul Glee Waner. No one has ever ascertained why they chose the middle name Glee, though later in life it became a running joke in light of Paul's footloose ways. Two years and eleven months later brother Lloyd joined him. The family would have five children—an older brother Ralph; two sisters, Alma and Ruth; and Paul and Lloyd.

In October that same year, the Boston Pilgrims and their great pitcher Cy Young defeated the Pittsburgh Pirates in the first-ever World Series. A new baseball league, the Pacific Coast League, took shape on the West Coast in 1903. Located in six cities from Seattle to Los Angeles, the league almost vanished when an earthquake and fire devastated San Francisco in 1906.

Beyond baseball, this was an age of innovation. The Wright brothers—another famous pair of siblings—made history with the first powered flight in Kitty Hawk, North Carolina. And the U.S. Congress approved an ambitious plan to build the Panama Canal in Latin America.

This was also an age of confidence—human potential reflected itself in the splendor of sport where body and mind conquered nature. At the turn of the century, Oklahoma put itself on the sporting map with one of its native sons, Jim Thorpe. A multi-talented football player, baseball player and track star, Thorpe was just starting a career that in five years would win him the acclaim as the greatest athlete since Hercules. He set the standard for a state that has bred top athletes like rabbits in its vast, wide spaces.

Much of Oklahoma is uninterrupted by towns or roads, and the towns are far apart on the plains and ranges. Oklahoma has always been a sparsely populated state. When the Waners started having their children, Harrah was a town of about 500 people. And it was an outdoor playground for two young brothers.

◆ ◆ ◆

In their twilight years, the Waners reflected on their upbringing with Lawrence Ritter in the *The Glory of Their Times* and Donald Honig in *The October Heroes*.

Paul Waner: *"I come from a little town right outside of Oklahoma City, a town by the name of Harrah. I went to State Teachers' College at Ada for three years, although I didn't really intend to be a teacher. Maybe for a little while, but not forever. What I wanted to be was a lawyer, and I figured sooner or later I'd go to law school. Eventually I was going to go to Harvard Law School, I reckon. That was my ambition, anyway."*

From the start, it helped to have a brother to pitch to and throw against.

Lloyd Waner: *"Well, the way I look at it, Paul and me had an advantage over most kids. There was only two years and eleven months difference in our ages, so we never lacked for somebody to play with."*

1. Corncob Balls and Branch Bats

The Waner family portrait. From the left: brother Paul, sister Alma, father Ora, brother Lloyd, mother Etta, sister Ruth, and brother Ralph (courtesy of Jim Knight).

Ora Waner understood the value of practice. One played the game not just for fun, but to be good at it, too.

Lloyd Waner: *"My dad had been a professional ball player himself you know, in Oklahoma City, when they first had the Western League. This was back in 1898. To get to the games he would ride his horse to Oklahoma City, leave it in the livery stable and then join the team.... He was a pretty good player, Dad was. As a matter of fact, at one time Cap Anson made him an offer to join the White Sox, but he didn't want to leave the farm.... He was a pitcher, and when he wasn't pitching, they would put him in the outfield."*

Ora Waner was a star pitcher for the Oklahoma City town team in the late 1800s. According to a 1927 *New York Times* story, Ora Waner turned down manager Cap Anson's offer to play for the Chicago White Sox. Instead, he bought his farm land and tended to his acreage and family. Why, he thought, he could play baseball in Oklahoma just as easily as he could back East.

Paul and Lloyd grew up in this house near Harrah, Oklahoma. Though some sportswriters portrayed the Waners as hillbilly "Okies," they were a prosperous family that owned hundreds of acres of farm land (courtesy of Jim Knight).

Ora and others in the family organized a Waner Nine baseball team—the "Keen Kutters"—in 1908. All the players were members of the Waner or Beaver families. Paul was six and Lloyd was four when they began to play. After the games Ora would give the baseball to his young sons.

One of the greatest images associated with the Waners is how they learned to hit against corn cobs. Imagination knows no limits on the plains of Oklahoma. At his Hall of Fame induction in 1967, Lloyd recalled that his father once carved a bat from a two-by-four, and the brothers hit with it for years. Other times they'd make a bat out of a tree limb, whittling it down to smooth perfection and allowing it to harden.

Lloyd Waner: *"Sometimes we'd cut saplings down in the woods and try to get a ball bat out of 'em, but they'd warp on you. We didn't have a real bat."*

Such images, corn cobs and branch-made bats, later fueled the popular misconception of the Waners as "barefoot Okies" and "dirt poor." They were neither, and in later years both of them resented this stereotype

1. Corncob Balls and Branch Bats

fostered mainly by Eastern sportswriters who understood little about the Midwest. Exasperated, they once had to defend their indoor plumbing conditions. Paul especially displayed a fierce pride about his origins. The country was a good place to grow up in, he noted.

Paul Waner: "My father was a man of breeding. We lived in the best house in our locality. We Waner children never knew anything but sanitary indoor plumbing, we always had plenty of good, wholesome food and if we went barefooted in the summer, it was because other Oklahoma kids also did that, not because there was any shortage of shoes in the Waner household. We ate well, and I was only a bit of a kid when I had my own horse and gun. There is no pauperism in my background, and I never went to bed hungry in my life. My father was a well-to-do prosperous farmer."

Drinking was a sign of manhood in those times, and it came early in a world of hard-drinking Plains men. "I never took a drink until I was eight," Paul wryly admitted. Growing up on the farm also introduced both brothers to chewing tobacco and pipe smoking.

Paul Waner: "I started smoking when I was just so high [pointing to two feet off the ground]. First, it was corn silk, next a corncob pipe, and after that, cigarettes. I grew up in Oklahoma, which was legally a dry state until recently. But us kids around Harrah and Ada knew early on where to get a jug of liquor."

They could always find a baseball game going on in those parts. Their older brother Ralph was a solid player, if not as gifted as Paul and Lloyd were. The Waner brothers graciously accorded their sister Alma as having the best power stroke in the family. Alma was the first to hit a corn cob far enough to break a barn window. "Our sister Alma was the best hitter in the family," Lloyd said.

Paul and Lloyd, though, seemed to have a special touch. Their father recalled stumbling upon this revelation of talent.

Ora Waner: "Well, I heard the two kids playing around the side of the barn and I took a peek, and I sure was amazed. There was Lloyd throwing corncobs at Paul and Paul was smacking those corncobs and sending them out on a line. He never missed one and he was using a hoe handle for a bat. Then came Lloyd's turn, and Paul would pitch to him. Same thing all over. Now I was considered a mighty good hitter myself, but when I saw those kids cracking away at corncobs I knew I was never in their class."

It was harder to hit corncobs than baseballs. Maybe this difficulty produced results.

The barn behind the Waner home in Harrah, Oklahoma (courtesy of Jim Knight).

Paul Waner: *"Those corncobs were hard to hit. Once you get so you can sock a corncob squarely—the way it comes flopping end over end at you—why a big round baseball, the same shape on all sides, is a cinch to hit."*

Lloyd said his father grew the corn for livestock, not to sell it. "The corn was ground, and we'd play with the cobs. We'd break a cob in half, soak it in water to make it harder, then take turns pitching at each other. We'd use a hoe or broom handle for a bat, and sometimes make one out of a two-by-four. I'd pitch until Paul missed, then we'd change sides. We'd scatter corn cobs all over the yard, and Dad would come and make us pick them all up."

Ora knew that speed counted in baseball as much as anything. The father used to set up footraces between his boys. Instructing them to run on their toes so as not to run flat-footed, he'd measure off a hundred yards or so, and then turn them loose. For a long while, Paul would beat Lloyd by a step or so. Then, after a while, Lloyd started beating his older brother by a step or two over a hundred yards.

Paul and Lloyd also developed their leg muscles walking nearly three miles from their farm to a one-room schoolhouse in the Dewey District. There Paul must have looked somewhat scholarly as he sometimes wore glasses when reading and doing homework. Paul probably could have

1. Corncob Balls and Branch Bats   15

picked up a baseball in a coal mine at night. But he needed help reading. When 14 and in the swing of teenhood, Paul abruptly ended wearing glasses. He stuffed his glasses in his back pocket while playing ice hockey on a lake where they were using a tin can for a goal and sticks for hockey sticks. Not surprisingly, Paul fell on his rear and broke the glasses. At least that must have been what he told his mother. After that, he did not use glasses again while playing any sport until age 37. He did use them for reading throughout his life.

Near the Waner farm was a river where the brothers went trout fishing. Other times they'd hunt possum. Their parents made sure the boys learned their lessons. In school, Lloyd even learned to play the violin—"I could carry a tune somewhat"—and Paul practiced the saxophone. While they did not receive formal instruction, they enjoyed the instruments well into adulthood.

There wasn't much time for musical lessons, as the farm chores were a relentless grind. Ora had 20 cows and would often have his children milk them. Years later Lloyd would say that the milking and other farm chores helped to strengthen their hands, thus making them better hitters.

As Paul and Lloyd grew older, they always seemed to be outside playing some kind of pick-up game with whomever they could find, if only themselves. There were few distractions from dawn until dusk when you live miles away from the closest town, a small one at that.

From their father the boys learned about the details of the game, whether it was making a bat, honing their swings or increasing their bat speed.

Paul Waner: *"I was about seven years old when my father, who was a pretty good ballplayer, although he never played professionally, ... cut himself a green hickory limb in the fall and left it back by the woodshed to season during the winter so he could make a bat for himself in the spring. By the time it was dried out and he made a bat of it, it was awfully heavy, especially for me. So when my father began to pitch to me from in close, I could hardly swing it. I was holding it out here, and a couple of times I nearly fell down. Then I just dropped the bat on my shoulder and when he pitched, I came off my shoulder with it, and was able to meet the ball."*

When a child first enters the adult world of ballplaying, embarrassing things can happen. Years later Lloyd recalled such an episode.

Lloyd Waner: *"Dad managed a local team for a while, and one day he put me into the game as a pinch hitter. I will never forget it. I was just 12 years* *old at the time and here I was getting into a game with grown men. I was so small at the time that the other team thought Dad had put me in to try and work out a bases on balls.*

"But I hit at the first pitch I saw and poked it over the third baseman's head down the left-field line. We were playing in a cow pasture and the ball rolled into some weeds and got lost. I started running, so excited I was shaking. When I got to third base, they were still out in the weeds looking for the ball. I stood there and didn't know what to do. Gee, I thought, the ball is lost. So I ran out there to help them look for it, too excited to hear my Dad yelling at me to come on across the plate. Well, they finally found the ball and whoever picked it up took one look at me, and tagged me out. Dad never let me forget that one."

The Waner boys seemed blessed with great bat control and running ability. As they grew older, the father was surprised that he could hardly ever throw a ball past them. Their left-handed swings were sweetly precise. Paul was left-handed in both batting and throwing. Lloyd threw right-handed and batted from the left side.

Paul had a good arm from the beginning. He started out as a left-handed catcher in grade school. As left-handed catchers face a non-existent future—right-handed batters presumably affect their throws down to second base—Paul got switched to pitcher. When he wasn't hurling, he played first base and the outfield.

In addition to baseball, Lloyd and Paul excelled in track in their high school career in Harrah. Lloyd even played football as a wide receiver—until his father forbade him to continue because of the risk of injury. Future Hall of Famer Carl Hubbell lived about 20 minutes away from the Waners and attended a rival high school in Meeker. Hubbell remembered that Lloyd's nickname back then was "Scratch" for the way he scratched hits out of any ground ball.

Carl Hubbell: *"Oh, my, he was a handful. 'Scratch,' I played against him in high school when I was at Meeker and he was at Harrah and I couldn't get him out then. He'd hit a high hopper back to the mound and beat it out. It was the damnedest thing I ever saw."*

After high school, Paul and Lloyd both attended East Central State Teachers' College in Ada, Oklahoma. Lloyd played ball for the Ada Independents and other town teams and for one year at East Central Teachers' College in Ada.

Paul's performance at Ada raised eyebrows. In 1922, he was 24–3 with 278 strikeouts and only 29 walks and a 1.70 ERA. In one 19-inning game,

1. Corncob Balls and Branch Bats

he struck out 36 hitters, with 29 of those being successive strikeouts. Other reports, perhaps more dubious, claim Paul won 40 out of the 43 games in one season at Ada.

With scouts taking interest in Paul Waner, an offer to play pro ball seemed imminent. One scout, identified as J. A. Hamilton, eventually signed him for the Joplin club in the Western League. Unlike the cool high-tech operations of today, professional scouting in the 1920s was cruder and more intuitive. Then, the life of a baseball scout was a sweltering odyssey through anonymous small towns with cockroaches, stomach-grinding foods, and humid hotel rooms. Driving an old automobile through countless miles of godforsaken back roads, a scout came upon hordes of young players and all he could do was live on his hopes and hunches one of them would pan out.

The Waner brothers often joked that sister Alma, shown here, was actually the best hitter in the family (courtesy of Jim Knight).

Indeed, Hamilton had a hunch this kid Paul Waner could turn out to be quite the player.

"Scouts don't scout in order to get rich," Kevin Kerrane wrote in the book, *Dollar Sign on the Muscle*. "They scout because they know baseball—from direct experience, not tests—and because they're opinionated men."

Hamilton's high opinion of Paul Waner was never tested at Joplin. The youngster did not get into one game with the club. Pressed by his parents to finish school, he did not report to the team and eventually was traded to Muskogee in the Southwestern League—where he didn't report either. He was just a player "on paper" for these clubs.

In a March 1927 letter to a friend identified simply as "Ernie," Hamilton recalled the details of Paul's first foray into the world of professional baseball.

J. A. Hamilton: "Yes, Ernie, I was the first guy to sign Paul Waner. Here is the story. In 1921 I was the manager of Joplin, Missouri [Class A

Western League]. On our last road trip, we registered in Oklahoma City. Some fellow—don't know his name or anything about him—approached me in the Colby Hotel and asked me if I wanted a young ballplayer. I naturally said, 'yes,' and in two hours he had Paul with me at the ball park. He worked out three days with us. He did not play as he was going to school and wanted to finish before playing any pro ball. I signed Paul for 1922 to Joplin. I left Joplin for Charleston, South Carolina, and lost all contact with Paul, until he was sold by San Francisco to Pittsburgh for lots of money."

Though he had signed a contract, Paul had the self-assurance to walk away from it and look for a better deal. He learned a lesson about keeping away from contracts with teams he didn't intend on playing for. It could have turned out much worse if all the legal machinery had kicked into gear.

Paul sensed opportunity beyond Joplin, Missouri.

In the early 1920s America was bursting with opportunity as the country abandoned its sleepy, rural origins and became an urban-based, free-spirited society. The end of the First World War and its senseless horrors marked a new era in self-actualization and a shift away from agrarian America. For the first time, more people were living in industrialized cities than in rural areas. Jobs in the big cities were plentiful, and the immigrant influx from Europe filled many of those low-paying jobs. Meanwhile, the rise of radio, motion pictures and the automobile were to become national rages during the coming decade, giving people more entertainment options and increased mobility—and a wide variety of distractions and temptations as well.

As the decade of the 1920s took its hold on the American imagination, oil gushers in Oklahoma brought a boom to the state. Tulsa is still proud of its roughneck heritage, and wanderers today in the downtown area will see the Golden Driller, a 76-foot-high bare-chested, hard-hatted oil man with one arm resting on a giant derrick.

Oklahoma's first entries into organized baseball came in 1904—three years before statehood. Ardmore fielded a team in the Texas League, and Guthrie, Oklahoma City, Enid, Shawnee and Chickasha were in the Southwestern League. In the Waners' time, the Oklahoma State League was the most popular, operating from 1908 through 1936, with 20 teams from different towns.

Baseball in Oklahoma goes back a long way, migrating westward from the East Coast in the 1850s.

Mark Twain once wrote of this connection between baseball and adolescent America: "Baseball is the very symbol, the outward and visible expression of the drive and push and rush and struggle of the raging, tearing, booming 19th century."

When New York's version of "town ball" arrived in Oklahoma, the Native American tribes in the eastern side of the state already had their own game—"stick ball." The Indians played the white man's game on the dusty parade grounds of Fort Gibson, Fort Davis, and Fort Towson. When the Apache warrior Geronimo and his band were finally caught and held as prisoners of war at Fort Sill in Oklahoma, they reportedly played a baseball game against soldiers.

Far from the factories of the Northeast and Chicago, baseball in the frontier days required some ingenuity. Traders sold balls made from calfskin-covered cork and yarn, and homesteaders settled for balls made from women's stockings and wrapping string. For bats, they sometimes used wagon tongues or the handles from rakes and pitchforks.

In the early 1880s, settlers from Illinois, Ohio and Pennsylvania flocked to the coal deposits near Krebs in the Indian territory. They brought with them a competitive spirit and passion for baseball. Krebs' star pitcher, Joe "Iron Man" McGinnity (originally spelled "McGinty")—a settler from Illinois like Ora Waner—has been credited as the "father of baseball in Oklahoma." During the week McGinnity was a muleskinner in the coal mines and on weekends played baseball, managed three Krebs teams, and organized other ball clubs in the area. He would enjoy a Hall of Fame career with the New York Giants.

On the Fourth of July, 1882, Krebs and Savanna played the first recorded baseball game in Oklahoma. Charles Saulsberry, a reporter for the *Daily Oklahoman* in the 1880s, was an eyewitness to the ingenuity of Oklahomans baseball pioneers who were also, fittingly, pioneers themselves.

"Krebs and Savanna," noted Saulsberry, "used anything they could find for bases—a sack full of hay or cans. Their baseballs were reddish colored and they were called 'dollar deads.' Four strikes were out and the catcher could stand far enough back to get the pitch on the second bounce."

The days of pioneers playing ball must have seemed like ancient history decades later when the Waners came of age. As baseball evolved and multiplied, so did the options awaiting young players—college, semi-pro or the minors. With his parents' emphasis on education, Paul and his brother chose college. The relative rarity of college-educated ballplayers in the major leagues during this era should be noted. Though he did not earn his degree, Paul was proud enough of his college experience to wear his Phi Delta Omega fraternity pin conspicuously on the lower corner of his suit vests when he was in the major leagues.

Once in the major leagues, the Waners found they had more schooling than the average ballplayer. Then, the college-educated player, even without degrees like Paul and Lloyd, was still the exception in the game. Presented with cold, hard cash to chase their boyhood dreams, most ballplayers opted to enter the minor leagues instead of going to college first. There was some foolishness espoused by diploma worshipers who thought the college-trained ballplayer could play the game smarter and improve the language, dress and manners of their teammates; the opposite could be true. Perhaps collegians in baseball might find their college polish dulling in the crude and coarse life of a professional baseball player.

Paul Waner's high school photograph (courtesy of Jim Knight).

Paul, however, wasn't affronted by the rough world awaiting him. He always got a kick out of how the San Francisco Seals of the Pacific Coast League discovered him, thus opening the door to the major leagues.

Paul Waner: "*How did they find me? Well, they found me because a scout went on a drunk. Yes, that's right, because a scout went on a bender.*"

Dick or "Nick" Williams was a well-known scout for the San Francisco Seals in the Pacific Coast League. Late in the summer of 1922 he was in Muskogee, Oklahoma, to take a look at a ballplayer named Roy Flaskamper. He looked him over, then sent in a recommendation via telegram, and promptly went on a drinking binge for the next ten days. The Seals never responded, so the scout just kept drinking.

When Williams finally sobered up he started back to the West Coast, worried his job might be in jeopardy for not bringing home some talent. On the train he bumped into a conductor with the last name of Burns. It just so happened that Paul Waner had dated the conductor's daughter at school.

Paul Waner: "*He couldn't wait to tell this scout how great I was. How I could pitch and hit and run and do just about everything. He was such a*

1. Corncob Balls and Branch Bats 21

convincing taker, and this scout needed an excuse so bad for where he'd been those ten days, that the scout decided, 'Doggone it, I've got something here.'"

Going on hearsay alone, Williams had no idea how Waner played. Blindly, he had stumbled upon a player with great promise. He was more lucky than good on this one, though scouts were paid for more than gut instincts. Leo Durocher once quoted Branch Rickey—as good a judge of baseball talent as any—on five qualities to be considered in measuring a ballplayer: hits for a good batting average, hits with power, runs fast, throws well, fields competently. While hitting and fielding can improve with coaching, running and throwing are natural talents. Any player with two out of the five traits can be a major league player. Any with four is a star—that was Paul Waner. All he lacked was long-ball power, and sometimes that develops with maturity.

Early on, however, the hitting wasn't even an issue. Williams wanted Paul as a pitcher, his regular position in high school and on the semi-pro clubs. When Williams returned to San Francisco, he told his superiors without flinching, "I've watched him for ten days and I don't see how he can miss."

The next spring Williams decided to learn more about his top prospect, so he wrote to Waner and asked him to send information about himself. Based on this, the Seals sent Waner a contract and waited for his reply.

San Francisco had just won the 1922 PCL pennant and were about to become a Pacific Coast League (PCL) powerhouse over the next several years. The league was embarking on its own Lively Ball Era patterned after Babe Ruth's colossal clouts in faraway New York. This would help Paul Waner make a statement about his own hitting.

In the 1920s, America as a nation was leaving childhood and becoming a powerful adult. It's therefore not coincidental that power was suddenly admired, appreciated and even demanded in our national pastime. The figure of Babe Ruth came to symbolize this new power.

Babe Ruth or not, the Waners' parents were ambivalent about baseball as a livelihood. Ora and Etta were practical people, and after all Ora had once himself decided against professional baseball as a career. Ballplaying was not a guaranteed money-making venture and it often resulted in a nomadic, family-denying lifestyle. Ora wanted the best for his sons, and he especially wanted college for them.

After much deliberation, Ora had Paul return the contract unsigned to the club. If Paul was going to risk his education—his own future—it had better be worth it. Besides, it bought them time to keep Paul in school awhile longer. The young Waner didn't like the decision, but he went along with his father, who could be tough as nails.

Ora Waner had worked himself up from a laborer to landowner in the heady days of the Oklahoma Land Rush. He was not about to toss adrift his sons after so much upward mobility. By the time the boys were born, the Waners were established landed gentry, and it was said, "they lived like kings on that big, old farm." Not even the Dust Bowl of the 1930s knocked them from their social and property moorings in Oklahoma.

Human nature tells us that money talks. When the Seals responded with a higher salary figure, the Waners suddenly reversed their positions.

Paul Waner: *"My father was a farmer and he wanted his sons to get a good education. But they sent the contract right back to me, and even upped the ante some. So I said, 'Dad, I'll ask them for $500 a month, and if they give it to me will you let me go?' He thought about it awhile, and finally said, 'Well, if they'll give you $500 a month starting off, and if you promise me that if you don't make good you'll come right back and finish college, then it's OK with me.' 'Why surely, I'll do that,' I said."*

College, ha. Paul Waner earned his degree in the philosophy of batting.

Go West, Young Seal

> During the past week we have passed the time in fixing wagon-covers, stowing property, etc., varied by hunting and fishing and playing base ball. It is comical to see mountain men and Indians playing the new game. I have the ball with me that we used back home (New York).
> — *Alexander Cartwright, heading to California, 1849*

The 1920s—it was the Jazz Age, Prohibition was the tongue-in-cheek law of the land, Jack Dempsey was the heavyweight champ of the world and Babe Ruth was a New York Yankee. But the optimism and glitter of the new decade was quickly tarnished when eight players from the Chicago White Sox were banned from baseball for life. The national pastime had faced its darkest hour in the Black Sox fixing of the 1919 World Series. Gambling at this point in baseball was a cancer eating away at its core. "It nearly wrecked baseball for all eternity," sportswriter John Lardner ruefully noted.

Reform of the game was paramount. The owners appointed a flamboyant federal judge Kenesaw Mountain Landis as baseball's first commissioner. And though Landis would rule in the next 24 years, baseball more than anything was reformed by a glittering galaxy of hitting stars.

Though no one knew it at the time, one of those would-be stars was Paul Waner. As the scrawny 19-year-old hopped off the train in San Francisco after a thousand-mile journey from his native Oklahoma, he stepped into a bustling, maddening world far from the solitude of alfalfa and wheat fields. By the turn of the century, San Francisco was the ninth largest city in America, a wealthy, cosmopolitan metropolis with the busiest port on the West Coast, the latest fashions from Paris, Cordon Bleu chefs and opera singers from Europe.

In the 1920s in San Francisco and elsewhere, the hemlines got higher, the morals got lower and the party never stopped—at least that's how the decade is portrayed. Beneath the carefree facade, the '20s were a complex and contradictory time, a mixture of innocence and decadence, brilliance and brutality.

Nowhere were these extremes any more in evidence than San Francisco. Despite the anti-drinking laws, San Francisco remained the wettest city in the West. The high-profile murder trial of Fatty Arbuckle fueled efforts to clean up red-light activities. The Anti-Booze Navy was created to try to prevent the illegal importation of liquor arriving in the San Francisco Bay, but it met with only limited success in these Prohibition days.

In San Francisco at the height of America's wildest decade, Paul Waner was living for the first time away from home, free in a big, burly city and given the opportunity of a lifetime to play professional ball. Deep down he knew he was good enough to make it—and enjoy himself while he did. There were some things, however, he had to learn about—like getting around town.

Paul Waner: *"So I went out to the Coast. And I'm an old country boy. When I got there I didn't even know they had a boat going across the San Francisco Bay to downtown San Francisco. Well, my ticket didn't include any boat trip from Oakland. To me, that ferry was a big, big ocean liner—I had never seen anything like it. Once I got to San Francisco, I took a cab to the Washington Hotel where the Seals had a room waiting for me. They had left instructions on where I was to go the next day to meet up with the team."*

Despite his optimism, it was slow going at first. Right away the veterans dubbed him "Okie" and shuffled him into the greenhorn ranks. Then Paul suffered an inauspicious beginning, one that could have thwarted his career right then. Indeed, it changed his life.

During one of the first Seal practices that spring in 1923, Waner pitched in an intrasquad game. To make a good first impression, he threw as hard as possible. The umpire was a Seals coach by the name of "Spider" Baum. Along about the sixth inning Waner's arm tightened up, causing a pain he had never felt before. Not sure what to do, Paul shouted into Spider that his arm was getting sore.

Spider Baum had no sympathy. He felt that young players had to get into shape and learn some things the hard way. He yelled back, "Make it or break!"

Paul winced, and threw. Something snapped.

2. Go West, Young Seal

Paul Waner: *"They don't say those things to youngsters nowadays. No, sir. And maybe it's just as well they don't, because what happened was that, sure enough I broke it. And the next day, I could hardly lift it."*

Paul was devastated and the Seals were disappointed. He could not pitch and figured his baseball career was finished. He expected to head back to Oklahoma on the train anytime. Few teams wait for arms to heal on unproven pitchers who haven't made it through one week of their first spring training. In truth, it is unclear if Paul actually broke his arm or suffered ligament or nerve damage. In any event, his future hung in the balance.

Lame-armed, Paul stood in the outfield, shagging flies for the Seals hitters. He lobbed the balls back underhanded, the only way he could throw. The pain was excruciating, but Paul suffered through it quietly and focused on the training sessions. Maybe he could salvage something out of this, he thought. After all, he always had been an excellent hitter and fielder, too. Finally, some of the veterans took pity on him and asked him if he wanted to hit.

It turned out his sore arm was the best thing that ever happened to him.

Paul Waner: *"So they threw, and I hit. They just let me hit and hit and hit, and I really belted the ball. There was a carpenter building a house out just beyond the right-field fence, about 360 or 370 feet from home plate. He was pounding shingles on the roof, and he had his back to us. Well, I hit one, and it landed on the roof, pretty close to him. He looked around, wondering what the devil was going on. The first thing, you know, I slammed another one out there and it darned near hit him. So he put his hammer down, and just sat there and watched. And I kept right on crashing line drives out there all around where he was sitting. Of course, they were lobbing the ball in just right, and heck—I just swished, and away it went."*

After Paul's fireworks, a Seals outfielder, Justin Fitzgerald, implored manager Jack "Dots" Miller to give the kid a chance at playing a position. As he told the *Los Angeles Examiner* years later—and maybe he took some liberty with credit—"Why waste this kid as a pitcher? Convert him to the outfield."

Ironically, Fitzgerald's own career ended prematurely when he suffered a sore arm.

Miller weighed his options on Paul. He was a good hitter, fast and had a good glove. That night the manager went out to dinner with Paul and told him, "Okie, tomorrow you fool around in the outfield. Don't throw hard, just toss them in. And you hit with the regulars."

This would showcase Paul, but he faced another obstacle because the Seals could only afford to carry a set number of players. While Paul practiced with the regulars through the rest of training, his status was still precarious. Like any player, Waner was signed on a trial basis and had to make the club. This was always a challenge for rookies, especially on a loaded team like the Seals.

The way it has been described, Paul didn't have the front office guys in his corner. Justifiably, they were concerned whether he would ever recover from his arm injury. Right before the season started, the team management told Miller he had to cut four recruits, and Waner's name was apparently among those. Miller argued with his bosses to keep Paul. He said he'd even pay the player's salary to keep him on the club. His swing was too sweet to let go, Miller said.

Miller had seen that kind of swing while he played in the majors from 1909 to 1921, splitting time with the Pittsburgh Pirates and St. Louis Cardinals. Miller had broken into the majors as a rookie second basemen for the world champion Pirates of 1909, playing alongside Honus Wagner. At St. Louis, Miller had played in the same infield as Rogers Hornsby.

Miller understood young talent. His defiance of the front office has been portrayed in heroic terms. As Paul put it, "They wanted to ship me back, but Miller said, 'no.' He would buy me himself first, like a white slave."

Paul Waner: *"Nobody was much impressed with me except Dots Miller. The top brass on the Seals was all for giving me my release before I started costing [them] a salary, but Miller had such faith in me that he offered to pay me out of his own pocket. Finally, in the first month of the season Dots played me in a doubleheader at Seattle, and I got eight hits in ten at bats. After that he finally convinced Charley Graham, owner of the Seals, that I might make a ball player."*

The front office backed down, and Miller found a roster spot for Paul. Once the season started, he eased him in gradually as a pinch hitter. Paul's debut came April 7, 1923, against Vernon at the San Francisco park. He pinch-hit for the pitcher, and lined out.

One of his next pinch hits was a grand slam over the right field wall. It was as emotionally charged as anything he had experienced. Then he went north to Seattle and Portland and worked his way into the regular lineup.

A month after the season started, tragedy struck the Seals. Miller was diagnosed with tuberculosis, usually a fatal condition in those days before antibiotics.

2. Go West, Young Seal

Miller called a team meeting to tell his players. As he spoke, a gloom hung over all those in the clubhouse, especially Paul who, stunned, almost cried. "We were all thinking, this is the end for poor Dots," he said.

Paul and Miller had just begun to establish a deep and meaningful relationship. When Miller left the club for treatment, Paul lost a friend and father figure. The rest of the club took it hard, for Miller was popular with the players, sticking up for them, as he had with Paul, when the front office tried to get tough or cheap, which was often.

Miller's wife took him to Saranac Lake, New York. Because of its pure air, the Adirondack mountain village was considered a haven for those afflicted with the "white plague." While Miller was there, Paul wrote him get-well letters. Three months later, Miller died. Decades later when Paul faced his own health challenges, he reflected back on Dots and the precious, fragile quality of life itself.

Back on the field, the Seals appointed first baseman Bert Ellison as manager. As he nursed his arm back to health, Paul waited for his opportunity. When player/manager Ellison broke his hand, Paul received playing time at first base. He stroked a hot bat through the rest of the summer, dividing time between the outfield and first base as the Seals debated his best position. The other Seals began to notice his gifts. Catcher Sam Agnew told the *San Francisco Bulletin* that Waner's arm trouble would keep him from becoming a pitcher but that he was "as good a hitter as there is in the league."

Paul got into a comfort zone in Recreation Park where the Seals played. Recreation Park was constructed after the San Francisco Earthquake of 1906 and located in the Mission District between 14th and 15th streets on Valencia. "Old Rec" was the home of the Seals from 1907 to 1930 before the all-concrete, lighted Seals Stadium opened in 1931. A wooden grandstand was raised to allow for several rows of bleachers built at ground level behind chicken-wire fencing. Designed for the rowdier fans, this area became known as the "booze cage," and that's where some of Paul's loudest fans cheered him on.

The dimensions of the field were 345 feet down the left field line, 385 feet to center field and—to Paul and other left-handed hitters' delight—only 235 feet down the right field line. However, a 50-foot-high chicken-wire fence in right field required fly balls to clear it for home runs.

By season's end, Paul held the highest batting average on the Seals. In 112 games with the Seals, he finished with a .369 batting average—second in the PCL and tops among his fellow Seals. In 325 at bats, he scored 54 runs, hit three home runs, and drove in 39 RBIs.

Waner's arm had gotten stronger, and he soon earned a reputation as a right fielder who could throw as well as anyone. He spent most of the season in the outfield, as the first base experiment yielded poor results with seven errors in 21 games.

Like most young hitters, he was streaky, and though he lacked deep power, he could reach the gaps with wicked line drives from his compact short swing. He was hitting best when he could pull the ball down the right field line. He did not overswing, displayed a total command of the strike zone, and rarely missed the ball.

San Francisco (124–77) won the PCL pennant in 1923 by 11 games. It was their second title in a row. The Seals were dominating, and the 1923 squad boasted a .319 team batting average. Like the Pirates that Waner would play for in two years, the Seals featured a high-average offense and few long-ball threats. Ellison led the team with 23 home runs.

Spending the off-season in Oklahoma, Paul went hunting and fishing with his father and brother. After his rookie season in San Francisco, he knew he could make it as a professional ballplayer. And he knew Lloyd had the same kind of right stuff. He encouraged his younger brother in his ballplaying at the college in Ada.

Back in San Francisco the next spring, Paul pulled a leg muscle that cost him several games at the start of the season. By May, he was a regular in the outfield, and that's when he found his stroke and began banging out hits like a veteran. Throughout his career, Waner tended to get off to a slow start and then typically picked up steam as the weather warmed.

Somebody told Speed Martin, a pitcher in the PCL and future major leaguer, that precocious Paul had no weaknesses.

"I believe them," Martin replied.

Another hurler, Bill Pierce, said he'd throw Paul pitches the average hitter could not handle "nine times out of ten, but he hit them right on the nose."

In early September, Waner's average peaked at .372, giving him an outside shot at the batting crown. But Paul was learning how to pace himself over a long season—the PCL played 200-game seasons—and he slowed to finish at .356, sixth best among PCL regulars. His final statistics showed 160 games, 46 doubles, 113 runs scored, 209 hits, 8 home runs, and 97 RBIs. In the field, he performed exceptionally, and his 28 assists tied for second place in the league.

In 1924, the Seals participated in one of the most dramatic finishes ever in PCL history. With almost the same team as the season before, San Francisco led Oakland, Seattle and Los Angeles for most of the season. On October 7, the Seals had a 4½-game lead over Seattle. Then Seattle took six out of seven against the Seals in a series highlighted by come-from-

2. Go West, Young Seal

behind performances and extra-inning games. At the end of the week, Seattle had a half-game lead over San Francisco and Los Angeles. In the last week of the season, Seattle defeated the hapless Portland Beavers six times in seven games, and though the Seals took five of seven from Oakland, Seattle wound up winning the pennant by 1½ games. San Francisco finished third at 108–93.

With two good seasons to his credit, Paul figured the future would only get better. He now had some capital with the Seals and lobbied them to sign his brother Lloyd. Paul felt a special obligation to make sure his kid brother had baseball playing opportunities. Though Lloyd would not make the big splash in San Francisco that Paul did, it got him some visibility that would prove useful in the future.

By 1925 a sense of reckless danger was in the air in America and abroad. That year Al Capone assumed control of the Chicago mob, Adolf Hitler published *Mein Kampf* and formed the SS guard, F. Scott Fitzgerald published his novel *The Great Gatsby*, John T. Scopes was arrested for teaching evolution in a Tennessee school in violation of state law, and 40,000 Ku Klux Klan members marched through Washington, D.C.

On the Pacific Coast, the PCL was recovering from its own dirty scandal of bribes and fixed games. Only five years before, in 1920, league president William McCarthy had expelled six players for throwing games and gambling. Seals pitcher Casey Smith was among those banned. So was Hal Chase, long one of baseball's most disreputable characters. Raised in Santa Cruz, Chase was a former PCL player who was also implicated in the Black Sox Scandal.

Surviving, the PCL boomed in the twenties and almost rivaled the major leagues in the quality of players and games. So acclaimed the PCL became that after World War II the major leagues debated incorporating the PCL as another league like the National and American varieties. Ultimately, the owners decided against this and opened the door for the New York Giants in 1958 to move to San Francisco and the Brooklyn Dodgers to Los Angeles, thereby dooming the PCL.

When Paul Waner played for the San Francisco Seals in the 1920s, attending a PCL game was a similar experience to a major league game. Fans either walked or took the street car to Recreation Park where games usually started at three o'clock. Adults would try to schedule their work day around games, and school children would often hurry from their last classes of the day to make the first pitch. The game usually lasted less than two hours, and people always seemed to make it home for dinner. Box seats cost $1, but some could save 15 cents by buying chair or grandstand seats, and the cheap bleacher seats cost only 30 cents. Ladies were admitted for free on weekdays but had to sit four rows deep in the grandstands unless a man accompanied them. The men all wore hats, coats, and ties.

Ballplayers received no special transportation to the park. They arrived at the game the same way their fans did. Most of them lived nearby. Wearing heavy wool uniforms, they talked and joked with fans, signing autographs. It was expected of them. Unlike today, the fans had tremendous access to the players, at the park or about town, and so they had their favorites. They'd chant or call out the names of those favorites as they stood around the field. Few of the players were college educated, and most of them dropped out of school to play ball. While they were better paid than many of their fans, they were not so well paid that they could forego jobs during the off-season. They worked all year round, playing ball and then back in the factory or warehouse or wherever they could find gainful employment. They had money worries like everyone else.

Then and now, a ballplayer's bat and glove were his pride and joy. In the '20s, a bat was lathed out of hardwood and bone-rubbed to depress any soft spots in the wood. Its thick handle might have been roughed up so the player's calloused hands (no batting gloves back then) could grip it more easily. Their fielding gloves were minuscule compared to those of today—two pieces of leather with some padding around the thumb, little finger and palm. After each inning, the players would leave their gloves on the field near their position. Sometimes a mischievous player would spit tobacco juice in the finger holes of his counterpart's glove.

Many good players preferred the PCL to the majors. The pay was comparable to the big leagues and the mild and sunny climate was better than back East. Besides, for West Coast native ballplayers, the East was far away in the days of rail transportation.

For Paul and others, the PCL was showcasing for the majors. Come the spring of 1925 several major league teams were intrigued with Paul Waner, including Detroit where player/manager Ty Cobb wanted him. But tightfisted Tigers owner Frank Navin wouldn't come up with the $40,000 the Seals were asking for a young ballplayer, who in those days might be lucky to make a few thousand a year. Other suitors included the New York Giants, Brooklyn and Pittsburgh.

The concern, of course, was his size.

Paul Waner: *"Joe Devine, a Pittsburgh scout, was trying to get the Pirates to buy me, but the San Francisco club wanted $100,000 for me, and the Pittsburgh higher-ups thought that that was a little too much for a small fellow like me. I only weighed 135 pounds then. I never weighed over 148 pounds ever, in all the years I played."*

2. Go West, Young Seal

The other concern was the price tag. Pittsburgh had recently been burned on this type of thing. In 1922, the Pirates signed Jimmy O'Connell for $75,000, a huge amount in those days. O'Connell quickly washed out of the majors, only playing in 139 games, all with the New York Giants. One might understand why Pittsburgh owner Barney Dreyfuss was hesitant to embark on another mega-acquisition.

But Devine continued to lobby the Pirates. One of the few major league scouts roaming the West before the 1930s, he lived in San Francisco and scouted for the Pirates and other teams at various times. Through Devine, the Pirates reaped a wealth of Bay Area talent during the 1920s, including the Waner brothers, Gus Suhr, Hal Rhyne, Ray Kremer, Dick Bartell, and Joe Cronin—all signed by Devine. In 1929, the scout went to work for the New York Yankees. In doing so, the Bay Area became Yankees territory, and Joe DiMaggio wore pinstripes instead of Pirates colors.

The question facing Paul Waner was how he could make a strong impression on a skeptical Pirates front office. With the Lively Ball of the PCL obscuring true offensive worth, Devine told Waner that he would have to hit .400 to make the big leagues. He wasn't really joking.

But no full-time PCL player had ever hit .400.

It seemed like an impossible request. Was Devine mad, Paul wondered? Even for the brazen young outfielder, the challenge of averaging two hits in every five at bats over a 200-game schedule was daunting.

Daunting, but not impossible. After some PCL batting titles early in the century were actually won with sub–.300 averages, the batting championships from 1922 to 1924 were won with averages of .384, .394, and .392, respectively. As the '25 season dawned, the .400 mark was ripe for assault.

As it turned out, Paul had company that season. Salt Lake City's Lefty O'Doul and Seattle's Frank Brazill joined Paul Waner in pursuit of the .400 mark. From June on, the three swapped the league lead in hitting nine different times. It looked like O'Doul, a native San Franciscan, was the odds-on favorite, commanding the top spot the longest, from July 25 through September 19.

About all the Seals had to worry about was Paul's drinking habits. And with major league scouts frequenting Recreation Park to look over talent, Waner included, Seals co-owner George Putnam became concerned about Paul's nightly adventures.

In 1957 Abe Kemp of the *San Francisco Examiner* revealed that Putnam and Ellison came up with a plan to curb Waner's "tonsil dusting." They figured if they could get Paul's girlfriend, a young lady named Dorothy, to stay away from him for the remainder of the season, Paul would slow down his drinking. Putnam gave $500 to Ellison to present to Dorothy on the condition she quit seeing Paul. It's hard to imagine the Seals were naive enough to blame Dorothy for Paul's imbibing, though this may just have been the way Kemp told the story.

Ellison, who later told Kemp it was the "most disagreeable assignment of his life," made an appointment to visit Dorothy at her place. Once there he told her the conditions and made her promise that she would never tell Paul about the agreement. She accepted.

Two years later, after Paul was on the Pirates, he bumped into Ellison at a Pirates-Seals exhibition game in San Francisco. That night they went out for dinner and drinks. They were exchanging small talk when Paul suddenly blurted out, "Bert, if I tell you something will you promise not to get mad?"

Bert, puzzled, agreed.

"Remember the $500," Paul paused, "you gave Dorothy?"

Bert attempted to interrupt, but Paul finished, "She didn't tell me, Bert, if that is what you are thinking." "If she didn't tell you," Bert asked, "then how did you know?"

Waner grinned, "Bert, I was hiding in the clothes closet."

One more obstacle arose to Waner's quest. In early August he began to feel dizzy and nauseated. Paul could not gather the strength for a single at bat in a 10-game series against Portland. After missing the first two games against Seattle, he returned to go 3 for 12 in a doubleheader.

Waner felt his batting title chances slipping away, and the Seals wondered what was wrong with him.

It took some investigation by the club, but they eventually figured out what was wrong with their young hitter. While hunting during the past winter in Oklahoma, Paul had accidentally been shot in the face. It wasn't clear if he had done it himself or if it was one of his hunting mates. Either way, a small amount of lead shot still remained in his jaw, and it was slowly poisoning him.

The Seals acted while in Portland for a series. A local doctor there removed the remnants of the bird shot. In a few days, Paul began to feel better.

But his rivals continued to pound the cowhide. O'Doul opened August with a .429 average. In one incredible series against Vernon, he went 19 for 21 with 11 consecutive hits. By August 24, O'Doul's .420 average was 22 points ahead of Waner's.

Then suddenly O'Doul went into a tailspin, and Waner and Brazill surged down the stretch. After seven months and 197 games—with three to go—Waner was slightly ahead of Brazill.

2. Go West, Young Seal

Going into that final weekend of play, Brazill had 278 hits in 703 at bats for a .395 average. Waner, though he would later claim he was batting .399 at that point (maybe it made for a slightly better story), was at an even .400 with 278 hits in 695 at bats. To pass Paul and snatch the title, Brazill would need to go 6 for 6 in his doubleheader against Portland.

With such odds in his favor, Paul could have sat out the doubleheader. But in a decision similar to that of Ted Williams on the last day of the 1941 season when the Splendid Splinter was cresting .400, Paul decided to play.

Paul Waner: *"Everybody on the team was pulling for me. I was nervous. My mark before that last game was .399, and I had to bat .500 that last day to reach .400 for the season. The first time up I hit safely, and felt better. Overeager, I struck out the second time at bat. The third time I tied into it and got a double to the right field fence."*

With two hits in four at bats, Paul had raised his average by one point to .401, winning the title. Brazill had gone 1 for 4.

To put this into context, the 1920s was one of bloated statistics in the PCL. With the Lively Ball, three players—Waner, Smead Jolley and Ike Boone—won batting championships with .400-plus averages from 1925 to 1929. In 1930, Earl Sheely batted .403.

Still, the 21-year-old Waner's performance was impressive. He had torched PCL pitchers in nearly every category. In 174 games, he compiled 699 at bats, 167 runs scored, 11 home runs, and 130 RBIs. His 75 doubles is a PCL all-time single-season record that stands to this day. With his gap line drives and speed, Paul was a prolific doubles hitter throughout his career.

Paul, despite being one of the lightest guys on the Seals, routinely hit in the number three spot. Behind him, clean-up hitter "Turkey" Brower cracked 36 home runs and posted a .361 average.

While Paul had a smash-up year, brother Lloyd could hardly get in the lineup. For him this was extremely disappointing, but he was not one to complain loudly. He just waited for his turn. Used mostly as a late-inning replacement and second baseman, Lloyd played in 31 games and hit .250 with only 1 RBI in 44 at bats. Few people realize that one day Lloyd Waner would arrive in the majors as a second baseman, but get switched to the outfield.

While their numbers were different that season, the twin-looking Waner brothers had similar stances at the plate. Throughout their careers, they both had the same unusual batting technique, resting the bat on their shoulder until the pitcher began his delivery.

If the delivery of a certain letter had been made, Lloyd might well have cut his losses with the Seals and joined another organization—making it unlikely he would have ever joined the Pittsburgh Pirates. All it took was one misplaced letter and the passing of 15 years.

According to a 1939 Associated Press wire story, George Stallings of the Boston Braves had written Lloyd in 1925 offering him a minor league spot in Rochester and "a shot at the big leagues." The eccentric Stallings had piloted the "Miracle Braves" of 1914, retiring seven years later to serve the team in an advisory capacity. Stallings' letter arrived somewhere in Ada, Oklahoma—likely at Lloyd's parents' house where he received mail at that time—but was subsequently lost. Finally, in June 1939 the unopened letter was discovered in a pile of rubbish. It was sent to Lloyd—a seasoned veteran by then—in Pittsburgh where he shared it with sportswriters amid a few chuckles.

As for Paul's batting title rivals that glorious season, it was a mixed bag. On one hand, Lefty O'Doul became a legendary figure in PCL circles as both a player and manager with the Seals. He enjoyed brief but brilliant success at the major league level, banging out a .349 lifetime average in 970 games. In 1929, O'Doul would hit a staggering .398 with a league-record 254 hits for the Philadelphia Phillies. On the other hand, Frank Brazill, an ex–major leaguer, had already tasted his only major league action of his career. In '21 and '22, he had played in a total of 72 games for the Philadelphia Athletics, with a .258 average and no home runs. But he found a home in the PCL as a productive hitter for many summers.

In 1925, the San Francisco Seals were peaking as a dynasty, winning a franchise-high 138 games as it claimed its third championship in four years. The Seals took the pennant by 12½ games over a powerful Salt Lake City Bees squad that featured O'Doul and a second baseman named Tony Lazzeri. The future New York Yankee Lazzeri took advantage of Salt Lake's rarefied climate and elevation—Salt Lake City was the Coors Field of the PCL—to smash an organized ball single-season record 60 home runs. In the majors Lazzeri would never hit more than 18 in a season.

After the season, the Seals faced an abundance of outfield talent. Smead Jolley, a late-season acquisition from the Texas bush leagues, had whacked 12 home runs and put up a .447 average in only 38 games. Another rookie outfielder named Earl Averill—a future Hall of Famer—also arrived that summer. Flushed with talent the next few years, the Seals could afford to sell off some players. Toward the end of the 1926 season and through 1928, the Seals would assemble one of the greatest ever minor league outfields with Jolley, Averill, and Roy Johnson. All had quality major league careers, though Jolley's defensive liabilities kept him from playing for long in the majors.

2. Go West, Young Seal

Paul Waner: *"We had such a terrific outfield that Lloyd didn't have a chance to break in the lineup, except pinch-running or pinch-hitting once in awhile."*

After the season ended, the Cincinnati Reds made a hard push for Paul. The Reds were also impressed with infielder Hal Rhyne, a terrific defender who had hit .285, 296, and .315 for the Seals in successive years.

Back in July, the Reds had offered $35,000 for Waner, Rhyne and one other unidentified player. However, as Paul appeared to be headed toward hitting .400 for the year, the Seals raised their asking price. It all came to a head in the fall. In a telegram on September 25, Seals co-owner Charles "Doc" Strub replied to Reds owner Garry Herrmann:

> Impossible for me to go East at this time. Putnam left Monday to meet several club owners who are interested in Rhyne and Waner. Believe Waner will be sold within a week. We are obligated to no club so far, but suggest you act at once in matter. Please do not construe this wire as giving you the rush act. Our proposition is $50,000, three players acceptable to us or $5,000 in lieu of each player not delivered. Cash to be paid. As you have suggested in letter August 11th you and I have had no trouble over players and know we can get together on players to be sent. Please keep this confidential and if deal is made wish to break story here same time with you.
>
> Charles Strub

Strub, a dentist, was a veteran in making such deals and made sure he got every last dollar he could. Through the years, Strub orchestrated the selling of O'Doul, Willie Kamm, Frankie Crosetti, Earl Averill, Lefty Gomez, Jimmy O'Connell, and Joe and Dom DiMaggio to major league ball clubs. Of all those players, he would say years later, he considered Paul Waner the best player he ever developed. That's what he told writer Joe Williams in 1954 when Strub published an autobiography.

With Paul drawing interest from Cincinnati and others, Devine kept Pittsburgh in the loop through October. As Cincinnati hesitated, the Pirates, feeling their bravado, and a few extra gate receipts from winning the World Series, pulled the trigger and made the deal. Owner Barney Dreyfuss paid the Seals $100,000 in cash for Waner and Rhyne. The Pirates had been scouting Rhyne for several years, and $60,000 was earmarked for Rhyne, $40,000 for Paul.

Back east in Pittsburgh, Paul was a virtual unknown alongside Rhyne, who was four years older than Paul and better known through the sports-writing grapevine. In any event, $100,000 was an eye-popping figure to spend on players in those days and one of the highest paid for minor league talent to that point.

Reflecting this, the *Pittsburgh Gazette Times* sports editor observed, "Rhyne should add much strength to the Pirate infield." Almost as an afterthought, he noted, "Scouts report that young Waner has considerable promise as an outfielder."

Pittsburgh salivated for Rhyne. The world champion Pirates thought enough of him to trade their starting second baseman Eddie Moore the next season. However, Rhyne fizzled and only saw action in 109 games in 1926 while hitting an unspectacular .251. He lasted in Pittsburgh a few more seasons, returned to the Pacific Coast League, and came back later for unsuccessful stints with the Boston Red Sox and Chicago White Sox.

In Paul, they got every penny's worth. And a kid brother to boot.

Smoky City Blues

> In a world fast reeling from the rural to the urban, in a country where one does not live where he grew up, in the ever-changing metropolis, loyalty to a baseball franchise offers the same assurance and stability that "home for the holidays" does.
> — *Tristram Potter Coffin, University of Pennsylvania professor*

In Pittsburgh, Paul Waner found a world vastly different than the harsh range lands of the Southwest. Pittsburgh was the nexus of steel manufacturing and a grand blue-collar tradition. Sprawled over a hilly area in the Appalachian Mountains, Pittsburgh sits at the convergence of the Monongahela, Allegheny and Ohio rivers, the latter of which spills far downstream into the Mississippi River. It was the perfect place to move steel throughout America as the country flexed its Industrial Age muscles.

In the mid–19th century Pittsburgh was considered—like Chicago and St. Louis—a "western" city. Then, the nation's population was especially condensed in the Northeast, especially the mid–Atlantic seaboard and New England. During the Civil War, the town boomed producing cannons, arms, coal and munitions for the Union forces. When the Civil War ended, young men returned home to Pittsburgh and, like their counterparts elsewhere, started swinging bats and throwing balls. For a country weary of war and bloodshed, "base ball," its phrasing then, was an instant hit, maddeningly so, first in the more affluent classes and then among the working classes of the omnipresent steel mills.

Work hard, play hard—so goes the creed in hard-hat Pittsburgh. By the 1870s, the city's blast furnaces accounted for almost 40 percent of the nation's iron and produced about half the nation's glass, shipping all this product out to the country through its massive railroad-marshaling yards. This meant workers—lots of them. Once it was said that on any given payday Friday, more money was spent in western Pennsylvania than anywhere else.

At the height of the mill activity, one was lucky to see across the street. Smoke from the ironworks, the glass factories, and the stern-wheelers and side-wheelers covered the city. Housewives had to brush the soot off their furniture and windows every day. The stuff clung to mirrors and tables, and sometimes during the day the air was so thick with smoke that one could not see the sun, as if a giant fog had enveloped the city, which gained a reputation as America's dirtiest city—the "Smoky City."

In Pittsburgh, in the midst of that metropolis of steel, there was always baseball. With its green grass and rituals redolent of old summer afternoons, the game had caught on meticulously and magically with a generation of boys at the start of the 20th century. Whether Pittsburgh or New York or Chicago, where populations were straining with the influx of European immigrants, baseball could tap into pastoral patterns and an unmoving clock so that youth could be recreated every afternoon at the ballpark. Though most Americans still lived on farms and in small towns, cities like Pittsburgh were throbbing with creative energy and industrial might, roaring up through the American dream with massive ambition. One chief diversion was baseball.

By the time Paul Waner arrived in Pittsburgh, baseball as an institution had momentum. In 1923, sports coverage in newspapers was one-sixth of the total space allocated to news, compared to only one-twenty-fifth back in 1890. It was the broadest sports coverage ever, and it was still expanding with the reach of radio. Baseball boomed as Sunday baseball— except in Pennsylvania for some years—came to be accepted.

The growth of cities like Pittsburgh allowed major league baseball to expand as populations increased. With more ticket buyers concentrated in dense urban areas, teams could afford to pay their players better and raise the talent level. The street car, railroad, telegraph, newspapers, and predictable factory hours in the large East Coast cities— unlike farming, which had different hours in different seasons—were perfect for baseball's growth. Fans could flock to the park because of the trolley line, secure in the knowledge of having steady jobs and regular paychecks.

Mass attendance at sporting events in America is as much an aftergrowth of industry and commercial society as anything. The game had arrived. And it seemed the fans yearned for an unknown American hero—

a Hercules or Siegfried of the diamond—to turn back the invading city's team. Heroes they could cheer and lavishly reward like Babe Ruth.

Before Ruth, there was the Dead Ball Era of Ty Cobb and John McGraw. The single run had more value because not many runs crossed the plate. Players and managers won games by outwitting the other team and trying to precisely aim their hits and maximize their base running opportunities. They even practiced getting hit by pitched balls. Defensive equipment was very crude, and the average fielder's glove was nothing more than what a farmer back in the Waners' Oklahoma might use for heavy work. Batters swung large bats, often up to three pounds. As hitters realized they could get more whip-like bat speed from lighter, thin-handled bats, this began to change. Ballparks were widely unpredictable, with some little better than pastures and others with rock-hard or soft and porous infields.

Baseball in Pittsburgh had a sense of history. In 1887, the Pittsburgh Alleghenies left the American Association to join the established National League. It earned the name Pirates after signing away infielder Lou Bierbauer from the Philadelphia club in the American Association. Throughout its history, Pittsburgh would treat its fans to unforgettable championships as well as stone-cold last-place finishes. Whole decades, even generations of fans, would pass by with the team at the top or bottom of its division.

At the summit of Pirate greats is the humble, hawk-nosed Honus Wagner, one of the most dignified stars the game has seen. Bow-legged and barrel-chested, Wagner played 21 summers and compiled a lifetime .327 average and 3,415 hits. Wagner, along with players like outfielder Tommy Leach and player-manager Fred Clarke, led Pittsburgh to pennants in 1901, 1902, 1903 and 1909. In the 1909 World Series, the Wagner-led Pirates prevailed over Ty Cobb's Detroit Tigers in a much ballyhooed showdown of rival stars.

Now, after winning the 1925 World Series victory against the Washington Senators, the Pittsburgh Pirates and their fans expected years of contending ball teams. The Bucs could really sting the ball, having led the National League with a .307 average that year.

One of Pittsburgh's emerging stars was shortstop Glenn Wright. He had one of the strongest arms of any shortstop in years. A surprisingly powerful hitter for a shortstop, he was the first National Leaguer with 100 RBIs in each of his first two years.

After the 1925 World Series, Wright met Paul Waner back in the Midwest. In vivid imagery, he described the encounter decades later in the book *Legends of Baseball*.

Glenn Wright: *"I helped Paul sign his first contract. I used to hunt with Fred Clarke, who owned part of the Pittsburgh club. In fact, I went with his younger daughter Muriel for a while. I would go to Kansas and hunt with him in quail season and he'd come to Missouri to hunt with me, and we both had good dogs. Fred had a little ranch out of Westfield, Kansas, with about 10 oil wells in the front yard. Anyway, I was down there and Paul wanted me to help him with his first contract in 1926. So I invited him over to Fred's place, with Fred's permission, of course. Paul got there in a Dodge coupe, which looked pretty beat up. When he got out of the car he had on the purplest suit I ever saw."*

Throughout his career, Paul was known for a loud fashion taste. On one hand, he might wear the brightest suit to a party, and on the other he might just show up in hip boots, jeans and his fishing duds. Years later, playing with Leo Durocher—another snappy dresser—Paul and Durocher would be photographed together in some of their more "dandy" attire. Some of this confused the Eastern writers, who expected the "rube" wardrobe from the Oklahoman. Havey J. Boyle noted, "Waner in a measure is a strange combination. Hailing from a small town in Oklahoma, he ought to present some western aspect either in dress, manner or speech. But he doesn't. He easily might be mistaken for a Princeton or Yale freshman."

For Wright, it wasn't Waner's wardrobe that impressed him. It was his sense of confidence and skill.

Glenn Wright: *"He had a couple of knocked-around bags, and I could tell one of them had a musical instrument in it. After dinner we were sitting around the fireplace and eating popcorn while Muriel played the piano. They had a big fireplace that would hold half a tree. After a while I said, 'Paul, why don't you get your instrument out and play along with Muriel?' He took it out and it was a saxophone and Muriel asked what she should play. 'Oh,' he said, 'play anything and I'll just follow along.' So she did and he did, and did a right good job too."*

Baseball is a game of razor-sharp precision. It's not a game of inches like you hear people say. It's a game of hundredths of inches. On a hunting trip, Paul demonstrated his skill in this area.

Glenn Wright: *"We got out in the field the next day and the dogs found a bird. I said, 'Paul, this is your bird.' And he said, 'All right.' So we kicked the bird out and Paul up and shot, and he didn't have his gun anywhere near his shoulder. Just shot from the hip, you know. But the bird fell deader than a door nail. Fred and I looked at each other and he said, 'We'd better stay behind this kid.'"*

"The dogs found another bird and I said, 'Paul, you take this one too.' But he said, 'No, this is yours or Mr. Clarke's.' So I told him, 'Well, to tell you the truth, we think that first shot was an accident.' 'Oh,' he said, 'all right.'

"We kicked the bird out and the same thing—gun still down by his hip, but the bird didn't even flutter after it fell. He didn't miss a bird all day. He was the best field shot I ever hunted with.

"Must have learned it where he was raised down in Oklahoma."

Roaring Baseball

> My being small has helped me more than anything.
> — *Paul Waner*

In 1926, the U.S. celebrated its 150th birthday, Richard Byrd and Floyd Bennett circled the North Pole by airplane, the Ford Company introduced the 40-hour work week, Carl Sandburg published *Abraham Lincoln, the Prairie Years*, Leroy "Satchel" Paige made his debut in the Negro Southern League, and Josef Stalin assumed dictatorial powers in the Soviet Union.

In Pittsburgh, plans were made to build the largest theater in the state that one day would be remade into Heinz Hall, 21 men died in an horrific mine explosion near Castle Shannon, the new Seventh Street Bridge opened, and Carnegie Tech's football team upset Notre Dame 19–0 at Forbes Field in the fall.

As the 1926 baseball season approached, Pirates owner Barney Dreyfuss publicly rejoiced in a World Series victory and his decision more than a year ago to bring some discipline to the club. Mischief-making ballplayers were his biggest problem, he surmised.

So, in late 1925, Dreyfuss had traded away his merry pranksters—first baseman Charlie Grimm, shortstop Rabbit Maranville, and, strangely enough, the serious-minded pitcher Wilbur Cooper—to the Chicago Cubs. Grimm and Maranville were notorious rowdies. And they drank heavily, especially Maranville.

"I got rid of my banjo players," Dreyfuss quipped.

While restoring discipline worked this time, Dreyfuss would not be so lucky the next time around.

4. Roaring Baseball

In many ways, Dreyfuss epitomized the "benevolent despots" who ran baseball in the early 1900s.

Temperamentally, the German-born Dreyfuss was passionate, impulsive, stubborn, and dictatorial. A former distillery worker who saved his money and worked his way up the company ladder, he owned the Pirates for 40 years and during much of that time was one of the National League's most powerful leaders. His best move ever was merging the Louisville Colonels of the American Association into the Pittsburgh Pirates in 1900, giving the Pittsburgh team Honus Wagner and all the talent they needed to field one of the strongest teams for years.

The Pirates owner had some quirks. He absolutely hated cigarettes. If Dreyfuss had known Paul Waner smoked cigarettes, he might not have signed him. In those days, the recruitment of players was haphazard and gleaned from tips from friends. Dreyfuss scouted a young Tris Speaker in Texas but refused to sign him after observing that Speaker smoked—even during baseball games.

"No man who smokes them will ever be a big league player," Dreyfuss would say.

Dreyfuss also ignored a letter by a cigar salesman recommending an undiscovered Walter Johnson. To him, people making their livelihoods in the tobacco industry were disreputable.

"What does a cigar salesman know about ballplayers?" snorted Dreyfuss.

Beyond the cigarette issue, the Pirates had some bad luck. In 1915, the Pirates also lost out to the St. Louis Browns in a dispute on who had the rights to a young rookie named George Sisler. The Hall of Fame firstsacker would have been a welcomed addition to a club that suffered a revolving door of light-hitting first basemen for much of the first half of the 20th century. The team enjoyed some brief stability there with Grimm in the early '20s and Gus Suhr in the '30s. But for the most part, Pittsburgh never reaped the offensive benefits of the prototypical first basemen.

Sometimes the front office exhibited a patronizing attitude. Once during the 1909 championship season Dreyfuss and Pirates management publicly scolded fans for their failure to encourage the players to do better—as if winning ball games were up to those sitting in the seats.

That didn't matter now, for Pittsburgh the past year had made it to the World Series where they defeated the reigning champion Washington Senators. The Series was one of the soggiest of all time as rain fell and the mud worsened in both Washington and Pittsburgh.

For the players, the Series was especially gratifying—in the pocketbook, too. Each one was rewarded with a tidy check for $5,332. Even adjusting for inflation, that sum was a nice increase over 1903 when the players received $1,182 and in 1909 when they got $1,825. The players voted full shares to one of the coaches, Jack Onslow, and road secretary Sam Waters.

At a players' meeting immediately after the Series in October 1925, the question came up as to whether a share should be given to Fred Clarke, the former manager and current stockholder in the Pirates as well as a "roving" coach of undefined sorts. Some players wanted to exclude Clarke as they thought he would reap other financial benefits from the championship. Simply, they found him disagreeable and sharp-tongued and just didn't like him. But the manager Bill McKechnie intervened, and eventually the players agreed to give $1,000 to Clarke—the same amount that scouts Bill Hinchman and Chick Frazer were to receive.

Clarke, miffed he did not receive a full share, returned the check. He considered it an insult. The roots of future discord were sown.

◆ ◆ ◆

In March 1926, with Lloyd back in San Francisco for another try at making the Seals as a regular, Paul arrived in Clearwater, Florida, for Pittsburgh's spring training camp. Along with Rhyne, Paul was the talk of the camp. The writer Tom Meany recalled how Dick Cox and Buzz Mc-Weeney, two Brooklyn Dodgers who had played against Paul in the PCL, bet Waner would hit over .300 that first season.

In acquiring Paul Waner, the Pirates were choosing a player perfectly suited for Forbes Field where extreme distances to the fences reduced home runs but made for tons of doubles and triples in the spacious gaps.

Home to the Pittsburgh Pirates from 1909 to 1970, Forbes Field played host to slashing, high-average players, and Paul Waner was the ultimate prototype. In their history the Pirates produced 24 batting champions, tops among all National League clubs. Three members of the 3,000-hit club—Honus Wagner, Paul Waner, and Roberto Clemente—played all or most of their careers in Forbes Field. While the Pirates boasted great batsmen, too often the franchise ignored pitching. No long-time Pirates pitcher from the 20th century is in the Hall of Fame. Pitching has always made the difference between great Pirates teams and merely good-hitting teams, and that is true of most franchises.

When Forbes Field opened in 1909, the 25,000-capacity steel-and-concrete park was pure state of the art, following on the heels of Philadelphia's Shibe Park, which had just opened that year. Named after John Forbes, a British officer in the French and Indian War, the park was located

4. Roaring Baseball

near the rolling hills of Schenley Park, the Carnegie Museum, the University of Pittsburgh's Cathedral of Learning, and Carnegie Mellon University.

In the early 1900s, the strikingly unique aspect of Forbes Field was its three tiers and an unusually large number of reserved grandstand seats for more affluent customers. Dreyfuss thought that his team's long-term prosperity rested with the higher-income crowd and not the rowdy bleacher fans. Believing the city was growing eastward—it was not—Dreyfuss built Forbes Field well east of downtown Pittsburgh. Though a bit far from the rest of the city, the result of Forbes Field on the edge of Schenley Park was magnificent—baseball in a hilly setting on the edge of a gritty city.

Tom Meany recounted how Dreyfuss tried to keep Forbes Field pure and pastoral.

Tom Meany: *"[Dreyfuss was proud that] no advertisement marred the blue-black of his fences, save during World War I when he permitted the painting of a legend on the left field fence recommending that the patrons buy war bonds and war savings stamps. Years afterward, when it rained, the tracing of the letters would gleam through the glistening fence."*

Several new features made their first appearance at Forbes. A wide promenade and inclined ramps replaced stairs as access to all levels of the triple-tiered pavilion. The third level, also accessible by elevators, housed spacious press facilities and private luxury-style boxes, the latter serving as precursors to today's skyboxes. The field was laid over a stratum of bedrock and covered by clay, soil and sod. This made for one of Forbes' most well-known characteristics—unpredictable bounces on hard-hit balls.

The other characteristic was the park's extreme dimensions. The fact that a no-hitter was never witnessed in 61 years of play at Forbes Field is testament to the acreage the outfielders had to cover. Though changes were subsequently made to bring in the far right field fence, in 1920 Forbes Field was 376 feet to right field, 410 to the right-center power alley, 447 to straightaway center, 462 to left-center, and 360 feet down the left field foul line. It was immense, and among today's baseball parks it would rank by far the largest.

In the context of their spacious park, the best Pirates teams featured players like Paul Waner who were fleet-footed and sprayed line drives into the gaps. Power was rare in the Forbes Field era, and speed, both on offense and defense, was highly valued. Especially in the seemingly endless outfield.

It wasn't decided for sure, however, that Paul Waner would exclusively play in the outfield when he first came up. He had some experience at first base with the Seals, and the Pirates tested him there during that first spring training. Stuffy McInnis, the first baseman in the Philadelphia Athletics' famed "$100,000 infield" during the mid–1910s, tutored Paul on how to play first base.

Paul Waner: "When I joined the Pirates in 1926, Stuffy was there as a substitute first baseman. He must have been close to forty at the time, and I think that was his last year in baseball. But he could still field that position like nobody's business, and he tried to teach me all he knew. I was his roommate in 1926, before Lloyd came up the next year, and Stuffy would spend hours with me in the room showing me how to play first base, using a pillow as a base."

The Pirates decided against Paul at first base, though. He was not tall enough. Later in the season outfielder Max Carey was sent to Brooklyn, and that permanently opened up an outfield spot. And, Paul was hardly a towering target at first base. "Actually, I was a little too small to make a good first baseman," he admitted.

As it was, Paul found it difficult to land a regular starting job that spring training, let alone a specific position. He didn't hit that well in the exhibition games leading up to Opening Day. On April 8, Charles "Chilly" Doyle of the *Pittsburgh Post-Gazette* indicated the jeopardy young Paul faced in an article under the ominous headline "Paul Must Improve Hitting Within Three Days or Be Benched."

In those days, the Pirates started spring training on the West Coast and headed back East, playing exhibitions with any number of amateur, semipro or pro teams along the way. At the outset in Los Angeles, Paul had lashed out four hits in one early game and appeared on his way to a triumphant spring. But as the days passed he showed little or nothing, and concern mounted after weak performances in Indianapolis, Indiana, and Hot Springs, Arkansas. Manager Bill McKechnie contemplated starting Carson Bigbee in left field and sitting Paul on the bench.

Doyle explained McKechnie's thinking.

Charles Doyle: "Skipper Bill is deeply concerned over left field. He realizes that Paul Waner is a great prospect, that he batted .400 in the Pacific Coast League, and that Paul will probably hit any kind of pitching when he is in form. But Waner has not been hitting consistently. The costly player explains his slump by stating that he never gets away to a good start in the spring."

Doyle noted that Paul was usually a late starter in spring training, and his best hitting came when he could really turn on the ball and pull it down the right field line. But so far that spring Paul was slapping hits like a banjo hitter to left field. Though the rookie smashed some solid line drives in a Louisville game late in the exhibition schedule, come Opening Day he was, as they say, riding the pine.

Doyle paints a picture of ballplayers warming up in the sleepy towns of America, with spring crackling beneath the still-hard ground and birds singing of the coming warmth of a new season. All of this happened on a grueling pace with constant travel.

Charles Doyle: *"The Pirates spent a perfect April afternoon in rushing about 200 miles from Hot Springs to Memphis. The champions were in fine spirits as they rolled into this thriving city at 7 o'clock. A two hour layover here was followed by a resumption of the journey to Louisville. There was a chill to the air when the Pirates aroused this morning. At 10 o'clock, however, the Pittsburgh athletes were on their way to Fordyce Field where for one and a-half hours they frolicked. The field was soggy from the recent rains, but everything worked out in a satisfactory manner. McKechnie wanted to give his players some work before they started on their long ride to Louisville. The sun was shining down on Hot Springs in a welcoming manner as the Pirates took leave of their old camping grounds."*

The Missouri Pacific train of sleepers left shortly after one o'clock and was in Little Rock two hours later after an up-and-down ride across the picturesque Ozark foothills.

Wrote Doyle, "With all the train rides, it felt good to stretch one's legs outside and toss the ball, swing the bat, no matter the weather. Soon enough, the Pirates arrived in Pittsburgh, ready to defend their world championship. Yet it would be a season that rocked the Corsair's ship like none other."

On April 13, 1926, Paul Waner made his first major league appearance. It came on Opening Day at Forbes Field against the St. Louis Cardinals. Pinch-hitting for pitcher Vic Aldridge in the seventh inning, Paul took a walk off St. Louis' Flint Rhem. The Cardinals went on to win the game, 7–6.

On April 16, Paul started his first game in left field. He walked twice and went hitless in two at bats. The next day, Paul collected his first hit, going 1 for 3. But the rest of April yielded few hits for Paul, and it was May until he began to heat up his stick, and when he did he kept hitting all season long.

That first season Paul tucked his small frame into the large and somber Pirates uniform. Like most other baseball uniforms of the 1920s, the Pirates uniforms consisted of standard whites at home, grays on the road, solid colors and simple graphics. The caps were navy blue with a red "P," and the fronts and backs of the jerseys had no lettering whatsoever. (Players' numbers weren't yet used either.) The sole identifier was a "P" on the upper arm sleeve, and socks were blue and red trimmed. This was the Pittsburgh uniform for most of the decade. The Pirates' familiar black and "gold" (yellow), would arrive in 1948, years after the Waners retired. By the 1970s, all the Pittsburgh sports teams would use the black-and-gold combination.

For both Paul and the Pirates, expectations ran high that spring. Some predicted Bill McKechnie's squad would dominate the National League for a few years, just as Fred Clarke's teams did winning four pennants at the turn of the century.

But the Bucs failed to start well. They languished in the National League cellar in April and May.

On May 8, Paul Waner smacked his first major league home run, coming against right-hander Skinny Graham of the Boston Braves. In his career, Paul's top home run target would be Clarence Mitchell, with five. He would also show greater power against right-handers, hitting 103 of his 113 lifetime homers against them. This is not uncommon for left-handed hitters, but his numbers overwhelmingly indicate that lefties had little trouble with giving up home runs to Paul.

On June 7, the Pirates won the first of several games to start a gradual climb from seventh place to first. The Cincinnati Reds and St. Louis Cardinals kept the pace with Pittsburgh. On June 24, however, the Cardinals beat the Pirates 6–2 as their player-manager Rogers Hornsby hit a grand slam—his 2,000th career hit—to win the game. Three days later St. Louis fortified their pitching in acquiring Grover Cleveland Alexander from the Cubs. On June 27, the epileptic, hard-drinking but still masterful Alexander tossed a four-hitter against Chicago to win 3–2 in his first appearance in a Cardinals uniform.

In adjusting to the major league routine, Paul Waner found life to be a constant hum of activity. On the last day of a home series—"getaway day"—the players returned to the clubhouse to shower and dress before leaving for the train station. Once aboard they usually gathered in the dining hall. After dinner they settled down in the club car or Pullman car to play poker, checkers, talk, drink, and read. After a few road trips even a rookie ballplayer like Paul became just another migrant worker in the baseball industry. First-class train passage could get boring and tiring. Trains, of course, had no air conditioning, and it was frequently difficult to sleep. The trips could be long. It was not uncommon for a team to play

4. Roaring Baseball 49

in Boston or New York on Saturday, take a train to Chicago or Pittsburgh on Sunday, and return to the Atlantic coast for a series opening Monday.

Amid all the travel and camaraderie some levity was expected. On the Pirates' first trip to Chicago's Wrigley Field that season—recently renamed in place of Weegham Field—the Pirates were told they'd be facing pitcher Charley Root.

Paul had played many times against Root in the Pacific Coast League. He knew what he threw and thought he could hit him well. Just before the game, however, the Cubs started Guy Bush instead of Root—and Bush was an unknown to Waner. Bush, a swarthy Mississippian with exaggerated sideburns, was thought by some baseball writers to resemble a riverboat card dealer—and to pitch like one too. Boasting a wicked curve and excellent control, Bush was thoroughly at home on the corners of the plate.

But Paul didn't notice any difference between Bush and Root. They might as well have been interchangeable. Apparently still thinking he was batting against Root, he smacked a couple line drives off the outfield wall for hits that afternoon. After the game he told his surprised teammates, "Hell, I never had any trouble hitting that guy in the Coast League."

His teammates just stared at him. Wonder boy, they thought.

To Paul, it was simple—watch the ball, not the pitcher. "Just keep your eye on the ball, and don't worry about who's pitching."

Paul didn't worry about picking up the tab, either. Even as a rookie, he was generous to a fault, driven by his desire to be out on the town with friends. The first time Paul visited New York with the Pirates, McInnis took him out to some expensive Broadway night spots. Somehow—whether by design or not—McInnis did not have the money to pay the $134 tab, and when closing time came, it was waiting for Paul. He paid it, and McInnis paid the smaller cab fare on the way home.

In the off hours, Paul practiced on his saxophone. His neighbors in his apartment building near Forbes Field never complained too loudly, though funky musicians, like crude ballplayers, were not among the brightest lights of proper society in those days. One beat writer observed that Paul Waner's saxophone habit "is an uncontrollable vice and there is little hope for reform."

◆ ◆ ◆

In San Francisco, Lloyd found it hard to carry a tune. With the Seals his performance had not improved from a year ago, and he saw little playing time in the first few weeks of the Pacific Coast League season. For 1926 he had collected only four hits in 20 at bats and six games. At the time, it looked bleak for the 19-year-old Lloyd. While fast and agile in the field, he just didn't hit with his brother's authority.

The Seals and Lloyd also had a disagreement over $2,500 or $1,250 as is sometimes reported. Apparently, the club had told Lloyd that if they kept him after May 1 he would get $2,500 in addition to his salary.

Paul Waner: *"Before the 1st of May came, they said, 'Paul, we want to keep Lloyd, but we haven't had a chance to see him. We'd like to keep him here if he'd just waive that $2,500.'"*

The older brother had to figure something out for the younger one. Paul served as his brother's hitting coach, agent, and manager. He made this point clear when the Seals asked Paul what he would like to do with Lloyd.

"Release him," Paul told the Seals. He didn't want Lloyd stuck there without getting paid the agreed upon amount. The Waners had too much pride for that.

Paul Waner: *"Lloyd went and got his things, and he left town. They were mad at him then. They said, 'Gee, we paid your salary all this time, and then you up and leave.' Lloyd said, 'Well, I got my release.' They said, 'What are you going to do?' And he said, 'I'm going to Pittsburgh.'"*

Paul made sure of this. He immediately visited Dreyfuss in his Forbes Field office, and with some brash salesmanship, sold the owner on giving Lloyd a tryout. When you consider that Lloyd had shown next to nothing in his stint with the Seals, this outcome was impressive. And it illustrated how the Waners stuck up for each other. If anything, Paul would have the rest of the world believe Lloyd was better than he.

Paul Waner: *"After I got to Pittsburgh early in 1926, I told Mr. Dreyfuss, the president of the club, that I had a younger brother who was a better ballplayer than I was. That kid can hit, run and field as well as I can."*

A "better ballplayer than I was." Those words reflected the brotherly devotion between the Waners. Paul was generous in his assessment, but it didn't matter to him. Dreyfuss agreed to look over Lloyd.

The bad feelings between Lloyd and San Francisco originated in 1925 when the Seals signed Lloyd, at Paul's urging. Then Paul had insisted on a "no option" clause in his brother's contract. It backfired when Lloyd got so little playing time, and the team didn't want to dish out the money.

Lloyd Waner: *"I was playing for a semipro team in Ada [Oklahoma] when I signed up. San Francisco promised to pay the team $1,250, and my*

4. Roaring Baseball

dad the same amount. Dad wanted to use the money to get me through college. I'd promised him I would go to college after the season. Well, San Francisco reneged on the agreement and wouldn't pay the money. Paul talked to Joe Devine who was a scout for Pittsburgh, and Devine said I should get my release and Pittsburgh would sign me. Paul advised me to do it and I did what he said. I got my release and the Pirates signed me. That suited me just fine because Paul was already with the Pirates and naturally I wanted to play with him."

The Pirates had little to lose and a lot to gain if Lloyd worked out.

The deal was for Lloyd to come to Pittsburgh so the Pirates could get a firsthand look at him. If they liked what they saw, they would send him to one of their minor league teams for development. All they had agreed to was paying his train fare and nothing else. For Dreyfuss, signing Lloyd on a trial basis represented an investment of only a few hundred dollars. If Lloyd didn't pan out, then the Pirates could release him. On the other hand, if he made the majors, he came in at low expense.

Arriving at Forbes Field in the wake of Paul's rampant bragging about him, Lloyd was told by Pirates manager Bill McKechnie to put a uniform on, take some swings and catch some flies.

If people thought Paul was small, Lloyd shocked them. Paul was about 5-foot 8½ inches. Lloyd was about the same height—some say he was an inch shorter—but he was real thin, and weighed 10 to 15 pounds less than Paul.

As McKechnie and Dreyfuss watched Lloyd in practice, the manager turned to the owner and said, "He isn't much bigger than a mosquito, but I think you'd make no mistake sending him to South Carolina."

Dreyfuss asked how much Lloyd weighed. About 130 pounds, he was told.

"Are you kidding?" Dreyfuss said when he saw Lloyd.

"Don't let his weight fool you," Paul quipped.

Today a ballplayer of 130 pounds seems downright freakish, but back then when the average American male was a smaller physical specimen the diminutive Waners were not so out of place. Many good players were small, notably Wee Willie Keeler (1892–1910) at 5 foot 4½ inches, and 140 pounds, and Rabbit Maranville (1912–1933) at 5 foot 5 inches and 155 pounds—both Hall of Famers.

Besides, Lloyd could run, field, and handle the bat. Not many pitches were thrown by him, and this was important to the generation of baseball men like Dreyfuss and McKechnie reared on Dead Ball strategies and Ty Cobb's gospel of contact hitting. Lloyd seemed to have the raw skills.

It was a matter of refining them with more minor league experience. The question for the Pirates was whether frail-looking Lloyd, if called up to the majors, could endure the grind of a 154-game season.

Originally, Paul lobbied Dreyfuss to place Lloyd on the Pirates' Triple-A team. But the owner preferred sending him to the "B" minor league team in Columbia, South Carolina. Dreyfuss figured Lloyd would spend a year at Columbia in the South Atlantic League, and if he did well enough, play the following season in Triple-A ball.

Lloyd would wear a Pirates uniform sooner than that.

The Pirates paid a boatload of money for Paul, but picking up Lloyd evened out the ledger sheet. Fred Lieb described Lloyd Waner as Dreyfuss's "greatest bargain ever." By 1933, some thought Lloyd Waner was worth a six-figure price if Pittsburgh were to trade him on the open market.

But in the spring of 1926 such accolades were unimaginable to Lloyd—all he wanted to do was crack Columbia's starting lineup—and plenty of doubters existed to make him second-guess his fledgling ballplaying career. Once he reported to Columbia, the team physician, Dr. William Marks, remarked, "He'll never make it through a season with a build like that."

Build and all, he made it through the 1926 season with a towering .345 average that won him the South Atlantic League's Most Valuable Player award. Finally, Lloyd had enjoyed a break-out season, just like Paul did when he hit .400 in the PCL. Now the Pirates would give him a chance next spring to make the major league club, skipping Triple-A altogether.

Speed was Lloyd's game, and many of his hits came on infield grounders. Quiet and polite otherwise, Lloyd was ruthless in hustling to make a hit out of anything. Wilcy Moore, a fellow Oklahoman and future Yankee pitcher, said facing Lloyd in 1926 was like watching a streaking blur.

Wilcy Moore: *"Look out for that little devil. I played against him in the South Atlantic League. He hits a ball that takes two hops and he's got a base hit."*

◆ ◆ ◆

While Lloyd learned to hit in Columbia, back in Pittsburgh Paul received some lessons in baseball etiquette from the men in blue.

Paul Waner: *"I remember my first year up. I was fussing at the plate umpire in St. Louis about his decisions. When I reached first base, [Bill] Klem was umpiring there, and he said, 'Young man, you're a great hitter, but you're* starting out wrong arguing with umpires. You're not going to get anywhere fighting with umpires. Knock it off, and it'll help you.' I took Bill's advice, and he was right. As for fighting with ballplayers, I'm too little to get nasty. Some big guy would break me into two."

Paul and Lloyd had solid reputations when it came to umpires. Once Paul explained how to tell the umpire they're wrong without showing them up.

Paul Waner: "If I thought it was a ball and the count was two strikes against me, I'd just say to the ump, 'Don't you think that one was a little bit wide,' or whatever. I'd say it out of the corner of my mouth without turning my head. That way fans don't know you're disputing his decision. It makes umpires sore when the batter turns and yells at him. Then the fans give the umps hell."

Paul also learned about National League pitchers that season. It reflected his cerebral approach to hitting that made him a successful batting instructor after retiring from play.

Paul Waner: "When I first broke into the majors, I kept a book on every pitch. I kept details on how many base runners were on base, what inning it was, what the pitcher got me out on, and what I hit. I didn't keep it in my head, I wrote it all down in a notebook that I carried around in my pocket. When the game was over, if I got a hit on a certain pitch, I wrote it down. It was all about knowing your strengths and weaknesses. After the first year, I didn't need the book. I knew the catchers pretty well, and would get to know the young pitchers coming—what they liked to throw to me."

Paul got to know the New York Giants' pitching a little two well for the tastes of their fiercely competitive manager, John McGraw. All summer long he slammed the Giants for hit after hit. Strangely, McGraw had heard from one of his scouts early that season not to worry about Paul Waner—"That little punk don't even know how to put on a uniform," the scout reported back to the Giants manager who had yet to see Paul.

After a few games of Paul stinging the Giants for hits, McGraw told the embarrassed scout, "That little punk don't know how to put on a uniform, but he's removed three of my pitches with line drives this week. I'm glad you didn't scout Christy Mathewson."

That season the Giants had another clean-cut Giants great, like Mathewson—17-year-old Mel Ott. On July 27 the rookie hit the first of 511 career home runs, an inside-the-park shot against Hal Carlson of the Cubs. While Ott was much more of a power hitter than Paul, both possessed strong arms in the outfield and hit for average.

Some animosity existed between the Giants and Pirates, a fall-out from a couple of decades before when the two clubs battled annually for the pennant and their owners feuded over league issues. And so it felt doubly good to Pirates like Paul to do well against the New York team. The fans at the Polo Grounds always made it tough on opposing players.

Paul Waner: *"I always hit well against the Giants, especially when John McGraw was managing them. He was a firm believer in curveball pitchers. When Bill Terry succeeded McGraw as manager in 1933, he plastered a $25 fine on any of his pitchers who threw me a curve ball. From then on I saw only one curve. Roy Parmelee threw it, in our last game with the Giants. I hit it right into the seats."*

More than New York, though, St. Louis was the roughest stop on the road trip circuit. The well-inebriated bleacher fans in St. Louis had a nasty reputation dating all the way back to the 19th century.

In a game between the Cardinals and Chicago Cubs on June 27, Cardinal fans launched a barrage of bottles and garbage on the field during the second game of a doubleheader against the Cubs when umpire Charlie Moran issued a catcher interference call against the Cardinals. It was par for the course and something that Paul Waner would soon experience.

Paul Waner: *"In all the 15 years I played with Pittsburgh I was never booed at home. Not even once. The same with Lloyd. No matter how bad we were, no booing. We never knew what it was like to be booed at home. I don't imagine it would help a fellow any. Now on the road, I liked to be booed. I really did. Because if they boo you on the road, it's either 'cause you're a sorehead or 'cause you're hurting them.*

"In my first year in the big leagues, the players all told me to watch out for the right-field fans in St. Louis. 'That right-field stand is tough,' they said. 'They ride everybody.' And, of course, the fellows didn't know whether I could take a riding in the majors or not."

The first time the Pirates visited St. Louis in 1926, Paul was prepared for the worst of heckling, perhaps even a showering of rotten fruit in the outfield. He figured, however, he would turn the tables.

Paul Waner: *"[They] gave me a terrible roasting. I turned around and yelled, 'They told me for years about all you fans in St. Louis, that all the drunken bums in the city come here. And now that I'm here, I see it's true.' I said it real serious and mad-like, you know, never cracked a smile."*

Provoked, the St. Louis bleacher rowdies unleashed a verbal tirade

4. Roaring Baseball 55

against the first-year ballplayer. It went on every game the Pirates played in St. Louis early that season. Then one day in mid-season the Pirates were pummeling the Cardinals in a game. After Waner smacked a triple and drove in a few runs, he took his place in right field the next half inning. The fans berated him incessantly.

He only laughed and waved to them. Then the unexpected happened.

Paul Waner: *"On the very last out of that game a fly ball was hit out to me. I caught it, and then ran over to the stands and handed it to some old fellow that I'd noticed out there every time we played in St. Louis."*

Stunned at first, the fans finally cheered and clapped. From that day on they did not harass Paul and even showed some affection for the out-of-town ballplayer. To keep them tame, every time Paul caught the last out of an inning he continued to run over and toss the ball the old guy's way. Peace was struck.

Visiting St. Louis required intestinal fortitude on all fronts. Ossie Bluege, the Washington Senators third baseman, recalled visiting Sportsman's Park in St. Louis when the Browns were sharing the field with the Cardinals.

Ossie Bluege: *"You should have been in the old St. Louis ballpark. It was a rat hole, that's what it was. You couldn't leave your shoes or gloves on the floor because rats would come up and chew them up. They had no shower stalls, one pipe in the middle of the room, hot and cold water, but it never got real cold because it was beastly hot in St. Louis. So you got tepid water coming out and still you had to wait in line, it was terrible, just terrible."*

That season Paul Waner played with three future Hall of Famers—Kiki Cuyler, Max Carey and Pie Traynor—and a fourth, if one counts a 19-year-old shortstop named Joe Cronin who saw action in 38 games. While Cronin would be traded to the Washington Senators in 1928 and blossom thereafter, Cuyler, Carey and Traynor were mainstays in the Pirates' attack.

Though in the twilight of his career, Carey was a considerable veteran influence on the Pirates. Born Maximilian George Carey, he had just completed a six-year ministerial program before deciding to embark on a ballplaying career. In 1910 he joined the Pirates and went on to become an established lead-off hitter and graceful center fielder. Not a strong hitter, his specialty was stealing bases, and he led the National League 10 times in that category. Carey was an innovator. He created sliding pads, much like the hip pads worn today in football. They prevented strawberries, though they absorbed sweat easily and got hot in the field. But "Max

Carey sliding pads" were highly popular as baseball's first protection for sliding.

Harold "Pie" Traynor, in his seventh season by 1926 and the Pirates captain, was acknowledged as the best third baseman ever for many decades until the arrival of power-hitting third basemen like Eddie Mathews and Mike Schmidt. In 1929, New York Giants manager John McGraw, himself a former third baseman, called Pie Traynor "the greatest team player of his time."

In Pittsburgh, the straight-laced, honest Traynor was the idol and embodiment of all that was good about the national pastime. Baseball was his whole life, and he never learned to drive a car, preferring to take the bus or train to the games. Despite all the adulation, he did not develop a big head.

Traynor took an interest in rookies, and in the spring of 1926 that meant Paul Waner.

Paul Waner: *"I remember soon after I came up, Pie Traynor said to me, 'Paul, you're going to be a very popular ball player. The people like to pull for a little fellow.'"*

Though he never hit more than 12 homers in a season, Traynor was a clutch hitter, driving in 100 or more runs seven times. He had good power to the gaps and seldom struck out. In the 1925 Series, he collected five hits—including a home run and a triple—against Walter Johnson of the Washington Senators. Blessed with supreme range, cat-like reflexes and a strong arm, he was the premier defensive third baseman in his era.

Pie Traynor: *"Nobody taught me how to play third base, and I'm glad they didn't. Every player handles situations differently and it's easy to be confused by players offering well-meaning advice. I know, I've tried to give advice to other players. The way I learned was simply to tackle each situation as it arose and master it before going on to something else. I think I learned more about playing third base in the morning bull sessions in the hotel lobby than I ever did out on the field. I picked up a lot of tips just keeping my ears open and the other players were always ready to discuss specific plays if I asked them."*

Charlie Grimm, the first baseman, remembered Traynor years later as a kind man who wanted to win.

Charlie Grimm: *"He used to field the ball down the line with his bare hand. No glove. Just his bare hand and that was it. As for the throw—well, he had the quickest hands and quickest arm of any third baseman I ever saw.*

4. Roaring Baseball

When he came up with the ball he came up with it real quick and you had to get over to the bag pretty doggone fast. He was the kind of guy who took things pretty easy in the clubhouse, and became a competitor the second he crossed those chalk lines. From a competitive standpoint, he was one of the real fighters of the game. He fought in a way that a lot of players fight today—all the way down the line. A lot of guys slid hard into him and that was the way he did his job—if he had a chance he'd slide hard too, though he never tried to injure anyone."

Traynor was raised in Somerville, Massachusetts, a melting pot of races, religions and ethnic backgrounds. The one thing most of the low-income families had in common there in the 1910s was a love of sports, especially baseball. How did he get the name "Pie"? One version holds that Harold got it from the neighborhood grocer after always ordering pie on weekly shopping trips. Another is that his father, a printer, pinned it on him after the boy came home all covered in dirt. "You look like pied type," said the elder Traynor, referring to a jumbled, ink-stained mess.

Traynor's teammate, the curly-haired, hazel-eyed Hazen "Kiki" Cuyler also played with competitive zeal. Like Traynor, he had won the respect of the other Pirates for his gentlemanly qualities and athletic gifts. In the seventh game of the 1925 World Series, Cuyler had laced an eighth-inning, two out, bases-loaded double off Washington's Walter Johnson to lead the Pirates to a 9–7 victory and their second World Championship. That hit ranks as one of the Pirates' greatest clutch hits of all time.

How did Kiki get his nickname? It appears he had a stutter, and hence "Kiki." Though a stutterer, Cuyler loved to sing—when stutterers sing, they do not stutter—and was notorious for locker room melodies.

It might come as a surprise that Cuyler holds the Pirates single-season record for total bases. Despite the presence of sluggers like Ralph Kiner, Honus Wagner, Barry Bonds, Willie Stargell and Roberto Clemente in Pirates history, Cuyler's 369 total bases in 1925 are the most ever for a Pirate. That year he hit .357, scored 144 runs, collected 220 hits, including 18 home runs, 26 triples, and 43 doubles.

Even with Hall of Famers like Cuyler and Traynor, and the arrival of the young phenom Paul Waner, the 1926 season would soon prove disastrous for the Pirates. In one of the most notorious player rebellions in baseball history, both the players and the front office let pride get in the way of fielding the best team. The trouble had originated in the off season when the players nearly refused to give Fred Clarke a share of World Series money.

The truth is it wasn't a rebellion against the manager, McKechnie, but a misunderstood effort to support him. Fred Clarke was in the center of it all. One could argue that Clarke was the most successful manager of the first decade or so of the 20th century. By 1909, he was 250 wins ahead of the Giants' John McGraw—and they were both about the same age. With that head start, if Clarke had kept on managing after 1915 he may have been more successful than McGraw during that decade. He wasn't. Though Clarke's Pirates won four pennants between 1901 and 1909 and won 90-plus games nine times, the Pirates slumped for several years thereafter. One reason was that Honus Wagner slowed down in the mid-1910s, and the Pirates failed to stockpile any new pitching talent or good young hitters. Soon enough, the player-manager Clarke was forced out in the winter of 1915 by owner Barney Dreyfuss. After 22 years and 2,703 hits, his playing and managing days were over.

When he fired Clarke, Barney Dreyfuss said, "Fred Clarke can't expect a first division manager's salary when he finishes in the second division."

Clarke packed up and left Pittsburgh. He owned ranch property in Kansas where oil would be discovered in a few years and where he could relax as a gentleman farmer. "After handling ball players for many years, handling mules should be easy," he observed.

By the early 1920s, Clarke was a millionaire and able to deal with Dreyfuss almost as a social equal. Even after losing the manager's job, he remained close with the Dreyfuss family, investing some of his oil money in the Pirates and rejoining the team as a vice president and minority partner. Despite his front office title, the dapper-suited Clarke sat on the bench during games offering advice, as Fred Lieb puts it, in the "salty language of a Pirate sea captain."

With his sharp tongue, Clarke started annoying the players. Two Pirates remained from Clarke's 1909 squad—Babe Adams, star of the 1909 Series, and Carey, the team captain in '25. Both had long played under Clarke, but as the 1926 season progressed and frustration mounted over the disappointing season, some Pirates players felt that Clarke was maneuvering to get his old job back. His "unofficial" coaching tips were evidence of this, they thought.

Early in the season Clarke had insulted second baseman George Grantham with some unsolicited advice. The player stood up to Clarke and told him to buzz off. The two exchanged angry words. The incident festered among the players already impatient with the chirping Clarke.

It's likely Clarke was picking on "Boots" Grantham for his poor fielding (he earned the nickname "Boots" for how he coughed up grounders). In 1924, the lifetime .302 hitter was one of the players acquired from Chicago when the Bucs sent Rabbit Maranville, Charlie Grimm, and Wilbur

Cooper to the Cubs. Pittsburgh fans criticized trading three popular players for an erratic fielder and strikeout-prone slugger like Grantham and two unknowns, but the trade paid off for the Pirates. In 1925, Grantham, switched from second base to first base, swatted a career-high .326 and reduced his strikeouts. Grantham batted over .300 in each of his seven seasons with Pittsburgh, splitting time between first base and second base. He was as good a power hitter as the Pirates had then.

The mutiny began on August 7. It couldn't have happened at a worse time, as the Pirates were in first place just ahead of Cincinnati and St. Louis. But that day the lowly Braves shut out Pittsburgh in a doubleheader. It got so bad that Boston sent in their shortstop, Bob Smith, to pitch. While Smith would give up position playing to become a decent pitcher, the Pirates were deeply embarrassed by the twin losses and the infielder-turned-pitcher. Lead-off man Carey was among the struggling Pirates with a .222 average and a sinus infection he could not lick. That's when Clarke lobbied McKechnie to get Carey out of the lineup.

Fred Clarke: "Why don't you get Carey out of there? He isn't hitting."

Bill McKechnie: "Well, who can I play in Max's place?"

Fred Clarke: "Anybody. Put in the bat boy. He can't do any worse than the fellow you are playing."

Outfielder Carson Bigbee told Carey about Clarke's lip-lashing. Carey was a proud veteran and not about to take the fall for the team's performance. The insulted team captain talked to several other players, and they shared gripes and complaints about Clarke and the operation of the team. Carey asked Adams, a soft-spoken man in his mid–40s, what he should do about it.

Babe Adams: "Well, I think the manager should manage and no one else should interfere."

Adams reportedly was on good terms with Clarke and may not have realized how his comments would be taken by the team brass. The Pittsburgh newspapers soon got wind of the dissension after Carey, speaking for the players, asked that Clarke be removed from the bench. This all forced the players to choose sides. The "ABCs"—Adams, Bigbee and Carey—stood by each other, and hence the "ABC" affair.

McKechnie and Clarke apparently had words, too. But they closed ranks quickly for public consumption.

Carey, thinking he represented the majority of the players, said publicly that he was speaking as the team captain—in support of McKechnie, the manager. The players even met with McKechnie before going public with their statement. At first he seemed to appreciate their support, but then quickly realized he could not go against the team brass, and that included Clarke. If he supported his players, he was criticizing Pirate management. Ultimately, he had to denounce the uprising—the irony being that the players were supporting McKechnie, not rising up against him. Like it or not, the manager had to lay down the law.

Bill McKechnie: *"[This is an] attempt to meddle in the administration of the team."*

Clarke removed himself from the bench for a few games. Then, after McKechnie had publicly branded the players, Clarke unwisely returned to the bench and demanded that the players be punished. If he had not done so, it's possible the team could have put the bickering behind them.

Barney Dreyfuss was traveling in Europe at the time. His son Sam was in charge of the team. Unfortunately, the players universally detested Sam as a silver-spooned little rich kid, thus he had no credibility to restore discipline on the team. He knew this and asked for help from his father.

Exchanging cables with Paris, on August 12 the Pirates front office decided to schedule a meeting the next day with the players. That day the players held their own tension-filled meeting, and many of them retreated from their prior positions. Only a few held their ground. As it turned out, the Pirates players came out in favor of Clarke by a 18–6 vote.

Paul Waner did not vote against Clarke. He was not the rock-the-boat type, and though he had a young man's confidence, he also seemed to respect authority. It was something his father had taught him. And, as a first-year player, Paul was extremely reluctant to rattle the cage. Let the veterans do that, if they wish.

The vote did little to restore harmony to the team—the Pirates were in chaos.

On the morning of August 13 the front office dealt swift punishment. Bigbee and Adams were given their unconditional releases. Carey was put on waivers and suspended without pay. Pie Traynor replaced him as team captain.

Through the whole mess, Paul Waner, just a first-year player, kept a tight lip. He was no dummy and could see that plenty of people were getting in trouble for saying the wrong thing.

The episode sent shock waves throughout Pittsburgh, and the fans could not understand what had torn apart their team so quickly. Babe Adams was the hero of the 1909 World Series and arguably the finest pitcher in Pirates' history. While in the last chapter of his career, Adams was a Pittsburgh favorite not deserving of such rash mistreatment.

Babe Adams: *"I am eighteen years in baseball without ever opening my mouth, and then when I answer a question, I find myself chucked off the club."*

The players appealed for reinstatement to Commissioner Kenesaw Mountain Landis. He only kicked the issue back to National League President John Heydler, who conducted a meeting of all the parties on August 17. Trying to find some middle ground, his ruling absolved the players of insubordination, but held that the Pirates had the right to get rid of any player they wanted to. The team's actions stood.

John Heydler: *"I cannot go back on the right of the officials of a league club to release, suspend or ask waivers on any of its players, not would I wish to do so if I had the right; but it is my opinion, after a most complete and thorough hearing of this case, that none of the three players—Carey, Bigbee and Adams—has been guilty of willful subordination or malicious intent to disrupt or injure his club."*

Carey moved on to the Dodgers, where he played, coached and managed for several years. As for Bigbee and Adams, their careers had come to an end.

Amid the turmoil, Paul was the team's bright spot. On August 26, he went 6 for 6 with two doubles and a triple in a game against the New York Giants, scoring one run and driving in two runners. Among Pirates, Ginger Beaumont and Kiki Cuyler had also achieved this feat before Waner. In 1975, Rennie Stennett, a second baseman with the Pirates, would go 7 for 7 to become the first player in the 20th century to collect seven hits in a nine-inning contest.

Baseball players are a superstitious lot, and years later Waner pointed to this game as proof that superstitions are much ado about nothing — and that he could adapt to any circumstance.

Paul Waner: *"I used six different bats, and swung six different times, and came up with six different hits. You just know there has to be a lot of luck in a thing like that. It so happened that Bill McKechnie, who was our manager that year, changed our batting order a little that day, and I was put hitting second instead of third, where I usually hit.*

"So I was in the corner of the dugout, smoking a cigarette, not figuring it was my turn yet, when somebody yelled, 'Hey, Paul, hurry up, you're holding up the parade. Get up to bat.'"

Waner hurried out to the plate, just grabbing a bat, any bat, along the way. He notched a hit that first time up, so the next time he did the same thing, not even looking at the bat he picked up. And again, and again, all day. He wound up with six hits. The next day Waner was immediately stymied in his attempt to notch a seventh consecutive hit—he even tried the "use a different bat" approach.

Though not superstitious, Paul admitted to having some presumptions.

Paul Waner: *"Well, if I got a hit the first time up in a game, then I'd throw my glove near a particular spot on the field after leaving the field to bat. If I got a hit again, I'd throw it to the same spot again. Now, if I didn't get a hit, then I'd throw it to another spot. This was about the only superstition I followed."*

Pittsburgh was following Cincinnati and St. Louis in the pennant race as the season unfolded. Then the team imploded. On the last weekend of August, Pittsburgh lost four out of five to the Cardinals in St. Louis. In an August 31 doubleheader against St. Louis, the Pirates lost both games, and in the second game were held to only three hits and one run by Redbirds pitcher Allan Sothoron, who in his last year of ball was serving more as a coach than pitcher. Though Pittsburgh briefly regained the league lead for a few days in early September, they soon faded away into third place behind Cincinnati.

Paul Waner kept hitting, though. He did not get involved in the ABC mess, and it helped him keep a white-hot focus for the remainder of the season. Into September he challenged for the batting title, an amazing feat for a rookie.

Almost as fatal to the Pirates' chances that season was a career-threatening injury to their hard-hitting shortstop, Glenn Wright. Pitcher Vic Keen of St. Louis hit him on the head with a pitch, and Wright went down limp. Wright eventually recovered but missed a lot of games. Keen, shaken by the incident, lost most of his effectiveness thereafter.

On September 19, the Cardinals tied the Reds for first place by thumping the Phillies in both ends of a doubleheader (23–3 and 10–2). Five days later at the Polo Grounds, the Cardinals won their first-ever NL pennant by beating the Giants, 6–4.

Though loaded with talent, the Pirates finished a disappointing third with a 84–69 record.

The front office promptly fired McKechnie. Dreyfuss also released first baseman McInnis who he thought was speaking out of both sides of his mouth in the ABC Affair.

The Pittsburgh press speculated that Clarke would crown his victory by grabbing the managerial reins. But Clarke mysteriously disappeared from view, perhaps told to do so by Dreyfuss who was sick of the whole affair. Clarke ended up liquidating his small interest in the Pirates. Now all the principals behind the scandal were gone, and Dreyfuss could move ahead with a new regime.

In later years, McKechnie, who became the first man to manage three different teams to the pennant, declined to talk about what went wrong on the 1926 Pirates. He would later win the title with St. Louis in 1928 and Cincinnati in 1939 and 1940.

Considering that the Pirates were World Champions in 1925 and added several outstanding players the next few seasons, this crisis ruined the possible rise of a Pittsburgh dynasty. And the player dissatisfaction with management was far from over.

On the positive side, the ABC Affair served to more accurately define the roles played by coaches and executives in the modern front office. Teams began to emphasize a clear separation of powers between the front office and the field staff.

Dreyfuss replaced McKechnie with Donie Bush, the former Detroit Tigers shortstop of the Ty Cobb era. The beetle-browed Bush only had one year of managerial experience, having piloted the Washington Senators to a 75–78 record and fourth-place finish in 1923. That the Senators won the American League pennant in the two seasons immediately following Bush's exit did not seem to bother Dreyfuss.

In hindsight, McKechnie was arguably the better manager than Bush. Good on the fundamentals, he was a mild-mannered strategist who favored middle infielders, defense and contact hitters. But his flat emotional style sometimes worked against him in receiving acclaim.

McKechnie and Bush differed greatly from the current favorite manager of the National League, Rogers Hornsby. The single-minded Hornsby, in guiding the Cardinals to the 1926 pennant, did not let much get in his way. He did not attend his own mother's funeral, which was held in Texas between the end of the regular season and the beginning of the World Series with the New York Yankees. He explained, "I've got a job to do here—getting this club primed for our games with the Yankees. Mother would have understood."

The Cardinals won the Series in seven games, and maybe Hornsby's mother smiled above. The years ahead, however, would prove disastrous for Hornsby as a manager.

After the World Series win, Hornsby demanded a three-year contract from the Cardinals. One of baseball's top hitters, he had batted more than .400 three times, including a 20th-century high of .424 in 1924. But on

December 20 the Cardinals pulled off a blockbuster trade by sending Hornsby to the New York Giants for Frankie Frisch and Jimmie Ring.

Back in Pittsburgh, Paul finished his rookie season in spectacular form. He posted a .336 average, almost winning the title, and scored 101 runs. His league-leading 22 triples were the third most all-time by a National League rookie, and his 35 doubles were the first of nine straight seasons with at least 30. In his *Historical Baseball Abstract*, Bill James argues that Paul had the best rookie season ever of any right fielder in baseball history and ranks him as the ninth best player of all-time at his position.

Paul Waner: *"I would have won a fourth championship under present rules, requiring the champion hitter to have a minimum of 477 appearances [in 154-game seasons] at the plate. But they gave it to Bubbles Hargrave, the Cincinnati catcher, who batted .353 in 105 games and only 326 at bats. I had 180 hits in 536 at bats."*

Another hard-hitting catcher that season was Earl "Oil" Smith of the Pirates. His .346 average was a career high and tops on the Pirates among those playing more than 100 games. Smith, the catcher for five NL pennant winners and reputedly the toughest man in baseball, received his nickname from columnist Westbrook Pegler's Brooklynese pronunciation of his first name. Traded to the Pirates, he hit .313 for the 1925 World Champions. In 1927, the National League would suspend him for smashing the jaw of Braves manager Dave Bancroft. Sold to the Cardinals the next year, he helped them to the 1928 NL pennant.

Ironically, these hard-hitting yet slow-footed catchers were getting in Paul's way of a batting title. Next year, Big Poison would smash a few more line drives and leg out a few more infield hits. He'd get some help from one of the best in beating out grounders—his younger brother.

Big and Little Poison

> Henry was always careful about names for they gave the league its sense of fulfillment and failure, its emotion. Names had to be chosen, therefore, that could bear the whole weight of perpetuity.
> — *Robert Coover, from the novel* Universal Baseball Association

The decade of the 1920s was dazzling with outrageous personalities in sports, politics, crime, society and entertainment. So much happened everywhere, especially in 1927.

In New York, Babe Ruth swatted home runs at a record rate, Charles Lindbergh flew the first solo flight from New York to Paris, and technology began to change the way people viewed the world around them. A contraption described as a "television" was demonstrated publicly in New York, *The Jazz Singer*, starring Al Jolson, was released as the first feature-length talking film, and the Dempsey–Tunney heavyweight fight was broadcast on the radio to record-setting audiences.

In Pittsburgh, the executive board of the Pittsburgh Symphony was arrested and fined after a Sunday concert on charges of violating the "blue laws"—the same law that kept the Pirates from playing on Sunday—and the U.S. Post Office began airmail service on the Pittsburgh–Youngstown–Cleveland route.

Starting in 1927, Pirates fans could now listen to regular broadcasts of home games on KDKA, the world's first commercial radio station. On August 5, 1921, KDKA had broadcast the first major league game when Harold Arlin called the Pirates' 8–5 win over the Phillies at Forbes Field. By 1922, the Series was being heard live by an estimated 5 million people.

Re-created games were heard by fans on three continents. Beginning this season, Charles Doyle of the *Pittsburgh Gazette-Times*—it became the *Post-Gazette* later in the year—reported away games via telephone to his editor, Chet Smith, who then set the story into print.

It was a new media age. America was reeling fast with innovation and opportunity, like a rising young prize fighter driven by ambition and hardly heeding the limits of time and space.

The timing for expanded sports coverage was fortuitous in Pittsburgh. The 1927 Pirates were filled with diamond talent—as well as big egos and stubborn pride. Among those veteran players, Paul and Lloyd Waner stood out like the sensible Midwesterners they were. They were more concerned about establishing themselves than in rebelling against authority.

Every ballplayer needs that one big break. Lloyd Waner received his two days before the 1927 season began.

In spring training, Lloyd's chances at making the lineup were slim as his build. Despite his MVP year at Columbia the season before, Lloyd had competition. The Pirates had plenty of outfielders—veterans Kiki Cuyler, Clyde "Pooch" Barnhart and now Paul Waner, and a talented rookie named Adam Comorosky—though the departure of Max Carey and Carson Bigbee had created openings.

Then, 48 hours before the Pirates were to begin the season in Cincinnati, left fielder Barnhart collided with another outfielder, Elmer Lane, while chasing a fly ball in an exhibition game in Houston. Both were injured and sat out Pittsburgh's last pre-season game in Shreveport, Louisiana. While Lane would not make the club, "Pooch" Barnhart was a seven-year veteran and, despite a weight problem, had posted a .325 average only two years ago. In 1926, ironically enough, Paul's hot bat took playing time away from Barnhart, who battled health issues as well.

Some thought Lloyd would have health issues, too. The Pirates' doctor, William Marks, said Lloyd, at 132 pounds, would not make it out of spring training in one piece. He hadn't gained any weight over the year before. Pirates third baseman Pie Traynor immediately pronounced him "too small, too thin and too scrawny."

What ultimately convinced skeptics was Lloyd's speed in tracking down fly balls in the outfield. No weakling could move that quick day after day. At the plate, Lloyd made contact without fail and hit down on the ball consistently for ground balls and short line drives.

Traynor would later change his mind. "Oh, he was fast," the great third baseman would say 40 years later, "He was the fastest man in the league and got a tremendous jump on balls hit to center field."

New manager Donie Bush was a mixed bag of enthusiasm and discipline. And he didn't mind infusing the dissension-riddled Pirates with some new blood that spring. To make this point clear, he played Lloyd in left field in an exhibition game in Shreveport, the last game of spring training. Lloyd banged out four hits in five at bats. He had won himself a starting job for Opening Day.

Paul Waner: *"Donie came over to me and he says, 'Paul, I'm putting your little brother out there in left field, and he's going to open the season for us.'*

"And I said, 'You haven't made a mistake.'"

Though Bush had just a sixth-grade education, he understood baseball talent. The former lead-off hitter for Ty Cobb's Tigers saw that Lloyd had the speed for a top-of-the-order position and the agility to snare just about anything in the field. Besides, the Pirates had already seen what one Waner could do in a Pittsburgh uniform.

Pittsburgh was a good situation for rookie Lloyd and sophomore Paul. The team had something to prove after the past season, and the fans were psyched. That season the Pirates would set a then-record attendance figure as 869,720 fans clicked the turnstiles at Forbes Field. After a red-hot start by the Giants, the Pirates led the National League from May 22 to July 6, but then Chicago set the pace through much of August. In September, the Giants and Cardinals closed strong on the Pirates, but Pittsburgh outlasted them with a strong September showing.

Still, the Pirates almost blew it for the second year in a row with more team chaos.

◆ ◆ ◆

The season opened in Cincinnati on April 12. Lloyd started the game in left field and Paul in right field, and between them in center roamed Kiki Cuyler.

The Waner brothers were together again, as they had been for years in Oklahoma and recently in San Francisco. It was the start of 14 summers together in the Pirates outfield for them—the longest-running such tenure in baseball history. They were the first brothers to play regularly in the same outfield since 1880 when John and Jim O'Rourke did so for Boston's National League club.

Lloyd quickly showed the impact of his 132 speed-demon pounds. In his first big league at bat he hit a routine grounder to shortstop. Legend has it he was four steps past first base when the throw arrived.

Lloyd Waner (courtesy of Jim Knight).

Lloyd Waner: *"No matter what your experience in the minor leagues has been, your first day in the majors always stands out. I crossed a big league plate with my first run, and what made it all the more enjoyable, it was brother Paul who drove me home. I was on second base. We were playing Cincinnati. Paul drove me home with a single to center. In my first game I got one hit and one run and was well satisfied that I wasn't a complete bust, the dread of every young fellow on his first day as a major leaguer."*

Paul knocked in Lloyd with the winning run in the first two games of the season, the second time with bases loaded against the Reds in the ninth inning. Lloyd made three sensational catches in the outfield, though he did make an error in that first game. One catch came in the ninth inning of that first game to save the a victory against Cincinnati.

In those first three games, Paul and Lloyd combined for seven hits in 21 at bats for a .333 average. Paul had four RBIs, with three of them coming on hits knocking in his younger brother. It would only get better from here, and one thing was clear to Bush and Pirates watchers—the one-two punch of the Waners worked. They had an uncanny sense of how the other brother was running the bases, or which pitch one would swing at. Paul aimed his line drives to right of left field, depending on which base Lloyd was on, just as Lloyd was suddenly breaking into a gallop. It established a pattern the two would follow throughout their careers.

In those early weeks together again, Paul, with one big-league season under his belt, tutored Lloyd on his hitting and gave him advice on different pitchers Lloyd was having trouble with. He got him to open up his stance against left-handers so he wouldn't pull away from them. And he told him to focus on the ball once it's delivered and not the pitcher's motion or wind-up beforehand.

Both Waners credited their wrist muscles, which resembled steel springs, for their fast swings. Paul reminded Lloyd to chop down on the ball and aim for the foul lines. As for his stance, he stood with his feet close together in the batter's box, about five inches from the back line. When starting his swing, he took a full stride, raising his right foot about four inches.

Lloyd Waner: *"The main thing he used to tell me was to hit down on the ball instead of up. He said that would give me a level stroke and I'd hit a lot of line drives. That's the way he did it and he'd hit them through that infield so fast they couldn't see them."*

Lloyd emulated how Paul used to lay the bat right on his shoulder and keep it motionless until the last second. Then with whip-like ferocity, he'd lash it around and smash the ball for short line drives.

The Waners made contact their policy, and they had great vision for seeing the ball as it arrived to home plate. "Cat's eyes," Brooklyn's manager Wilbert Robinson once said, "that's what both of them have. No wonder they can hit. Can probably see in the dark, too."

Beyond introducing the Waner brothers to the National League, Pittsburgh made some other headlines early that season. In the first game of a May 30 doubleheader at Forbes Field, Cubs shortstop Jimmy Cooney pulled off an unassisted triple play in the fourth inning against the Pirates. With runners on first and second, Paul Waner lined to Cooney, who stepped on second base to get brother Lloyd Waner and then tagged Clyde Barnhart as he came down from first. The Cubs went on to win the game, 7–6, in 10 innings and then edged the Pirates, 6–5, in the second game. Cooney and the Cubs snapped an 11-game Pirates winning streak. Eight days later Chicago traded Cooney—hitting .242 at the time—to the Phillies. It was proof yet again that baseball rewards hitters more than fielders.

As the Waners began visiting cities around the league, it became clear that the two brothers on the same team should have nicknames. After all, they looked almost like twins, both played the outfield, and both collected hits by the bucketfuls. What kind of nickname would apply to these brothers, wondered sportswriters? No nicknames existed until a 1927 newspaper article.

The nicknames "Big Poison" and "Little Poison" stuck with them throughout their careers. Much speculation has focused on their origins. How did these monikers, some of baseball's most memorable, arise? Was it because the Waners were "poison" to National League pitching? While they were, that was not a likely source, though the magic of the nicknames alluded to this effect as well.

Lloyd Waner: *"It started in 1927, in New York. We were playing the Giants in the Polo Grounds. There used to be this Italian fellow who always*

Lloyd Waner (courtesy of Jim Knight).

sat in the center-field bleachers. He had a voice on him you could hear all over the ball park. When he hollered out you heard him no matter where you were. Well, Paul and I were hitting well against the Giants. This one day we came out of the clubhouse between games of a doubleheader and this fellow started hollering at us. What it sounded like was 'Big and Little Poison,' but what he was really saying was 'Big and Little Person.' He was a real nice fellow and we would wave at him and he finally became our biggest rooter in the Polo Grounds. We got him an autographed baseball one time. But whenever we came in there he would yell that and the newspapermen finally picked it up, except they thought he was saying 'Poison' instead of 'Person.' It became a newspaper nickname, because no ball players ever called us that."

Paul confirmed Lloyd's recollection. In a 1941 *Sporting News* questionnaire, Paul wrote in his own handwriting regarding the nickname: an "Italian fan wanted to see the Big + Little Persons and pronounced it like poison." In numerous other interviews, he said the nicknames arose in Brooklyn's Ebbets Field.

So, who was that "Italian fan?" Some newspapers accounts identify him as either Tony or Abie. He either sat behind the visitors dugout, or as Lloyd said, in the outfield bleachers. He may have been a newspaper vendor outside Ebbets Field.

In 1962, an Associated Press story quoted Paul on the origins of "Poison."

Paul Waner: *"It was given to me by a fellow named Abie who sold newspapers outside Ebbets Field in Brooklyn. It was in 1927, my second year with Pittsburgh. Lloyd, my kid brother, had just joined the club. I weighed 145 pounds then, and Lloyd, 135.*

"We both got off to a fast start and by the time we played our first game in Brooklyn, Lloyd and I were hitting around .450 apiece. A reporter saw Abie in the park and was surprised because Abie rarely left his newsstand.

5. Big and Little Poison

'What are you doing at the game, Abie,' the reporter asked.
'I came to see those poisons,' Abie said.
'Poisons, what poisons?'
'You know, the big poison and the little poison on the Pittsburghers,' Abie explained.
"Abie meant to say 'persons,' of course, but from that day on Lloyd and I became known as 'Little and Big Poison.'"

The Waner nicknames were perpetuated by sportswriters who heard a fan (maybe Abie) holler it out in some form, as Lloyd and Paul both attested to. As a pun and play on words, Big Poison and Little Poison emphasized different meanings or applications—for example, "poison for pitchers," and the brother aspect of "big" and "little" brother. Thus, the name was a perfect fit.

To be sure, the poison twins were lethal to National League pitchers that season. By June 8, Paul was batting .363 with 52 RBIs in only 44 games. Lloyd's .315 average and 35 runs scored was impressive for a first-year recruit.

But poison other than the Waners seeped into the Pirates clubhouse that spring. When the club staggered and demonstrated what Bush thought was a lack of enthusiasm, the manager tinkered with the lineup. One of the changes involved switching Kiki Cuyler from the third spot to the second spot and moving him from center field to left field. No matter the sugar-coating, it was a demotion for him.

Cuyler exploded. He saw himself as a speed merchant and a slugger, not a move-the-runner-along type of hitter who sacrificed himself a lot. Why, he could steal bases, leading the league four times. He swung from the heels, drove in RBIs in bunches, and struck out more often than the average player of the era. Not much of a bunter or someone who could slice hits behind the runner, Cuyler was uncomfortable making the switch to the second spot. And he let it be known.

When Bush demoted him, Cuyler was hitting .309 in 85 games and had already swiped 20 bases. It wasn't only the batting order decision that rankled him. He didn't like giving up the center field spot. But Lloyd Waner had proved splendid in chasing flies in left field, and Bush was determined to play Lloyd, now batting .329, in the most valuable outfield spot.

Without his heart in it, Cuyler went 0 for 5 in his first game as a number two hitter. In the clubhouse after the game, Cuyler complained to Bush that the move was not going to work. The manager only responded, "You'll get used to it."

Cuyler complained to the media about his unhappiness and kept chattering at Bush, which only seemed to toughen the rookie manager's stance. During an especially poor showing in Cincinnati, Cuyler slammed his bat into the ground and demanded of Bush, "Take me out of that second slot before I become the worst flop on the team."

Bush retorted, "You'll stay there until I am ready to change you."

Earl Smith, the catcher, didn't help matters by kidding Cuyler in front of Bush, "Doesn't Kiki like where the manager wants to bat him? Too bad."

A few days later Cuyler failed to slide on a force out at second base in a game against the Giants. Bush promptly fined him $50. The two got into a shouting match, and Bush benched the outfielder in favor of Clyde Barnhart. The issue soon became a major topic among Pittsburgh newspapers and fans. Many of them sided with Cuyler, roasting Bush in the daily sports sections.

At Forbes Field, fans screamed, "We want Kiki," at the games. The most vocal and violent of the fans tended to sit in the 50-cent bleacher seats in left field. After throwing empty beer bottles at Bush, several of them were kicked out of the game.

Other players around the league joined in the fray. Bill Terry, the Giants first baseman, defended Cuyler on his "slide." To any objective observer, Cuyler was one of the league's most gifted players. Unfortunately, the criticism seemed only to harden Bush's resolve to bench Cuyler permanently. And Dreyfuss toed the hard line for a second year in a row when it came to discipline.

"We're not going to let the fans or even those fellows up in the press box pick our lineup," the owner said.

They never relented, and Cuyler never played another inning with the Pirates. He didn't even pinch-hit for the rest of the year.

With Cuyler benched, Lloyd now assumed center field duties for Pittsburgh, a position he would hold for the next decade or so.

After the season, Pittsburgh would trade Cuyler to the Chicago Cubs for two undistinguished players. One of the club's most lopsided trades ever, the dumping ignited another firestorm of criticism against the Pirates brass. As Fred Lieb wrote, "A star in the making, his meteoric career was to flash over Pittsburgh skies for only four brief but tumultuous seasons, when the brilliant Cuyler was to become the fickle Dreyfuss' gift to the Chicago fans."

Had Cuyler remained in Pittsburgh, there was no telling how strong the team would have been with three Hall of Famers playing side by side in the outfield. But the man known as "Kiki" had his idiosyncrasies.

Woody English, the Chicago shortstop, played with Cuyler on the Cubs from 1928 to 1934.

5. Big and Little Poison

Woody English: *"Cuyler was a lifetime .321 hitter and he could steal bases, and we were able to get him because he got into a feud with Donie Bush in Pittsburgh. There was a close play in a crucial game, and Cuyler didn't slide into second base. And that's why Donie got rid of Cuyler. You know, Cuyler wasn't too popular with the players, either. He was a loner. There were several things about him that I could see where people wouldn't like him. For instance, he put suntan powder on his face to make it look like he was sunburned. And as good as he could throw, he never threw anybody out in a close game, and he never seemed to get the winning hit for the Cubs when I was there. He was an 'average' guy. He liked to get his average up. Probably didn't know who won the game, but he did all right. He could run. But I'd have to say he wasn't very popular with the majority of the players. He kept to himself. He liked to dance, and he'd go out, never palled around with a single player on the club. They didn't really dislike him, but he wasn't one of the boys."*

English's scathing claims aside, no one doubted the extent of Cuyler's talent. He also stole bases at a time when few did. Neither of the Waners stole many bases during their careers.

As author Donald Honig puts it, "The stolen base was a lost art form in the '20s and '30s. Maybe the top base stealer in the league would swipe 30 bases a year. The ball was so lively that Ty Cobb's style of play soon went out. There was no need to steal lots of bases. The players started going for the long ball."

The "what ifs" of baseball are never-ending. What if, like Cuyler, the Waners had stolen more bases? They had the speed to do so, especially Lloyd. If the Waners had also offered a running game to complement their high-average attacks, hindsight historians might consider them as greater offensive players. Lloyd's career high in stolen bases was 14 in his rookie season. Paul once stole 18 bases.

At the time, however, baseball strategy was based on station-to-station scoring, with runs coming from a flurry of singles and maybe an extra base hit. Why take a chance on a stolen base ending an inning? Most lineups had guys who could hit singles and usually had one big power hitter. Today, lineups are designed just the opposite, with a plethora of power hitters and few table setters—guys like the Waners.

"Stealing was just not part of the game," Honig noted.

Speed and eyes gave the Waners their edge. Once Paul's phenomenal eye-hand coordination aroused one reporter's curiosity. Paul was prone to telling the writers that his eyes could actually magnify an object like a baseball as it was hurtling towards him, thus making it easier to hit. It was utter nonsense, of course, but the writer took the bait and wrote a story on the subject of Paul's eyesight.

Pittsburgh physician, Dr. Robert F. Room, was quoted in the story. He had a more plausible theory than Paul's yarn spinning.

"Waner didn't have eyes that magnified because there are no such things," Dr. Room said. "What he might have had was extraordinary power of concentration. His eyes would pick up the ball the instant it left the pitcher's hand and focus on it intently that it actually looked to him as though it was increasing in size as it approached the plate. This ability to concentrate would serve the same purpose as a magnifying eye."

The powers of concentration served Paul well in putting together a power-hitting record unequaled by any other hitter in baseball history.

Starting on June 3, Waner managed to get an extra-base hit in 14 straight games—a little-known major league record that stands to this day. While it doesn't have the Hollywood brilliance of Joe DiMaggio's 56-game hitting streak, it may be just as formidable to break.

That wasn't all. During this extra-base spree, Paul Waner set the Pirate franchise record of 12 straight games with at least one RBI. Paul drove in 23 runners during the 12 games starting on June 2, the day before the extra-base bender began. The all-time major league record is 17 straight games with at least one RBI, set by Oscar Grimes of the 1923 Chicago Cubs (27 RBIs total).

Throughout his career, Paul's specialty was to make long hits of the two-bag and three-bag variety. His lifetime total of 605 doubles ranks 11th all-time, and his 191 triples are 10th all-time in baseball history. That's even including the 19th-century players.

In the first game of his streak, Waner rallied his club against Philadelphia 11-1 with a home run and two singles. After a rain-out and day off, the Pirates resumed the series against Philadelphia on June 6. The Pirates won 7–5 with Paul stroking another home run and a double.

On June 7 against New York, the Pirates won 9–6 as Waner smashed a double and New York's Rogers Hornsby hit his 200th career home run. Giants third baseman Fred Lindstrom robbed Paul of another extra-base knock on a brilliant grab of a wicked line drive. The Pirates were manhandling New York that season, winning all first five games to date against the Giants.

New York, however, soon had its revenge. The following day Hornsby homered in the ninth inning for a 8–7 victory. But Paul extended his extra-base hitting streak to four with a triple. On June 9, he stretched it to five with a double as New York beat the Pirates 12–1.

On June 10, Paul's bachelor days came to an end when he married

Corinne Moore. The two had grown up a "stone's throw" from each other in Oklahoma and had attended grade and high schools together. They had begun dating when Paul was attending East Central State Teachers' College. Moore eventually graduated from Columbia University, in 1924, and afterwards taught physical education in Port Arthur, Texas, schools.

Corinne Waner: *"We knew each other a little growing up. Then he came down to Ada to go to school, where I was going at the time to get my degree in physical education. He was a good student there. After he went on to the major leagues, we got married and we traveled quite a bit around, during his Pittsburgh and Boston days."*

The ceremony was performed at the home of John Hughes, a friend of Paul's. Hughes lived in Dormont, just outside the Pittsburgh city limits. The Rev. E. C. McGown of the Mt. Lebanon Presbyterian Church married the couple. Local fans and the Pirates chipped in and bought the newlyweds a new automobile, which was presented to Paul before the next home game. The new car came with some strings attached.

Paul Waner: *"They made the presentation all right, and a friend handed me the keys to the car. Later I learned he had made the first payment and I had to make the rest."*

After the wedding, the Waners took up residence in the Morrowfield apartments near Forbes Field.

Paul didn't let marriage get in the way of his streak. On the same day he got married, he celebrated with a pair of doubles, a triple, and five RBIs. The Pirates stymied the Giants 13–4 in the last game of the four-game set.

On June 11, the nation hailed not Waner's marriage but the return of Charles Lindbergh from Paris after his historic transatlantic flight. While President Calvin Coolidge pinned a Flying Cross to Lindbergh's chest, Paul Waner knocked a double in an 11–10 loss to Brooklyn.

The next day the Pirates lost again to Brooklyn as Paul extended his extra-base hitting streak to eight games with a double and triple. On June 13, the Pirates edged Brooklyn 4–3 as Paul managed an inside-the-park home run that proved the decisive blow. Brooklyn's outfielder Jigger Statz nearly snared the ball, but it sailed over his head and Paul galloped home.

Paul's next extra-base hit was a double on June 15 against the Boston Braves in Pittsburgh. The two-bagger enabled Pirates pitcher Carmen Hill to win his eighth straight game.

The next day, Pittsburgh blanked last-place Boston 6–0. Lloyd got three hits and scored twice while Paul tripled and singled. At this point he also had a 19-game hitting streak to go along with his 11-game extra-base streak.

On June 17, Paul doubled to extend his long-hit record, yet the lowly Braves managed two runs in the ninth inning to win the game. In the final game of the Braves series, Paul banged out a triple to help his team beat Boston 7–4.

The Pirates visited Chicago for a series starting June 19. They lost the first game 14–7 though Waner cracked two doubles and a single in five plate appearances. It would be the last game in his extra-base hitting streak.

The next day, June 20, Paul managed two hits—only singles. The extra-base streak ended, though Paul had also by then hit in 23 straight games, which would remain a career high. In his 14-game extra-base streak, he went 32 for 61 with 11 two-baggers, five triples, and three home runs.

Meanwhile, Lloyd had compiled a 10-game hitting streak in the midst of his brother's streaks.

On June 27, Paul became the season's first player to get 100 hits when he knocked two doubles off Flint Rhem of the Cardinals. At the time, Frankie Frisch of the Cardinals and Lou Gehrig of the Yankees each had 99 safeties.

Paul was making a name for himself in a city still fresh with the memory of the great Honus Wagner. Though Wagner had had a falling out with Dreyfuss upon retirement over money issues and was not involved with the club at that point, the Flying Dutchman was still very much a presence in the Steel City.

That summer the writer Tom Meany was at Forbes Field when a familiar-looking figure strode to the plate.

Tom Meany: *"One evening in Pittsburgh, after a Dodger-Pirate game, there was a twilight game scheduled between the Homestead Grays, a well-known Negro team, and the Green Cab Co. Some of us in the press box lingered to watch an inning or two of the game, principally because Wagner was playing first base for the cabbies. On his first time at bat, Honus tripled to the top of the exit gate in right center at Forbes Field. In all the games I have seen at that park in a quarter of a century, that exit gate was cleared only once, by Bill Terry with the Giants. And this was in 1927 when Honus hit the top of it, when he was 53 years old!"*

Honus Wagner had played with some tough characters in baseball's early days, but the 1927 Pirates were among the rowdiest, and it seemed a tradition with the Pittsburgh clubs for some years. If they weren't fighting, they were drinking, or both. (The Waners preferred the drinking.)

Ed Froelich became a bat boy for the Chicago Cubs in 1924. His remembrances of the Pirates were included in Peter Golenbock's *Wrigleyville*.

Ed Froelich: "One of the best teams around that time was the Pittsburgh Pirates, who won the pennant in 1927. The Pittsburgh team was a hell-bent drinking crowd. The Waner brothers, Paul and Lloyd, were on that team, with Joe Harris on first base, George Grantham at second, and catching were Johnny Gooch and Earl Smith, Oil Smith, who may have been the toughest character of them all.

"Smith was the guy who when he was with the Giants picked McGraw up, stuck him up against the wall, and beat him up pretty badly. He was also the guy who was catching when [Boston Brave] Dave Bancroft slid to score a run, and Smith punched him in the face and knocked him out cold. He was a tough man, hard as nails. Nobody wanted to challenge him because he was so unpredictable. He'd hit you first and argue later. Earl Smith was a silent guy, had those cold, blue eyes, blond hair, and he'd always be chewing tobacco. He didn't mind taking a drink or two, either."

Smith's blow to Bancroft took place on June 18 in the midst of Paul Waner's extra-base streak. It didn't affect Paul's line-drive binge, but it caused Bancroft to lose consciousness and turn white. Boston's player-manager was carried off the field and taken into the clubhouse for medical treatment.

Smith and Bancroft had bad blood going back to 1923 when Bancroft levied a $500 fine on Smith—then on the Braves—for throwing a chair out of a hotel window. Smith always wanted his $500 back, but Bancroft, a fiery shortstop in his Hall of Fame career, wouldn't budge. When the Pirates visited Boston in 1927 the next time, Bancroft attempted to have Oil served papers for $15,000 in damages. The catcher climbed over the Braves Field outfield fence to avoid the process server, leading to *The Sporting News* to observe in a headline: "Blackguards Always Are Cowards."

Author Robert Creamer once described Smith, from Arkansas, as "a hard-drinking tough-guy catcher who had no fear of anybody." With the champion Giants of 1921–22, he ignored manager John McGraw's signals and defied, of all things, bed checks. The Giants traded Smith away as McGraw screeched he was a "goddamned anarchist" with "no respect for law and order."

Law and order was in shorter supply than booze in those Prohibition days. Some of the drinking must have fueled tempers at times.

Ed Froelich: "The Pirates came into Chicago one time, and it was Prohibition days and the club was faltering a little at the time, and manager Donie

Bush decided he would search everybody's suitcase. Everybody's suitcase was frisked, and Bush found whiskey in practically everybody's suitcase. Players would get good Canadian whiskey when they came to Chicago through Al Capone. Capone got the whiskey into the country inside cans of ham. You'd take a can opener and open up the ham can, and there inside would be a nice bottle of Canadian whiskey. Well, Donie Bush found ham cans in practically every suitcase. He didn't take their ham cans away, but he did fine them."

One wonders if Bush dared to fine Earl Smith.

While it is unclear whether the Waners were involved in the mischief-making, they had no qualms about quenching a good thirst, especially Big Poison.

Fred Lieb once wrote about Barney Dreyfuss's reaction to Paul's thirst for the bottle. While Dreyfuss hated cigarettes, he did make his pre–Prohibition fortune in beer and distilleries, a fact not lost upon the Pirates players. When told about Paul's midnight adventures, Lieb wrote, "There is a story that Barney Dreyfuss once repeated a variation of Lincoln's famous remark about General Grant when gossips brought reports of Paul's imbibing. 'Find out what brand he drinks. I want to send some of it to some of my other players.'"

By July, baseball writers were plucking descriptions and predictions from thin air as they tried to describe the Waners and their unique outfield combination as brothers. Some said they were baseball's best "brother act." The more skeptical doubted that Lloyd could make it through the entire season. *Baseball Magazine* intoned that "Lloyd is still quite young and under weight, and may not be able to stand the hot pace as the season ripens."

Some of the Pirates dubbed their scrawny center fielder, "Sprouts," in the hope Lloyd would grow like a weed. Others teased him with the tag, "Muscles."

Lloyd muscled up and smacked his first career home run on August 11. The pitcher was no less than the great Grover Cleveland Alexander of St. Louis. Of Lloyd's 27 lifetime home runs, 13 would be inside the park. His first one went over the fence.

Speed, not power, gave the Waners their edge, noted Rud Rennie of the *New York Herald Tribune*. They played smart baseball, seemingly able to ascertain each other's moves.

Rud Rennie: *"It may be imagination, but it seems that every time one looks up one of the Waners is on base and the other is hitting the ball. Sometimes one is sure there must be more than two of them. You see, Lloyd leads* *off and not infrequently gets on base. Paul bats third, and also has a habit of getting on base. The result is that Lloyd moves around ahead of Paul. Once again, as in fielding, they never get in each other's way. There is no danger of Paul's being delayed in transit due to Lloyd's slowness, not unless he breaks a leg. They are two of the speediest base runners in the business."*

Heinie Groh, a veteran of six World Series clubs, played on that 1927 team with the Waners.

Heinie Groh: *"That was the first year both the Waner boys were in the outfield for Pittsburgh, and it sure was a delight to watch those two play baseball. Could they ever hit. No bloopers, either. All line drives. And both of them fast as antelopes."*

But they weren't gods with wing-tipped shoes. Early in August when the Pirates were playing the Giants in the Polo Grounds, the Waners were doubled up. Lloyd started the inning off with a single. Second baseman George Grantham fanned next. Then Paul stung a sharp grounder to first baseman Bill Terry, who whipped the ball to second base to nail Lloyd by a few inches, and then stood back on first base to take the throw from shortstop Travis Jackson to barely nip Paul.

The brothers connected for their share of baseball oddities. On September 4, the Waners became the first brothers to homer in the same game and same inning, connecting off Cincinnati's Dolf Luque, "The Pride of Havana" and one of the finest players ever to come out of Cuba. For the Waners, it wasn't so much the distance of their home runs—these balls bounced into the stands. Until 1930, balls that bounced into the stands were deemed home runs.

Lloyd Waner: *"Paul had wonderful bat control. I'll never forget one day in Cincinnati. The old park there had a low fence in front of the box seats down behind third base. I swung at a pitch and sliced it about a foot inside the foul line, and it went into the seats on one bounce. In those days it was a home run. And as I crossed the plate, Paul, who was the next hitter, said to me, 'Now I'll show you how to hit one, too.'"*

He did, hitting the same line of trajectory that Lloyd had. Eppa Rixey, Cincinnati's tall left-handed pitcher, watched from the bench. "Those were the only two times in my life I ever saw a ball hit in that spot twice and go into the stands," he said.

Rixey was 6 foot 4 inches and wore size 13 shoes. Once he was pitching against the Pirates in Pittsburgh when snow began to fall. "A fellow," Rixey said, "ought to have snowshoes to play here."

Paul Waner pointed to Rixey's huge feet and said, "Ep, you've already got yours on."

Twice more the Waners would homer in the same game—in 1929 and 1938. Other brothers to homer in the same game include Jason and Jeremy Giambi, Aaron and Bret Boone, Hank and Tommie Aaron, Billy and Tony Conigliaro, Graig and Jim Nettles, Cal and Billy Ripken, Rick and Wes Ferrell, Al and Tony Cuccinello, and Matty and Jesus Alou.

Toward the end of the season, the Waners sat down and talked money with Dreyfuss—and found it harder to drive the long ball there. In the days of the reserve clause, and no agents, young ballplayers were hardly a match for shrewd businessman who had years of experienced negotiating and protecting their interests. They marched up to Dreyfuss' office and listened to the owner tell them the facts of life.

Paul Waner: *"I sat down in the chair and he said, 'You're a pretty good hitter, but you can't come in on a ball very well from right field, and you can't bunt.'*

"I don't know what made me say this, but I told Barney, 'Neither can Babe Ruth, and he's making $80,000 a year.' He was stunned and for a minute didn't have an answer for me. I used to accuse Bill Benswanger [Dreyfuss's son-in-law who became the owner years later] of keeping a book for the old man. Barney would pull it out when he wanted to talk about the contract. He never mentioned the good days, only the bad ones. If you hit four straight homers and popped out the fifth time, that's the one he would talk about."

Salary talks were a source of chronic tension between Paul Waner and Barney Dreyfuss. Paul was a confident ballplayer and not one to blindly accept authority, especially when it mattered in the pocketbook. Two years later in 1928 Dreyfuss told Paul to become a slugger.

"Why don't you hit home runs like Ruth," squawked Dreyfuss.

Paul replied, "You want me to hit home runs, Barney? Okay, I'll hit them."

The next season Paul would hit a career-high 15 home runs. But his average dropped to .336. When contract time rolled around, Dreyfuss refused to give Paul a raise.

"Why should I give you a raise?" Dreyfuss said. "Look what happened to your batting average. It dropped," the owner complained.

Paul gave up on hitting home runs.

Somebody once told Kiki Cuyler that Dreyfuss kept figures on everything. So come contract time Cuyler armed himself with all kinds of glowing statistics and made his appointment to see the owner.

Paul Waner: *"Kiki walked in and had the paper in hand. Barney told him to sit down and before Cuyler could say a word, Dreyfuss said, 'Now, Hazen, I don't believe in figures.' Well, that was the end of Cuyler's chance to argue about his play."*

After Paul retired, he looked more fondly upon Dreyfuss and his cheap ways. After all, by then Paul had played some under other owners more tight-fisted, like Branch Rickey.

Paul Waner: *"Barney didn't treat me badly, though. I earned $5,400 my first year, and got a $1,100 raise the next year. After I hit .380 that second year, the old man boosted me to $11,500. That was a pretty big pay raise in those days."*

In September, the Pirates torched the league for a 22–9 record, clinching the pennant. At the end, Pittsburgh's season record stood at 94–60, a game and a-half over the Cardinals—last year's champions—and two games over the Giants.

The Pirates clouted their way to the top with a league-leading team average of .305. Their 817 runs scored tied the New York Giants for the league high.

The precocious Waners made all the difference.

If you're not talking power, Lloyd's was one of the greatest rookie seasons in baseball history. His .355 average was only second to Paul's in the league. He also hammered out a National League rookie record 223 hits and scored 133 runs. Of his hits, 198 of them were singles, thus setting a record that exists today. Willie Keeler's 202 singles in 1898 with the Baltimore Orioles stand as the 19th-century high. Before Lloyd, Jack Tobin of the St. Louis Browns had notched 179 singles in 1921 for the best 20th-century mark. In 1985, Wade Boggs of the Boston Red Sox set the American League mark with 187 singles in 240 hits.

Lloyd was the first rookie to ever collect 200 hits. A classic singles-hitter, his 17 doubles and 6 triples that season were indications he would never have much power. He only struck out 23 times—and this would be the most Lloyd ever struck out in one season.

Baseball writers didn't begin picking rookies of the year until 1947, but the Society for American Baseball Research maintains that Lloyd would have been the NL Rookie of the Year in '27 and Paul would have been the pick in '26.

Paul hit a blistering .380 to win the league batting championship. He also led the NL in RBIs with 131 and in triples for the second year in a row with 18. The awesome numbers go on—his 237 hits set an all-time Pirates

Paul Waner standing near his favorite spot to slice line drives—the right field foul line (courtesy of Jim Knight).

record, and he also racked up 42 doubles, 9 home runs, and 114 runs. He only struck out 14 times. After his stunning rookie year, Paul had followed it up with a tour de force campaign.

Paul credited the "use the whole field" approach.

Paul Waner: *"Look, there are three men in the outfield. Why should we hit it where they are? Shoot for the foul lines. If you miss, it's just a foul ball; if you get it in, it's a double. And if it goes into the stands, don't worry. We don't pay for the baseball."*

That season the Waners set records for teammate brothers that still exist today—combined at bats (1,258), batting average (.367), doubles, triples, runs, and fewest Ks. They hit for more than their poundage. With less than 300 pounds between them, they cracked out 460 hits.

The 1927 *Spalding Official Baseball Guide* noted, "One of the greatest personal artistic efforts of the season was the skill displayed by the Waner brothers. Their work was polished, capable and successful, and two better natural ballplayers have not come into major league ranks since the war."

While there would have been no 1927 pennant without the Waners, the Pirates had other heavy contributors. Sparkling third baseman Pie Traynor hit .342 and could scoop up a ground ball, get it out of his glove, and rifle it to first base faster than anybody in the league. The agile Traynor earned the nickname, "the Pirates' second shortstop," for his range. It's been said of Traynor that batters would hit a double down the left field line, but Traynor would throw them out at first.

The Pirates had depth. With a distinct recollection of Joe Harris's stick work in the 1925 World Series, Dreyfuss purchased "Moon" from the Senators. Harris compiled a .326 average and played most of the season

5. Big and Little Poison

at first base. Barnhart hit .319 in 108 games, and Grantham, returning to second base, clipped along at .305. Shortstop Glenn Wright knocked in 105 RBIs, and part-time outfielder Clyde Barnhart finished up with a .319 average after losing his spot in spring training and then regaining it after the Cuyler fiasco. Despite all the good hitters, the Pirates played lots of small ball with bunts and the hit-and-run, setting a team record for sacrifice hits that season with 214.

This was one of those rare years for the Pirates when good hitting and good pitching converged. Carmen Hill, a previous unknown, enjoyed a career year in leading the Pirates with a 22–11 record. Rey Kremer, in winning 19 games, paced the league with a 2.47 ERA, and Lee Meadows pocketed 19 victories. Pittsburgh's combination of plate prowess and strong arms carried them into the postseason.

In October's World Series, the slashing Corsairs would confront the slugging Yankees, a team built diametrically opposite them. The showdown was an exclamation point on the arrival of the Lively Ball Era, and Goliath would prevail over David.

Appalachian Stomp

> Ever since the first caveman picked up the first cudgel, went to his front door and smacked the first nosy saber-toothed tiger in the snout, mankind has known the atavistic power and pleasure of the bat.
> — *Thomas Boswell, from* How Life Imitates the World Series

A few days before the 1927 regular season ended, the Commissioner's Office of Major League Baseball designated the Hotel Schenley in Pittsburgh its headquarters for the upcoming World Series. Because the trip between New York and Pittsburgh could be made overnight, it was agreed that it was not necessary to have a day off.

Many in baseball's higher circles had been hoping for a Yankees–Pirates series. The Yankees had the star power, and Pittsburgh had the AM radio power in the local KDKA station—and a good team as well for a solid match-up. While other fall classics had been heard sporadically on radio, the 1927 Series would be the first to be broadcast uniformly on a nationwide radio hookup with an estimated listening audience of 35 million people.

Late on Sunday night of October 1, the Yankees boarded a Pullman train—dubbed the "Yankee Special"—and pulled out of Pennsylvania Station in New York amid thousands of cheering fans jammed around the gate. Their train chugged westward across the Appalachian Mountains, headed to Pittsburgh.

The Yankees arrived in Pittsburgh early Monday morning and proceeded to the Roosevelt Hotel to check in and eat breakfast. Both teams would have two days to relax and practice before the Series started at Forbes Field on Wednesday.

6. Appalachian Stomp

The Waner family at the opening game of the 1927 World Series vs. the New York Yankees. From the left: Paul Waner, Etta Waner, Ruth Waner, Ora Waner, Lloyd Waner (courtesy of the Oklahoma Sports Museum).

Pirates manager Donie Bush asked Yankees manager Miller Huggins whether he wanted his team to take batting practice in the morning or afternoon. Huggins, looking at the darkening skies, chose morning, and it was a wise choice. So late that morning, Wilcy Moore and Waite Hoyt threw batting practice. Ruth was the first at bat. He bunted a few times, popped up several balls, and then smacked a couple over the right field stands. Lou Gehrig followed and did much the same. The New York writers noted that Ruth seemed to be getting under the ball too much.

After 45 minutes it started to rain, and the Yankees stopped their batting practice. The Pirates never got to take batting practice that day. Back at the hotel, both the Yankees and the Pirates entertained themselves—separately—by playing cards, poker and pinochle the rest of the afternoon. Later that evening players of both teams gathered at the Nixon Theater to watch a mystery play.

Away from the world of baseball, Yankees slugger Lou Gehrig had serious worries. His mother had undergone surgery for a goiter at St. Vincent's Hospital back in New York. When Gehrig was notified by telegram that his mother was OK after the operation, he reportedly tossed his cap in the air and did a "dance."

The rain got everything off track, though. Baseball Commissioner Judge Kenesaw Mountain Landis looked out the window of his Hotel Schenley room just a couple blocks from Forbes Field. It was damp and drizzling outside.

"Does it always rain in Pittsburgh?" Landis asked, recalling the mud-filled World Series between Washington and Pittsburgh of only two years ago. Just in from wind-bitten Chicago, Landis hoped no games would have to be postponed.

Rain or no rain, the odds makers favored New York at 7–5, which might sound a bit favorable to Pittsburgh in hindsight. But Pittsburgh fielded a strong club, and the 1927 Yankees were not as yet acclaimed as the greatest team ever, despite being the first team in history to lead wire to wire and winning an American League record 110 games to finish a record 19 games ahead of the Philadelphia Athletics. The Yankees had led the American League in nearly every offensive category, setting major league records with 975 runs scored, 158 home runs, 908 runs batted in, and a .489 slugging average. Babe Ruth (60 home runs) and Lou Gehrig (47 home runs) formed the most devastating one-two punch in baseball history to that point.

After hitting his record 60th home run, Ruth said, "Sixty, count 'em, sixty. Let's see some son-of-a-bitch match that." On another occasion, the Bambino observed, "If I'd just tried for them dinky singles, I could've batted around .600." On the other hand, the Pirates had hit 54 home runs as a team—and no one player had more than nine.

Confronting this pinstripe buzzsaw were baby-faced Paul and Lloyd Waner. These young phenoms had taken the baseball world by storm that summer, and the sporting press had discovered fascination in the brotherly tandem's rise to stardom. The narrative was set—Ruth and Gehrig versus Paul and Lloyd Waner.

To witness this grand encounter, the Waners brought their mother, father and sister to the East Coast for the Series. Other Oklahomans making the trek included "Arb" Green, the organizer of the Ada Independents, the amateur team on which Paul and Lloyd played after high school.

With the autograph hounds out in full force, the press chuckled at some of the fair-weather fans. One enthusiastic fan revealed his dearth of knowledge about the game when he thanked Pirates outfielder Clyde Barnhart for an autograph, and then told him, "I hope the Pirates win all seven games."

6. Appalachian Stomp

Throughout the Series, baseball comedians Al Schacht and Nick Altrock would captivate the crowds with tricks and skits. They rolled baseballs up and down their arms and backs, clowned around in slow motion, staged a mock Tunney–Dempsey fight, and played a tennis match dressed in women's clothing.

Ghostwritten columns from the players began to appear in the press. One Yankee observed the Pirates "had bunches of columns," and Lloyd's byline was among them. His first piece, just before the Series opened in Pittsburgh, carried the headline, "Lloyd Waner Unexcited Over His First World Series Game."

He was just so mild mannered. In the article Lloyd assured readers he approached these games just like any others and that it was important for a ballplayer to "keep his feelings and his nerves under control."

As Lloyd put it, "Coolness is a highly essential part of the National Pastime."

Both brothers followed this strategy, at least in rhetoric. Paul said years later that he forced himself to "not think about playing in a World Series, so I wouldn't get nervous."

On Tuesday, October 4th, the Yankees took batting practice again. This time Ruth hit five in a row over the fence, Gehrig two, and Bob Meusel, Ben Paschal, and Johnny Grabowski also hit several each.

Thus begat one of baseball's most widely circulated myths.

The myth holds that the New York Yankees won the World Series before the first pitch was even thrown. Supposedly, with Ruth and Gehrig launching moonshot after moonshot, the Yankees had intimidated the singles-hitting Pirates into submission. An unattributed quote to Lloyd Waner had him saying to Paul, "Gee, they're big, aren't they?" The Pirates stood there, mouths opened, watching the balls fly beyond the fences, the tale goes. One by one, they got up and left the park. Some of them were shaking their heads while leaving the field.

This never happened, and the myth is ripe for debunking. The difficulty is that like Ruth's called shot in the 1932 World Series, the story reinforces the popularly held perception of Ruth and the Yankees, something that melodramatic sportswriting feasts upon at the expense of the facts. The other obstacle is locating any eyewitnesses to that batting practice held so many years ago.

Granted, the Pirates and their fans at Forbes Field that afternoon were impressed with the Yankees' batting prowess. But being impressed is much different from being scared into submission. These were professional ballplayers who knew they had a job to do and had experience playing against many tough opponents. While some teams lose confidence, the resulting Series was closely played in three out of the four games, proof that the Pirates played gutsy.

Wilbert Robinson, the Brooklyn manager, wrote a *New York Times* column on the Series. He was an eyewitness to the second day of batting practice and may have contributed to the rise of this tale.

Wilbert Robinson: *"Babe Ruth came up, and whang! he blazed a homer into the right field grandstand. Before he was through he hit four more, and I could see some of the Pittsburgh boys' eyes open when they saw those shots crash into the seats. Gehrig also cracked a couple.*

"On the other hand, while the Pirates looked on in open admiration at the manner in which the Babe and Lou cracked the ball, I don't believe it frightened them in the least. After the workouts I ran into Paul Waner and said, 'Well, Paul, did the big fellows scare you any?'

"'Not a bit, Robbie,' he replied. 'After all they are only ballplayers.'"

Robinson added, "That seems to me to be the attitude of the entire Pittsburgh club."

The Pirates, Lloyd and Paul among them, always refuted the charge they gave up before the Series started.

Lloyd Waner: *"Well, I don't know how that got started. If you want to know the truth, I never even saw the Yankees work out that day. We had our workout first and I dressed and was leaving the ballpark just as they were coming out on the field. I don't think Paul stayed out there either. We never spoke of it. I know some of our players stayed, but I never heard anybody talk about what they saw. I don't know where the story came from. Somebody made it up out of thin air, that's all I can say."*

Paul Waner: *"That's just silly. For one thing, we didn't scare as a club. Why should we have been scared? We had just beaten out the Cardinals, the same team that had taken the Yankees in the 1926 Series. The story is that after we had our workout the day before the Series, we stayed in the stands to look over the Yankees and got scared stiff watching Ruth, Gehrig, Meusel, and Lazzeri belt balls out of the park. Lloyd is supposed to have said to me, 'Aren't those awfully big guys?' The only thing is I wasn't even in the stands. I left the park as soon as I dressed, as did most of us. I doubt Lloyd was there, as we usually left the park together. And, as a matter of record, we weren't over-powered. There were only two home runs in the Series, both by Babe Ruth. We weren't disgraced."*

Paul and Lloyd's recollections hold up under scrutiny. The Pittsburgh and New York newspapers only mention an impressive batting practice show by the Yankees and do not reference any signs of intimidation among the Pittsburghers.

We do know that Lloyd Waner was concerned about the American League's livelier ball. Unlike today, back then the AL and NL used differently manufactured balls, and for years the AL ball was considered more juiced. In the World Series the rules called for the home team to use their league ball, thus theoretically erasing any advantage.

Lloyd did contradict his later assertion that he never saw the Yankees practice (maybe his ghostwriter did, however) but expressed confidence the Pirates would beat New York anyhow: "The ball used in the American League undoubtedly is more lively than the official ball of the National League. This was apparent in the practice sessions yesterday. Their smashes always appeared to bound higher than ours."

And he noted, "After closely watching the New York Yankees all through their practice yesterday, I could not help but feel that they are just another good baseball club."

Lloyd poked fun at the "Homer Gap."

"As a home run hitter," he said, "I finished just 58 circuit slams behind Babe Ruth and I was beaten out by Lou Gehrig with a margin of 46 such drives, but the two roundtrippers I produced certainly afford me all the pride of a small boy wearing his first pair of boots."

Small boys is exactly what Babe Ruth thought about the Waners after first seeing them. He was widely quoted as saying, "Why they're just little kids. If I was that little I'd be afraid of getting hurt."

Beyond Ruth and Gehrig, the Yankees featured Earle Combs, the best lead-off hitter in baseball. He batted .356 and led the league with 231 hits and 23 triples. Bob Meusel hit .337 with eight HRs and 103 RBIs and finished second with 24 stolen bases. Tony Lazzeri compiled a .309 average, finished third in the league with 18 HRs, had 102 RBIs, and tied for third with 22 steals. The switch-hitting Mark Koenig clipped at .285 and scored 99 runs from the number two spot in the order. Joe Dugan, a solid fielding third basemen, hit .269 average. The catching trio of Pat Collins, John Grabowski and Benny Bengough combined to hit .271 with seven HRs and 71 RBIs.

Yankees pitchers also dominated the league, posting a league-leading 3.20 ERA and 11 shutouts. Waite Hoyt, the ace of the staff, won 22 and lost only 7 and had a 2.64 ERA. Thirty-year-old rookie Wilcy Moore burst into the majors as the best relief pitcher in baseball, posting a 19–7 record and leading the league with a 2.28 ERA, while tying for the league lead with 13 saves. Herb Pennock, one of the best southpaws in the game, finished 19–8 with a 3.00 ERA. Urban Shocker, one of the few pitchers still

Sportswriters billed the 1927 World Series between the Yankees and Pirates as the clash of baseball titans, large and small, or Ruth and Gehrig vs. the "Waner Act." From the left: Paul Waner, Babe Ruth, Lloyd Waner, Lou Gehrig (courtesy of Jim Knight).

legally allowed to throw a spitball, finished 18–6 and was third in the league with a 2.84 ERA. Dutch Ruether, in his final season in the major leagues, and the hard-throwing George Pipgras, after being eased into the starting rotation in mid season, combined for a 23–9 record, with a 3.73 ERA.

In the regular season Pittsburgh seemed prone to playing to the level of its competition, dominating the stronger NL teams but getting upset too often by the woeful Phillies and Braves.

Like the Yankees, the Pirates had recent Series experience, having won in 1925 over Walter Johnson and the Washington Senators. The Yankees had won four pennants, though only one World Series, in 1923.

In the match-ups, the Yankees had an ominous edge. The Pirates only had two left-handers on the staff, Mike Cvengros and Emil Yde, both of them predominantly relievers. Against the Pirates' right-handed staff, the Yankees featured four left-handed swingers in their first four guys in the lineup. Much was made of the fact the Yankees hadn't seen curveball pitchers like the Pirates, and that the Pirates feasted on left-handed

6. Appalachian Stomp

pitchers like Herb Pennock despite having a bunch of lefty swingers themselves.

At Forbes Field in 1927—and these distances were apt to change periodically—the distance down the left field line was 375 feet, the deepest corner at the flag pole in left center was 462 feet, straight away center field was 442 feet. In 1925, the 86-foot-high right field grandstand was built. Beyond the wooden left field and center field walls was Schenley Park. Seating capacity was around 35,000, but extra bleachers had been built for the Series behind the wall in left and center, raising capacity to 42,000. Forbes Field was decorated with red, white and blue buntings.

All of the Yankees pitchers tossed batting practice Tuesday except Game One starter Hoyt. The Yankees got worried when Pennock was cracked on the knee while throwing batting practice. He was listed immediately as questionable for starting Game Three. The Yankees wrapped up their workout by snapping and flipping the ball around in infield practice. To gauge the amount of foul area, Gehrig paced off the distance from first base to the new temporary field boxes in the stands.

The Yankees quickly got acclimated with the notorious infield at Forbes Field. Dugan remarked, "It's hard as a rock and you will see some fast shots going through during the next two games. If Ruth and Gehrig played a season on this field they would kill some infielder."

That second day of practice Ruth was the last position player to leave the field. The world-famous Bambino paused briefly to shake hands and pose for a photograph with Honus Wagner and other local VIPs. Fans crowded outside the gates after the Yankees afternoon session to try to get a glimpse of Ruth. One veterans group in Pittsburgh presented Ruth with an award of appreciation in his hotel room during the Series. The Waners even asked for his autograph.

The night before Game One New York's Waite Hoyt prepared to face the Pirates. He studied the Pirates lineup and scouting report in his hotel room. Years later he recalled the "book against" the Waners.

Waite Hoyt: *"I went over the scouting reports with my catcher. The Waners were slash hitters. Late to put the bat on the ball, last minute swingers—and they always got a piece of the ball. More to left field than to right. 'Pitch inside to them,' the reports said. 'Even then play the third baseman close to the line.'"*

The next morning Forbes Field's gates opened at 10 A.M. Before the game, the traditional pre-game photos were taken of Huggins and Bush, and another famous one of Ruth and Gehrig shaking hands with Lloyd and Paul Waner. The Waners and Pirates appeared in white uniforms with dark blue and red striped stirrups, while the visiting Yankees appeared in their road gray uniforms, with navy blue and rust colored stirrups. Governor Fisher of Pennsylvania threw out the first pitch.

The temperature was in the 70s at game time, a mild, clear-sky October day in western Pennsylvania. Starting pitchers were New York's Waite Hoyt and Pittsburgh's Ray Kremer.

Earle Combs swung at Kremer's first pitch and flew out to Clyde Barnhart in deep left field. After Ruth walked, the Yankees then took a 1-0 lead on Gehrig's triple to right field where Paul attempted a shoestring catch but missed, the ball skipping past him to score Ruth from first. In the Pirates' turn, Hoyt accidentally plunked Lloyd on the shoulder with a pitch. Paul then doubled him around to third, and Lloyd eventually scored on Glenn Wright's fly ball. Paul was stranded at third after Traynor flied out to right.

In the third inning, the Yankees scored three times on Pirates fielding gaffes. Grantham, playing first base, made an error on Mark Koenig's grounder to begin the inning. After Ruth stung a single, Kremer walked Gehrig and Meusel to force home a run. Lazzeri bounced into a force out that scored Ruth and moved Gehrig to third base. The Pirates nailed Gehrig in a rundown between third and home, but catcher Earl Smith misplayed Traynor's throw for the second error of the inning.

New York won the first game, 5–4. The two errors and misplays hurt the Pirates more than anything. In such a close game, if the Pirates had just fielded one of those plays successfully, they might have won.

Paul Waner: *"We knocked Hoyt out of the box in the first game, and lost when a double play ball took a bad bounce and hit George Grantham, our second baseman, in the chest."*

The Yankees, meanwhile, showed gracefulness on the field. Babe Ruth made an outstanding catch that Paul Waner rhapsodized about years later.

Paul Waner: *"I saw what I'll always recall as the greatest catch ever in that World Series. I was on third base when Pie Traynor hit a sinking liner to right. There were two out, and Babe Ruth came running in to make a backhand catch just off the ground. Don't let anyone tell you all Ruth could do was hit. That catch had plenty to do with the Yanks beating us four straight."*

In covering the games, the Associated Press played up the showdown between the Waner brothers and the Ruth-Gehrig combo. After every game the wire service ran a story titled: "Home Run Twins vs. the Waner Act."

6. Appalachian Stomp

Every day the wire service listed the offensive production of Ruth, Gehrig and the two Waners.

In Game Two, New York pitcher George Pipgras analyzed the Pirates lineup before he took the mound. The Yankees hurlers were into studying their opponents.

George Pipgras: *"I'll tell you what I did. I went back to the hotel and began studying that Pirate lineup until my eyes started to hurt. How was I going to pitch to them? They had some good hitters— the Waner brothers, Pie Traynor, Joe Harris, Glenn Wright. I guess I was a bit nervous when I got to the ball park the next day. Heck, I was pitching for a team that had won 110 games. I was expected to win. I got some great encouragement from Urban Shocker in the clubhouse— he was going to be the first out of the bullpen if I got into trouble.*

"'Listen,' he said, 'when you leave the game, leave the ball rough.' He was a spitball artist, you see. 'Sure,' I said, 'I'll do that.'"

"I was fast that day," he said. "Didn't throw but three curves. They kept coming up there looking for the curve but never got it."

Though Pipgras started off shaky—Lloyd Waner led off with a triple in the first, and then scored—the Yankees roared back with three runs in the third. One of the runs scored because Lloyd allowed a ball to go between his legs. New York added three more in the eighth.

Lloyd's error symbolized the Pirates' shoddy fielding the first two games. After Game One, Ora Waner, in a brilliant example of baseball-minded paternalism, talked with his sons on "how to play the Yankee sluggers" in the outfield. Lloyd, however, redeemed himself somewhat later in Game Two by catching a deep fly by Combs.

The greatest outburst of the Series took place in the stands at Forbes Field in Game Two. Down four runs in the eighth inning, Pirates fans went bonkers when they realized that Bush had to choose a pinch hitter for relief pitcher Cvengros. They started chanting for the long-exiled Kiki Cuyler to pinch-hit. The *Pittsburgh Post-Gazette* noted, "Scanning the bench for a pinch hitter, Bush heard, even as a deaf man would hear, the tumultuous demand that Cuyler be sent to the plate to fill the role."

Bush, instead, tapped Earl Smith. But the fans kept yelling and chanting. "And even with Smith at the plate, the booming of, 'Put Cuyler in,' reverberated from the bleacher ramparts," observed the *Post-Gazette*.

Smith grounded out, and the Pirates went down meekly in the ninth as New York held on to win the second game, 6–2.

The Series moved to Yankee Stadium for Game Three with the Pirates down two games to none. The *Post-Gazette* sounded panic, called the cause as "practically hopeless," and described the Pirates as the "Dr. Jekyll and Mr. Hyde" of baseball clubs. During the season they were unbeatable for stretches and then entirely vulnerable—like now—in others.

It was one thing for the Pirates to give up runs. It was another thing, utterly foreign, for their bats to go silent. And they did in Game Three.

A crowd of 60,695 watched as New York's Herb Pennock retired the first 22 Pirates batters. He had a perfect game going until one out in the eighth when Pie Traynor broke it up with a solid single to left. Barnhart followed with a double to break up the shutout, but the game belonged to Pennock. Gehrig's two-run triple in the first inning provided Pennock all the cushion he needed that afternoon.

The Pirates' defense again let them down. Twice in the seventh inning, Pirates infielders decided to try to throw out lead runners on ground balls, and both times the runners made it safely to the next bag. Had they chosen instead to go for the surer out at first base, they may have prevented runs from scoring. As it was, the Yankees knocked pitcher Lee Meadows out of the inning with six runs, three of them on a Ruth home run.

New York won Game Three 8–1 in the only blowout of the Series. Pennock's three-hit performance that day was memorable in the annals of the World Series.

Lloyd Waner: *"Pennock had fine stuff and A-1 control. Remember, our club had a .305 team batting average that season, but Pennock smooted us out with very little trouble. He wasn't the type who threw it past you—he just made you hit it at somebody."*

Lloyd acknowledged the Pirates' batting slump. "I believe almost anybody could have held us helpless today when we were touching the ball so gently."

Paul Waner: *"I've got to admit Pennock was mighty good that afternoon. Before Herb died years later, I got to know him quite well, and we often discussed how he pitched to me that day. And we both got a big laugh out of it. Remember, I had been the National League batting champion that season, hitting .380, and the league's Most Valuable Player. I had knocked out 237 hits and drove in 131 runs. And you know what he fed me? A ball with nothing on it. It came floating in like a balloon waist high. He kept it on the outside, so I couldn't pull it into the right field. All I did was hit four long flies to the outfield."*

Pie Traynor was upset.

"Our pitching has been good," Traynor said, "yet we have lost three games, and our fielding has been only average if not worse, which puts the

6. Appalachian Stomp

pitchers in the hole. But it's our hitting that has been terrible. We have not made three hits in a row since the Series started. That shows how weak we have been."

Not making three hits in a row was a problem for a team like Pittsburgh that depended on stringing together a series of hits instead of bopping out three-run homers like New York did to score runs.

Down three games to none, the Pirates suddenly risked embarrassing the National League at a time when league rivalries were serious matters, unimaginable in today's fraternity-minded baseball world. Pittsburgh faced the prospect of New York becoming the first American League team to sweep a National League team in the autumn classic. The Chicago Cubs had performed the first Series sweep back in 1907 when they manhandled the Detroit club in four games straight. The "Miracle Braves" of 1914 also had swept their Series from the Athletics, and the New York Giants had accomplished the feat against their cross-town rivals, the Yankees, in 1922.

Getting swept by the American League was something that loyal National League patriots like John McGraw could not stand. In the 1920s, if McGraw's team wasn't in the Series he was often observed advising the NL manager on how to beat the competition. He did so when the Pirates were in the 1925 Series.

Before Game Four—with his club's fate on the brink—Bush tried to whip up the enthusiasm among his downcast Pirates. In glowing terms, he reminded them of their glorious comeback in 1925—done under McKechnie, however, and not Bush. He urged them to stage a similar effort. One wonders whether Bush had the clubhouse in his corner after the Cuyler affair, though.

In Game Four at imperial Yankee Stadium, the Pirates opened with a run in the first inning. But the Yankees responded with a run of their own in the bottom of the inning. It was quiet until the fifth inning when New York went ahead 3–1 on a towering home run by Ruth into the long October shadows at Yankee Stadium. It was his second of the Series. But the scrappy Pirates responded in the seventh inning by tying it 3–3. Winning the first game in New York could set a new tone, the Pirates faithful hoped.

The game remained tied until the ninth inning. The Pirates were unable to score in the top half. In the bottom of the inning the situation turned grave. With the Pirates' Johnny Miljus pitching in relief of Hill, Combs walked to lead off, Koenig beat out a bunt, Combs went to third and Koenig to second on a wild pitch, and then Ruth was intentionally walked. The Yankees had loaded the bases with none out.

Suddenly Miljus got the next two outs, striking out Lou Gehrig and

Bob Meusel. If he could close out the inning, the Pirates would send the game into extra innings and get another chance. All Miljus had to do was get out the next Yankee batter, Tony Lazzeri. He got the sign from Pirates catcher Johnny Gooch and threw.

Paul Waner: *"While he was working on Tony Lazzeri, though, Johnny [Miljus] suddenly let loose a high pitch that sailed over catcher Johnny Gooch's shoulder, and in came Combs with the run that won the game, and the Series, for the Yankees."*

It was Miljus' second wild pitch of the inning. Combs had faked breaking for the plate from third. Maybe it threw off Miljus, or maybe he was tired from two-plus innings in relief.

Out in right field, Waner was stunned. Years later he said the run crossing the plate jolted him into realizing he had just played in a World Series. And it was now over.

As Lloyd saw the fateful wild pitch, "Gooch reached out after the ball, but simply turned it off with his glove. I believe I have seen more than one such offering caught, but they are very hard to handle and hard as he tried, Gooch was not able to get hold of it."

Lloyd Waner: *"The World Series was over. For a couple of seconds I didn't budge, just stood out there in center field. Couldn't believe it, really. It's no way to end a ball game, much less a World Series, on a doggone wild pitch."*

"Shell shocked" was how the *Post-Gazette* described the Pirates team. Their heads hung low as they trooped off the field, the writers noted.

In Pittsburgh that winter the post-mortem debate was fierce. Many debated whether it was Miljus' or Gooch's fault on the errant pitch.

It didn't really matter, for the Pirates faced terrific odds if they were to battle back from being three games down. The real explosive issue concerned the Cuyler benching and how the Pirates failed out of spite to use their star player when they needed his bat the most. In the entire Series he never so much as made an appearance. The Pittsburgh sporting press had jumped all over the Pirates for this, and one editorial cartoon showed a swarthy, loud-mouthed fan yelling, "Put Cuyler In!"

None of the Pirates' pinch hitters during the Series hit the ball out of the infield.

Bush never answered reporters' questions on Cuyler throughout the entire Series, and Cuyler himself kept quiet. After the final out in Game Four, however, he released a rambling statement to the media in New York. As he saw it, given his future in Pittsburgh was over he had nothing to lose.

6. Appalachian Stomp   97

Kiki Cuyler: "To tell the downright and whole truth, the whole thing is a mystery to me. There are some things to be told, without doubt, but it is not I who can tell them. In my own heart I have felt some things, and they may or may not be true, but as for what might be called the facts of the case, they will have to come from my employers."

About the source of the fall-out, Cuyler sounded both regret and innocence.

Kiki Cuyler: "I had paid for my mistake, whether I thought it right or not, and felt that I should be permitted to start with a clean slate. But things didn't seem to work out that way. I was being played in left field and batting second. I had what ballplayers call a 'yen' against batting in that position, and playing left field is about the worst thing I do.... And yet I tried as hard as I ever tried in my life. I made the mistake, I see now, of speaking about these things. I should have batted second and played left field without saying anything, but I wanted to help and felt I could be of more help in center and batting in any other position than second."

Upon hearing of Cuyler's statement to reports, Bush responded that the player had a "temperament" problem.

Donie Bush: "Cuyler is not my style of ballplayer. He wants to do what he wants to do, not what he is told. Cuyler was the sort of ballplayer who had to be handled with kid gloves. Cuyler said he could not play left field and would not bat second in the lineup."

A contemporary ballplayer might tell team management about playing preferences whether through the press or behind closed doors. And management might well listen. But in the 1920s players, even stars like Cuyler, were expected to be much more submissive to management.

One writer observed of Cuyler that he "seems to have come out of this Series a martyr and covered with some sort of synthetic glory." If he were truly a team player, the implication was, he would have shut up and played wherever Bush wanted him.

Cuyler or not, Lloyd thought that by Game Four the Pirates were beginning to play better. Too little, too late, though.

Lloyd Waner: "It's true the Yankees beat us four straight, but they didn't run us off the field. There was only one lopsided game, where they beat us 8–1. Otherwise two of those games were settled by one run, and it seems to me that every game was close going into the late innings."

Lloyd said Babe Ruth and Lou Gehrig were the ones who defeated

Pittsburgh in the World Series. "Outside of those two individuals, the Yanks were not nearly as dangerous as we thought they would be."

As a team, New York had batted .279 and slugged .397 to Pittsburgh's .223 batting and .285 slugging averages. And the Yankees outscored the Pirates 23–10. Yankees shortstop Mark Koenig batted .500 for the Series high.

Paul had hit .333, and Lloyd, .400. Ruth had hit .400, and Gehrig, .208. But Ruth had two homers and Gehrig had two doubles. Lloyd had a double and a triple, and Paul, a double. The Ruth–Gehrig combo had five walks between them to the one free pass by the Waners.

Dreyfuss steamed about the defeat. Chagrined over the rough play of his club, he had also lost potential gate money, as Pittsburgh would not be hosting the sixth and seventh games at Forbes Field. More than economics, though, was the pride issue.

"No team that is good enough to win the championship of a major league should lose four straight games to the pennant winner of the rival league," Dreyfuss snarled.

For the players, the Series meant a little extra income. The winning player's share was $5,592 and the losing player's share was $3,728. The total attendance was 201,105 for the four games.

After the "disastrous" Series, as Paul termed it, the Waner family went back to Oklahoma. Lloyd characterized the mood.

Lloyd Waner: *"We were a little unhappy with the way things had gone. We thought we were going to give a better showing than we did because we were a good hitting team...."*

For Lloyd, 21, and Paul, 24, the World Series experience was too brief— and came too soon in their careers.

Lloyd Waner: *"My first year up to the majors was 1927 and darn if we didn't win the pennant. Boy, I thought to myself, this looks like a cinch. But I hung around 18 more years and never saw another one."*

Strangely, the four-game sweep may have helped fortify baseball's integrity, which was still a lingering question only seven years after the Black Sox scandal revelation. Not a lot of gambling money is made on sweeps by the favored team. The *Post-Gazette* quoted one fan anonymously on this effect.

"I had been doubtful about the honesty of baseball ever since the Black Sox scandal," the fan told the reporter, "but since the Yankees won out in four straight games this year, the fact begins to dawn in my mind that while an occasional player may be tempted into making a misstep, the game itself is on the level."

6. Appalachian Stomp

In Oklahoma, the town of Harrah responded with a welcome back parade for the famous brothers. To Paul, everyone seemed a bit too joyous in light of the Pirates defeat. Then he found out that his townspeople had placed some huge sums of betting money on the Series—but not on the Pirates to win. Instead, they had bet on the Waners to out-hit Ruth and Gehrig in batting average—not slugging, not home runs, but batting average.

The Waners did—.367 to .357. It was small consolation, however, for losing the Series.

In 1998, the *Shawnee News-Star* in Oklahoma asked readers to write in about their favorite baseball memories. One reader wrote in about the Waners versus Ruth-Gehrig showdown:

> In December 1951 it was a pleasure to be in the same Pullman car for two days with Lloyd Waner and other baseball men going to the baseball annual meeting in Columbus, Ohio. If you had a tape recording of the yarns and incidents, both going and coming, it would have made an interesting book.
>
> The Yankees won in four straight games, but the betting was all on the hitting contest between Ruth and Gehrig versus the Waner Brothers. The brothers won by a tiny margin, and Lloyd told of his amazement at the warmth of a homecoming after a brutal loss.
>
> Everyone in this area figured the Yankees to win, but all the betting was on the contest between famous sluggers. The natives were loyal and all bet on the Waners. The following winter, the four men toured together in a Vaudeville Act which survived for 14 weeks.
>
> Both of the Waner brothers had been track stars in high school, and this speed was handy in the outfield and in beating out grounders for a hit.... A lot of memories.
>
> Irvin Owen
Shawnee

The Pirates lost to a legendary team.

George Pipgras: "Those '27 Yankees had everything. I don't think any ball club in history could beat them. They were tops. Any team that has Ruth and Gehrig has a head start, doesn't it? They gave the pitcher confidence. You knew that if you were behind a run or two late in the game, it didn't matter; Ruth would hit one, or Gehrig would, or they both would. Then we had Earle Combs, Tony Lazzeri, Joe Dugan, Bob Meusel. Every one a great ballplayer."

To have reached the pinnacle so early—Paul in his second year and Lloyd in his first—the Waners expected more World Series appearances the rest of their careers. But they never materialized. In later years, Paul admitted his disappointment.

Paul Waner: "*Gee, that was tough to take. It'd just tear you apart. We'd make a good start, but before the season was over they'd always catch up with us. And when you're not in the race anymore, it gets to be a long season, really long.*"

Lloyd Waner: "*It looked like we hit the jackpot. We figured we were in it the first year, and we'd be in it plenty of times.*"

During the Waner era in Pittsburgh, the Pirates finished second four times, despite the presence of terrific hitters like Pie Traynor, Arky Vaughan, Gus Suhr, Glenn Wright, Bob Elliott, and Dick Bartell. The old franchise nemesis—lack of good starting pitching and a genuine power threat—hurt the Bucs during the late '20s and '30s.

After the Series, Lloyd and Paul decided to capitalize on their near-fame. They joined a vaudeville tour, billed themselves as the "Waner Wonders," and toured theaters in St. Louis, Baltimore, New York, Pittsburgh, San Francisco, and Los Angeles, among other cities. Paul played saxophone, Lloyd pretended to play violin, and both told baseball jokes.

"Every so often," Lloyd once said, "we'd hit the same notes as the orchestra."

The brothers would come out on stage in their Pirates uniforms and talk about Babe Ruth and the recent World Series. As an aside, a young violin player by the name of Jack Benny, who would go on to become a famous radio and TV comedian, was the master of ceremonies for the Waner skits.

One entry had Paul on stage, and Lloyd rushing in, breathless.

"Where you been?" Big Poison would ask.

"Chasing down the last ball Babe Ruth hit in the World Series," Little Poison would answer.

Like many players in that day and age, the Waners made more money on their winter vaudeville gig than they did playing baseball for six months. They were each paid $2,100 a week, far more than they'd so far made in baseball.

Lloyd Waner: "*We did all right. They wanted us to go on for ten more weeks. But that would have thrown us over into spring training and the Pittsburgh ball club wouldn't let us do it. Paul was disappointed; he loved getting out there on stage. But as far as I was concerned it was just as well. It had been a long season and I figured it was time to get on back home.*"

6. Appalachian Stomp 101

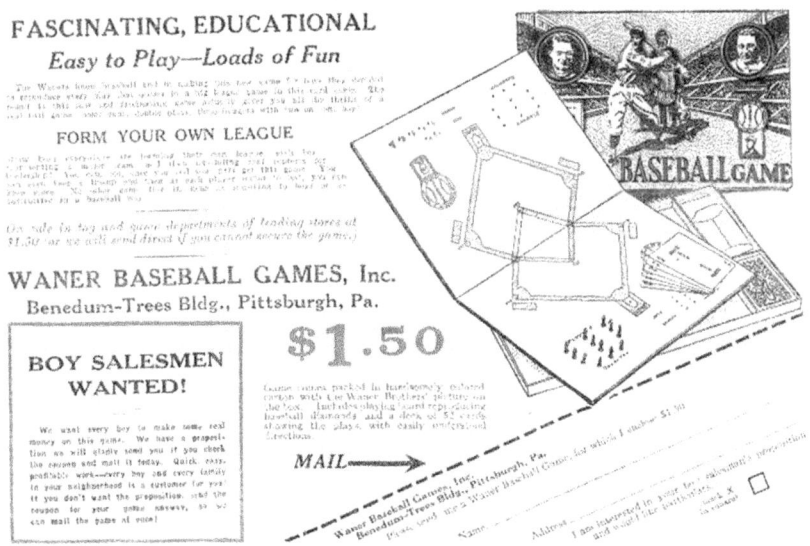

After the 1927 World Series the Waner brothers marked their own baseball game (courtesy of Jim Knight).

As Lloyd realized, "We were better ball players than vaudevillians."

Their sister, Ruth, who had taken time away from her college studies at the University of Oklahoma to attend the World Series, said, "They talked about it and said they had a good time, but neither of them had any professional training in music."

After the Series clamor had died down, the Baseball Writers Association of America selected Paul as the league's Most Valuable Player. In a close vote, Paul received a total of 72 points out of a possible 80, with Frankie Frisch of the Cardinals second with 66 and Rogers Hornsby of the Giants third with 54. Lloyd finished in sixth place with 25 points. A change in one ballot would have given the fiery Frisch the award.

Vaudeville wasn't the only creative spirit the Waner brothers showed that winter. Lloyd and Paul teamed up with their older brother, Ralph, who had created a table baseball game played with a special deck of cards. Newspaper reports indicated they expected to go to market with the game by spring. The first table baseball game had been patented in 1868 by Francis C. Sebring. Since then, thousands of games have been invented, with the first real-life simulation coming in 1931 when Clifford A. Van Beek of Green Bay, Wisconsin, marketed "National Pastime" in *Baseball Magazine.* It's hard to imagine the Waners' game as statistically reflective of actual ballplayers like the current games Strat-O-Matic and APBA are. The fate of their effort is not known.

On the real field of baseball, the game was changing, and each year more hitters tried to emulate Ruth, if not for the statistics, then for the salary potential. When Cleveland's Ray Chapman was killed by a pitched ball on August 16, 1920, major league baseball quickly enforced a rule requiring clean baseballs during a game. No longer were balls muddy and discolored, difficult to see, and mushy by the fifth inning. As a result, offensive production during the '20s and '30s was up by about two runs per game. The league averages hovered around .280, by far the highest of any era. It's no accident many Hall of Fame hitters played during this period. Usually when home runs increase, strikeouts do as well, reflecting the big, looping swings of power hitters.

Yet it took decades and new generations of ballplayers to erode the influence of people like Cobb, McGraw, and their legions of students who advocated "inside baseball." Students of this game like the Waners strived for the hit-and-run, hitting behind the runner, aiming the location line drives, and would usually consider a home run just a fluke.

Rough Seas for the Pirate Ship

Lloyd led off and Paul batted third, and it seemed that every time a visiting team held a one-run lead, one, or both, of the Waners was coming to bat in the ninth inning. It is frightening to think of the many cases of ulcers they must have caused National League pitchers.
— *Tom Meany, sportswriter*

In 1928, Herbert Hoover defeated Al Smith for the U.S. presidency, Amelia Earhart became the first woman to fly the Atlantic, Walt Disney introduced Mickey Mouse in the animated film *Steamboat Willie*, Margaret Mead published *Coming of Age* in Samoa, and in the midst of the Prohibition physicians were found to be writing prescriptions for whiskey.

In Pittsburgh, the state superior court approved Sunday symphony concerts for Pittsburgh, but the Sabbath Association announced it would demand enforcement of the Blue Laws.

But the real fun in the Steel City was discussing the Pirates. Lloyd Waner had a rookie season that rated extremely high in baseball history at that point. The precocious gazelle from Oklahoma prompted Clifford Bloodgood of *Baseball Magazine* to wonder what lay ahead for the younger Waner.

Clifford Bloodgood: "When Lloyd Waner made 223 hits in his first year in the majors he became the first player in baseball history to accumulate over 200 bingles on his first maiden voyage. The coming campaigns may not treat young Waner so kindly. His batting may shrink. Time may dull the *memory of his solo flight to fame—but he made the flight. A Little Poison sure went a long way."*

Bloodgood pointed out that Waner had racked up more first-year hits than Ty Cobb, Eddie Collins, Babe Ruth, Harry Heilmann, Rogers Hornsby, Cap Anson, George Sisler, Ed Delahanty, and Tris Speaker. Would Lloyd one day rank among these great ballplayers? Only time would tell.

Meanwhile, the Pirates retooled in the wake of their Series defeat to the Yankees. In November, they shipped Kiki Cuyler to the Chicago Cubs for infielder Earl "Sparky" Adams and outfielder Pete Scott. The writer Fred Lieb noted, "Barney put on white whiskers and his Santa Claus coat when he made his Cuyler deal."

At 5 foot 5 inches, Sparky Adams was even smaller than the Waners. A mediocre hitter at best, Adams played in Pittsburgh for one and a half years before being jettisoned to the St. Louis Cardinals.

Pete Scott was an accident-prone outfielder who would never play again after the '28 season. Replacing Cuyler in the Pirates outfield was the fleet-footed Adam Comorosky.

Cuyler, meanwhile, began an outstanding seven-year run for Chicago, piling up Hall of Fame statistics.

On the other hand, the Pirates snookered an aging John McGraw by trading Vic Aldridge for Burleigh Grimes. Alridge had made the mistake of asking Dreyfuss for a raise after a poor season. The owner, noting that Alridge's ERA had ballooned to more than four runs a game, put him on the trading block. As it developed, Grimes would win 25 games for the Pirates in '28 while Aldridge was a holdout for half the season.

Grimes admired Paul Waner. In 1955 when Grimes was coaching the Kansas City Athletics, he recalled facing Paul Waner back in the '20s.

Burleigh Grimes: *"I saw a lot of good hitters but I never saw a better one than Paul Waner. I mean I once threw a side-arm spitter right into his belly and he hit it into the upper deck. I may have gotten Waner out but I never fooled him."*

The deal for Grimes was one of the few things that Dreyfuss could smile about that season. The Pirates would struggle to follow up their historic '27 campaign.

◆ ◆ ◆

As the 1928 season opened in Pittsburgh, Pirates fans were teased with news of yet another Waner. Travia Waner—sometimes spelled "Travea"—

was a cousin of Lloyd and Paul's, and he signed on as an outfielder with the Johnstown team in the Mid-Atlantic League. That put him just a couple hours from Pittsburgh. But he was never called up. In 1929, Travia played with Des Moines of the Western League as an outfielder but ended the season as a pitcher, compiling a 14–11 record for Keokuk in the Mississippi Valley League. The idea of three Waners, maybe in the same outfield, must have been inconceivable to Pittsburgh followers.

But that's all we know of Travia Waner. By 1938, he was living in Harrah, Oklahoma, starring on a softball team when reporters tracked him down again. The manager of the club, Jack Vannosdoll, told inquiring reporters, "Travea is too good a softball player to spend time up in the major leagues. He's our clean-up man, and how he smacks that ball."

With no more Waners to the rescue, the Pirates staggered through April and May, a disappointing performance for a team that had just played in the most recent World Series.

Though the Pirates gave up too many runs, they were among the best hitting clubs once again, with Paul leading the charge. Big Poison hit safely in 22 of his first 24 games that season, with a dozen being multiple-hit games. His best performance in the early going came on May 4th when he went 4 for 6 with two doubles and a triple. Those eight total bases didn't yield an RBI though, and Paul seemed to scratch for RBIs all season long. Sometimes the pitchers were afraid of pitching to Paul's scorching bat in run-scoring situations. In one game he got four walks.

Lloyd, too, slapped the ball around prodigiously. By June 2, he had 19 multiple-hit games and was batting .333 to Paul's .358. It looked as if he was forever having two or three hits a game, mostly singles. In one June stretch he racked up 27 consecutive singles without an extra-base hit among them.

The hits came from all directions in the Pirates lineup. On June 12, Pittsburgh set a major league record when seven Pirates collected at least three hits each in a 15–4 rout of the Philadelphia Phillies.

While most of Paul's hits were falling in between fielders that season, he got robbed of at least one, and by Brooklyn's Babe Herman of all people.

In a June game, Herman, a notorious erratic fielder, had made the mistake of not moving back when Paul came to the plate after he had played light-hitting Sparky Adams extremely close in. Paul wound up smashing a line drive right at Herman, who caught what otherwise would have been a hit. Former Pirates Max Carey was in center field that day for the Dodgers. The incident illustrated the "daffy" reputation of Babe Herman, Brooklyn's Babe.

Max Carey: *"I yelled at him [Herman], but he didn't hear me. I whistled at him. Still, he didn't hear me. I waved my arms frantically, trying to catch his attention, but he was looking at the stands ... at a bird flying overhead ... everywhere but at me. Then Paul hit the first pitch. He drove it on a line to right field. If Babe had been playing him properly, it had to be a base hit. But he caught it and tossed it back to the infield and went back to daydreaming. Even from where I stood, I could hear Paul screaming. I didn't blame him, of course. I think if I had been in his place I would have gone back and got my bat and run out to right field and hit Babe over the head."*

Paul played 24 games at first base that season, filling in whenever the stone-handed George Grantham was injured. He responded like the prototypical slugging first-sacker, blasting his first career grand slam on June 28. Every game it seemed like Paul got a hit—that season he recorded hitting streaks of 20, 15, 15, and 13 games. He hit safely in 128 of the 152 games he played in 1928. And he hit well from either the second or third spot in the lineup. On July 10, the Pirates came from behind to beat Philadelphia on back-to-back hits by Paul and Lloyd.

Paul showed some power, too. On August 6, Paul homered to help Burleigh Grimes win his 20th game.

If the Pirates had always been a team more gifted with hitters than pitchers, the emphasis became even more stark beginning in 1928.

Pittsburgh's only 20-game winners until the middle of World War II were Burleigh Grimes' 25 wins in 1928 and Ray Kremer's 20 wins in 1930. Pressed to come up with an annual ace, every season the Pirates brought in new arms and turned out old ones, making for unreliability on the mound and heartburn in the dugout. The only Pirates pitcher who consistently earned respect around the league was reliever Mace Brown—and one day he would give up the most notorious home run in club history.

And so, Pirates pitchers depended on run support and a steady defense behind them. Catcher Al Lopez of Brooklyn, a rookie in 1928, recalled the stingy Pirates defense during a Dodgers–Pirates doubleheader on the last weekend of the season.

Al Lopez: *"This is when the Pirates had Pie Traynor and Glenn Wright on the left side of their infield. Well, I was strictly a pull hitter and I hit some good hard shots to the left side. I'd take off for first figuring I had myself a hit, but each time to my astonishment I saw that peg zinging into the first baseman's glove. It was practically impossible to hit a ball past Traynor or Wright. I was zero for eight in that doubleheader and went home that fall wondering what a fellow had to do to get a base hit in the big leagues."*

7. Rough Seas for the Pirate Ship 107

Wright played in only 108 games due to an army injury that season. The Pittsburgh writers whispered that Wright had let himself get badly out of shape after getting hurt. Despite efforts by trainers and physicians, his once-powerful arm seemed reduced to that of a sandlot player. After the season Dreyfuss would trade the popular Wright to the Dodgers for pitcher Jesse Petty and infielder Harry Riconda. Though the fans were displeased with the move, the Pirates were rich in young middle infielders as they were in outfielders like the Waners. One of them was Dick Bartell.

Bartell got into his first game with Pittsburgh in 1927 and then hit .305 in 1928 as a part-timer. For his fierce, scrappy style, the Chicago native earned the nickname "Rowdy Richard." He got into many fistfights with teammates and opponents alike during his well-traveled career. Yet he was a winner, playing on three championship teams and on the Pirates from '28 to '30.

There was no denying Bartell came to the ballpark to play hard every day. Cincinnati infielder Tony Cuccinello remembered a howling Dick Bartell crashing into him to break up double plays.

Tony Cuccinello: *"He was the absolute toughest ... he enjoyed the contact out there. No one ever took me out as hard at second base as Dick Bartell. He almost broke my legs out there and made me feel as if I had all my bones broken. He could play."*

If Bartell told you something, you listened and got it right the first time. He once punched Paul Waner for spitting tobacco juice on his shoe after warning him not to. He had his own stories about the Waners, especially Paul, as he recounted with Norman Macht in *Rowdy Richard.*

Dick Bartell: *"Lloyd didn't drink much when he was playing, but Paul was another story. There were plenty of times he showed up at the ball park and he wasn't sober. In the dugout we had an ice chest. He'd stick a pint of whiskey in there and take a swig between innings, before he'd go up to bat."*

In his own mind, Bartell had paid his dues. At 5 foot 9 inches and 160 pounds, it was never easy for him, and in a way he was the small-man antithesis of the Waners. While they were peacemakers and polite, he was the fighter with a chip on his shoulder. Bartell, however, was gracious enough to remember those who had supported him on the way up.

Dick Bartell: *"I signed my contract with the Pirates, and as I was still a teenager, I had my Dad with me when I arrived in Paso Robles, California. The first thing I saw when I put on my practice uniform and trotted out to the infield to take a few ground balls was six infielders hanging around* second and short. I trotted out there, but it was a veterans' convention, and they wouldn't let me take any practice—the field was theirs. The big six were Glenn Wright, Pie Traynor, Johnny Rawlings, George Grantham, and even Joe Cronin and Hal Rhyne, who had paid their dues as rookies in 1926.

"I called my Dad and said, 'Get me outta here.' Pirates executive Joe Devine heard the conversation and chewed me out for being a baby and making waves. Then Donie Bush called me into his office, and he chewed me out. So I took the field feeling as low as I could get.

"We were playing a spring training game against the Yankees and I guess Babe Ruth was watching me try to get my grounders at short and second and getting pushed around by the vets. I looked at him, he waved a finger at me and called me over. Here's a 19-year-old being called over by the greatest player in baseball.

"I went over to him and stuttered, 'D-d-do you want me, Mr. Ruth?'

"He just smiled and looked at me and said, 'I know you're a rookie and the old guys are giving you a hard time. Put up with it. Work hard and don't worry about other guys. Don't say too much and just let your play do the talking. I've watched you, kid, and I think you're gonna make it big in the Big Leagues. Just be careful and let those old guys do what they want. Soon it'll be your turn.'

"I never forgot the advice and whenever I was down or in a slump or was mistreated by other ballplayers or owners, Babe's advice kept me going and kept me in baseball. I never would have had an 18-year career without that advice. When I saw him at the first All-Star game in 1933 in Chicago, even though I was playing for the National League and he was with the American League, after the game [which Ruth won 4–2 with a home run] I went over and congratulated him.

"He remembered the earlier incident, gave me a broad laugh and a hearty slap on the back and said, 'See what I told ya? Ya made me right.' That was the most pleased I have ever been."

Bartell wasn't the only new face in the NL that season who enjoyed a distinguished career. On July 28, a 25-year-old Oklahoman named Carl Hubbell made his first major league start. It came against the Pirates. Maybe the Waners gave their Pirates teammates the scouting report on their old high school rival. Pittsburgh knocked out Hubbell in the second inning of his debut.

Hubbell got back on his feet quickly. On August 11, he recorded his first major league winning in shutting out the Phillies. Featuring a deadly screwball that broke down and away from right-handed batters, the left-handed Hubbell was arguably the best National League pitcher in the 1930s.

Still, Hubbell seemed to have his hands full with the Waners. On left-handed hitters like the Waners, Hubbell's screwball moved in toward them instead of away, making it somewhat easier to hit.

Carl Hubbell: *"Paul had the best bat control of any hitter I faced. He could foul off your best pitch, your 'out' pitch. Then he had you. Paul is one of the few fellows I never really learned how pitch to. A breaking ball usually bothers most hitters, but Waner seems to follow one perfectly and almost picks the field he wants to hit to. I don't care how you pitched him. You could pitch him slow stuff inside and he could still hit that hole in left center."*

Hubbell's greatest moment came in the 1934 All-Star game when he successively struck out Babe Ruth, Lou Gehrig, Jimmie Foxx, Al Simmons, and Joe Cronin. Those sluggers aside, he always took care when pitching to Little Poison. Keeping the pesky Pirates off the bases was challenging enough.

Carl Hubbell: *"Lloyd never hit many home runs ... but when I pitched against Lloyd, I always tried to pitch him away. I wanted him to hit a fly ball because I didn't think he could hit it out on me."*

Lloyd's best game that season came on September 20th when he hit a rare home run and went 4 for 5 with a double and three RBIs.

Paul Waner came close to winning his second consecutive batting title, battling Rogers Hornsby down the stretch. Waner entered September with a .375 average, but the long, hot summer was wearing him down in the last few weeks.

Hornsby was now playing for the Boston Braves after an off-season trade from New York where he had once again had a falling out with management. "The trade was made in the best interests of the New York Giants," observed the Giants front office.

Cantankerous or not, Hornsby had won six batting titles and compiled an astounding .400-plus average from 1921 to 1925—five straight years!

So confident was Hornsby of his ability he once said, "I don't like to sound egotistical, but every time I stepped up to the plate with a bat in my hands, I couldn't help but feel sorry for the pitcher."

The writer Lee Allen said of Hornsby, "He was frank to the point of being cruel, and subtle as a belch."

Hornsby ruthlessly asserted his power and prestige. Thirty-one games into the '28 season, Hornsby had maneuvered himself into being named manager of Boston when the former manager, Jack Slattery, was fired. Boston owner Judge Fuchs asked the Rajah what kind of team he has. "Mostly bums," Hornsby replied.

In the final weeks of the campaign, Pittsburgh visited Boston for a series, the batting race in a dead heat. The local newspapers billed it in Armageddon-like terms as a showdown between the two best hitters in the National League: "The Battle for the Batting Championship."

It turned out to be firecrackers versus a howitzer. Hornsby whacked out several hits and Paul wound up hitting poorly in the series. In his last 23 at bats, Waner had managed only two hits, going hitless in his final 8 at bats. When it was over, Hornsby came upon Big Poison in the runway underneath the clubhouse.

Paul Waner: *"Well, Rog, it looks like you're going to beat me."*

Rogers Hornsby scowled at him. "You didn't doubt for a minute that I would, did you?"

Hornsby won the NL batting title at .387 to Waner's .370.

Odd and historic events headlined the 1928 baseball season. In the American League the aging Ty Cobb finally hung up his spikes after 24 years and 4,191 hits. The great Tris Speaker also retired with 20 years and 3,514 hits under his belt. In Philadelphia, a 20-year-old Jimmie Foxx clubbed a ball completely out of Shibe Park, the first ever. On July 29, the Cleveland Indians demolished the mighty New York Yankees, 24–6. They pounded out 27 hits (an AL record 24 singles) in scoring the most runs ever against the Yankees.

Back in the National League in Chicago, Cubs center fielder Hack Wilson jumped into the stands to attack a heckler, one Edward Young, a milkman. His teammates restrained him from doing severe damage. National League president John Heydler slapped Wilson with a $100 fine, but in court Judge Francis P. Allgretti—a Cub fan—imposed a $1 fine on the milkman.

At season's end, Pittsburgh had finished with 85 wins and in fourth place behind the Cardinals. The Yankees again destroyed their competition, the Cardinals, in a four-game sweep. Maybe the Pirates players took solace in the powerful Murderers' Row sweeping another NL team for the second year in a row. It reaffirmed how good those Yankees really were.

In Pittsburgh, the club's poor showing put manager Donie Bush's job in jeopardy. Dreyfuss had expected to repeat after winning the pennant the year before. But the '28 club flopped even worse than did the '26 squad after having gone to the World Series the year before.

It would be a winter of discontent in the Smoky City.

On the positive side, Paul and Lloyd continued their prolific batsmanship. Paul led the league with 142 runs and 50 doubles. Entrusted with the almighty number three hitter's position, Paul was the muscle behind the Pirates offensive attack as he also banged out 19 triples and drove in 86 RBIs—all done with only six home runs.

Lead-off hitter Lloyd Waner scored 121 runs and batted .335 with 14 triples and five home runs, with three of them coming on inside-the-park gallops. Amazingly, Little Poison struck out only 13 times in a league-leading 659 at bats, tying Carson Bigbee (1922) for the franchise record of fewest strikeouts in 150 or more games.

The primary beneficiary of the Waners at the top of the order was clean-up hitter Pie Traynor, who knocked in 124 RBIs and compiled a .337 average. For the second year in a row, the Pirates led the league in runs scored. Their team average of .309 and record of nine players hitting over .300 that year remain all-time franchise highs.

The Pittsburgh club also pounded out 100 triples, tops in the NL and an incredible 48 more than their home run total. The Waners and Pirates were perennially among league leaders in three-baggers, especially Paul with his extra-base thunder.

Big Poison was a triple machine. In his first 10 years of play, he notched 10 or more triples each year. His lifetime total of 190 triples is the highest for any player whose career began after 1920. For the fans in the seats, Paul seemed eternally chugging around second base and headed toward third where he slid and kicked up dust with Oklahoman gusto.

While Paul was one of the best triples hitters, it was true that the shape and dimensions of Forbes Field resulted in many batted balls rolling a long way and outfielders running to no end after them. In any event, the triple may be the most exciting play in baseball. Unlike the over-the-fence home run where the end result is known immediately, the triple holds drama and suspense for observers as the runner heads into third on what is usually always a close play.

Since 1900, the Pirates have dominated the National League in triples, topped off by Owen Wilson's staggering 36 triples (24 at home) in 1912, a major league record unlikely to be threatened. That was also the year the Pirates set the all-time single-season team record of 129 triples. In the 1921–1946 era, 1 of every 14 Pirates hits were triples, compared to 1 of about 18 for all of major league baseball.

Aside from the Forbes Field effect, another reason for so many Pirates triples is the type of ballplayer Pittsburgh traditionally recruited—swift-running, line-drive hitters like the Waners. That's the conclusion of Richard L. Field Burtt in *Insider's Baseball*, edited by L. Robert Davids, founder of the Society for American Baseball Research. On a career basis, no fewer than a dozen Pirates hit 100 or more triples dating back to the 1890s: Lloyd and Paul Waner, Jake Beckley, Fred Clarke, Tommy Leach, Max Carey,

Pie Traynor, Arky Vaughan, Roberto Clemente, and Honus Wagner. Wagner is the all-time NL leader with 231 triples. These were all fast running men who could handle the bat exceptionally.

The Pirates weren't the only ones at Forbes Field banging out three-baggers. Visitors enjoyed the same benefit of a spacious park. Enos Slaughter of the Cardinals recalled plenty of dramatic three-base clouts in Pittsburgh.

Enos Slaughter: *"I got a lot of triples there. I hit 148 triples, though I spent three years in the service. At Forbes, right-center was 395 feet away with a high screen, and center-field was 428, and it was 435 in left-center.*

"If you hit the ball in one of those spaces, you run to daylight for a triple."

The Cruel Business

> The sooner these boys realize there is no chance of getting what they've asked, the sooner they will use their common sense and report for work under the terms we've made them.
> —Barney Dreyfuss, Pirates owner on the Waners' holdout

Whether the conspicuously consuming wealthy, the bootleggers, the booboisie, or the silk-shirted stockbrokers knew it or not, the year 1929 was the last hurrah of the Roaring Twenties. Like the Rock of Gibraltar in the world economy, America was the foundation of a seemingly boundless stock market that kept going upward. No one suspected all hell would soon break loose.

But all things that go up must come down. The author Edmund Wilson observed, "It was difficult for those born later to believe it really occurred, that between 1929 and 1933, the whole structure of American society seemed to be going to pieces." The problem wasn't only financial—the violence in American society seemed unprecedented. In the past six years such brazen crime figures as Al Capone, Legs Diamond, and Bugs Moran racked up unimaginable profits in the illegal booze trade and littered the landscape with corpses.

In the year ahead America would endure the bloody St. Valentine's Day Massacre in Chicago, the "Black Tuesday" Stock Market Crash on October 29, the continuing consolidation of Joseph Stalin's power in the Soviet Union, and the first term of the Herbert Hoover administration that unwisely promised, "two cars in every garage, two chickens in every pot."

Whether booze, stocks or dictators abroad, America was up to its collective neck in forces that would shape its destiny the next couple of decades. "Everything nailed down is coming loose," said Gabriel to De Lawd in the novel *Green Pastures*.

Before everything came loose, Pittsburgh continued to stabilize its image as America's industrial capital. The United States Steel company announced a $20 million expansion program for plants in Duquesne, McKeesport and Braddock. The Grant Building—at 37 stories the city's tallest and topped with an airplane beacon spelling out "Pittsburgh" in Morse Code—opened. And, Allegheny County residents rejected the Pittsburgh Metropolitan District Charter, which would have made Pittsburgh the country's fifth-largest city with a population of more than 1.3 million.

◆ ◆ ◆

As if the reckless forces of society rising up wasn't enough, hell almost broke loose between the Waner brothers and their beloved Pittsburgh Pirates.

That winter both Paul and Lloyd reflected on their sterling accomplishments in their first few years of ball. They ranked among the best young players in the National League. They could hit and field and run, and they were good clubhouse guys. It was time to cash in on their talents, for they were a relative bargain for the Pirates, especially as Lloyd had come in at such an inexpensive price tag.

So that spring both brothers decided to hold out from the Pirates, returning their original contract offers, which called for a modest $1,000 raise collectively, unsigned to owner Barney Dreyfuss. Back in Oklahoma, the Waners let it be known that they were seeking a combined $30,000 in salary, with $18,000 for Big Poison and $12,000 for Little Poison. The previous year Paul had made $12,000 and Lloyd $11,000.

Players back then had little leverage under the reserve clause, but both Lloyd and Paul played hardball—at first. They leaked the possibility they might quit the game if unsatisfied with their contracts. The Pittsburgh newspapers billed it in less than flattering headlines: "Thirty Thousand or We Quit!"

It was the biggest publicity crisis of their young careers, with the Pirates spin machine working in overdrive to cast them in a greedy light. Team officials said the Waners told them they would sign together or not at all. Pittsburgh then funneled a story to sympathetic Joe Vila of the *New York Sun*, who then wrote about the brothers' contract strategy and implied their lack of remorse over the team's dismal 1928 season.

8. The Cruel Business

"The Waners were not responsible for the Pirates' poor showing last season and they have formed a sort of co-partnership agreement to hold up Dreyfuss until he comes to terms," Vila wrote.

As it would unfold, Lloyd and Paul were not quite united in their grand stand. If they had been at the outset, they went their separate ways.

In the Pirates offices, Dreyfuss took the hard line in public but worried in private. No way, he told the writers, would he give the brothers a penny more than his final offer of a combined $24,000. Yet Dreyfuss was smart enough to know his club would be severely weakened if one or both of the Waners walked away for the season.

Paul returned three contract offers unsigned. He called Dreyfuss's bluff, highlighting the fun he enjoyed away from spring training.

Paul Waner: *"I know of several good fishing places around here, and it is my intention to stay here until they place the figure on my contract that I am entitled to."*

Dreyfuss's son, Sam, was the club treasurer at the time. He played the bad cop. "Paul Waner is going to be a hard man to sign. He has made demands which are so far above what the club offered him that he'll have to come down considerably before we can reach a business basis," he told writers.

Strangely, the younger Dreyfuss even appeared to blame the contract trouble on the "devilish saxophone" that Paul had learned to play. That instrument and the vaudeville tour after the 1927 season had enlarged the egos of the Waners, he said. Pirates management believed that the entertainment world had infected the Waners with self-importance—as if the baseball limelight didn't do that as well to young ballplayers.

This was misleading. At the team's request the Waners had given up vaudeville after the 1928 season. But the Pirates still tried to portray them as juvenile and immature, with Lloyd clearly dependent on his older brother. The tactic was to split their ranks.

Sam Dreyfuss: *"Paul is responsible for Lloyd. Whatever he does, he takes care of the younger brother with a fatherly oversight that is good to see. If Paul says, 'no,' Lloyd says 'no,' too. But Lloyd will grieve even more than Paul if he remains idle. If Lloyd does not play ball in 1929, he would perish of nostalgia. Paul will have to think of that. Paul likes to play ball, too, but Paul thinks he has to look out for Lloyd."*

An element of truth existed in what Sam Dreyfuss said. Paul was the carefree type who didn't worry much about tomorrow and always knew he could make it as a ballplayer no matter what. Lloyd, on the other hand, knew that his best career track was baseball, and he didn't want to lose this opportunity. As spring training neared, the prospects for a quick settlement with Paul looked dim. But the Pirates had a feeling they could get Lloyd on board first, thus quashing the brothers' dual negotiating strategy.

Then suddenly, rumors started coming out of New York that the Giants were interested in the Waners for the combined sum of $225,000. Maybe Dreyfuss was putting pressure on the Waners by initiating trade talks. Yet his historical animosity towards the Giants would appear to make that two-pronged sale a remote possibility. It seemed an obvious leak to the sporting press, one that would never turn out.

In early March, both Waners were staying put in Oklahoma. Paul's wife Corinne was about eight months pregnant, and that may have been keeping him there as well. When training camp opened on the West Coast the Pirates were without the Poisons. Manager Donie Bush had to scramble to assemble an outfield.

Replacing the Waners were Adam Comorosky, Freddie Brickell and George Grantham. The early results were discouraging, observed Ralph S. Davis of the *Pittsburgh Press*. The new outfield trio produced only one hit in 12 at bats in an exhibition game against the San Francisco Seals. While that was only one game, there was also the issue of the Pittsburgh fans and the type of ballplaying they had come to expect. This was several months before the Great Depression struck the nation, and most people did not begrudge ballplayers their just deserts. People starting getting anxious.

Ralph S. Davis: *"Fans have shown a deep interest in the case, and the majority of them here sided with the Waners, feeling that their demands have not been unreasonable in view of the salaries paid to other players who are not considered the stars that the Waners are."*

Beyond the Waner flare-up, training camp had plenty of distractions. Bush, who seemed to attract player rebellions like horse flies, dished out a $50 fine to several Pirates in a hotel in Paso Robles, California, for gambling and tossing cigarette butts on the carpeted floor. Right after he had told the players they couldn't play cards, Bush had walked in on them doing just that.

While the most celebrated, the Waners weren't the only Pirates holdouts. Heine Meine, a young unknown pitcher who had only pitched in one major league game back in 1921, rejected his salary offer. Meine did not join the team on the train headed to camp, and the front office took a hard line on him too. He wound up agreeing to the terms and saw little

8. The Cruel Business

action that season. For the Pirates front office, it was one thing for stars like the Waners to hold out, it was another for bench-warmers to do so.

The outfield wasn't the only trouble spot for Pittsburgh—the infield had yet to be settled. Bush contemplated moving Pie Traynor to shortstop, a position Pittsburgh needed to fill with a quality glove. As spring training rolled along, the manager tried all sorts of combinations with Traynor and the veteran third baseman Sparky Adams. Finally, come Opening Day, Bush would decide on the brash Dick Bartell at shortstop, a good choice. He would also fill in at second for the perilous glove of George Grantham. By hitting .302 in full-time duty that upcoming season, Bartell would make the league take notice.

The club was undergoing a facelift from their 1927 championship team. In their perennial hunt for a good first baseman, the Pirates acquired Earl Sheely, a former Chicago White Sox and Pacific Coast League star. One of Sheely's legs was a bit shorter than the other, but that

Paul Waner and the long-gone days when players stuffed their gloves in their back pockets (courtesy of Jim Knight).

didn't stop the lifetime .300 hitter from being one of the best clutch-hitting and fielding first basemen of his era. Unfortunately for the Pirates, Sheely's era had already passed, and he hit only six home runs for the Pirates that season. At 36, he would be back with Sacramento in the PCL the next season to wind down his career.

Rookie outfielder Adam Comorosky was the possible heir apparent to one of the disgruntled Waners if they chose to stay away. Some of the veterans gave the 24-year-old Comorosky a rough hazing.

"The young outfielder was made the victim of a number of jokes after he had reported," one writer noted. Ironically, Comorosky had also received similar "treatment" the season before in the minors at Indianapolis. It got so bad with the Pirates that spring that Bush had to issue orders for everyone to leave the kid alone.

The contract squabbling seemed harassing to Lloyd, too. Confrontation just wasn't his style, not like Paul who overflowed with gutsy self-determination. Sometimes their differences were stark. The writer Maury Allen pointed out that Paul "wasn't much of a talker but had a droll sense of humor and was not above treating his baby brother as a baby brother when they both had long been starring in the big leagues."

On March 18, Lloyd finally relented, signed for $10,000, and joined the club four days later. He had talked it over with Paul, of course, and the older brother appeared to have given the younger one the support he needed to make his own decision. Right before signing, Lloyd had spent several days fishing and camping with Paul in the backwaters of Oklahoma. When he got back from the trip and opened another telegram from Pirates asking him to sign, he wired them back affirmatively. He came to terms for $2,000 less than what he had originally sought.

That was one hurdle cleared. The other was whether Lloyd could get back in shape quick enough. In those days, spring training really was about getting a ballplayer into shape after a presumably idle winter. Today, players have the luxury of training year-round in the best facilities and don't have to work other jobs to make ends meet.

So, once Lloyd arrived at the Pirates camp, the writers asked if he was in shape. He told them he was five pounds above his normal weight of 145 and that he'd done some throwing and catching during the winter, but had played in only one sandlot game in Oklahoma. He needed some conditioning, in other words. Bush eased him into the lineup sparingly in the rest of the exhibition games—perhaps sending a message, too, that the Pirates did not take his hold-out lightly.

Some bridges had to be rebuilt between the Pirates and Lloyd. Little Poison first attempted to dispel the "double hold-out" strategy. He was his own man, he strongly stated, and not his brother's man.

Lloyd Waner: *"Brother Paul and I have not been working together in our efforts to secure larger salaries. I have nothing to say about him. All I know is that it was my belief that I should get more money, and so I acted on my own initiative. I signed because the terms suited me. It seemed like everybody in the country offered me something nice, some urging me that I do this, and others suggesting that I do that, but I decided to handle my own business."*

Certainly one reason for his signing was Lloyd's upcoming marriage. During the 1928 season he had become engaged to Frances Mae Snyder of

8. The Cruel Business

407 Oakland Avenue in Pittsburgh. A stenographer at the United States Casualty Company in Pittsburgh, Frances had met Lloyd while working at her mother's flower shop on Atwood Street in Oakland near Forbes Field. The Pirates bought flowers at the store for team occasions. Apparently, Paul and Lloyd used to frequent the flower store, and that's when romance between Lloyd and Frances blossomed.

A few days after Lloyd signed, the Pirates caved to Paul and offered him the $18,000 he wanted. He packed his gear and hurried to camp. Once in Fort Worth, Texas, on the Pirates' spring training route, Paul learned that his wife had given birth to a baby boy—Paul Jr.—back in Oklahoma City. Upon hearing the news, Paul rushed back to Oklahoma and stayed there a few days with the baby and his wife, and then returned for a second time to the Pirates. Paul Jr. would be his only child.

With the baseball season about to begin, *Baseball Magazine*'s F. C. Lane took inventory of Lloyd Waner.

F. C. Lane: "*Lloyd has an uncanny fielding sense and a flawless technique which approaches perfection. He does seemingly impossible things and does them with such apparent ease that the spectator is amazed. One of the fleetest men who ever trod a baseball field, he never seems to exert himself. He drifts, rather than runs. The eye will glimpse him in one part of the outfield where it would seem he could not possibly be, and a few seconds later he will appear at a distant spot in the very nick of time to spoil a slashing hit.*"

While Lane pointed out that Lloyd was not an accomplished base stealer, his speed on the base paths was phenomenal. "Let the defense lapse ever so little, let a shortstop juggle the ball momentarily, and Lloyd Waner scores a hit," wrote the scribe.

Lloyd always faced comparisons with his better-hitting brother, Lane noted. It never seemed to annoy Lloyd who Lane described as a "most reticent young man." Not a word on record exists to indicate any sibling jealousy between the two baseball brothers. For others, however, the comparisons were inevitable.

F. C. Lane: "*One handicap was Big Brother Paul. Paul was older and already had made his mark. He had proved, that in spite of his lack of weight and inches, he was one of the greatest hitters baseball had uncovered in a decade. But baseball has its proverbs and superstitions. No great ball player has an equally great ball player for a brother has become a baseball truism. Paul Waner was a great player. It was a foregone conclusion Lloyd would make but an indifferent comparison.*"

But Lloyd's numbers were excellent early in his career, and it looked

Lloyd Waner catching a fly (courtesy of Jim Knight).

as if he would chase the coattails of his brother through the rest of their careers. Lane admits Lloyd surprised baseball experts with the hits that popped out from his "frail looking" build. Rogers Hornsby once admitted his first couple of years in the majors were not as productive because he was so skinny and lacked a man's strength.

In a way, Lloyd seemed physically built for a middle infield position, and he had the quick reflexes and range. Second base was his original high school position and one he played with the San Francisco Seals. In his first year with the Pirates he played one game at second.

Lane revealed that Lloyd often thought of playing the keystone base.

Lloyd Waner: "I believe that I could learn to play second base well enough to get by in the big leagues. I was naturally a good ground coverer and a good fielder. I have a satisfactory throwing arm. The throw at second base is relatively easy. Besides, a second baseman usually plays rather deep and has time enough to handle the ball. In my opinion, second baseball is the easiest position on the infield, easier than shortstop, and preferable even to first."

Lloyd was too valuable of a fly-catcher in monstrous Forbes Field, and that's where team management wanted him. It would be another two years, in 1931, until Lloyd had a brief chance to play some second base again, and it would be his last time doing so.

❖ ❖ ❖

The 1929 season had some magic in it. On May 5, the Pirates' Burleigh Grimes defeated Boston, 7–2, with the help of a triple play—Grimes to Pie

8. The Cruel Business

Traynor to Chuck Hargreaves, back to Traynor, to Dick Bartell, and back to Hargreaves. Score that, 1–5–2–5–4–2.

Once again, the Waners were the hit men of the National League. They sprinted from Opening Day on and never looked back. Lloyd's performance this season would rival his rookie year results, and Paul would enjoy one of his better power and RBI-producing seasons.

Little Poison began the season hitting safely in 38 out of his first 44 games. Scoring nearly a run per game, the lead-off hitter seemed forever on base. He would put together 10-game hitting streaks, get stymied for one game, and then restart another 10-game hitting streak.

One of the games Lloyd did not get on base came on May 8 when Carl Hubbell of the Giants tossed a no-hitter against the Waner brothers and the Pirates, winning 11–0. The fellow Oklahoman walked only one and struck out four. The game had a climactic ninth inning, when two straight Giants errors put the first two Pirates on base, bringing up the Waner brothers in succession. Hubbell, who seemed to have started in the majors as though he'd always been there, got coolly back to work.

He struck out Lloyd — no small feat — and then got Paul to ground out, as the *New York Times* reported: "The senior Waner slashed the ball along the ground between the pitcher's box and first base. Like a flash Hubbell dived for the ball and scooped it cleanly. Whirling and without waiting to recover balance, he fired the ball to second base."

Fully recovered from the Hubbell no-hitter, Lloyd and Paul Waner cracked home runs in the same game for the second time. These shots came on June 9 against Brooklyn's Doug McWeeny — Paul in the fifth inning, Lloyd in the seventh. Before retiring, the Waners would turn the trick once more, in 1938. Then it would be back to back, the first time brothers had struck consecutive homers.

Paul was smacking longer hits that season — reflecting Dreyfuss's demand for more power — but his average hovered "only" around .330 for much of the season — which was well below his lifetime average at that point. With batting average the all-important indicator in those days, Paul took this hard when he went a few games in June without a hit. So he took the extraordinary step of benching himself. According to the story, Paul went to Donie Bush and told him a couple days off might help his game. Bush agreed and sat Big Poison on the bench. Pittsburgh fans not privy to the dugout talk were dumbstruck — was Paul receiving his punishment over his spring training hold-out? In the wake of the Kiki Cuyler fiasco of a couple years ago, this caused a mild sensation for a few days in the Pittsburgh newspapers until Paul returned to the lineup and the familiar crack of his bat rang through Forbes Field again.

These days hits fell by the bucketfuls on the Waner brothers—even from the scorekeeper's office. As both Waners could run, scarcely a day went by that one or both of them wasn't involved in a close decision at first base. The Forbes Field scorer in those days was John Gruber, a bearded old-timer who frequently called the entire press box into consultation on a knotty decision.

Eddie Murphy, the *New York Sun* Dodgers beat writer, once lamented, "Have you ever noticed that, no matter how many people John asks for an opinion, his decision always winds up as a hit for one of the Waners?"

Maybe the hometown bias wasn't quite this flagrant, but it seemed that way to out-of-town writers. With the Waners averaging 400 hits together in a season those days, close calls would sometimes result in hits.

Beyond anti–home-run screens, baseball was feeling innovative that summer. The New York Giants installed the first-ever loudspeaker system at the Polo Grounds. At most ballparks a man with a megaphone—just like the kind a high school glee club would use—bellowed the batteries before the game three or four different times in different sections of the bleachers and grandstand.

From radio to loudspeakers, the sounds of the game were changing. Some experiments did not take hold, though. On August 25 at a Pirates-Giants game at Forbes Field, home plate umpire Cy Rigler was wired for sound so that fans could hear his calls. He had a microphone plugged into his mask and wires inside his uniform. Metal plates were affixed to his shoes, and he stood on a metal sheet. The Giants won the game 10–5, but the wired-up umpire experiment is lost to the ages.

In late July the pressure mounted on Bush after the Pirates fell out of first place. The consensus was that the Pirates had talent—six of the eight regular position players would hit over .300 that season—and Pittsburgh should win the pennant. Ralph Davis of the *Pittsburgh Press* asked Dreyfuss if Bush was secure in his job.

"Why should I make a change?" the owner replied. "I don't know where I can find a better man than Donie Bush."

Somehow it sounded too much like public relations. Rumors abounded of Bush getting the axe.

Doubtless Bush's eyebrows turned downward in disappointment that season. The fans by and large never forgave him for the Cuyler benching, and the team suffered its share of injuries in '29. A poor road trip during late August had dropped the Pirates far behind the Cubs. Bush's Pirates had failed to win a pennant in his brief tenure, and it appeared this year's version would not do so either.

On August 29, Dreyfuss cut his losses and forced Bush to resign after

8. The Cruel Business

a tense one-hour meeting. Exactly 119 games into the season, the Bush exit popularized the kiss-of-death interpretation of public votes of confidence in a manager. In double-talk fashion, Dreyfuss also carried on the Pittsburgh tradition—in a company town dominated by Big Steel—of managers "resigning" rather than being fired. It looked better for the company if its soldiers fell on their swords like good corporate citizens, as if they accepted their own failure in letting down the whole organization. And so, Dreyfuss released the following public statement:

> Owen Bush has tendered his resignation as manager of the Pirates club, and I accepted it. There is nothing further to say, except that Jewel Ens has been named to succeed Bush for the remainder of the season.

The Pirates' new manager, Jewel Willoughby Ens, had been a manager for years in Cincinnati's farm system and had once played second base with the Pirates. He was probably most similar in approach and strategy to Bill McKechnie. Ens surprised the Pittsburgh faithful by winning 21 of the remaining 35 games that season.

Toward the end of the season on September 17, Lloyd and his fiancée Frances were married at the home of a relative in Swissvale near Pittsburgh. The Rev. Homer C. Renton of the Oakland Methodist Episcopal Church gave the vows. Paul was, of course, Lloyd's best man. Others present included close relatives and owner Barney Dreyfuss.

Lloyd, like Paul, actually played baseball on his wedding day. He went 2 for 4 with two runs scored, one RBI, and one walk. Both Waners seemed to benefit from their nuptials on game day.

While wedding bells sounded in Pittsburgh, the championship lager was flowing in Chicago. In 1929, the Chicago Cubs were aiming to win the pennant for the first time in 11 years. Threatening since 1926, Joe McCarthy's squad had finished third the season before, and extra punch was infused into an already formidable lineup with the addition of Rogers Hornsby. On his fourth club in as many years, Hornsby sparked the Cubs by hitting .380, belting 39 home runs, and driving in 149 runs. The Bruins' all-star outfield included Hack Wilson (39 home runs and 159 RBIs), Riggs Stephenson (.362 and 110 RBIs), and—Pirates take note—Kiki Cuyler (.360 and 102 RBIs). Their offense was overwhelming.

The Pirates finished in second place with an 88–65 record, 10½ games behind Chicago. Pittsburgh was in the pennant race for about two-thirds of the season and held first place for 37 days and as late as July 24. But the hard-swatting Cubs pushed aside Pittsburgh as they grabbed the pennant. The Pirates' 13–16 record in August allowed the Cubs to draw away with the league lead. In the World Series, Chicago would lose to the Philadelphia Athletics of Jimmie Foxx, Al Simmons, Mickey Cochrane, and Lefty Grove.

At season's end, Lloyd had put together a career year and would finish fifth in the National League Most Valuable Player running—his highest placement ever and the only time he outranked his brother. Lloyd belted out a .353 average and he posted career highs with 74 RBIs, 134 runs, and a league-leading 20 triples. Perhaps most impressive were his 234 hits, and while that did not lead the league in this offensively saturated era, the total reflected his determination at getting on base.

In his first three years of play, Lloyd had tallied 678 hits—a major league record. No hit master, from Ty Cobb to Pete Rose and Tony Gwynn, had ever made so many hits in their first three years of play. The future looked bright for little brother, and though he would never win a batting title like Paul, his annual pace baffled earlier skeptics. The skinny kid was making it big.

One reason Lloyd got so many hits was that he took very few bases on balls. He swung at most anything, and rarely missed. Decades later, statisticians would downgrade Lloyd's performance due to his low on-base percentage (OBP) for someone with a .316 lifetime average. (Walks plus hits divided by official at bats equals on-base percentage, the contemporary statistical heir to batting average in determining how successful a player is reaching base.) In his career, Lloyd walked once every 18 or so at bats, far below the average player. In the 1920s and 1930s the yardsticks of batting average and total hits received more attention than the hidden game of baseball found in walks and their correlation to run scoring. On this point, Lloyd was fallible.

On the other hand, Lloyd had many other strengths beyond OBP as an offensive player. He was the second-hardest guy to strike out in major league history—once every 44.9 at bats. Incredibly, his season strikeout totals were 23, 13, and 20 in his first three years of play, which in today's baseball is about how many times an average player strikes out each month. Aggressive at the plate, Lloyd followed the conventional wisdom of the day—collect as many hits as possible, and always make contact. It's hard to fault a guy for not seeing into the future to determine what statistical yardstick would be most popular. As Lloyd saw it, bases on balls got in the way of making hits—and hits have the potential to move runners two and sometimes three bases at a time compared to one for a walk.

Lloyd, the obedient brother, deferred to Paul's view on the matter.

Lloyd Waner: *"The reason I never walked much was Paul told me if a pitch was so close it could be called either a ball or strike, it was good enough to hit and that many of his hits were made off pitches of that kind."*

As a lead-off hitter, Lloyd knew his role. Getting on base meant getting a hit. "Every manager I ever played for always told me the same thing—your job is to get on base. There were always some pretty good hitters coming up behind me."

Funny, though Paul advocated to his little brother to go for the hits, he displayed more patience at the plate and would lay off the marginal pitch. His walk totals are much higher than Lloyd's. It's also probably true that pitchers threw more carefully, and sometimes off the plate, to Big Poison. Paul believed that a consistent .300 hitter should be able to hit four out of ten pitches safely, but he'd be lucky to connect for a hit on one of ten bad pitches.

Paul Waner: *"But a walk is often as good to the team as a hit, and the odds are against the batter when he chases a bad ball."*

Paul was tricky. Sometimes he would intentionally swing poorly on pitches to make the hurler over-confident. Then once the pitcher laid one in there, he'd whack it.

Paul Waner: *"Most games are close enough so that at any one time they can be decided by a long hit. I want to make sure I get the pitch I want in that spot, no matter how many hits it costs me to build up to it."*

In 1929, for the third year in a row, Paul banged out 200 hits. Though his average fell to .336, he boosted his run production with 100 RBIs, scored 131 runs, and connected for 43 doubles and 15 triples. The season also marked a career best in walks with 89 and in home runs with 15.

Could Paul Waner have hit more home runs in his career? Maybe, if he put his mind to it, but it likely would have lowered his average, just as it did that season. Years later Paul talked about the "what ifs" of his career and the game changing toward more power hitting.

Paul Waner: *"If I could start over again, there's one thing I'd do—use a lighter bat. I believe I could hit 35 home runs a year. When I played I used a 42½ ounce bat. A home run was mighty nice but it was strictly an accident then."*

Contemporary hitters would be shocked that a 150-pound man like Paul Waner used such a large bat. Today, mammoth 200-pound hitters prefer using bats weighing about 32 ounces. Yet Paul's best years came using 40-plus-ounce bats.

Even for his era, Paul used an unusually heavy bat, especially for a lightweight guy. In 1942, the Hillerich & Bradsby company, the makers of Louisville Slugger bats, reviewed Paul's bat usage. As noted, the company found that he used a heavier bat than the average player. Hillerich & Bradsby executive Henry Morrow noted that when Paul was with the San Francisco Seals in 1923 he used a 40-ounce bat—a Reb Russell model with a medium-size barrel and thick handle. In 1926, his first year in Pittsburgh, Paul kept using the Russell model, this time with a slightly smaller handle, weighing about 38 to 40 ounces.

Sometimes different players used the same bat in those days—they lasted far longer than the easily breakable ones of today. Supposedly Paul Waner and Pie Traynor shared the same bat for the entire 1927 season. Paul once claimed he used a 42-ounce bat in the 1927 World Series.

When pressed for time, Paul wasn't always discriminating on bat choice. Joe Cronin recalled once seeing Paul Waner picked up a massive 40-ounce bat as he raced out of the dugout to face fire-balling Dazzy Vance. He whacked four hits off of Vance that day using the heavy wood.

As the years passed, Paul experimented with bat selection, and ordered different types, preferring lighter bats as he got older. By 1932, the weights had dropped to 37 and 38 ounces, in 1933 to 35 and 36 ounces, and in 1934 to 34 and 36 ounces. By 1935, he had 10 different models of bats. None of his bats were over 35 inches long. According to Morrow, Paul Waner noticed what bats other players used, and if something worked well, he gave it a try.

As eyes turned toward the 1930 season, they might have seen one giant bat swatting line drive after line drive and the demoralized looks of chagrined pitchers trudging back and forth from the mound. Like the guns of summer, 1930 would be a season unlike any other in the Lively Ball Era.

9

The Exploding Universe

The only real game in the world is baseball.
—*Babe Ruth*

As New Year's Day dawned on January 1, 1930, and trumpeted a new decade about to unfold, Paul Waner would have been surprised to know that he would collect more hits—1,959—than anyone in baseball during that 10-year period. He had some good competition, for a galaxy of stars swirled throughout those long-ago summers.

Paul also never would have imagined that people back in Oklahoma were actually lobbying him to run for Congress. But they were. He was that popular back in his home state—where he didn't always reside during the winter, preferring sunny Florida.

Despite the October 1929 stock market crash, early in 1930 the country was more preoccupied with yanking the yoke of Prohibition off than with foreseeing the Great Depression. President Herbert Hoover described the anti-drinking law as a "great social and economic experiment" of the past 10 years. In dissent, Congressman Oliver of New York railed that Prohibition had "driven liquor from the bar to the boudoir, from the saloon, from hops to hips, from keg to kitchen." By now, it was clear that a huge criminal industry was preying on the demand for beer, and disagreements were settled with machine guns and concrete shoes. And so a weary public called for appeal of the Prohibition law in one poll after another.

While people worried about their entertainment lubricant, the U.S. government quietly assisted the emerging Depression by passing the Smoot-Hawley Act, a bill that included some of the highest tariff rates in history on manufactured products. It set off a flurry of economic nationalism. Soon countries around the world retaliated by raising tariff rates on the U.S., thus deepening the worldwide depression. The year saw a crackdown on many things—a copy of James Joyce's novel *Ulysses* was seized by custom officials on the grounds that it was obscene, and the works of Leon Trotsky were banned in Boston. The world seemed to be going backward, not forward.

In Pittsburgh, the Better Traffic Commission recommended a ban on all curb parking downtown and urged Mayor Charles H. Kline to eliminate the practice of fixing traffic tickets. In November, the Stanley Theater hosted a benefit show for the increasing numbers of unemployed and needy families—and it was standing-room only, testament to the worsening conditions in the area.

Joining the ranks of the so-called "needy" were major league pitchers that season. The Lively Ball Era would reach its ultimate extreme as several factors converged to give hitters all the advantages and pitchers none.

Going into the season Paul Waner had a lifetime .355 average and was averaging 210 hits and 122 runs scored per season. Lloyd had a .344 career average and averaged 226 hits and 129 runs scored each season. Proof of their consistency, neither brother had failed to score 100 runs in any one season, and in only one year—Paul's rookie year—did one of them miss 200 hits. And that was because Paul had fewer plate appearances than was typical for him later on.

James J. Long of the *Pittsburgh Sun-Telegraph* compared the Waners to baseball's other brother acts.

James J. Long: *"For all the annual fixtures that have graced the stage of the national game in recent years, none has stood out with such consistent brilliance as the Oklahoma brothers who combine their efforts to help Pittsburgh win ball games. With all due respect to the Delahantys, the O'Neills, the Meusels, the Johnsons, the Tannehills, the Schmidts, the Coveleskies, the Ferrells, and others, the Pirates duo must be called the most valuable brother combination that ever performed along the main line. As a double force in the same lineup, they are in a class of their own."*

Lloyd had surprised his critics by grinding through the past few seasons without any major challenges to his delicate physique. Except this season he would not be so lucky, and it would mark the first health setback of many in his career.

In January, Lloyd was in Pittsburgh visiting with his wife's relatives when he began experiencing stomach pain. When he checked in with the

9. The Exploding Universe

Pirates physician, an X-ray was taken. They discovered he had appendicitis. Lloyd had been feeling internal pain since late 1929 and seemed to need frequent rest and a bland diet. Still, he had played many days when the pain tortured him.

On January 20, Lloyd was taken into surgery at the Presbyterian Hospital in Pittsburgh. So widely known were the Waners that wire reports carried the news of Lloyd's condition. An hour after the appendectomy Lloyd regained consciousness and seemed OK.

The question for the Pirates was whether Lloyd would recover soon enough to play center field and play for the entire season. Spring training was a month around the corner. As the days passed, the already skinny Lloyd lost even more weight and was extremely weakened once the bell rang for spring training. With Lloyd unable to make it to camp, the Pirates opened spring training with relative unknowns, Ira Flagstead and Fred Brickell, alternating in center field, not good news for Pirates fans.

Paul with his weapon in hand (courtesy of Jim Knight).

One Buc newcomer, Gus Suhr, took over at first base, and he would be the first baseman the Pirates had always lacked. Like Paul, Suhr had formerly starred with the San Francisco Seals in the Pacific Coast League—in '29 he hit .381 with 51 home runs and 177 RBIs. The next season he was playing for the Pirates, the start of an 11-year career in which he set a National League record for consecutive games played. During WWII, the Iron Man Suhr returned to the Seals.

Paul Waner recalled a story about how National League pitchers welcomed the rookie Suhr into the league.

__Paul Waner:__ "Once we were playing the Chicago Cubs in about 20 spring training games stretching through Los Angeles, San Francisco, El Paso, Tucson, Phoenix, and Amarillo. Suhr was the new man we bought. The Cubs had a tough pitching staff—Pat Malone, Guy Bush, Charlie Root, and Lon Warneke. Well, they just knocked Gus down, one after the other. Just—BAM!—down he'd go, and he didn't know what had hit him. He must have thought they didn't like him for some reason.

"Well, these Cub pitchers were testing him. They wanted to see if he got scared. If they discovered that he got scared or angry at being thrown at, then they could handle him more easily. But Gus didn't fall for it; he just ducked when they threw at him. And then our pitchers tried to bust some of their hitters in return."

One day an emaciated Lloyd Waner showed up at the Pirates camp, but he could not exert himself. By Opening Day, he should have recovered under normal circumstances. His sole contribution came on April 28 when he—astonishingly—collected a hit in a pinch-hitting appearance. After that, he wouldn't see regular action until July.

On May 2, with Lloyd's pain getting worse and the season well under way, the Pirates sent him to Johns Hopkins Hospital in Baltimore, one of the finest medical institutions in the country. They were not taking chances on Lloyd at this point. He was eventually transferred to the Union Memorial Hospital in Baltimore. There he had additional surgery involving the removal of his tonsils and adenoids.

With rumors growing that Lloyd was in seriously bad shape and might not play again, Waner's physicians spoke out on the matter. The Pirates must have asked them to dispel the more harrowing rumors that Lloyd was somehow finished as a ballplayer or his life was in jeopardy.

Lloyd's physician, Dr. Bertram Bernheim, branded such reports as ridiculous and spun an optimistic message. "He soon will be as well as ever. We're anxious to get him back to the Pirates. We know he's badly needed there."

Incidentally, at the same time third baseman Pie Traynor was in another Baltimore hospital receiving eye treatment. He returned to the Pirates soon thereafter.

With two operations literally under his belt, Lloyd did not play regularly until early July, and then he gingerly eased his way back. He became a "real lightweight," in sportswriter Fred Lieb's words, and played in only 65 games. His hitting, however, picked up a couple weeks after returning, and he made up for lost time in stringing together prolific hit totals.

Lloyd was just getting in on the fun that his brother Paul and other major league hitters were enjoying in 1930. On April 29, suspicions arose that the ball was unusually lively that year as 123 runs were scored in seven major league games—that's 17.5 runs total per game. That same day Suhr walked six times in one baseball game, tying a major league record that stands today. The season was strange from the start.

Upon examination, the National League ball had stitches so low they were almost countersunk, which kept the pitchers from getting the kind

9. The Exploding Universe

of grip they needed to throw sharp breaking pitches. Plus, the ball bounced farther, indicating it was more tightly wound inside.

But it was more than the ball. History shows that the summer of 1930 was an unusually hot and humid one on the East Coast, and such weather generally helps hitters more than pitchers. Also, the pitching may have been thinner. Only two rookie pitchers of any quality reached the major leagues that season and both were in the American League—Left Gomez of New York and Mel Harder of Cleveland.

Like his National League peers, Paul got off to a whippet-like start. He knocked out four singles in four at bats in his first game, and after that there was no stopping him. Paul went 35 for 74 (.473) in his first 19 contests up to the first week of May.

He wasn't alone. Four other National League batters were batting over .400 in that same period. Ironically, one of them was Paul's old PCL rival, Lefty O'Doul. He was now playing for the Philadelphia Phillies and posted a .478 average in his first 16 games.

Hitters everywhere were crushing the ball. On May 12, Giants pitcher Larry Benton set a modern major league record by surrendering six home runs in a single game, but he still got credit for the win (14–12) and hit a home run himself.

One unidentified Phillies pitcher said, "It's gotta end sometime. Come November there'll be snow on the field."

In mid-season, John McGraw, whose own New York hitters were giving pitchers an unprecedented drubbing, called for reducing the distance between home plate to the mound to 58 feet instead of 60. His startling public pronouncement focused new attention on the plight of the pitcher. But no action was taken on his recommendation.

The offense may have been good for attendance. Despite the October stock-market nightmare, Americans showed up at the ballparks in record numbers. For the first time in history, major league baseball drew more than 10 million. The National League enjoyed its most profitable season ever—this was not a season to miss.

In analyzing the record attendance, bear in mind that the Depression didn't start overnight in October 1929. In the spring and early summer of 1930, there were a few bank failures, some slowdown in business activity, and rising unemployment. But it appeared gradually and none of this affected the fortunes of major league baseball. Even the worst case of pessimism could not have predicted what lay ahead.

One thing was certain—hitting was rampant. Through July 1, Paul Waner had put together hitting streaks of 16, 9, 8, and 7 games. One of his best days came on June 16 when he smacked three doubles.

While National League fans had an exciting pennant race to cheer on—St. Louis, Chicago, New York and Brooklyn all contended until late in the season—the fifth-place Pirates struggled early on. Once again, the pitching was the main culprit.

In a four-game series against the New York Giants at Forbes Field, the Pirates scored 30 runs, 29 of them in three games alone. Yet Pittsburgh still lost three out of four of the games. Why? Pitching.

Paul Waner: *"There was a lot of happiness and sadness in the Pirates in those days. When I was with Pittsburgh fighting for the pennant that was fun. But it just tears you down when you get three, four or five runs ahead of the opposing team, and then— BAM!— they start scoring runs off our pitchers and beat us."*

Paul Waner thinking baseball (courtesy of Jim Knight).

Inflated box scores abounded around the league. On successive days in early May, the Cubs blew two extra-inning games to Brooklyn by identical scores of 11–10. The next day they staggered past the Phillies, 16–11.

Away from this crazy summer of baseball, Paul Waner waited for Lloyd to heal and get back on the field, and he pursued his other interests, some of them surprising for a ballplayer if Roscoe McGowen of the *New York Times* is to be believed.

Roscoe McGowen: *"Paul was a free soul who couldn't abide restrictions. He ate and drank as he pleased, as long as he pleased. Sleep was something he didn't seem to need because even when he went to bed he often stayed awake for hours reading. He wasn't reading comic books, 'whodunits' or Wild West tomes either. His taste ran to books in philosophy, science and other subjects allegedly beyond the ken of baseball players."*

While that may be true, the writer John Lardner may have captured

9. The Exploding Universe

Paul's mien on and off the field better when he once remarked that "Paul Waner set the spiritual, or spirituous, pace for the Pittsburgh club in those days. He was the wrong sort of example from a medical point of view, because no matter what kind of tea he drank, he remained the best and sharpest-eyed hitter in the National League. In Pittsburgh, though, several of the others did drink the same brand as Paul, but without any noticeable benefit to their batting averages."

Paul had several memorable games that mid-summer. On June 26, he scored four runs as he made three hits in four at bats with a double and triple. On July 6, he posted a perfect 5-for-5 day with another double and triple. A few days later, on July 11, he again enjoyed a flawless 4-for-4 performance.

On July 23, the Pirates played a role in a game that symbolized the Lively Ball of 1930. In the first game of a doubleheader in Philadelphia, the Pirates gave up 48 total bases on 27 hits to the Phillies and still won, 16–15, in 13 innings. Don Hurst homered twice for the Phillies, and his team's 48 total bases tied a major league record. Pie Traynor homered in the ninth inning of the first game and in the 13th inning of the second one for the decisive blows. Paul went 2 for 4 and Lloyd, 3 for 6. Incidentally, this game marked Lloyd's return to form, and while he played an abbreviated season, from this point on he stroked his share of hits.

For Paul, having Lloyd back made him more comfortable. The Waners intuitively knew how each other played, whether on the bases, at the plate, or in the field. The way they shared the outfield was uncanny, as they never crashed into each other or went after the same fly ball without seeing the other.

Lloyd once told a reporter that he and his brother had agreed that any fly ball hit into center or right-center was Lloyd's. But if a ball bounded between them and rolled to the wall, Lloyd would run it down and then flip it to Paul, who would throw it to the cut-off man.

Lloyd Waner: *"Paul had the better arm and he caught a lot of hitters at second. We played together in the outfield 14 years and, in going for a fly ball, we never even touched one another. Not once. We just had a feel for one another."*

The 1930 offensive deluge wasn't limited to the major leagues. Gene Rye of Waco in the Texas League hit three home runs against Beaumont in one inning on August 6. Entering the bottom of the eighth inning, Beaumont was leading, 6–2, but Waco pummeled them for 18 runs. Rye smacked a solo homer, a two-run shot, and a grand slam for seven RBIs that inning.

Lloyd, left, and Paul, right (courtesy of the Pittsburgh Pirates).

In Pittsburgh, what puzzled the Pirates was how they could dominate the best teams in the league but get trounced by the worst ones. The good-hit, no-pitch Pirates won the same number of games against the champion Cardinals as the miserable Phillies.

In late August, the Pirates caught fire and proved pesky down the stretch, beating Brooklyn twice in a significant series toward the end of the season. Lloyd was locked on the ball, crafting a 17-game hitting streak to end the season that had started so precariously for him.

The pennant race was as hot as the air outside. That month a record heat wave was punishing the entire country and had killed as many as 72 people in Chicago. Temperatures were above 100 in many of the major league cities, including Pittsburgh.

This was back when players did not drink water to hydrate like they do today. Old-fashioned thinking held that drinking lots of water on a hot day would only make a person susceptible to the effects of the heat. Unbelievably, players would drink sodas and other beverages that would actually dehydrate them.

The night before the season ended in 1930, the Pirates all partied deep into the night at a supper club in East St. Louis. They were terribly hung over for the next day's game with the Cardinals, the first Dizzy Dean pitched in the majors, and they didn't care who won or lost, losing 3–1.

9. The Exploding Universe

"What'd we get off you, Dizzy," asked Paul, recalling the game years later. "Three hits? We were lucky to get those."

Dizzy blurted out, "Well, Paul, you was the greatest drunk ball player I ever struck out."

The 1930 pennant went to the St. Louis Cardinals, led by new manager Gabby Street. St. Louis scored a mind-boggling 1,004 runs with eight regulars hitting over .300. With a decent pitching staff, the Cardinals compiled a 92–62 record. The Pirates finished fifth at 80–74, only 12 games behind St. Louis. Not bad for a fifth-place finish.

Paul and Lloyd could look back on successful seasons. Paul's 217 hits and .368 average were accompanied by 32 doubles, 18 triples, and 8 home runs. His RBIs fell off to only 77, however. Due to his illness early on, Lloyd got into only 68 games but made the most of his presence by batting .362 with 94 hits.

Every team could hit that year, so balanced pitching was the key. In hindsight, the Pirates missed the spitballer Burleigh Grimes. The Pirates had angered Grimes by trying to cut his pay on the eve of the 1930 season. So Grimes held out and after a couple of trades ended up on the Cardinals, pitching the Redbirds to the pennant, though the powerful Philadelphia Athletics later won the World Series. The Pirates took solace in Rey Kremer winning 20 games despite a 5.02 ERA—the only time in history this has happened.

Yet the Pirates gave up a franchise-high 928 runs while scoring 891.

The 1930 season was the greatest offensive explosion in the 20th century. The entire NL hit .303 and set all kinds of offensive records (the AL hit .288). Hack Wilson of Chicago blasted a record 56 home runs and drove in a record 191 RBIs, and Bill Terry of New York stood as the last man to hit .400 in the NL. The Giants set a modern record with a team batting average of .319.

Amazingly, in 1929 and 1930 Pittsburgh had a record six players in double figures for triples. This has never been done in the 20th century by any other ball club. The Pirates as a team hit 116 triples in 1929 and 119 in 1930, post–Dead Ball Era highs.

But triples did not win pennants.

The Return of the Dead Ball

> The guy with the biggest stomach will be the first to take his shirt off at a baseball game.
>
> — *Glenn Dickey, sportswriter*

In 1931, it was increasingly hard enough to keep the shirt on your back, let alone at the baseball game. Nearly five million Americans were unemployed, and the numbers were growing every month. Other news also filled the newspapers that year. Atomic-fission research yielded discoveries that in a few years would be applied in production of the atomic bomb, stellar radio emissions from the Milky Way were first detected, NBC in New York began the first regularly scheduled TV broadcasts, the "Star Spangled Banner" became the official national anthem, and George Gershwin's hit musical *Of Thee I Sing* reflected widespread disillusionment with politics and the state of the nation.

Pittsburgh faced its share of misery. With their funds exhausted, relief agencies warned that nearly 48,000 Pittsburgh area residents would "begin starving" immediately. It didn't happen, but the hunger was real for many people.

Baseball owners, facing a worldwide economic collapse, prospects of declining gate attendance, and absurdly inflated offensive statistics, took strong measures to slow down the game. They introduced a deader ball by raising the stitches, canceled the sacrifice-fly rule and decreed that balls that bounced into the stands would now be ground-rule doubles and not home runs. More radical proposals—such as moving the pitcher closer to the plate or restoring the spitball—were fortunately shelved.

The result was the Great Depression of Baseball as averages and run-scoring plummeted in 1931 to post–Dead Ball Era lows.

Pirates fans might have found cause for depression, too. During the winter, Pittsburgh owner Barney Dreyfuss made a bad trade when he gave up shortstop Dick Bartell to the Philadelphia Phillies for light-hitting shortstop Tommy Thevenow and pitcher Claude Willoughby. While Bartell went on to enjoy an 18-year career, Thevenow would play five years for the Pirates and only once collect more than 100 hits, and Willoughby would appear in only nine games in 1931 before retiring.

On the positive side, the Pirates signed a young hard-hitting shortstop from Fullerton, California. His name was Floyd "Arky" Vaughan, and one day he became the Pirates' greatest shortstop since Honus Wagner and a juggernaut in the Waner-led Pirates lineup.

That winter Lloyd Waner gave an interview to *Pittsburgh Press* sportswriter Fred Wertenbach, who was curious about Waner's ability to bounce back from the appendicitis problem the season before. His weight loss and his skipping of meals on game day had many wondering if he was somehow losing strength. For Lloyd, it was a chance to show the baseball world he was healthy and fit.

Lloyd Waner: *"I have three things that keep me busy—fishing, hunting, and golf. Golf to me doesn't have the thrill socking the old apple has. I like the feeling I get when I dump the ball down and beat the pitcher's throw to the bag. It's like the games we used to play when we were kids, when you outrun someone."*

While Paul spent the winters in Florida and Oklahoma—and as the years passed, Florida became his preference—Lloyd frequently trudged around the woods of Oklahoma.

Lloyd Waner: *"Much of my hunting has been in the Kimichi Mountains not so far from my home in Oklahoma. It's real work climbing and if I don't get any game, I think, 'Oh, well, that's that much more toward being in shape when the season begins.' I've recovered my health and felt better than I have for years. I spent two weeks in the Kimichi Mountains, but we mostly fished. I spent several days visiting my folks at Harrah, Oklahoma, and am expecting to make another trip to the mountains in late January."*

A cartoon alongside the piece was dubbed "Lloyd 'Pee Wee' Waner." In it Lloyd's muscles burst through a tank top with the caption reading, "The Wee One states that he is in the pink and thinking of challenging Hack

Wilson in a telephone book tearing contest." Hack Wilson was the preeminent home run hitter in the National League and seemed to pack as much muscle into a 5-foot 6-inch, 200-pound body as was possible.

As the season opened, John Leonard "Pepper" Martin and Dizzy Dean of St. Louis captured the baseball world with their down-home charm and diamond splendor.

A stocky 5-foot 8-inch Oklahoman from rural parts, Pepper Martin grabbed at everything with a Depression type of despair, stealing bases and sliding headfirst into bases like a crazed man—the "Wild Hoss of the Osage." While Pepper played in the outfield in '31, he would later play third base, knocking balls off his chest and whipping them over, sometimes erratically, to first. It could be dangerous for the batter.

Lloyd Waner: *"When I bunted on Pepper, I always ran down the line with my hands covering my head."*

Dizzy Dean was a man of terrific pitching talent and even more words, some of which actually were standard English. Dizzy often made good on his outrageous boasts. As he put it, "It ain't bragging if you can do it."

Lloyd Waner described Dizzy as, "one of those boys who you knew was never coached anywhere, who was born to decorate a mound just the way you saw it."

In Pittsburgh, the season and cast of characters were not nearly so colorful, and without the few Waner highlights it would have been a dismal year.

In April, Paul hit in 12 straight games. But while in other seasons he had an abundance of two- and three-hit games, this season he seemed unable to break the mold of one-hit games. In one stretch he hit in six consecutive games but only managed one hit in each, so his average actually fell a little. By June 6, his batting average stood at .311, low for the renowned Big Poison. Lloyd's .304 then was further evidence that the ball bounced differently than last year's. On May 24, he did collect four hits in five at bats with two doubles.

With the Waners seemingly joined at the hip, sometimes the sporting press recorded their collective accomplishments along with their individual ones. They had cause to do so on July 9, 1931, when Lloyd stroked two hits against the Chicago Cubs. It was the 2000th hit of the brothers' combined careers, and it had come in only 1,409 games played. The Waner duo had a lifetime .349 average and had scored exactly 1,107 times.

There seemed a business-like proficiency with the way the brothers executed their craft. The *New York Herald Tribune* noted, "With all this

10. The Return of the Dead Ball

Depression talk, the firm of Waner & Waner, manufacturers of safe hits and brilliant fielding, reports its business booming as usual."

Such talk was prophetic. On July 18, Paul broke out of his one-hit-per-game routine to smash two home runs in a single game for the first time. He hit them off of Brooklyn's Pea Ridge Day, an Arkansas farm boy whose real name was Clyde Henry Day.

Paul Waner: *"Pea Ridge Day, the hog caller, was pitching against us. He was watching us take batting practice. The batting practice pitcher threw low balls to me and I was bouncing them around. Pea Ridge, who was eyeing from the dugout, sang out, 'So that's your weakness, low balls. Well, I finally found out how to pitch to you Waner.'*

"Just before the game, I told Oscar Stanage, our coach, that I was going to hit the first pitch over the exit sign in the upper right field deck. Just as I expected, the first pitch was downstairs. I hit it exactly where I said I would, right through the exit hole for a home run.

"I knew Pea Ridge would not be expecting me to look for another low ball. Sure enough, my next time at bat, he threw me another low pitch and I hit that one in the same place, just missing the exit opening by a foot or two. Pea Ridge stormed around the mound, fit to be tied. Then he suddenly burst out laughing. 'You framed me, Waner,' he hollered at me. 'I'm never going to believe you again.'"

Pea Ridge Day lasted parts of four seasons in the big leagues. Mostly working in relief, he posted a 5–7 record and 5.30 ERA. In 1934, three years out of baseball, he died at the age of 35.

Paul would pull off the two-homers-in-a-game feat three more times in his career. But the long ball wasn't his forte.

This point was made on August 18 when Paul collected a season-high five hits—all singles. Still, the hits were harder to come by than in prior years. Paul was only 28, and his brother, 25, so they weren't losing bat speed due to age. All hitters shared this frustration, especially newcomers eager for quick success in the majors.

One of those newcomers on the 1931 Pirates was outfielder Forrest "Woody" Jensen. Through the mid–1930s he played alongside Lloyd and Paul in many games.

Woody Jensen: *"I'll be honest with you, I was a heck of a center fielder myself. But I never got to play it because of Lloyd. He was so quick, he got to balls nobody else did. And I can never remember any of us running into each other. We were too busy running back to the fences with that pitching staff we had in those days.*

"Forbes Field was the biggest park in baseball. In center, it was almost 500 feet. Oh, you'd get an inside-the-park homer once in a while, but not many. They kept a batting cage in center field, and I don't remember anybody ever reaching it. But Lloyd won games with speed. That's what won it for you in that park."

In *Fenway: From Frazee to Fisk*, Martin F. Nolan writes, "The ballpark is the star. In the age of Tris Speaker and Babe Ruth, the era of Jimmie Foxx and Ted Williams, through the empty-seats epoch of Don Buddin and Willie Tasby and into the decades of Carl Yastrzemski and Jim Rice, the ballpark is the star."

For all their country-boy practicalities, the Waners shared such sentiments about their home turf. The urban park of Forbes Field replaced the Oklahoma where the breeze whistled ruefully through wheat and alfalfa fields. Here in hilly, smoggy Pittsburgh, the landscape looked different but the ball field still played like a ball field, and it was home away from home for the Waners for almost two decades. As the smokestacks from Homestead to South Side bellowed and belched grit in the distance, and the machinery of the city clicked and clacked under thousands of scurrying feet, the Waners were at home in Pittsburgh's version of Industrial Age baseball.

If anything, it was just fun at the park, even in batting practice.

Lloyd Waner: *"We loved Pittsburgh and Forbes Field. Paul and I used to practice throwing our gloves down in the outfield in batting practice and then would try to hit them. Once in awhile we would hit them, too. It took a lot of practice to hit where we wanted to. Paul could. He could really call his shots. I could hit the ball where I wanted to—but I had to wait for my pitch, or go with the ball where it was pitched."*

Paul and Lloyd were often referred to as the "Waner Act," as if they were some Hollywood skit that put fannies in the seats. Indeed, the twin-looking brothers were a rare act. They came in a pair, and if you could tell them apart on the field, which wasn't always, you would notice some of their personality differences. Paul was a bit more brash and Lloyd, the quiet trooper. Yet they both demonstrated a certain laid-back style, and this served to catch the opposition off guard.

The writer Kaspar Monahan described the "Waner Act" in one of his columns.

Kaspar Monahan: *"Lloyd Waner, the younger and the smaller of the two, would go to bat with a moist, mild and inoffensive look on his face and a gentle beam in his eye. That mild expression fools nobody save young*

10. The Return of the Dead Ball

bushers, just up from the sticks. No sir. The infielders shift uneasily and sort of tighten up. The pitcher takes an extra hitch in his pants— nervously. The outfielders edge in toward the diamond, praying they can snag the little line drive that is pretty apt to come zinging out toward one of 'em.

"Lloyd just lets that first one cut the corner of the plate. 'Strike one,' hoarsely rumbling from an umpire's throat, never bothering Lloyd, or for that matter, big brother Paul. The next appeals to Lloyd's somewhat fastidious taste. Then, smack, just like that— a nice crisp, clean sound. And the ball heads on a line over the second baseman or shortstop's head to meet the turf some 15 feet away in front of the center or left fielder. Nice, sharp little single.

Paul Waner (courtesy of Jim Knight).

"Brother Paul now up. Smack, again— and there it goes, this time probably to right, which is the ideal place to knock the ball if your brother is on first. Even if he's not your brother, he'll appreciate your forethought because it's a long heave for the outfielder from right field to third. So brother Paul deliberately aims for right and he has an uncanny knack of 'placing' his hits. Brother Lloyd is off as brother Paul's bat meets the ball. Lloyd rounds second like the devil is after him and by the time the right fielder gets the ball via an infielder to third, why there'll be little Lloyd perched on the bag, breathing easy."

With Lloyd leading off and Paul batting in either the second or third spot in those years, the Waners had honed their "act" for scoring runs.

But 1931 was an off year for runs. In late August, National League president Heydler blamed the reduced scoring on "the new ball with raised stitches and a heavier cover." Next year the two leagues would reverse themselves on favoring a "deader" ball and agree to adopt a uniform ball for the first time, choosing the American League version because it was considered livelier.

Big and Little Poison

Paul Waner's baseball card, year unknown, with an intriguing Lou Gehrig reference (courtesy of Jim Knight).

However, it took until 1933 to finally introduce the standardized ball into play. In the midst of the Depression with shrinking attendance, the owners made no bones about their goal—to increase scoring and thus fan turnout. If only they had kept the 1930 ball. Some games in 1931 were just plain strange.

On September 22, in a 13-inning game at Forbes Field, Pirates catcher Hal Finney had no put outs in a 3–2 win over Philadelphia. Paul Waner drew five walks, and 20 runners were left on base as pitcher Heine Meine won his 19th game to tie for the lead in the NL.

When the dust settled on 1931, it turned out that baseball's most offensive season (1930) was followed immediately by one of the weakest ones in recent memory. The National League's cumulative average fell 26 points from the year before to .277 and scoring dropped 21 percent. Bill Terry fell from .401 to .349, and Hack Wilson plummeted from 56 home runs and 191 RBIs to 13 home runs and 61 RBIs. The decline was less drastic in the AL where runs decreased by only 5 percent total.

No matter how the ball bounced, the 1931 season was more of the same for the Pirates. For the second straight year the Bucs finished in fifth place but fell to 75–79, 26 games behind St. Louis. In the World Series, the Cardinals would triumph against the Philadelphia A's.

The Waners joined the retro–Dead Ball parade as they tallied their lowest batting averages thus far. Lloyd led the league in hits for the first and only time with 214 safeties while batting .314. His runs scored dropped to 90, but he only struck out 16 times in 681 at bats, an exceptional testament to his bat control. As he grew older, Lloyd struck out less often, a sign of his experience.

Paul's .322 mark topped the Pirates—demonstrating what kind of year it was for hitters. But his streak of four years with 200 or more hits came to an end as he garnered but 180 safeties. And for the first time his

10. The Return of the Dead Ball

Paul and Lloyd Waner on tour in Japan during the 1930s.

runs scored dropped below 100 to 88. All indications that the Waners and others weren't battling just themselves, or better pitching, but the tinkering of the game and ball by the owners.

No matter the retro Dead Ball, Paul and Lloyd were the pride of Pittsburgh and were untouchable when it came to the Pirates making changes after the season. Once the season ended, the Pirates fired Jewel Ens and replaced him with George Gibson, the catcher from the golden years of the Fred Clarke Pirates. Son-in-law William Benswanger handled the transition for Dreyfuss.

Third baseman Pie Traynor nearly landed the managing job as a player-manager, according to Ralph Davis of the *Pittsburgh Press* who noted a few years later: "When Jewel Ens was relieved after the 1932 season, the first reports were that Traynor would get the post, but it is understood that Mrs. Dreyfuss prevailed on Benswanger to give Gibson another chance."

In the winter of 1931, Paul Waner toured Japan on a major league All-Star team featuring Lou Gehrig, Lefty Grove, Mickey Cochrane, Frankie Frisch, Rabbit Maranville, Lefty O'Doul, and Al Simmons. (Babe Ruth was busy making a movie.) The trip was sponsored by the newspaper *Yomiuri Shimbun* as part of a circulation-boosting campaign. From all indications, it was the first time Paul Waner had ever visited a foreign country.

The American All-Stars won all 17 games they played against the mostly Japanese college players. In baseball-crazy Japan, the games were held before large, enthusiastic crowds who marveled at the power and speed of the "gaijins"—or foreigners. The Americans won with such scores as 20–3, 22–4, and 19–1. The Japanese admitted their embarrassment at even being on the same field as the big leaguers, and even at one point asked for a 20-run handicap. This did not impress the gaijins.

Lou Gehrig: *"I had heard about yamata damashi [Japanese fighting spirit] and I thought I could learn something from it. But unfortunately, all I saw were players jogging to first on ordinary grounders. When I saw a runner coming down the line at me, grinning, I felt like punching him."*

Some of the Japanese, while acknowledging the physical superiority of the Americans, thought they lacked other intangibles. Suishi Tobita, a Japanese sportswriter and former player, said, "They have power and ability, but they weren't serious."

During the tour, the ballplayers were treated like lords and constantly hounded for autographs by the baseball-loving Japanese. Evidently, Paul Waner signed a few himself. Years later at the height of World War II and Japanese-American fighting in the Pacific Theater, a dead Japanese soldier on Namur Island was found with a Paul Waner–signed baseball bat. The United Press headlined the story in the insensitive language of that day and age: "Dead Jap Carried Waner's Autograph."

Made in Japan, the bat was forwarded to Paul Waner in April of 1944. By then, Waner was playing for Brooklyn in the twilight of his career. Marine Corporal Charles E. Truiitt, a former post man from Wilmington, Delaware, sent the bat to Big Poison, and presumably he was the one who found it.

Paul Waner was famous around the world. Not like Babe Ruth or Lou Gehrig, but not bad for a country boy from Oklahoma who played baseball away from the New York limelight and slashed doubles and triples and not the long ball.

Pennant Hopes and Misadventures

> I am the city of Pittsburgh.
> I am the city of rivers.
> Smoke city,
> Steel city,
> Coal city,
> Once.
> During the War I gave to the world:
> Out of my furnaces, red with flame,
> White with heat,
> Damp with sweat,
> I gave my steel.
> Out of my mines, I gave my coal.
> I gave my men.
> I gave my life in the lives of men.
> In sweat,
> In labor;
> In blood;
> I gave.
>
> *— From "Pittsburgh 1932" by Eleanor Graham*

While Pittsburgh gave steel to America, the giving mood across the country seemed to retreat with the shrinking economy that had by 1932 filled the streets with 13 million unemployed people. It was a tragic year in many regards, especially for the Pirates' ownership family.

President Hoover appointed Pittsburgh's Andrew W. Mellon as ambassador to Great Britain. Mellon was the richest man ever to hold that post and a tireless advocate of the trickle-down theory as Secretary of the Treasury. The reason Hoover actually sent Mellon to England was to get him out of the country after critics charged him with mismanaging the economy and possibly contributing to the Depression.

Later that year in October, New York Governor Franklin D. Roosevelt, the Democratic presidential candidate, spoke to 30,000 people at Forbes Field. Three weeks later he was elected, pledging a "New Deal" for all Americans. In November, free milk was distributed to 50,000 needy and undernourished students in 500 schools in Pittsburgh's Allegheny County. Beyond the Smoky City, Amelia Earhart became the first women to fly solo across the Atlantic, Radio City Music Hall opened in New York, Babe Didrikson won a gold medal at the Olympics in Los Angeles, and Buck Rodgers came to the radio.

And Paul Waner nearly went to New York.

Waner's near trade to New York had its roots in the sudden demise of the Dreyfuss family. Pirates owner Barney Dreyfuss's son, Sam, had died in 1931 with pneumonia at the age of 36. His father suffered emotionally for months afterwards. Then in January 1932, Barney was operated on for a glandular condition and somehow contracted pneumonia. After a one-month battle, he died too.

It was a sudden, huge loss for Pittsburgh.

During Dreyfuss' 32 years owning the Pirates, the club had won two World Series and six pennants and finished in the second division only four times. He had been generous to players who remained loyal to him and could be stern when crossed or when players did not mirror his somewhat puritanical ways.

For much of his ownership career, Dreyfuss was a major shaper and architect of the National League. He had fought against the potentially disastrous move to "syndicate base-

Paul Waner ready to go (courtesy of Jim Knight).

11. Pennant Hopes and Misadventures

ball" advocated by another group of owners, helped get the single commissioner structure set up in the wake of the Black Sox scandal, and warned that the Lively Ball would diminish baseball.

Replacing Dreyfuss at the helm of the Pittsburgh club was his son-in-law, William Benswanger. An incessant pipe smoker and insurance company executive by profession, Benswanger had consented to run the club after Sam's death. With less than a year's experience, he withdrew from his insurance business and took over the team on a full-time basis. While he gave a nod to baseball, he loved classical and opera music.

Bill Benswanger: *"To me, music is the highest form of expression—a universal language. You may not understand Italian, Hungarian, or Russian, but attend a concert where the music of those countries is played and you feel a kinship with the composer, the grief of the country he knew, also its joy, hopes, and aspirations."*

He had a taste for fashion, too. Benswanger would add a large blue "P" on the front of the bare Pirates jerseys that season. It wasn't much, but next season the "P" was red, and road jerseys actually emblazoned "Pirates" across the chest. Ironically, uniforms across baseball were generally drab and dreary during the rollicking 1920s, and then became more innovative and colorful during the down-and-out 1930s.

Not long after Benswanger sat in the big leather chair, rumors starting swirling about the possible trade of Paul Waner, still barely 30 years old and at peak market value. Though Big Poison and Barney Dreyfuss had bickered now and then over salary, the two had always respected each other. Now that Barney was no longer in the picture, the Pirates front office seemed reluctant to endure Paul's salary demands and drinking escapades.

The New York Giants were the most frequently mentioned suitor. The New York newspapers delighted in this and quoted an unidentified Pittsburgh team official as saying that Paul "had played his last game as a Pirate."

The prospect of Paul Waner alongside Mel Ott in New York's outfield seemed too good to be true. The Giants were offering infielders Sam Leslie and Eddie Marshall and outfielder Fred Leach for Big Poison. But the Pirates were demanding first baseman Bill Terry in a one-for-one swap. The Giants appeared reluctant as John McGraw, who greatly favored Terry, was running the club. Indeed, 1932 was the last year of McGraw's 33-year managerial career. Terry succeeded McGraw as manager in early 1932 despite being a brief hold-out that spring training.

Paul seemed unfazed about the trade rumors. The nonchalant

Oklahoman felt at one with the Pittsburgh Pirates, but knew he'd play ball anywhere. Besides, he was enjoying learning how to fly an airplane back in Oklahoma. In February he flew solo in a training plane for the first time after 10 hours of practice with an instructor, Paul Hinds, a former Army pilot.

Paul and Hinds once had to make a forced landing, which no doubt would have shocked the Pirates. Hinds said later he was impressed by Paul's "coolness" at the controls as the plane slipped in an air bank and nearly scraped the ground. Big Poison was heard to say, "Ride 'em, cowboy!"

The day after his solo flight Paul and Lloyd left Ada to join the Pirates in Kansas City for spring training. No trade had been made.

With all the trade rumors swirling, if John McGraw were choosing between Waners, he'd probably have picked Lloyd. At least that's what he said to the *New York World Telegram* on February 24, 1932, though he may have been trying to drive down Paul's market value.

John McGraw: *"If we got Paul, where would we use him? He couldn't displace Ott in right, he would not be adequate in center, and from what I hear about [Len] Koenecke, Paul could not keep that young man out of left. Lloyd Waner would be quite a different proposition. He is the greater of the pair."*

Whether McGraw was obfuscating to deny trade rumors or not, it was an odd statement. True, Koenecke was an impressive athlete. Maybe more importantly he was the last player personally scouted by McGraw, who had arranged for his purchase from Indianapolis of the American Association in 1931 for $75,000. But he was no Paul Waner.

Koenecke's was a strange, tragic story. After playing briefly for the Giants in 1932, and failing to live up to his potential, he was shuffled around the majors and minors. In 1935, on a flight from St. Louis to Detroit, Koenecke, who had been drinking and getting loud, got himself kicked off the plane once it landed at the next airport. It was late in the evening, and he decided to charter a flight to Buffalo where he had some friends to party with some more. While the plane was in the air, Koenecke tried to wrestle the controls from pilot William Mulqueeny.

The copilot, Irwin Davis, tried to restrain the brawny ballplayer but was pushed to the floor. Mulqueeny, with one hand on the controls, picked up a fire extinguisher with the other and bludgeoned Koenecke in the head until he was dead. Both pilots were cleared of charges. Speculation at the trial focused on whether Koenecke was trying to commit suicide in a "grand and glorious manner."

11. Pennant Hopes and Misadventures

His future so hotly debated, Paul nearly missed the beginning of the 1932 season. During the winter Paul went to Florida on a golfing and fishing trip. He was standing just off shore when "an unidentified creature," as it was reported, bit Waner on his left ankle. The wound did not heal properly, and an infection resulted in his leg swelling up. He missed some games that spring training. By the time the season opened, his ankle had healed.

Before Opening Day of the 1932 season, the Waner brothers appeared on the local KMOX radio station in St. Louis where they opened with the Cardinals. *Pittsburgh Press* sportswriter Ralph S. Davis and KMOX announcer France Laux interviewed the two outfielders. Paul told them that Bill Walker was the toughest pitcher he had faced—his choice was always changing—while Lloyd said all of the NL pitchers were hard at times. The younger Waner attributed his hitting success to "balance" at the plate. Each said that the Cardinals and New York Giants were the teams to beat that season.

With the addition of 20-year-old shortstop Arky Vaughan, strong contributions by the Waners and Pie Traynor, and some decent pitching for a change, the Pirates arose as a contender for the National League flag in '32. The club was in first place for 44 days of the campaign, and it wasn't until August 1 that the Cubs took a stranglehold on first.

This season, the Waners truly lived up to the "double dose" aura. Between them they would knock out 99 doubles for the year. On Opening Day, Lloyd cranked out three doubles to set the pace. But it was Paul who took the lead in setting one of the hottest two-bagger seasons in history. On Opening Day, he belted a double, and from there on in April it was sock! bang! smash! whack! wallop! By the end of the month he had nine doubles in only 15 games.

That was just a warm-up for May. The first three games that month Paul pounded out three more two-baggers, and then after going two games without a hit, punched out two more in four days. On May 17, he slammed out two doubles in one game, another one the next day, and then two more on the 19th.

That was nothing until May 20.

That day the Pirates were in St. Louis to play the Cardinals. Paul had stayed up the night before drinking with friends at a party hosted by Pirates pitcher, Heine Meine, who owned a saloon south of St. Louis in Luxembourg. The next afternoon, as he wobbled to the plate in batting practice, he asked Cardinals manager Gabby Street to have his pitcher take it easy on him.

"I didn't get too much sleep last night," Paul said.

"Sure, Paul, sure," Street said, patting Paul on the back. As the Cardinals' manager headed back to the dugout, he thought to himself, "This is one day Big Poison won't hurt us."

Instead, Paul walloped four doubles that day to tie a major league record and lead the Pirates to a 5–0 victory over St. Louis. Pirates pitcher Larry French twirled a two-hitter.

Robert E. Hood, in his book *The Gashouse Gang*, revealed another tale about that day.

Robert E. Hood: *"During the course of that game, Waner sneaked a drink or two in the dugout. And, at one point, umpire Bill Klem, who did not look unkindly upon the grape, held up the game to wait for Waner to appear at the plate. This was the afternoon that Paul Waner tied the National League record for most doubles in a game. He hit four doubles off Tex Carleton—and he did a handspring at second base after each one!"*

Paul's quartet of doubles was a sign of things to come. The next day, May 20, he belted out another double for good show. Then he rapped out doubles in back-to-back games on May 27 and 28, slapped out one in each of the next two days in successive doubleheaders, and socked another one the next day.

Paul Waner ended May with a preposterous 29 two-baggers. In only a month and a-half of play, 182 at bats and 44 games, the elder Waner had swatted as many doubles as many players might in an entire season.

By June 13, Paul was hitting .400, and a week later was clipping along at .406, 16 points higher than runner-up Chick Hafey of the Cardinals. On June 25 in the second game of a doubleheader, he had one of his best days ever, going 5-for-5 with a double, two home runs, four RBIs, four runs scored, and 12 total bases. Lloyd helped his brother out in that game by slapping out three hits and scoring three times.

Lloyd Waner (courtesy of Jim Knight).

Lloyd was in the midst of a 22-

11. Pennant Hopes and Misadventures

game hitting streak that ended June 23. He had been given that day off—we do not know if he was not feeling well or was simply rested—but was eventually called upon to pinch-hit that day. He walked, and scored a run, but without a hit his streak ended.

Lloyd got a bum deal on this one. Though he missed 20 games to various ailments, he was in a groove this season, tapping out singles almost at the rate of his vaunted rookie year. From May 30 to June 19, he notched a 14-game hitting streak. Missing a hit on June 20, he restarted his hitting and it eventually became his 22-gamer. After two pinch-hitting appearances on June 23 and June 26, he hit safely in the next five games. In August, Lloyd put together a 13-consecutive-game hitting streak. This season he had two four-hit games.

Paul had three four-hit games, two of them back to back in that torrid month of May. No matter how much Big Poison drank, he liquidated National League pitching. Sportswriters noted to their younger fans that "Paul's habits are not recommended to boys. He enjoyed parties and laughed at curfews."

Though Paul Waner may not have been an ideal hero for youth, he was a man determined to make a better life and he had energy and unusual intelligence. He was also fair and unselfish and had a silent strength that emanated from his small body and sharp mind. Like his brother Lloyd, he fought to survive in a tough world, trying to shape the best possible life using only the tools available to him—his uncanny talent and perseverance. Maybe he differed from the popular teen heroes in the '20s and '30s, and maybe he retained the fierce competitive urge to do better than anybody else, but he understood that bad times afflicted everybody and that all were in the same boat.

But ballplayers are no statesmen. They are players. Crude or rude or lewd, they are players first and foremost. Mastering their craft is the highest badge of honor a player can hope for, and this is done through the relentless perfecting of technique and attitude. This is what Bob Broeg, the St. Louis sportswriter, captured in a May 1970 column on Paul Waner.

Bob Broeg: *"A sharp-featured, thin-lipped little man, tanned the color of an acorn and as lean as an Indian pony from his native Oklahoma, Paul seemed constructed entirely of bone and gristle. A left-handed hitter, he'd stand well back of the plate, his feet almost together, toes parallel to the line of the batter's box, about five inches inside the chalk marks. He raised his right leg as he stepped into the plate, nothing like the exaggerated leg-lift of Mel Ott. Tomahawking the ball, Waner was a clothesline hitter, hitting sharply to all fields, and so straight that his wife could have hung out a week's wash* *on one of his liners. He wasn't a roisterer on the scale of Babe Ruth, nor was he a rowdy, but he liked late hours, liquor and convivial company."*

Tributes aside, Paul had some sensitive fans. After Broeg wrote that column, the *Sporting News* received a letter from Joel M. Ponder of, ironically, Oklahoma City, Oklahoma. It read in part:

> I cannot believe that one of baseball's greatest stars could have consumed as much booze as mentioned and still hold himself together so dynamically for 20 years in the big leagues. In fact, the records prove that he was really an Iron Man, to say the least. Yes, I believe that Paul Waner was indeed the Mighty Mite of baseball, but I'll never agree that he nearly drank the well dry while racking up so great a record.

One might "ponder" if Mr. Ponder was an Oklahoman acquaintance of Paul's.

Once during 1932 Paul frustrated the easy-going Chicago manager Charlie Grimm with his ability to perform under the weather. "Jolly Cholly," as Grimm was called, made this story into one of his favorites.

As it goes, Paul had partaken in a night of heavy drinking and felt extremely ill in the morning, unusual even by his standards. Some say he had never gotten to bed and was still reeling when he came to the ballpark. A cold shower helped little. But his name was in the lineup that day.

In his first at bat, Paul missed the ball by "18 inches," reportedly. In the second at bat, he improved, missing it only by six inches. In the ninth, with the score tied between the two contending teams, Paul came to bat again. He rifled a triple down the right-field line to drive in the winning run. Big Poison slid triumphantly into third base, a big cloud of dust engulfing him.

Grimm was unable to contain himself. He burst from the Cubs dugout and glared at Paul, lying there on the ground.

"It's just like you, you little punk, to sober up at a time like this," snorted Grimm.

One time Paul hit two home runs off Pat Malone, the tall, hard-throwing Cubs hurler. But Malone didn't feel sorry for the hung-over Waner and would not dust him off, telling him instead, "I'll twist the head off your shoulders, Waner."

Paul, not the fighter type, said of Malone, "He was so tough he wanted to embed the ball in your skull above the ear so the undertaker would have to have a chisel to get it out."

Nothing stopped Paul, however, from his two-bagger delights. On September 25, he banged out his 62nd double to establish a new NL record

11. Pennant Hopes and Misadventures

as the Pirates defeated the Cardinals 7–1. The record would last until 1936 when Joe Medwick doubled 64 times for the still-standing record. Earl Webb's 67 doubles for the 1931 Boston Red Sox is the major league record.

The Pirates narrowly missed the pennant that season, finishing in second place, four games behind the Chicago Cubs. They dominated the league in July, winning an all-time franchise-high 25 games in a month. But the rest of the way they were unable to close the gap.

Vaughan blossomed at shortstop, smacking out a .318 average. He never fell below .300 for the Pirates the next 10 years. Gus Suhr got a vote of confidence from manager George Gibson, and he finished the first season of his Iron Man consecutive-games-played streak. The Pirates were a good-hitting club again that year, and the pitching was much improved, though they suffered from the loss of ace Steve Swetonic for weeks. Larry French was the same old workhorse, winning 18 games and losing 16.

Paul finished fourth in the league in batting with a .341 average. He also knocked out 215 hits, played in all 154 games, and ranked fourth to Chuck Klein in the National League's Most Valuable Player award voting.

Lloyd missed 20 games due to a variety of aches and pains, and that was a sign of things to come. Still, he hit .333 and collected 188 hits and scored 90 runs.

With Benswanger running the Pirates, there was more loose talk of trades and rumors about the Waners circulated through the sporting press. While Benswanger would prove hesitant to pull the trigger on any deals, at least it gave an idea of the worth of the players and what they had meant to the franchise since their arrival. For example, the *Sporting News* considered Lloyd a steal:

"Representing no investment (by the Pirates) whatsoever, Lloyd probably would bring a six-figure price in open ivory market, were the Pirates to dispose of him. Fortune, indeed, smiled on the Pirates when Paul asked that Lloyd be given a trial six years ago."

The Curiosity of the League

> B is for
> Base-ball
> The Ball once struck off,
> Away flies the Boy
> To the next destin'd Post,
> And then Home with Joy
> —*John Newberry, published in "A Little Pretty Pocket-Book"
> in London, England, 1744*

    Baseball is an ancient game, one that depends on heroes and heroics, and gradually in the 1930s organized baseball realized the attraction of star power, past and present.

    In 1933, baseball owners established the All-Star game, hoping to heighten declining fan interest in the national pastime. It was a mastermind of imaginative fantasy, pitting the game's finest players against each other, plunk in the middle of the Depression. One had to find ways to uplift the spirits of the restless natives.

    This thinking went beyond white America, too. In Pittsburgh, A. G. "Gus" Greenlee, owner of the Pittsburgh Crawfords, answered the black community's interest in baseball by establishing the Negro National Leagues, which would last a glorious 12 years and feature stars like Josh Gibson and Satchel Paige.

    This year modern professional football began in Pittsburgh when the Pittsburgh Pirates, owned by Arthur J. Rooney, lost to the New York Giants, 23–2, before a crowd of 25,000 at Forbes Field. Eventually Pittsburgh's professional team would become the Steelers, woeful for decades then splendid in the '70s and afterward.

In baseball, the Pirates finally brought back one of their all-time stars—Honus Wagner—as a coach. Strapped for funds, Wagner had asked the Pirates for gainful employment and received support from around baseball, including the writer Fred Lieb, who publicized Wagner's plight in the most sentimental way.

Wagner's return seemed to motivate the Pirates players as Pittsburgh led the league in batting and won 87 games to finish second once again, only five games behind New York. Although there would be periodic rumors of Wagner taking over the manager's position, he remained only as a coach for some 20 years, willy-nilly becoming an enduring reminder of the Barney Dreyfuss regime. He worked well with the youngsters, teaching Arky Vaughan about the nuances of shortstop, for example. All this made an impression on the veterans like Paul Waner.

Paul Waner: *"Honus came back as a coach with the Pirates during the thirties. He must have been sixty years old easy, but darned if that old boy didn't get out there at shortstop every once in a while during fielding practice and play that position. When he did that, a hush would come over the whole ball park, and every player on both teams would just stand there, like a bunch of little kids, and watch every move he made. I'll never forget it.*

"Honus was a wonderful guy, so good-natured and friendly to everyone. Gee, we loved that guy. And the fans were crazy about him. Yeah, everybody loved that old Dutchman! If anyone told a good joke or a funny story, Honus would slap his knee and let out a loud roar and say, 'What about that?' So whenever I would see him, the first thing I'd say would be, 'What about that, Honus,' and both of us would laugh. I guess there's no doubt at all that Honus was the most popular player who ever put on a Pittsburgh Pirates uniform."

Another new face on the Pirates was Fred Lindstrom. Before the season the Pirates made the trade for Lindstrom, a third baseman and outfielder. Once promised the Giants' managing job, Lindstrom was expendable after New York instead hired Bill Terry to replace McGraw. After learning he would not be the Giants' manager, Lindstrom, who was prone to talking back to McGraw, saw even less reason to heed McGraw's tough talk. So when he retired, McGraw convinced the front office to get rid of Lindstrom in a three-way swap with the Pirates and Phillies in December 1932. A future Hall of Famer—but one who critics frequently mention as not deserving of it—Lindstrom had a .311 average in a 13-year career. Only playing full-time for seven of those years, his two best years came in 1928 and 1930 when everyone else was pounding the cowhide.

When the Pirates picked up Lindstrom, Paul quipped, "My goodness, we need pitching." But it turned out he and Lindstrom became good friends and golfing buddies.

Once Lindstrom arrived at the Waner home for a morning golf game. When he got there, Paul's wife told him, "Paul's gone to the store for a loaf of bread."

Lindstrom waited and waited. Finally, he asked Mrs. Waner, "When did he leave for the store?"

"Last night," she replied, accustomed to her husband's carousing.

Another time after an all-night tour of New York's watering holes with Lindstrom, Paul showed up bleary-eyed and tired for a doubleheader the next day at the Polo Grounds. Lindstrom thought Paul should take the day off. Instead Paul knocked a double, home run, and single in the first game. In the second game, he whacked two doubles, a home run, and a single.

Lindstrom was also at the heart of another drinking story. Once the Pirates were in Chicago to play the Cubs. In the mid-afternoon before the game, just as the Pirates players were leaving the hotel for the ballpark, Paul Waner was stumbling back into the hotel after a long night out on the town.

Manager George Gibson did not see Waner make his inebriated entrance, as Lindstrom and a couple other Pirates spun Paul right out the revolving door and into a taxi cab. When the cab stopped at a red light near Wrigley Field, Paul spied an onion-reeking hamburger joint.

He jumped out, saying, "Haven't had breakfast. Gotta have a couple hamburgers."

In the clubhouse before the game, Big Poison's teammates screened him from Gibson. When it came time to play, they thought the hot sun would sober him up. Not soon enough, however, as the onion-smelling and hung-over Paul Waner muffed a fly ball in the first inning. He went hitless—until the ninth inning.

Down by one run, the Pirates had runners on second and third—and Paul due up. Some of the Pirates on the bench whispered that maybe Gibson should send up a pinch hitter. But the manager demurred.

Facing the hard-throwing Guy Bush, the bleary-eyed Waner stood up to the plate. Bush delivered a high, tight fastball, and Paul, jammed, swung with all the might he could muster. He poked a blooper just over the third baseman's head, scoring the tying and go-ahead runs. The Pirates went on to shut out the Cubs in the bottom of the ninth, winning the game.

Gibson grinned and put his arm around Paul afterwards. "Maybe

12. The Curiosity of the League

the rest of you guys would be great hitters like Paul—if you ate onions," he said.

Waite Hoyt, the old New York Yankee foe from the 1927 World Series, signed on with Pittsburgh in 1933 in the twilight of a career that included 237 victories. Years later in 1948 Hoyt was one of the 56 honorary pallbearers at Babe Ruth's funeral in New York's St. Patrick's Cathedral. It was a sweltering summer day, and former Yankee teammate Joe Dugan remarked to Hoyt, "I'd give anything for a beer."

Hoyt responded, "So would the Babe."

In some of the best recollections of the brotherly Waner tandem, Hoyt recalled the modesty and decency of Lloyd and the libertine and sharp-minded Paul.

Waite Hoyt: *"I didn't see much of the Waners until I joined them as a Pittsburgh teammate in 1933. You didn't hear much about Lloyd, as Little Poison seemed to be the half of the brother team who seriously applied himself to baseball, and was never guilty of antics like his brother Paul. Lloyd was never a conversationalist—very self-effacing, quite modest, never given to boasting. Paul himself never mentioned his league-leading abilities. He never complained about anything on the ball field, never questioned an umpire, never made alibis. He got his hits, then stood in the outfield and kept up an incessant line of encouraging chatter. Never failing. He was always there, playing every minute. Paul worked and labored at the game. He was smart—well-groomed and a perfect gentleman.*

"He was the curiosity of the league, the guy who amazed all others. Little Lloyd tagged along like the kid brother going to the swimming hole. Lloyd was like him in a more quiet way. There the resemblance ended."

As Hoyt illustrated, Paul lived life on his own terms. He had boundless energy and hardly wore down.

Waite Hoyt: *"Paul was a man of the world, who loved life and all there is, animate and inanimate, plus a generous dash of the flowing bowl. Paul, like Babe Ruth, was never handicapped by a night on the town."*

One time when the Pirates played a spring training game against the White Sox in Oklahoma City, the Waner brothers invited Hoyt and some other teammates back to the family farm in Harrah to meet the folks.

Waite Hoyt: *"Lloyd said to me, 'Watch Paul. Then watch Dad. Dad doesn't like him to drink highballs or straight drinks. Cocktails are all right.'*

"I watched Paul. His Dad watched him. Paul poured a rather generous dash of unadulterated corn. He added a wee drop of lemon. His Dad was satisfied. That constituted a cocktail."

Lloyd Waner (courtesy of Jim Knight).

Hoyt recalled when Lloyd finally had to give up rooming with his brother. Now 27, Lloyd preferred going to bed earlier than his night owl brother. And it wasn't just a question of bedtime.

Waite Hoyt: "*There was a series in Boston with the Braves. I went to my room about 10 P.M. I was due to pitch the next day's game. But I didn't get to sleep. That's because in the room above me there was this constant rumbling and racket.*"

So Hoyt marched upstairs and knocked on the door. The door flew open, and inside the room were Paul Waner and teammates Steve Swetonic, Larry French, and Heine Meine. Evidently, they were playing a football game with pillows inside the hotel room. Paul, holding a pillow tight, would crash up the middle. Each time, he'd be thrown back against the wall for a five-yard loss. He finally dove under the bed and scrambled up on the other side for six points.

When Lloyd asked waivers on Paul as a roommate, he was heard to say, "I never get any sleep."

Paul replied, "Sleep—who needs it?"

Another time Hoyt and teammates Bill Swift and French went to pick up Paul at his hotel. They had a round of golf scheduled for that day. Paul was practicing all right.

Waite Hoyt: "*We walked down to his room, and we heard this odd noise—kaloom, kaloom. We knocked on the door. 'C'mon in,' Paul yelled. 'I'm practicing.' He had had scrambled eggs for breakfast. The platter was on the floor inverted, being used as a tee. Paul was knocking golf balls off it with a nine iron. 'See that rose in the wallpaper—watch,' he'd say.*"

When he wasn't monkeying around, Paul took time to represent the National League on July 6 in Chicago's Comiskey Park at the first All-Star game ever. Lloyd was not selected for an All-Star game until 1938.

Dressed in specially designed uniforms with "National League" emblazoned across the chest, Paul Waner and the senior circuit looked a cut above the junior circuit competition. But on the field of play the AL demonstrated its long-ball prowess as Babe Ruth clouted a two-run homer to lead his league to a 4–2 win.

Paul did not start the game, as Chuck Klein of Philadelphia was the National League's right fielder and batted in the third spot. Waner later filled in as a defensive substitution. Paul would also be selected to the All-Star roster for 1934, 1935 and 1937—four times altogether. In those games he went hitless in eight at bats with one RBI and one strikeout.

"I guess those American League pitchers didn't think I was too hot a hitter," Paul told sportswriter Fred Lieb.

When regular season play resumed, Lloyd was battling a hitting slump. When the season opened he had been shifted to left field that season as Lindstrom took over center field duties. The switch seemed to affect Lloyd's batting, as he slumped to the mid–.250s through much of the spring. On July 12 the lifetime .340 hitter was benched by manager George Gibson. Lindstrom moved to left, and Adam Comorosky assumed center field duties, and earned himself more playing time by hitting .305 during Lloyd's absence. Lloyd never complained to the press nor made any trouble, but his competitive fire burned to get back into the lineup and he may have felt insulted by the move to left field. When he returned to the lineup six days later, he hit in eight straight games.

On July 19, the Pirates hosted the Giants when a near riot took place. It happened with runners on first and third and two out in the top of the fourth. Giants pitcher Freddie Fitzsimmons lined to center fielder Fred Lindstrom who scooped the ball off the ground and held it up for the umpire George Barr to see. Barr called it a fair catch, causing Giants manager Bill Terry to rush out and protest. Umpire-in-chief Augie Moran held a conference and reversed the call, allowing Gus Mancuso to score.

The fans began yelling at Moran and hurled bottles and garbage at him. There was more to come. Three days later in another Pirates-Giants game, fans at Forbes Field rained bottles and projectiles onto the field when umpire Moran called the Pirates' Tony Piet out at first base on a close play.

The season marked another first in terms of brothers in baseball. In the AL, Red Sox catcher Rick Ferrell homered off his brother, Indians pitcher Wes Ferrell. Wes, perhaps baseball's best-hitting pitcher, also smacked a home run. It marked the only time the Ferrells homered in the same game.

When the bell rang on the 1933 season, Paul had barely cleared the .300 hurdle—at .309—and Lloyd did not at all. Though he wrapped up the year with a 14-game hitting streak, Lloyd's .276 average was the lowest of his career to that point. While Paul scored 101 runs and notched 16 triples, demonstrating his speed and bat were still threatening, Lloyd's major problem was games played. He saw action in only 121 games. Of his 138 hits, only 19 were of the extra-base variety.

The Pirates fared better than the Waners. In 1933 the club finished in second place, just missing the pennant by five games. They boasted five regulars hitting over .300—Arky Vaughan (who also led the league with 19 triples), Fred Lindstrom, Tony Piet, Pie Traynor, and Paul Waner. Workhorse Larry French won 18 games for the second year in a row and shined on an otherwise weak pitching staff.

Philadelphia's Chuck Klein eclipsed all the hitters in the league that year. Not only did the former steel worker from Indiana win the Triple Crown (.368, 28 HRs, and 120 RBIs), but he also topped the league in slugging average, hits and doubles. Showing little appreciation for his Ruthian effort, the Phillies traded him in the off season for three journeymen players, making Klein the only Triple Crown winner traded after his big season.

The pennant-winning New York Giants—who only had one .300 hitter in Bill Terry but a wealth of good pitching—defeated the Washington Senators in the World Series.

In the Negro National League, the American Giants of Chicago beat out the Pittsburgh Crawfords to win the league's first half championship. The second half of the season was not completed, and this led to an amusing episode. Author Robert Peterson observed, "W.A. (Gus) Greenlee, league president, awarded the pennant to his club, the Pittsburgh Crawfords. This was, of course, disputed by the American Giants."

If it were only that easy for the Pittsburgh Pirates.

Celebrating the Common Man

> I would rather see steel poured than hear a great symphony.
> —*Mary Heaton Vorse*, Men and Steel, *1919*

In America, 1934 was a down and dirty year. Ravaged by economic doom, the country celebrated the common man in the roughneck St. Louis Cardinals, and Pennsylvania finally passed a law making Sunday baseball legal, thus allowing working men and women in Pittsburgh and Philadelphia a chance to watch baseball on their days off. Outlaw heroes—Pretty Boy Floyd, Baby Face Nelson, Bonnie and Clyde, and John Dillinger—were all slain by lawmen this year. In New York City, former major leaguer Billy Sunday held a fiery revival meeting to bring God to the people. In San Francisco Alcatraz Prison opened to bring convicts to maximum security. In Pittsburgh professor Albert Einstein lectured at Carnegie Tech on the weighty subject of the equivalence of mass and energy, and back in Einstein's native land, Hitler's storm troopers brought terror to the streets of Germany.

Hurling the Cardinals into October, the Deans were baseball's best-pitching brothers, usurping the Waner Act as the game's most renowned sibling pair, at least for that season. Before Opening Day, Dizzy boldly predicted he and brother Paul would win 45 games together—they did, and a few more. Yet Paul and Lloyd would not be outdone, for Big Poison rebounded from last year's lukewarm effort to win yet another batting championship. While wielding the stick as well as ever, his life off the field seemed to rival that on the field.

161

In *The Gashouse Gang*, author Robert E. Hood wrote about a game in Chicago where Paul once smashed a ball off the fence and, as it bounded between the fielders, he steamed around second heading for third. "Unfortunately, he was still woozy from a long, strenuous evening on the town, so when he made a long, swooping slide he wound up in the left-field bullpen, yards away from third base."

In *Big Sticks*, William Curran wrote of the "wealth of merry tales" that followed Paul Waner and became his legacy off the field. Exaggeration has it that the blurry-eyed Paul saw three baseballs on every pitch and swung at the middle one. Another says that Waner attended a revival meeting in St. Louis and was so moved that he took the pledge—and promptly suffered a batting slump.

◆ ◆ ◆

On April 29, in their seventh game of the 1934 season, the Pirates won their historic first Sunday ball game, beating the Cincinnati Reds 9–5 before some 20,000 shivering fans. Paul slammed a two-run home run, and Lloyd slapped out three singles to drive in two runs himself. For the rank-and-file hometown crowd—especially the mill workers in the Homestead, West Homestead, Rankin, Munhall, Braddock, Duquesne, McKeesport, Monongahela, and Clairton—this gave them a chance to watch baseball on the weekend after hot and heavy work all week long.

Oddly enough, the late owner Barney Dreyfuss had never lobbied for Sunday ball in Pennsylvania. "It'll kill our Saturday afternoon business," he was heard to say.

Owner Bill Benswanger thought differently. Once the state legislature had passed the new law, he made the decisive break with the Dreyfuss tradition to encourage Sunday ball. A new era was dawning, and Pennsylvania professional baseball could well afford Sunday ball, as had been exemplified in all the other cities that allowed Sunday games. It gave the average citizen a chance to see ball games without playing hooky from work—and that often meant the mills throughout western Pennsylvania.

In the shadows of the city's smokestacks, the rank-and-file movement grappled with big labor issues, ferocious red-baiters who labeled them "Communists," and disorganization. Above all, labor leaders wanted the right to organize independent unions. There was talk across the nation of a huge steel strike that spring. The steel companies in Pittsburgh and elsewhere began stringing barbed wire around their mills and purchasing munitions. A strike date was set for June 14, but President Roosevelt intervened, and the steel workers would have to wait for their right to form unions.

13. Celebrating the Common Man

A steel strike would have potentially devastated the Pittsburgh Pirates' gate attendance, as many of their fans worked directly or indirectly with and for the steel companies and their suppliers. Faced with precarious prospects in this regard, Benswanger could not afford another mediocre club that failed to satisfy the masses and put the fannies in the seats. In June, with the Pirates in fourth place at 27–24, Benswanger fired manager George Gibson and replaced him with the popular Pie Traynor. This might have been considered a rash move, but the entry of Traynor was a shot in the arm to the club.

The two-time All-Star Traynor was a local legend, renowned for field leadership and his personable nature. Everyone, from the low-level grunt to the business executive, found him easy to talk to and get along with. For Benswanger, he seemed the perfect choice—a ballplayer who had the respect of his teammates and baseball insiders around the league. But the sudden ousting of Gibson made Traynor wary of looking like he wanted the manager's job too badly. In those days, that would have been considered bad form. Baseball is so much about respect that pitchers throw at batters and umpires toss out managers and players if they don't show enough respect.

So Pie had his alibi.

Pie Traynor: *"I wasn't looking for a job. Managers are worth a dime a dozen, and I knew the job wouldn't be steady."*

The timing was good for Traynor. At 36, he had seen his best playing days. In a game that season against the Phillies he overslid home, and as he reached back to touch the plate, the Philadelphia catcher fell on his right arm, hurting it badly. He never fully recovered from it, and that season he would hit .309 in 119 games. The next year he would only play in 57 games, hanging up his spikes thereafter to manage full-time.

Billy Herman, one of the National League's best second basemen in the 1930s, recalled Traynor's twilight as a player. His arm injury made him an erratic thrower.

Billy Herman: *"I saw quite a bit of Pie Traynor, though he'd been around for a while by the time I came into the league. Son of a gun, he was a great player. Most marvelous pair of hands you'd ever want to see. The only problem he had was throwing. He was wild. They told me he was always wild. But the thing that helped Traynor was his quick release. You'd hit a shot at him, a play that he could take his time on, and he'd catch it and throw it right quick, so that if his peg was wild, the first baseman had time to get off the bag, take the throw and get back on again. It was the only way Traynor could throw; if he took his time, he was really wild."*

While Traynor left the ranks of the everyday player to manage, Paul Waner continued scorching line drives around the league.

Billy Herman: *"Pound for pound, Paul was the best hitter I ever saw. Nothing worked on him—we never found a way to get him out."*

After going hitless on Opening Day, Paul hit safely in 16 straight games, was snuffed out for one game, and then picked up where he left off with a 7-game hitting streak. In July, after 87 games, he was banging away at .369, almost 100 points above Lloyd's .273.

At midseason, Paul had a chance encounter with a "magical bat."

Paul Waner: *"All the players who reported to the All-Star game in New York last July brought along their own bats. The bats were stacked in front of the dugout before practice started. When I looked for mine, I happened to pick up Gabby Hartnett's [the Chicago catcher] favorite bat. It was lighter than mine, maybe only 34 or 35 ounces, but for some reason it felt good in my hands. Hartnett let me use it during the game, and while I didn't set the world on fire with my hitting, I became attached to Gabby's bat—in more ways than one."*

Surprise, surprise, when Paul unpacked his suitcase after returning home from the All-Star game, he discovered Gabby's bat. Maybe he had meant to bring it with him. At the time he was hitting .331, good but still only 20th best in the NL during a year of greater offense.

So the practical-minded Paul Waner started using Hartnett's bat in games, and in a month his average had climbed to .360.

When Hartnett found out when the two met for a Pirates-Cubs series, he good-naturedly chastened Paul as a "bat thief." Then he gave in and told Paul to keep the bat.

The bat actually cracked a couple times while Paul was using it, so he used nails and tape to hold it together. "Don't tell (National League President) John Heydler," Paul chuckled.

In due course, the bat completely broke into pieces, and Paul was left to order duplicate versions of the same weight and length from the bat factory.

That season the Pirates got into the routine of winning one and then losing one, never making much headway in the standings.

But Paul kept up his pace down the stretch, finishing at .362 to win his second batting title. It came seven years after securing his first title, and to Paul that seemed too long of a wait. But in those days of league averages hovering in the .280s, he had plenty of hard-hitting rivals to contend with—the Medwicks, the Terrys, the Hornsbys.

Big Poison also topped the league in hits (217) and runs scored (122) and posted solid extra-base numbers (36 doubles, 16 triples, 14 homers). He finished second to Dizzy Dean in the National League's Most Valuable Player award selection.

While a banner year for Big Poison, 1934 was unremarkable for Little Poison. He did not get above .300 for the second year in a row. Despite a 21-game hitting streak in midsummer, Lloyd finished at .282 with 95 runs scored and one home run.

Eclipsing some of the other Pirates hitters that season was 22-year-old shortstop Arky Vaughan. He banged out a .333 average and scored 112 runs. He seemed primed for a big season, though no one would have guessed what numbers the Arkansas native would compile next year.

Almost sighing in relief it seemed, Paul relished the return of a livelier ball in 1934.

Paul Waner: *"It's foolish for someone of my weight to try for home runs. I haven't got the power. So I make up for my lack of strength by using some judgment. I try to place my hits. The opposing teams know that I don't always hit to the same field, and so the players have to spread out, and I have a good chance to find a hole. It is easier for me, a left-handed batter, to hit an inside ball to left and an outside ball to right. But to a certain extent I determine whether the delivery will be inside or outside. I do this by stepping into, or away from, the plate when swinging."*

Paul studied the catchers as well as the pitchers.

Paul Waner: *"I went a lot by the catchers. You could almost say I hit by the catcher that was facing me. I knew these catchers—what they liked their pitchers to throw—and I watched where they placed their gloves."*

Paul said the 1934 ball seemed faster, shot past infielders quicker, and bounced harder between the outfielders. Though not like 1930's combustible version, the ball boosted the confidence of hitters in the National League at a time when attendance was down and baseball was pressed financially. The previous year the major leagues had adopted the AL's more juiced ball as the major's uniform ball, and maybe it had taken some time for the effects to be noticed in the NL.

Paul Waner: *"With the fast ball in play, I had more confidence in myself. If I went hitless three or four times in a row, I knew I'd get a hit before long. In 1933, my slumps were longer and extended over several days."*

With the Cardinals powered by the Dean brothers' pitching that summer, the tough-hitting Cardinals bareknuckled their way to the World

Series, prevailing against the Hank Greenberg–led Detroit Tigers in seven games—no small feat. The Pirates could take solace in beating the Cardinals 13 times in their 22 encounters during the regular season.

Traynor steered the Pirates to a fifth-place finish in 1934, winning 74 games. The Pirates seemed perpetually frozen out of the pennant chase in those days. It had been seven long years since 1927 when the Pirates last went to the World Series.

Paul Waner: *"Oh, it's a long season. When you're out of fighting for the pennant, it becomes monotonous."*

Paul wished the Pirates had ace pitchers like Carl Hubbell and Dizzy Dean, two of the best pitchers he—or anyone else for that matter—had ever seen. He also experienced difficulty against Ray Benge of Brooklyn and Bill Walker of St. Louis. "Both of those fellows gave me lots of good balls to hit at, but I couldn't connect against them like I would against others."

While much is made of the happy-go-lucky image of Dizzy Dean, the flame-throwing right-hander was an intimidating presence on the mound and was not averse to throwing at batters if they got the best of him, which was seldom. In those days, batters almost expected to get hit for success at the plate.

Lloyd knew all about this unwritten rule and accepted it as part of baseball's code. Today, it seems hitters take it personally when pitched inside.

Lloyd Waner: *"When I played, a pitcher could throw at you any time he wanted to. In fact, he could tell you he was going to throw at you and there was nothing said. You had to take it. If he hit ya, he hit ya. You just got a base on balls. But now they want to fight if they even come close."*

Back then, Little Poison noted, the pitcher-batter duel was different. "A hitter goes up there now and he gets his gloves on and gets his pants all in shape. But when I was playing a pitcher'd have three strikes on you before you got up there, because when I played, when you got one foot in the box, the pitcher could pitch."

Not many pitchers were fazed by the Pirates' long-ball threats. There weren't any.

Recent annual Pirates team totals in home runs included 52 homers in 1934, 39 homers in 1933, 48 homers in 1932, and 41 homers in 1931. To put this into perspective, many league leaders—guys like Foxx, Ott, Klein, Gehrig, Ruth—hit as many home runs in a season as the entire Buccaneer squad.

13. Celebrating the Common Man

This lack of might was an irony for Pittsburgh baseball, at least in some quarters. After all, the city had some stout sluggers playing just over the hill from Forbes Field—in the Hill District, home of the Negro National League.

Josh Gibson, the powerful catcher for the Pittsburgh Crawfords, is reported to have smashed 69 home runs in 1934. According to the eyewitness testimony of Jack Marshall of the Chicago Giants—reported in Robert Peterson's *Only the Ball Was White*—Gibson hit a fair ball out of Yankee Stadium this season. "Josh hit the ball over the triple deck next to the bullpen in left field. Over and out!" If accurate, it made Gibson the only player ever to accomplish that feat in a regular game.

Gibson's battery mate, Satchel Paige, showed he had one of the best arms in Pittsburgh if not in America. His many feats included winning two games on July 4—but in two different cities. Paige no-hit the Homestead Grays in Pittsburgh, 4–0, and then jumped in the car and drove to Chicago where he defeated the American Giants, 1–0, in 12 innings.

An arm like Paige's and a bat like Gibson's would be a fortune to any team.

One augur of good fortune for Pirates fans, though no one knew it at the time, came on August 18. A young baby was born in the back streets of Carolina, Puerto Rico. His name—Roberto Clemente Walker.

The Bambino's Last Hurrah

> It fell across our city like a curtain of black rolled down. We thought it was our judgment, we thought it was our doom.
> — *Woody Guthrie*

Two days before Opening Day in the 1935 baseball season, the blackest day ever fell upon Paul and Lloyd's native Oklahoma. The Dust Bowl came on April 14, 1935, when winds and dust gathered in a huge, sprawling storm, and ravaged the landscape across many states. So dark were the skies that it was as if the sun had stopped shining and night had come — and it stayed that way.

The Dust Bowl was an ecological and human disaster that took place in the southwestern Great Plains region of the United States in the 1930s, including parts of Kansas, Oklahoma, Texas, New Mexico, and Colorado. When the drought and dust storms showed no signs of letting up, many people abandoned their land in a nightmarish case of the dispossessed. Others would have stayed but were forced out by banks and landlords when they lost their land in foreclosures.

In all, one-quarter of the population left, packing everything they owned into their cars and trucks, and heading west toward California. The mass exodus, some lured by false promises of jobs, depleted the population drastically in certain areas. In the rural area outside Boise City, Oklahoma, the population dropped 40 percent, with 1,642 small farmers and their families pulling up stakes.

14. The Bambino's Last Hurrah

As Lloyd Waner told author Donald Honig, the two brothers were aware of the hardship back home. They saw it in the off-season when journeying back to Oklahoma. It made them appreciate the chance for a better life that baseball had given them.

Lloyd Waner: *"It did seem like a miracle. We were the beneficiaries of it, and sometimes we'd forget there was a real world out there. Remember, we went from hotel to the ball park, back to the hotel, and then onto the train for the next go-round. All of our reservations were made for us, all of our meals were paid for. Did that for six months. Then the season would be over and my brother Paul and me would go back to Oklahoma, and then we would realize how bad things were. The farms were abandoned, the owners off to Lord knew where. Stores that had been doing business in the spring were boarded up. People were glum and poor. That was the real world."*

The Dust Bowl exodus was the largest migration in American history. By 1940, 2.5 million people had moved out of the Plains states. Arriving in California, the migrants were faced with a life almost as difficult as the one they had left. Many California farms were corporate owned. They were larger, and more modernized, than those of the southern plains, and the crops were unfamiliar. The rolling fields of wheat were replaced by crops of fruit, nuts and vegetables. Like the Joad family in John Steinbeck's classic, *The Grapes of Wrath*, some farmers wound up in the San Joaquin Valley picking grapes and cotton. They built their houses from scavenged scraps and lived without plumbing and electricity. Polluted water and a lack of trash and waste facilities led to outbreaks of typhoid, malaria, smallpox and tuberculosis. Their lives there were almost as harsh as back in the Dust Bowl.

In Harrah, Ora and Etta Waner were able to keep their large farmhouse where Paul and Lloyd had grown up. They were fortunate to have owned their property outright and not been dependent on bank loans or working for others. This distinction set the Waners apart from the corn-fed poor Okie image that the Eastern writers gravitated toward in describing them. While farmers, they were landed gentry for all intents and purposes.

But like everyone else, Paul and Lloyd Waner were not immune from the Depression. Ball clubs were quick to reduce players' salaries during this period, and many players just barely made enough to get by on. Though well-established stars, Paul and Lloyd understood their finances were affected by the general drop in attendance at baseball games. Since the Depression began, the Pirates had trouble breaking 300,000 annually at the gate. During the twenties they had averaged twice that amount, and one had to go back to the lean World War I years to find similarly low figures for the club.

It was a time to spend money wisely.

On his dad's advice, Lloyd put some of his money into real estate around Oklahoma City. Paul, however, thought little of investments. Not much of a saver, he lived the good life, and owned a 50-foot yacht in Florida with expensive fishing equipment, and he often took it out deep sea fishing in the Gulf of Mexico. Big Poison also reportedly rode large sea turtles for fun, and marched to his own drum beat. At parties, Lloyd would humbly say how glad he was to be invited, and then turn over the entertainment to loquacious Paul—"he always pinch hits for me"—who would spin yarns into the night.

Spinning some positive news that year, the wealthy Pittsburgh banker Andrew Mellon donated vast sums of money and art for the construction of the National Gallery of Art in Washington, D.C., Pittsburgh-area voters approved Sunday movies, following on the heels of the successful "Sunday experiment" in baseball from the prior year, and three weeks later, large crowds filled theaters for the first-ever Sunday films in Allegheny County. On the labor front, Pittsburgh steel workers made some headway at last as the Committee for Industrial Organization (CIO) was formed to expand industrial unionism.

That summer, the most exciting event in Pittsburgh was the Bambino's last hurrah.

On May 25, Babe Ruth came to Forbes Field as a member of the Boston Braves. At 40, he was tired, sluggish and unhappy with his break with the Yankees, who he felt had treated him badly. The Babe, however, went out with a bang in one of the most sublime farewells in baseball history.

Lloyd Waner: *"He was old, he was fat, he couldn't run, and he had lost a lot of his ability at the plate. But he was still Babe Ruth. He came into Pittsburgh to play, and after one of the games, I was leaving the ball park to go home and there's Babe signing autographs, surrounded by this big crowd. I'll swear that half the people who were at the game were waiting for him to sign. I stood there for a while watching and marveling at it. When I went home that crowd was still around him. The next day when I came to the park, somebody told me that Babe finally asked one of the policemen to get him a folding chair and Babe just sat there signing autographs.*

"'Till how long?' I asked.

"'Till nearly ten o'clock at night,' the fellow said. 'He just sat and sat and sat til he'd made everybody happy.'

14. The Bambino's Last Hurrah

"You could see he was nearly finished. He still had that beautiful swing, but he just wasn't hitting them anymore. But this one day he upped and amazed everybody. He hit three of them out in one game. The last one was hit farther than any ball I've ever seen. It went over the roof. I was standing in center field watching it go. You would have thought it had a little engine in it. It became a dot against the sky and then disappeared. My, did he hit it. But he could hardly get around the bases. His legs were shot, you see. We hit several balls out to Babe in right field in that game and he could hardly move after them. It was sad watching him out there."

Pirates pitcher Guy Bush recalled giving up Babe Ruth's final two home runs.

Guy Bush: "He [Ruth] came up again in the ninth. I was a little mad. I told my catcher, Tommy Padden, that he was not good enough to hit my fastball. I came through with a fastball for strike one. I missed with the second. The next pitch I nodded to Tommy. I was going to throw the ball past Mr. Ruth. It was on the outside corner. As he went around third, Ruth gave me the hand sign meaning 'to hell with you.' He was better than me. He was the best that ever lived. That big joker hit it clear out of the ball park for his third home run of the game. It was the longest home run I'd ever seen in baseball."

Legend has it the last shot went 600 feet, the longest ever hit at Forbes Field. Maybe. The ball soared over the heads of a group of kids on the corner of Boquet and Joncire and into a construction lot. Henry "Wiggy" Diorio retrieved the ball and Ruth autographed it for him at the Schenley Hotel later that night.

In fitting irony, the Pirates won that last game Ruth homered in, 11–7. Lloyd went 3 for 5 with one triple—it shot past the slow-footed Ruth—and scored two runs. Paul knocked out two hits in four at bats, scoring twice. Perhaps there was some redemption from the earlier 1927 World Series.

Six days later Ruth would take his last at bat in the majors, grounding out against Phillies Jim Bivin to first baseman Dolf Camilli.

Both Lloyd and Paul held the old home run king in the highest esteem. The Babe also respected the Waners, especially Paul. Before the season Ruth, goaded on by sportswriters, had picked his "All-America" team. His infield included Lou Gehrig at first, Charley Gehringer at second, Arky Vaughn at shortstop, and Billy Werber at third. In the outfield, it was Al Simmons, Mel Ott and—yes—Paul Waner.

While the choice of Paul was obvious, in choosing Vaughan the Babe was eerily prescient. Vaughan was not yet an established star, though in May of 1935 he was on the brink of a season of Hall of Fame proportions. While not the greatest gloveman, the mild-mannered Vaughan was a selective hitter with some power who hit for average—and he quickly became a star in Pittsburgh's lineup.

On June 10, Vaughan joined Paul Waner and second baseman Pep Young as the three smacked successive homers in the eighth inning against the Reds.

In 1935, Vaughan pummeled National League pitching for a .385 average, which won him the batting title that year and set an all-time high for shortstops. He won baseball's "other" Triple Crown—leading the league in batting average, on-base percentage, and slugging average. In doing so, Vaughan was chosen the Most Valuable Player in the National League, the first of the Pirates since Paul Waner in 1927.

An extremely fast runner, the left-handed Vaughan was a dead pull-hitter who, like Ted Williams, battled countless defensive shifts against him. In 1935 it got so bad that Vaughan made himself—late in the season—hit to left field. For most of the season he cruised along above .400.

Lloyd Waner marveled at Vaughan's raw abilities.

Lloyd Waner: *"We had a fellow with us on the Pirates throughout the 1930s who sure was an outstanding hitter and a fine shortstop. Arky Vaughan. He could hit and he could run. I'll say he could run. We had a contest on in Pittsburgh one time, things like running to first base, bunting and running, and so on. Arky and I tied in going to first base in bunting and running. Three and two-tenths seconds. Don't think that Arky Vaughan couldn't scamper. For going from home plate to second base I don't think there was anybody who could match him."*

Rip Sewell was pitcher for the Pirates from 1938 to 1949. He was famous for the "eephus" pitch, a blooper ball that confounded most hitters except Ted Williams, who smacked an eephus for a home run in the 1946 All-Star game. Though he saw Vaughan later in his career, he, too, had vivid recollections. As Vaughan matured, he became a better fielder.

Rip Sewell: *"Arky Vaughan was in his heyday at shortstop for the Pirates when I got there. I'd say that he was as good a man at short as I ever saw. He could do it all. And he was a good hitter. He could hit for power, and he could hit for average. And he could fly around those bases! I never saw anybody who could go from first to third or from second to home faster than Vaughan. Like we used to say, when he went around second his hip pocket was dipping sand. That's how sharp he cut those corners."*

14. The Bambino's Last Hurrah

Probably the most famous story about Arky Vaughan is when he once made Leo Durocher speechless, and that was hard to do.

By 1943 Vaughan was no longer with the Pirates and was playing for the Brooklyn Dodgers, lured out of early retirement by Dodger general manager Branch Rickey. Billy Herman was with the Dodgers as their second baseman, and the irascible Durocher was managing. One day around midseason Durocher and Dodger pitcher Bobo Newsom, another colorful personality, got into a loud argument after Newsom threw a wild pitch that lost that day's game. Durocher then fined and suspended Newsom.

Herman recalled the next day's chain of events.

Billy Herman: *"The next morning I was having breakfast together with [Augie] Galan and Arky Vaughan at the New Yorker Hotel, where we were staying. Vaughan, you know, was a guy who always had everybody's respect, as a ballplayer and as a man. He never said much, but everybody admired and respected him. ... Arky's reading the paper. Durocher had given an interview saying that Newsom had crossed [catcher Bobby] Bragan up, giving him a spitball, and that was why Bobo was suspended. But it had been building up, you see. Newsom had been getting to Durocher for weeks, throwing cutting little remarks at him. Bobo didn't mean any harm, but Leo was getting madder and madder. So finally he had a chance to stick it to Bobo, and he did."*

What happened next is amazing by Durocher standards.

Billy Herman: *"So Vaughan's reading this, and he's very quiet, not saying anything to anybody. But something's bothering him, we could tell. So we go to the ball park. Durocher isn't there yet. We put on our uniforms and went out and loosened up. But this time Durocher is in his office. Well, Arky had been waiting all this time to ask Durocher if he'd been quoted correctly.*

"He goes into the office, with a newspaper in his hand. 'Leo,' he said, 'did you tell this to the writers?' 'Yeah,' Durocher said, 'I told them that.' Arky didn't say another word. He went back to his locker and took off his uniform—pant, blouse, socks, cap—made a big bundle of it and went back to the office. 'Take this uniform,' he said, 'and shove it right up your ass.' And he threw it in Durocher's face. 'If you would lie about Bobo,' he said, 'then you would lie about me and everybody else. I'm not playing for you.'"

The effect was profound on the rest of the Dodgers players. After talking it over they decided to boycott the game, a stunning rebellion against Durocher. About 10 minutes before game time, Durocher started running around, pleading with his players to play, and that everything would be straightened out. Finally, he got nine players to suit up. But not Vaughan. He would not play.

Billy Herman: *"Around the seventh inning Branch Rickey came down to the clubhouse. Vaughan was still sitting there. He told Arky that he understood the situation, that he could sympathize, and one thing and another. Rickey could be very persuasive when he wanted to. But Vaughan wouldn't budge. Then Rickey said, 'All I want you to do is put on your uniform, go out and sit on the bench for a few minutes and then come back. If you don't at least make an appearance, we'll have to discipline you. We'll have no alternative.' Finally Vaughan agreed. He put on his uniform, walked into the dugout, and then turned around and walked right back out again. Well, they straightened it out as best they could. I think they rescinded the action against Bobo. But it seemed to me like they got rid of Newsom pretty quick after that."*

Another Babe—and another Herman—made a brief stint with Pittsburgh that season. Before the season the Pirates had picked up the hard-hitting Babe Herman who at 32 should have had some hits left in his bat after batting .304 for Chicago the past year. He did, but not for Pittsburgh. In spring training, Herman, a right-fielder most of his career, had been touted as the Pirates' best left-field option. Watching from his spring training perch, Volney Walsh of the *Pittsburgh Press* noted Traynor's enthusiasm for Herman.

"Babe is a better fielder than most people will admit," Walsh wrote. "He can throw and he is now learning to throw from the strange position of left field. He can run the bases and Traynor predicts he will startle Pittsburgh fans by his feats on the lines. In order to get Herman's punch into the lineup, Traynor is willing to sacrifice a bit of fielding skill."

Herman, however, had injured his foot in spring training and never got off on the right foot. Then he pulled a leg tendon in May and found himself on the bench and seeing rare duty as a pinch-hitter. On June 12, the Pirates moved Herman to Cincinnati for the waiver price of $7,500 after the Babe had posted a meek .235 average with no homers in 26 games. Recovering his health, he attacked the ball with ferocity for the Reds and smacked out a .335 average the rest of the year.

In 1935, the Brooklyn Dodgers called up 19-year-old Harry Eisenstat from the minor leagues. In the pitcher's first appearance against the Pittsburgh Pirates, he faced Paul Waner. This is what he told sportswriters at the time:

Harry Eisenstat: *"I looked at Waner when I was ready to pitch, and*

14. The Bambino's Last Hurrah

his eyes were closed. It looked as if he was falling asleep. But as I let the ball go, those eyes popped open all right."

Waner smashed a triple into the outfield, scoring two runs. The rookie Eisenstat, who specialized in the screwball, just shook his head at the nonchalance of Paul, a 10-year veteran by then.

Harry Eisenstat: *"If you were to walk over to the Pirates bench, and ask him whether I was a right-hander or left-hander, he wouldn't know. He didn't even look at me."*

Now in his mid–80s and living in Ohio, Eisenstat recalled the rookie experience and baseball in the 1930s.

Harry Eisenstat: *"We're going back a few years, now. But both of them—Paul and Lloyd—were class guys, great ballplayers. Paul had more power than Lloyd, though Lloyd was the better outfielder defensively. They were both very pleasant, especially with young rookies. They took the time to show them the ropes, what to do and what not to do. They were credits to the game. You don't see many like them around today. I played against them a few games, and though I didn't know anything about them off the field, their families and so forth, I could tell they were good guys. I saw them helping rookies all the time."*

Once Eisenstat had to cover first base on a ground ball by Paul. When he got to the bag, Big Poison had a few kind words for the left-hander that have stuck in his memory.

Harry Eisenstat: *"I covered first base once, and he complimented me on the screwball that I threw. I recall him saying, 'It's tough to hit.' But he could hit it anyhow. He was such a great hitter, able to place line drives to any part of the field. He didn't just hit to one field. You didn't strike him out very often. They never chased bad balls. They made you throw the ball they wanted to hit."*

It was hard to get to know opposing players back then, Eisenstat said. Unlike today when the country club atmosphere exists, most ball clubs in the early part of the past century had a no-fraternizing policy, unwritten or not, about mingling with opponents. Teams would fine players for making a public spectacle of friendship with opposing players.

Eisenstat remembered Forbes Field. "It was a tough field, not like the nice ones they have around today. The grass and the fences and everything were not as smooth as they are in parks today."

In 1938 Eisenstat, primarily a reliever, was traded to the Detroit Tigers.

There the 22-year-old Brooklyn native roomed with Hank Greenberg. In the twilight of his career, Greenberg would sign with the Pirates for the 1947 season and mentor the young slugger Ralph Kiner while rejuvenating fan interest in the Pirates.

Harry Eisenstat: *"I was lucky to room with Hank, who was a great player. When I was pitching, I had great players behind me, too, like Charlie Gehringer, Billy Rogell, and Mickey Cochrane [a player-manager then]. With them on the field, you looked forward to going to the ball park every day. These were guys determined to be successful, and that was contagious for the whole team. They, too, worked well with the rookies, especially Hank."*

Eisenstat's greatest claim to fame came October 2, 1938. That day he beat Bob Feller, 4–1, on the same day Feller struck out 18 Detroit Tigers to establish a major league record. Feller's effort also thwarted Greenberg's chances of surpassing Babe Ruth's 60-homer mark (Hank finished with 58). Incredibly, Eisenstat only gave up four hits but became a historical footnote alongside the exploits of the legendary Greenberg and Feller.

In 1939, Detroit traded him to the Indians for an aging Earl Averill and some cash. As was the case with so many ballplayers, the Second World War interrupted Eisenstat's career. Rather than return to baseball after 1942, Eisenstat considered it his patriotic duty to keep working in his defense plant job. After he got out of the military, he returned to live in the Cleveland area. He believes the players of yesteryear are overlooked today.

Harry Eisenstat: *"The sportswriters today don't know who these guys were. They know about the present day ballplayers, but they don't know the background of these guys who built the game into what it is. For one, it was just tougher to be a player back then. But if you had the ability, and hung in there, you'd make it."*

The season of 1935 was filled with history-making events that would shape the game for decades.

On May 24, a crowd of 20,422 at Crosley Field witnessed the first night major league baseball game. With nearly a million watts of light, Crosley Field was illuminated when President Franklin Roosevelt flipped a switch in the White House. The Reds won, 2–1. Later, Washington Senators owner Clark Griffith predicted, "Night baseball is a passing fad. There is no chance of night baseball ever becoming popular."

The bright lights shone on a few Pirates that season. Vaughan's performance has been cited. But it was the rare masterful seasons by two Pirates pitchers that gave fans hope for the future. Cy Blanton and Bill Swift

14. The Bambino's Last Hurrah

boasted the NL's two lowest ERAs. The Oklahoman Blanton's 2.59 mark won the ERA title, edging out his teammate and other stalwarts like Dizzy Dean and Carl Hubbell. In Blanton, it seemed the Pirates might have finally found the mound ace they had been searching for. Blanton's story, however, turned tragic—he suffered from mental problems during his career, and in 1945 he died in an Oklahoma state mental hospital. He was only 37 years old.

The Waners also contributed their potent sticks. In August, Lloyd hit safely in 23 straight games, an all-time high for him, and Paul banged out a 15-game hitting streak. The odd thing about Lloyd's streak was that he missed two weeks during the beginning of it and two weeks near the end due to injury. But he collected his hits every game he was in the lineup. Back in centerfield full-time, Little Poison ran the outfield like a gazelle.

Lloyd Waner (courtesy of Jim Knight).

This was evident on June 26 when Lloyd set the record for put outs in a doubleheader with 18. He made nine in the first game and nine in the second one. At the plate, Lloyd also excelled, going 5 for 9. It was a highlight film day for Little Poison.

Lloyd's .309 average and graceful outfield play that season showed he still had plenty left in his legs. He slapped out 14 triples and scored 83 runs in the lead-off spot.

Paul turned in his annual batting tutorial. He socked out a .321 average with 29 doubles, 12 triples, 11 home runs, 98 runs scored, and 78 RBIs.

For the first time in their nine years of playing together, neither Waner led the Pirates in total hits. It had been routine for one of them to bang out 200 or more hits, or at least to top the club in hits for the year. It didn't happen this time around. Outfielder Woody Jensen's 203 hits paced the Pirates.

In 1935, the Bucs finished in fourth place, 13½ games behind the Chicago Cubs. The Chicago squad put up a 21-game winning streak in September to overtake the Giants and head to the World Series where they lost to the Detroit Tigers. The Pirates even had five future Hall of Famers on their roster—the two Waners, Traynor, Waite Hoyt, and Vaughan.

So did the cross-town Pittsburgh Crawfords—Satchel Paige, Josh Gibson, Judy Johnson, Cool Papa Bell and Oscar Charleston. The Crawfords defeated the New York Cubans for the 1935 Negro National League championship.

As every veteran player knows, holding down a full-time position is a matter of fending off the constant competition of younger, more affordable players. Lloyd played in only 122 games, and Paul, 139, his lowest total in 10 years of play.

It's difficult to assess drinking's toll on Paul, or even Lloyd for that matter. Then it was hard for a major league ballplayer to find the support system—outside of or within himself—to stop the self-destructive act of excessive drinking. Baseball players were grounded in a tradition of hard drinking, and few had the skills to make the changes they needed to. One player of Paul Waner's era who eventually learned coping mechanisms—and actually played with the Waners—was Rollie Hemsley.

In 1935, Alcoholics Anonymous (AA) was founded in Ohio, and it gave hope to those seeking to escape alcohol dependency. And Hemsley was a big part of putting AA on the American map.

Hemsley had come up with the Pirates in 1928 and became the regular catcher in 1929. He had great potential for, unlike many catchers, his speed early on was above average. In his 19-year career, the five-time All-Star Hemsley appeared in 1,593 games and batted .262 while establishing himself as a premier defensive catcher—and sadly, a notorious hard drinker like Paul Waner. In fact, the two often reveled into the night together when Hemsley was a member of the Pittsburgh Pirates.

Hemsley drank himself off four clubs before temporarily whipping alcoholism with the help of Alcoholics Anonymous. Hemsley began sobering up soon after his trade to Cleveland in 1938, meeting with a group of recovering drinkers in Akron, Ohio.

In the spring of 1940, Hemsley went public about his AA membership. Newspapers and magazines published articles about his recovery and accompanied him as he traveled around the country talking about getting sober. The publicity resulted in many new members joining AA. The June 27, 1940, issue of the *Sporting News* featured an extensive article on Hemsley:

Hemsley's Own Story of His Wagon Ride
Strangers helped him make greatest decision. Former rollicker smiles over past flings but is serious about aid he received from organization known as "Alcoholics Anonymous." Not a Prohibition group. High and dry for more than a year. Backstop agrees he's in tip-top shape and records agree. Now Rollie wants to aid others in the way he has been helped.

It's hard to imagine the breakthrough this represented in that day and age. In terms of social experimentation, it was clear that Prohibition had not worked. Now the roots of the recovery movement were planted with the help of a reborn catcher, a refugee from a sport where drinking was considered macho and almost expected as entertainment for players bored with life away from the diamond. For Hemsley, his work in establishing Alcoholics Anonymous and own story of recovery is a tribute to his great personal courage. But it had an unhappy ending. Bill James reports in his *Historical Baseball Abstract* that Hemsley ultimately "fell off the wagon." Still, he went on to a post-playing career as a coach and scout.

Hoisting the Black Flag

> Every normal man must be tempted at times to spit upon his hands, hoist the black flag, and begin slitting throats.
>
> —H. L. Mencken

The year 1936 was a complicated one. The Dust Bowl continued to grip Paul and Lloyd Waner's native Plains in extreme hardship, and President Roosevelt's New Deal policies came under fire for not working fast enough, if at all.

In Pittsburgh, the worst-ever flood in city history swamped the city's low-level streets on St. Patrick's Day, killing 74 and leaving 50,000 homeless. On other fronts, the Steel Workers Organizing Committee held its first meeting, Allegheny General Hospital was dedicated, and the University of Pittsburgh's John Woodruff of Connellsville near Pittsburgh won a gold medal in the 800-meter race at the 1936 Summer Olympics in Berlin. Woodruff joined Jesse Owens as one of two American black Olympians who repudiated Nazi leader Adolf Hitler's racial supremacy theories by virtue of their amazing performances.

Movies enjoyed their most prosperous year since the advent of the Depression, and the blockbuster novel *Gone with the Wind* by Margaret Mitchell demonstrated the appetite of Americans for quality entertainment during even the toughest of times.

Baseball was one of the Depression's most available forms of entertainment. Along with the first annual selection that year of members for the National Baseball Hall of Fame in Cooperstown, New York—Ty Cobb, Babe Ruth, Honus Wagner, Christy Mathewson, and Walter Johnson—

15. Hoisting the Black Flag

the sport counted on upcoming stars to continue to inspire the national pastime. This season rookies Joe DiMaggio and Bob Feller would usher in a new era of fandom.

Unlike the mid-1920s when the World Series–flushed Pittsburgh Pirates could afford pricey rookies such as Paul Waner, in the midst of the Depression the club could no longer recruit such golden talent on a whim. So the front office counted on veterans like Paul and Lloyd Waner for pennant-winning contributions. One of the brothers almost didn't make the 1936 season.

That winter back in frigid Oklahoma, Lloyd, 30, contracted pneumonia. It escalated and landed him in the hospital's critical-condition ward. He eventually recovered, though it was weeks before Little Poison first stepped outside since getting pneumonia. As spring training approached, he sat down and penned a letter to Pirates chief Bill Benswanger.

"I'm feeling fine," Lloyd wrote, "but I sure was sick. When do you want me to report?"

Benswanger told Lloyd to take whatever time he needed before reporting. On April 1, weeks after training camp had opened, an underweight Lloyd Waner joined the Pirates in Longview, Texas. He did not put on a uniform or play in the exhibition game that day, which the Pirates won 9–7 against the White Sox.

After Opening Day on April 14, there were some Pirates heroics early on. On April 20, Gus Suhr's two-out, three-run, ninth-inning homer defeated Chicago 9–8.

For Paul, the season began badly.

Waner ended up suing Stevens and the sponsors of the broadcast for $150,000 on the grounds of libel. We do not know what was said about Paul Waner. Newspapers were protective of private lives, especially when lawsuits were involved. All the *New York Times* said was, "The suit was based on the allegation that the broadcast falsely criticized his playing as a member of the baseball team, and injured his reputation and had exposed him to 'public hatred, contempt and ridicule.'"

After much research involving newspaper microfilm, the basis for this lawsuit has not been determined. Unfortunately, learning the truth behind this episode would have revealed much about Paul's state of mind at the time. He was not a fighter, and so taking the extraordinary step of legal action was unusual.

In any event, the criticism seemed to inspire Paul. He went on to smoke the ball that season, starting with a 13-game hitting streak in late May and a flurry of doubles. He banged out eight two-baggers, eight in one

11-game stretch in June, and had a neat 30 by the All-Star break. Big Poison's average kept rising that season like a thermometer on a hot day—.331 on June 9, .349 on July 28, .368 on September 9.

On June 3, Paul made an unbelievable one-handed grab of Boston's Hal Lee's warning-track drive in the eighth inning to save a 7–5 win over the Bees.

Alas, it was the year of no respect for Paul Waner. For the first time in four years, he got left off the All-Star roster, even though he was among the league leaders in batting average and doubles. Pittsburgh got snubbed all around.

At the All-Star game in Boston on July 7, Chicago manager Charlie Grimm drew the wrath of Pirates fans for not using either Arky Vaughan or Gus Suhr in the game. Manager Pie Traynor served as one of Grimm's coaches and pitcher Lefty Birkofer threw batting practice—but that was all. Though the National League won the game, no Pirates saw action, and that caused consternation in the Steel City. Some faulted Grimm for holding a grudge against his old team after he was traded back in the mid-1920s.

Paul responded to his lack of attention with high voltage performances. On July 9, in the first game back after the All-Star break, Paul banged out four hits with two doubles and a triple with a season-high six RBIs.

On July 10, Phillies slugger Chuck Klein became the fourth major leaguer to hit four home runs in one game—the irony being that Klein performed this rare feat in expansive Forbes Field and not the cozy Baker Bowl, his home turf for years. Klein's homers powered Philadelphia past the Pirates 9–6 in 10 innings. All of his shots went over Paul Waner's head into the right field stands. Klein nearly launched a fifth homer—Paul caught his last drive at the wall.

On July 14, Paul accomplished the rare feat of stroking two triples in one game. At the time, the Pirates were in second place, six games behind St. Louis. Paul, atop the league in batting average, visited the Craft Club in suburban Pittsburgh one evening for a fan banquet, and talked about the Pirates season thus far.

Paul Waner: *"We have the best ball club this year that I've played on. It's better than our 1927 club, which won the pennant. That may sound like a strange statement ... but don't forget that the league is a whole lot stronger than it was in 1927. Both St. Louis and Chicago are stronger now than then.*

"It's going to be a bitter battle right down to the wire, and we're going to be in the thick of it. In a race like this, the outfit that gets the better breaks will be the ultimate winner. We've had all the worst of the breaks so far. Take

15. Hoisting the Black Flag

our games with New York. We lost four out of five to the Polo Grounders on our last Eastern trip. Yet a single break in our favor would have reversed every one of those games. Had we taken four of five, we would have been that much closer to the Cardinals now. But we'll get our share, and the sooner the better. It's anybody's race as I see it."

The Bucs made their presence felt. On August 24, their bats roasted St. Louis for 25 hits in a 17–5 donnybrook.

Three days later the Pirates beat the Dodgers 6–3 as Brooklyn made four errors behind pitcher Van Lingle Mungo. Mungo became outraged at what he perceived to be a lack of support by his teammates. The former Pirates player then deserted the team in Pittsburgh and returned to Brooklyn. Eventually Dodgers president Steve McKeever convinced Mungo to rejoin the team.

Mungo wasn't the only overheated player that hot summer. The heat weakened several Pirates, and pitcher Bill Swift suffered a bout of hay fever. The aging pitcher Waite Hoyt had surgery and after recovery returned for bullpen duty.

In Pittsburgh, tempers boiled over among the fans and sporting press. When the team struggled late in the season, there were calls for Traynor's removal as manager. Critics pointed out he had hardly improved the team during his three years at the helm. Results were demanded, even of the popular Traynor. Like Mel Ott, he was one of the National League's "nice guys." But a feisty manager type like Leo Durocher always said, "nice guys finish last."

The Pirates scuffled to stay in the race until mid–September. Carl Hubbell's 16-game winning streak was one reason the New York Giants won the pennant before going down in defeat in the World Series to their rivals the New York Yankees.

In 1936, the Pirates finished at 84–70, eight games behind New York. They could not close the gap after playing only .500 ball from June on.

That season Paul's .373 average won him his third and last batting title. Though he had no invitation from the Major League All-Star team back in July, *The Sporting News* named him to its All-Star team after the season. Paul finished with 53 doubles, 218 hits, and 107 runs scored, and his 94 RBIs were his highest total in seven years. All around, 1936 was vintage Big Poison.

It was the third consecutive year a Pirates player had won the league's highest hitting honor—Paul in '34, Vaughn in '35, and Paul again in '36. Paul also tied Rogers Hornsby for the NL record with seven 200-hit seasons. Pete Rose later broke this mark with 10 seasons. And his 53 doubles made him one of two National Leaguers ever to hit 50 or more two-baggers in three different seasons. Stan Musial is the other.

As for Lloyd, his playing time had dropped due to his late start and general frail condition that season. Still, in his 106 games, he poked out a solid .321 average with 13 doubles, eight triples and one home run. In yet another stunning reminder of his bat control, Lloyd struck out only five times in 414 at bats.

Replacing Lloyd in the lead-off spot that season for the Pirates was 28-year-old outfielder Woody Jensen, who set a major league record with 696 official at bats that season (since broken). Jensen didn't like to draw walks any more, if not less, than Lloyd Waner. He walked only 16 times in 1936. Lloyd had 31 bases on balls in many fewer plate appearances.

Like other baseball players, the Waners were increasingly active in golfing. From the swing to the stick and ball aspects, the game had many things in common with baseball and yet was different. It was more individualistic, for example. One could practice and play alone, or with a group, and the outcome was not based on anything like the pitcher-batter duel of baseball. In many ways the games complement each other.

After the 1936 season, Paul won the National Baseball Players' Golfing Tournament in Tampa. It was the second such golfing championship for Paul, who had also won the same tournament, which he had helped organize back in 1934.

In a fitting case of irony, Paul Waner beat Babe Ruth—his 1927 World Series nemesis and now retired—in the final round to win the match outright. If only, he later said, this took place on the diamond and not the fairways and greens.

The Last Great One

Poverty is the great reality. That is why the artist seeks it.
—*Anaïs Nin*

In 1937, America's confidence in its future lagged despite some of the period's most ambitious creative efforts, especially in architecture. That year the majestic Golden Gate Bridge in San Francisco opened and was hailed right away as one of the more stunning engineering feats of the 20th century. Though a bit lower on the architectural radar map and on the other side of the continent, the University of Pittsburgh's towering Cathedral of Learning opened across the street from the Pirates' Forbes Field. Forty-two stories high, the Cathedral looked like a Gothic-drip sandcastle, casting a medieval glow upon the east end of Pittsburgh.

Elsewhere tragedy erupted in the fiery downing of the Hindenberg airship in New Jersey and in the mysterious disappearance of the beloved Amelia Earhart and her airplane. The master architect Frank Lloyd Wright completed his "Fallingwater" home near Pittsburgh and the world debated the merits of functional design. Abroad, civil war raged in Spain, Germany continued to rearm, and an imperialistic Japan took military action on the behemoth China.

While ballplayers had no union, the Steel Workers Organizing Committee secured a minimum daily wage and benefits for Pittsburgh steel workers. In just nine years, Pittsburgh would become the hotbed for the first union movement in baseball, though both Waners would be out of baseball by then.

Wintering in Sarasota, Paul may have looked favorably on the concept of player unity when he received his first contract offer. Even though Big Poison had won the batting title the season before, Pittsburgh had sent him a contract calling for a "steep reduction" of about 15 percent.

Paul balked. Sounding a gracious note in the hardest of times for Americans, he told reporters he would have been satisfied with the same pay as the year before. But taking a cut was another matter, as he explained. Besides, he charged the club with breaking its promise to him.

Paul Waner: *"The management called me by telephone from Pittsburgh nearly a week ago, and agreed to pay me so much. I said, okay. Then they sent me a contract, but they cut $500 out of it. I sent it right back. They wired me claiming they had witnesses listening in on our conversation over the telephone, and I'd have to sign."*

Waner told the Pirates, "I don't have to sign for that, and I'm not going to."

Team president Bill Benswanger quickly pinned the blame on Paul before leaving for spring training in California. "When a man makes an agreement and then repudiates it that man is hard to figure out," he told reporters.

Then it got nasty. Benswanger coolly observed, "This may be a break for some young outfielder. We have won only one pennant in Waner's 11 years with the club, despite his fine hitting. I think he is being badly advised."

The two talked back and forth through the sporting press, and it did little if any good. Bemused by Benswanger's tone, Paul tried to keep the bottom line in sight. "Don't put me down as a stubborn hold-out. I don't want to be sitting down very long. We aren't far apart as to salary."

Surprisingly, Paul did not continue to fight. Doubtlessly, he factored into the negotiations the hard times afflicting people across the country and the slumping gate attendance of the Pirates. So he eventually accepted a small cut from his last year's salary and reported to camp.

After the season opened, Paul boosted himself well above the .300 mark and seemed to have improved his fielding, which was a concern the season before, according to team officials. On his hitting one good sign was his pulling the ball down the right field line, indicating renewed bat speed. By June 10, his .339 average had all the signs of upward mobility. Meanwhile, little brother Lloyd was clipping along at .311, though he missed almost all of April to one ailment or another. As the poison spat from their bats, the Waners looked like they were back at full strength as the game's best-hitting brother duo.

Paul Waner may not have liked what he was getting paid, but he didn't kid himself—life was good, relatively speaking, for ballplayers in the Depression. He and others in the elite major league fraternity didn't stand around in bread lines, work dirty and dangerous jobs for little pay, or try to sell apples on street corners.

Paul Waner: *"You could buy a wheelbarrow full of groceries for a few dollars in those days. And for $100 a month, I had the best apartment in the Schenley Hotel that you ever saw."*

Peter Beagle, the author of such fantasy classics as *The Last Unicorn*, recalled staying in the same room that Paul Waner had as a ballplayer. As a student at nearby Carnegie Mellon University in the 1950s, Beagle rented a room from the proprietors, Mr. and Mrs. Stone.

Peter Beagle: *"My roommate and I rented a room there for the last three years of school. Mr. Stone was a cop, and in fact was Eleanor Roosevelt's favorite traffic cop. She always asked Mr. Stone to direct traffic when she came to Pittsburgh. Anyhow, the Stones rented to students and to the Pittsburgh Pirates. The hotel was a couple of blocks from Forbes Field, easy walking distance.*

"I remember Mrs. Stone saying that Paul Waner was her favorite. No matter how drunk or hung-over he was, she said, he was always a gentleman. Even then I knew, of course, who Paul Waner was. I don't think Lloyd was staying with him when he rented there. Well, it turned out that my roommate and I found the apartment, sometime in 1957. It was a pleasant room, about the size of the bedroom I shared with my brother growing up in the Bronx. There were two beds. It had access to a bathroom around the corner. The place was right across from the police station. It was a good thing [chuckles]. Once I got seriously sick, and was taken to a hospital in a police wagon from just across the street.

"Mr. Stone was the policeman they used to send for when Billy Conn got drunk. The Conns, you know, were an Irish family of fighters from Pittsburgh. And when Billy Conn got drunk, that 14th round with Joe Louis never happened."

On June 14, 1946, Joe Louis knocked out Conn in the 14th round before 45,000 at Yankee Stadium to retain his heavyweight crown.

Peter Beagle: *"Literally, Conn would stand on the sidewalks swinging at everybody in the world. So they'd send for fat, gray-haired Mr. Stone, who'd walk straight up to Billy and say, 'C'mon, Billy, I know who you are. Let's go home now and sleep it off.' Later, in the '60s when I heard all the cries of 'off the pig,' I thought, you mean poor Mr. Stone?*

Lloyd, left, and Paul, right (courtesy of Jim Knight).

"*In those days in Pittsburgh you really did see people like Vern Law and Elroy Face walking the streets in Oakland. Face ran a bar named The Bullpen. Roberto Clemente's hobby was ceramics.*"

In the 1950s Paul Waner would visit Pittsburgh as a hitting coach for other teams when they played the Pirates. Beagle saw some of the magic left in that poisonous bat.

"I saw Paul Waner in batting practice. As a hitting coach, he was legendary for hitting fungoes and could place a ball anywhere. He'd put a handkerchief in the outfield, and hit a ball right to it. He was well-known for that."

Peter Beagle: "*Paul stayed at the Stones' toward the end of his career. Mrs. Stone used to tell him that she worried his eyes were going bad, and he'd get hurt by a ball, thrown or hit. He would say to Mrs. Stone, 'I've been at this a long time, and if I know who's pitching, and who's at bat, and a few other factors such as the wind direction, I should be able to stand where I can catch the ball.'*"

◆ ◆ ◆

In 1937, Paul was batting champion emeritus in the National League—the only three-time batting champion still playing in the senior circuit. The writers would ask him about the pitchers around the league and who was the toughest to hit. "Cliff Melton," replied Paul this time. Melton would win 86 games with the Giants in eight years, including a 20-win season as a rookie in 1937. He must have made a quick impression on Paul Waner that season.

Paul Waner: "*I couldn't hit him with a paddle. He always crossed me*

16. The Last Great One

Paul Waner at an oldtimers game in 1950, sixth from the right (courtesy of Jim Knight).

up. I got to him once, though. Jim Tobin of our club and Melton were in a knockdown contest. Big Jim hit Jim Ripple and Mel Ott with pitches. So Melton buzzed one over my head. I said if he knocked me down again I'd slam the next one into the upper deck. He did—and I did."

On July 7, Paul Waner led off and played right field for the National League in the All-Star game at Washington's Griffith Park. He went hitless in five at bats, but squeaked out an RBI. The American League won 8–3 on the strength of Lou Gehrig's four RBIs, a double and homer. In all, the five New York Yankees on the All-Star squad needed little help from the rest of the American Leaguers.

After his usual All-Star let down, Paul Waner seemed to rebound with force. In the next game after the All-Star break, he went 4 for 4 with a triple and two RBIs. By July 29, Big Poison looked as if he might challenge the .400 mark with his .383 average.

The Pirates missed out on a big opportunity that season.

In 1937 a young man with the awkward name of Stanislaus Musial tried out for the Monessen team in the Class D Penn State League. "Stan the Man" Musial would become a Hall of Famer during his career with the St. Louis Cardinals. He almost ended up with the Pirates, though.

Musial grew up in Donora, Pennsylvania, downwind from the Pittsburgh blast furnaces and steel mills and not far from Forbes Field. His father, Lukasz, and his mother, Mary, were immigrants from Poland and Czechoslovakia. Like many immigrant parents—and even the Waners' parents—they worried about the future earning potential of baseball, a sport that few made it in. But Stan's father didn't want his son to work in the steel mills. He wanted Stan to go to college. Musial could have gone to the University of Pittsburgh on a basketball scholarship, but during the 1937 summer he decided to play in the Penn League.

Musial won an assignment on the team. But after Baseball Commissioner Judge Kenesaw Mountain Landis freed a massive number of Cardinal minor leaguers, Musial wondered if he had made a mistake getting involved with Branch Rickey and the Cardinals. In those years, St. Louis searched for young talent across the country, signing hordes of kids for little money up front. The Cardinals claimed it was the only way they could compete with rich clubs like the Yankees and Giants, but Landis argued that St. Louis manipulated the major league futures of these players. He had a point, as many of these players got lost in the Cardinals' farm system for years. On the other hand, the development of the farm system in organized baseball brought baseball to many small towns across the country and served as a development pipeline for players—a way to teach them uniformly about the fundamentals of the game.

Wary of the Cardinals, however, Musial, a pitcher then, went to a tryout with the Pirates. But when manager Pie Traynor found out Musial had already signed with the Cardinals, he backed away. Musial explained.

Stan Musial: *"After I signed with the Cardinals, I didn't hear from them for a while. I wondered if they had forgotten about me. That spring Judge Landis released 91 Cardinal minor league players. I honestly hoped I had been among them. If the Cardinals really were as bad as Judge Landis said they were, I didn't want to be part of their organization. I had a friend in Donora, Irv Weiss, who knew Pie Traynor. He took me to Pittsburgh, and I worked out with the Pirates a couple of days. I was pitching batting practice to the Pirates when I got notice to report to their [the Cardinals'] farm club at Williamston, West Virginia. Well, I had to tell Traynor.*

"He said, 'Did your dad sign your contract?' I said, 'Yeah.'

"He said, 'That sort of makes it official, but if you're ever out of a job, come back and see us.' Pie Traynor liked me."

Stan the Man was never out of a job again.

Johnny Dickshot was a back-up outfielder with the Pirates in 1937. As a child, his favorite memory was driving thirty minutes from his home in Waukegan, Illinois, to Wrigley Field to watch the Cubs of Hack Wilson and Gabby Hartnett.

16. The Last Great One

As a player, Dickshot recalled a series between Pittsburgh and the New York Giants in August 1937.

Johnny Dickshot: *"We were facing the Giants in a four-game series and Pie Traynor told me I'd be starting all four. That meant I'd be facing Carl Hubbell for the first time, and he had a 24-game winning streak earlier in the season [over two years]. My roomie, Pee Gee [Paul Waner], gave me sage advice. He said, 'Just hit what you see. Don't expect anything and don't wait until you're at three balls and two strikes.' I took his advice and went 3 for 4.*

"During the series with the Giants, it got exciting. Hal Schumacher was pitching against us, and every time home plate umpire Bill Klem would call a strike, Woody Jensen would yell from the dugout, 'Catfish,' a nickname Klem hated. You see, Klem had big lips and sprayed the air when he talked, so he had this nickname and he hated it. Every time Jensen would yell 'Catfish,' he would hide, and Klem would look over and throw someone else out of the game. He emptied our bench three times and never did get Woody."

That season Dickshot once ran in to catch a fly ball, but lost his cap. Instead of chasing the ball, Dickshot chased his cap, and two runners circled the bases.

Gus Suhr, the slick-fielding first baseman, ended his Iron Man streak that season. From September 11, 1931, to June 5, 1937, Suhr had played in 822 straight games, a National League record at the time. It might come as a surprise to some that Suhr ended his streak to attend his mother's funeral in San Francisco.

Bernie "Frenchie" Uhalt was one of Suhr's teammates, and in Dick Dobbins's *The Grand Minor League* about the Pacific Coast League he recalled playing alongside Suhr.

Frenchie Uhalt: *"Gussie was a wonderful person, a relaxed sort of fella. Nothing bothered him, just went out and played the game. He gave it his all. He actually came back [out of retirement] and played for the Seals when the war broke out and we lost [first baseman] Ferris Fain."*

In August, Lloyd went on a hot streak. In a game on the 12th, he singled five times in five at bats, scoring four times. In all, he registered 16 multi-hit games that month, bringing his average up to .329. He pushed it up another point to .330 by the end of the season for one of his finest campaigns in recent memory—129 games, 177 hits, and 80 runs. If he had not missed so many games early on, 200 hits and 100 runs were within reach.

Paul was above .370 going into September, but he dipped a bit down the stretch. On September 18, he went 3 for 4 and collected his 200th hit of the season, thus establishing a 20th-century NL record with his eighth year of 200 or more hits.

The 1937 season was the last highly productive one of Paul Waner's 20-year career. Now 34, Paul had played in every one of the Pirates' 154 games, slashing out a .354 average, 219 hits, 30 doubles, 9 triples, 2 home runs and 74 RBIs. Tired at the end, he only managed to play all those games by entering the last two as a pinch hitter and defensive substitution. Other players had done that, but Paul was lagging as the bell rung on the 1937 season. It would not detract from what was his last, great season in the majors.

At the end, Paul tied with Gabby Hartnett of Chicago for the third highest average in the league after St. Louis' Joe Medwick's .374. For the first time in three years, the Pirates could not claim the batting champion. Arky Vaughan finished at .322 behind the Waners.

With their usual blend of strong hitting and weak pitching, Pittsburgh popped up to third place with an 86–67 record. They pounded the weaker clubs in the league, taking 21 of 22 against the last-place Cincinnati Reds, for example. The New York Giants won their second consecutive pennant, and for the second year in a row lost to the Yankees in the World Series. Again, the Yankees were seemingly invincible as in the days of Ruth and Gehrig. This time it was DiMaggio and Gehrig.

For several years now, Pittsburgh had been inching up on the pennant. They would get their chance next season in one of baseball's most dramatic climaxes.

Shadow Ball and the Gloamin'

It breaks your heart. It is designed to break your heart. The game begins in the spring, when everything else begins again, and it blossoms in the summer, filling the afternoons and evenings, and then as soon as the chill rain comes, it stops and leaves you to face the fall all alone.
—A. Bartlett Giamatti, from The Green Fields of the Mind

Bart Giamatti could have been describing the Pittsburgh Pirates of 1938. It was one of the more heartbreaking seasons in the history of baseball—and the Pirates were at the epicenter.

Suddenly that year the world got more dangerous. Germany sent troops into Austria and looked hungrily on Czechoslovakia, and the democratic nations of the world seemed paralyzed between intervention and isolationism. In America, Orson Welles scared an already jittery nation into a panic with his science fiction radio show, War of the Worlds, about a Martian landing. To the rescue came Superman in comic book debut form, and Dust Bowl refugee Woody Guthrie took his folk music show on the road to reach hearts and minds across the land.

In Pittsburgh, Post-Gazette reporter Ray Sprigle was awarded the Pulitzer Prize for his exposé of Supreme Court Justice Hugo Black's affiliation with the Ku Klux Klan, and the Pittsburgh Housing Authority announced that its first low-cost housing project would be located in the Hill District, the initial step in a $40 million slum-clearance project.

At baseball's winter meetings in Chicago, the Pirates again attempted to trade Paul Waner. This time it was a straight-up deal for Brooklyn's Van Lingle Mungo, the fire-balling right-hander with a high leg kick. His unusual name inspired a clever, jazzy, early-'70s ditty by songwriter David Frishberg.

Mungo was wild and mean. He got visibly upset when his teammates made mistakes, and as he spent his peak years on abysmal Dodgers teams, this happened frequently. A heavy drinker who frolicked with the girls, Mungo once had to be smuggled out of Cuba to escape a machete-wielding husband.

The Pirates brass desperately wanted Mungo. Only 27, he was riding the crest of several good seasons in Brooklyn. Problem was, he had suffered an injury in the 1937 All-Star game, and no one was sure how well he would recover. Before the injury his 238 strikeouts in 1936 were the most in the majors since Dazzy Vance fanned 262 for the 1924 Dodgers.

Benswanger sent Jim Mulvey, the vice president of the Dodgers, a telegram offering Waner for Mungo. The Dodgers scoffed, even suggesting that part of the message was left out—surely, the Pirates were offering more than just Waner, who would turn 35 this season. The *New York World Telegram* ran the story under the headline: "Pirates Bid for Mungo Brings Laugh—Flatbush Ignores Offer of Paul Waner."

Jim Mulvey: *"Benswanger says he will trade star for star—and then he offers to give us an outfielder who is on the wane for a pitcher who may have it in him to become the outstanding performer in our league."*

Clearly, the Dodgers were trying to sweeten the deal, and they were careful not to rule out a trade. But the Pirates balked, and the talks were off in a matter of days. There would be no trading of Paul Waner.

Just as well. It would have been disastrous for Pittsburgh. Mungo never recovered from his injury in '37 and did not win more than four games in a season until war-weary 1945 when he notched 14 victories for the Giants. Besides, he held out the following season and was chronically at odds with his team on salary issues.

Reflecting on the publicity it caused, Mulvey sighed and noted, "Pittsburgh is tough to negotiate with. It seems to be afflicted with trading timidity."

If Pittsburgh was hesitant to trade big-name players like Paul Waner, that was understandable. At the winter meetings every year, lots of good and bad deals alike were proposed, and just as quickly nixed.

Pittsburgh, however, missed out on a chance to become the first franchise to break the color barrier as the winter meetings also revealed. While Pittsburgh should not have been expected to do this any more than another major league club, it did have the homegrown talent if it chose to do so.

17. Shadow Ball and the Gloamin'

Lloyd, left, and Paul, right (courtesy of Jim Knight).

For some time the Pittsburgh black newspapers had written about opening up the majors to black ballplayers, and Pittsburgh seemed a possibility with the local talent on the Pittsburgh Crawfords and the Homestead Grays. This would have given the Pirates a greater infusion of talent than the Louisville Colonels did when they brought Honus Wagner, Tommy Leach, and Fred Clarke to the Smoky City in 1900. All it required was intestinal fortitude.

Reporter Chester Washington of the *Pittsburgh Courier*, a black newspaper, decided to put the Pirates on the spot to make history. He sent a telegram to Pirates manager Pie Traynor at his hotel in Chicago during the winter meetings.

> PIE TRAYNOR. PITTSBURGH PIRATES. CONGRESS HOTEL. KNOW YOUR CLUB NEEDS PLAYERS. HAVE ANSWERS TO YOUR PRAYERS RIGHT HERE IN PITTSBURGH. JOSH GIBSON CATCHER. B. LEONARD 1B AND RAY BROWN PITCHER OF HOMESTEAD GRAYS AND S. PAIGE PITCHER COOL PAPA BELL OF PITTSBURGH CRAWFORDS ALL AVAILABLE AT REASONABLE FIGURES. WOULD MAKE PIRATES FORMIDABLE PENNANT CONTENDERS. WHAT IS YOUR ATTITUDE? WIRE ANSWER.

Washington waited, and waited. But no reply came. Baseball historians and those whose minds thrive on speculation and endless "what if" propositions can only dream about what the 1938 Pirates would have been with that kind of black talent. Maybe one of the strongest clubs ever?

In Pittsburgh and elsewhere, major league baseball did not appear ready to face its own demons.

During the season the Washington Senator's owner Clark Griffith told writer Sam Lacy of the *Washington Tribune*, "There are a few big league magnates who are not aware of the fact that the time is not far off when colored players will take their places besides those of other races in the major leagues. However, I'm not sure that time has arrived yet. A lone Negro in the game will face caustic comments. He will be made the target of cruel, filthy epithets. Of course, I know the time will come when the ice will have to be broken. Both by the organized game and the colored player who is willing to volunteer and thus become a sort of martyr to the cause."

In any event, ominous signs pointed to problems in the Pirates clubhouse. Paul, commenting on team president Bill Benswanger's public pronouncement that fans would see more "new faces" in the Pirates' roster, said that Pittsburgh management was only interested in cutting payroll.

"They don't want new faces, they want cheap faces," Paul said.

Paul was again taken back by the Pirates' low contract offer. He called it a "two-for-a-nickel bum."

The public rift, coming on the heels of the Waner-Mungo trade rumors, was too much for Benswanger to bear. This time he relented. On February 18, he inked Paul to a new contract and tried to smooth out his star's ruffled feathers. Meanwhile, low-maintenance Lloyd had duly signed and returned his contract without question.

Bill Benswanger: *"I told him, 'Paul, say anything you want about your contract if it's unsatisfactory, but please let's don't have any more personal fights in the newspapers about cheapness.' He agreed, and that's all there was to it."*

Benswanger didn't want the headache of Yankees owner Jacob Ruppert and general manager Ed Barrow in dealing with Joe DiMaggio. After rejecting the Yankees' initial offer, DiMaggio had it pointed out to him by Barrow that he was asking for more than the great Lou Gehrig earned.

DiMaggio responded, "It's too bad that Gehrig is so underpaid." Faced with a personal public relations nightmare, DiMaggio missed the first 12 games of the season before signing the Yankees' original offer.

Disunity threatened Pittsburgh's clubhouse, the scene of many player rebellions in the past. Oddly, it seemed the best Pirates teams played with an edgy clubhouse, from the 1920s through the 1970s. This time it was Woody Jensen who took a shot at manager Pie Traynor. Unwisely, the young player ranted to a Pittsburgh newspaper that "the Pirates don't win championships because Traynor fails to make the best use of his available talent, keeping too many players cold on the bench and over-working the regulars."

Traynor's reply didn't help matters. "Since when did newspapers start playing up .270 hitters? And who is this Jensen? Just a mediocre ballplayer at best."

Traynor, feeling the heat, thought he had the talent to win the pennant. Just before the season, he was eating dinner with his friend Jimmie Dykes, manager of the Chicago White Sox. Remember, the New York Yankees had won the World Series in both 1936 and 1937 and were loaded to the gills with talent.

"Jimmie," said Traynor, "I'd sure like to win this year and beat those Yankees."

Dykes almost choked on his steak. "What's wrong with you, Pie? Don't you feel well?"

Actually, Traynor was more prescient than Dykes. A good team on the field, the Pirates took their quirky clubhouse into the season and plowed ahead toward that ever-elusive pennant.

♦ ♦ ♦

The Pirates won their first seven games of the season. With all eyes on the pennant—it had been a long 11 years since the last one—manager Pie Traynor felt that a sober Paul Waner would be more valuable to the team. So he asked his star to curtail his thirst while the season was underway, and so began one of the most widely circulated tales about Waner.

The story goes that once he quit drinking, Paul went into the worst slump of his career and found himself spending time on an unfamiliar bench. It is true that he began 1938 in the worst slump of his career. Six weeks into the schedule, he was hitting .120. Pressed to explain his sudden demise at the plate, Paul spun it in the best light.

Paul Waner: *"This looks very serious, but I really believe that before many weeks have passed a lot of us will look back on my slip and smile. I feel great, I have picked up five pounds on the bench, which ought to benefit me in that I've been a bit light. All in all, I feel that I will soon be back where I was. A batting slump is a terrible thing, but on the other hand, when the batter holds the whip hand, he often wonders how the pitcher gets him out."*

Years later Traynor said he sometimes kept Paul on the bench in the first half of doubleheaders. He was afraid that a hung-over Paul would not be able to see the ball and would be skulled by a pitch. Some pitchers said they were afraid to throw to a wobbly Paul Waner because he might not be able to get out of the way of an inside pitch. If Paul failed to chase down a fly ball in the outfield, it was blamed on the effects of alcohol and looking up into a blazing, high sky.

While it rang of sentimentality, the Buc clubhouse guy in those days, "Socko" McCarey, said Paul somehow functioned just as well hung-over. "He never staggered out there. It never affected his playing," McCarey said.

Once Traynor recognized that a sober Paul Waner was of no help to the club, he reportedly took the right fielder out for a drink. From that day on Paul drank like the days of old, and his batting average began to climb. It's possible that Paul, in the jittery throes of withdrawal, was not as relaxed at the plate as when drinking—drinking on his free time, that is. This sounds ludicrous, though, when one considers the health effects of alcoholism.

Lloyd, on the other hand, wallowed in success at the plate. On May 4, he went 4 for 4 with two triples and five RBIs and three runs scored. On August 16, he smacked a three-run homer and drove in four runs, and the next day knocked out two doubles.

In their efforts to field the 1938 team, Traynor and owner Benswanger walked a tightrope between youth and experience.

Bill Benswanger: *"We must keep enough of the veterans in the lineup to hold a balance, but Traynor and I both agree that we must now show preference to young players in some of the key positions, as some of the veterans in some of these spots appear to have gone over the top in the matter of their skill."*

Dark clouds seemed to follow the Pirates. One newspaper charged the team had a number of "malcontents" that were unhappy with Traynor's stewardship. The unidentified players quickly disputed the charge and backed Traynor publicly.

In June and July the Pirates ransacked their opponents, winning 40 of 54 games. They appeared on a pennant pace as they fought off the Giants, the champions of the past two years. The club took first place on June 12 on the momentum of a 13-game winning streak and settled into leading the senior circuit pack.

Benswanger was so sure the Pirates would play in the World Series that he had a press stand built on the roof of Forbes Field and he printed 1,000 press buttons. For years afterward those buttons remained quaint souvenirs of the club's bittersweet season.

17. Shadow Ball and the Gloamin'

This season was not so easily predictable. Few could have imagined Cincinnati's Johnny Vander Meer would throw two consecutive no-hitters, that Lou Gehrig would have played in his 2,000th straight game, and that a 19-year-old Ted Williams had the audacity to tell the Red Sox veterans who jeered him, "I'll be back, and I'm going to wind up making more money in this game than all three of them put together."

Paul, 35, and Lloyd, 32, counted themselves among the grizzled veteran class. They made an impression on a rookie Max Lanier of the Cardinals. One of the best left-handed pitchers in the National League in the late '30s and '40s, Lanier remembered with levity the sting of Paul Waner's bat that season.

Max Lanier: *"[Frankie] Frisch was managing [the Cardinals] then. He was tough on young ballplayers ... I remember one time Paul Waner was wearing us out with line drives. Finally, Frisch stood up in disgust and yelled, 'Who on this ball club can get that Waner out?' Max Macon was sitting on the bench—this was before he went to the Dodgers. Well, Max liked to pop off a little anyway, and he said, 'I can get him out.' Frisch was delighted to hear that. He clapped his hands and said, 'Atta boy. Get down there and warm up.' Waner comes up again. Frisch brings in Macon. The first pitch Waner hits a line drive and breaks Macon's little finger. Frisch couldn't help but lie down on the bench and laugh himself silly."*

Beyond the Waner brothers, and stalwarts Arky Vaughan, Gus Suhr, Pep Young and Lee Handley, the Pirates benefited from important new blood that season. Outfielder Johnny Rizzo, brought over from the Cardinals' Columbus farm club, immediately started producing in Pittsburgh that season. He had the kind of power usually absent from the Pirates lineup and would set a team record with 23 home runs his rookie year. It's hard to imagine 23 home runs being the Pirates' season record in the first three decades of the 20th century, but it was an indication of their lack of power as an organization and the expansiveness of Forbes Field.

The story behind the rise of Rizzo involves one of the great masterminds of player development, Branch Rickey. Rizzo was traded to the Pirates when Rickey had to decide between Rizzo and a young player named Enos Slaughter. At the time, Commissioner Landis was hounding Rickey to declare some of his minor league players free agents. So Rickey dealt the much-heralded Rizzo, and Cardinal fans went bonkers.

It turned out that Rickey had hyped up Rizzo over Slaughter because he wanted to keep Slaughter. Rizzo would be a one-season wonder, and Slaughter would enjoy a Hall of Fame career for the Redbirds.

Breaking into the majors that same season as Rizzo, Slaughter looked back on the days of the Pirates and the Waner brothers.

Enos Slaughter: *"Paul was a great hitter, he was better than Lloyd. He could hit that ball down over third base—even if you were hugging the bag—and he'd still slide one through for two. They tell me that Dizzy Dean used to take Paul out drinking the night before ol' Diz would pitch against the Pirates. And Paul would still go 5 for 5.*

"Back in those days, they would fine us if we associated with other players on the field. I was just fresh up from the minor leagues. Those beer joints and clubs weren't on my list. I stayed at the hotel, and went to the park and played ball. Both of them were quiet. But they came out to win. Play to win, yes sir. Different than today.

"The game today, it's all home runs. I wouldn't go see these games today. You'd have to pay my way. These players don't give a dang for nobody, all they know is the dollar."

With Rizzo and unusually good pitching for a change, they coasted into midsummer. Traynor, while resting his pitchers enough, gave his position players little rest before September. It would come back to haunt the club. Despite Pittsburgh's lead in the mid–September standings, the torrid Chicago Cubs were closing on the Bucs.

On September 15, Lloyd and Paul hit consecutive home runs off Cliff Melton of the Giants in the fifth inning of a game at the Polo Grounds. In their 14 years of play together, it was the only time the pair had hit successive home runs in a major league game. It would be Lloyd's last career home run.

The first time brothers on opposing teams homered against each other was on July 5, 1935, when Brooklyn's Tony Cuccinello and New York's Al Cuccinello did it in a game at the Polo Grounds. Joe and Dominic DiMaggio would also perform the feat in a New York-Boston game on June 30, 1950.

Beyond brotherly bashes, September was rough on the Pirates. On their last East Coast trip, they were rained out of several games by a hurricane looming off the coast. Sitting around in the hotels, the players got edgy and began thinking too much about the few weeks ahead. It appeared to zap them of their sense of momentum by the time they got back on the field. While the rain fell, all they could do was watch their lead narrow.

Bill Benswanger: *"We went east on the final trip, good and hot. Everybody knows that when a club is hot, it can make wrong plays and win. When it is cold, nothing turns out right.... But as we sat around hotel lobbies dur-*

17. Shadow Ball and the Gloamin'

ing the storm, a hot team cooled off and never regained its winning momentum."

One must understand the second-guessing inherent in this perspective. Sometimes a team needs to relax, and a few days off is often welcomed at the end of a season when players are tired.

Meanwhile, that summer Chicago had replaced manager Charley Grimm with Gabby Hartnett, and it gave the Bruins a shot in the arm, and they continued their march on the Pirates. Still, all the Bucs had to do was play .500 ball in September to win the pennant. But by the 26th of the month the Cubs had cut Pittsburgh's lead to a game and a half.

The stage was set for a three-game series showdown between the Pirates and the Cubs in Chicago. Billed as a "make-it or break-it" series in Wrigley Field, nothing seemed to go right for the team from the Steel City.

On September 27, in the first game, Chicago started a lame-armed Dizzy Dean who hadn't had his good stuff in a couple years. It was Dizzy's first start since August 20. Hartnett's pitching staff was worn thin, and the new skipper had been forced to go with Dean, who had been used fewer than a dozen times since being acquired from the Cardinals in April.

It has been said that baseball is a funny game, and Dean ended up baffling the powerful Pirates hitters who weren't used to the slow and cute stuff. Paul Waner knew right away an opportunity had been missed.

Paul Waner: *"I think we still could have won if we'd beaten Diz in that big series. It was the year after Dean had hurt his arm. He didn't have a prayer, but was just pitching with guts alone, winning seven games along the way. We kept swinging at his soft stuff all day. By the time I came up in the eighth, we were trailing, 2–0. But the runners on third and first, and only one out, we had a chance to rally. It was up to me to keep it going. I had noticed they were playing me with a fairly open spot in right-center. Now, if there was one thing I could usually do, it was place a hit. By this time I thought I knew exactly what Diz was throwing, and decided I could bring those runners home by rolling a drive into the right-center alley. Sure enough, when Diz let go his pitch, it came up to the plate big as a grapefruit. I timed my swing, thinking I would get the fat end of the bat on the ball. Just as I made contact, that big grapefruit dropped down. Instead of meeting the ball solidly, I topped it and bounced it to Dean's right. One run came in, as he forced a runner at second, but our rally was dead, and we lost, 2–1."*

As it turned out, a bigger climax lay ahead.

After Dean's victory over the Pirates, Pittsburgh had a skinny half-game lead over Chicago. On September 28, in the second game of the series, Chicago and Pittsburgh were tied 3–3 for most of the game. One huge missed opportunity occurred when the first base umpire called a balk—with Lloyd on third and Paul on first, the Pirates would have scored the lead run. But, incredibly, the other umpires overruled the first base ump. It doesn't often happen that way. The Pirates were enraged, and in later years would point to this as an act of umpire malfeasance.

Paul Waner: *"I will always think the balk they didn't enforce on pitcher Vance Page of the Cubs cost us the pennant."*

The Pirates took a 5–3 lead in the eighth, and then Chicago struck back to tie the game. In the bottom of the ninth inning with two outs and the scored tied at 5–5, the Cubs had their last chance. Darkness was falling fast. Phil Cavaretta was playing first base for Chicago that day.

Phil Cavaretta: *"It was fall, the days were getting shorter, and it was an extra long game. There had been a lot of hitting, a lot of bases on balls. It was one of those two-and-a-half, three-hour games. I remember so well how tough it was to hit up there. The batter and the pitcher and almost all the infield were in the shade. But in the bleachers the sun was still out."*

Mace Brown, the ace reliever, had been pitching for the Pirates since the eighth. Catcher Gabby Hartnett was the batter. Brown had a real good fast ball and slider. His 50 appearances in 1937 without a complete game had established him as one of baseball's first pure relief specialists. Earlier in 1938 he had been the first reliever selected in the then six-year history of the All-Star game. His record was 15–8 as he faced the Cubs to preserve Pittsburgh's hopes of a pennant.

The beefy, tomato-red faced Hartnett was a good high-ball hitter and future Hall of Famer. His former manager Joe McCarthy called him the "perfect" catcher—hard-hitting and strong-armed. His 236 home runs lasted as a career record for catchers until Roy Campanella, Yogi Berra, Johnny Bench and Carlton Fisk came along.

Joe McCarthy: *"He had everything except speed. He was super smart. Nobody ever had more hustle. Nobody could throw with him. There have been few clutch hitters and he was the best."*

But time was running out. Umpire Jocko Conlan had wanted to call the game in the eighth, but agreed to go nine, and that would be it. He knew how important the game was to both teams.

There were two strikes on Hartnett. All Brown needed was one more, and he threw the pitch of his life.

17. Shadow Ball and the Gloamin' 203

Paul Waner: *"But he didn't get it. Hartnett swung, and the damn ball landed in the left-field stands. I could hardly believe my eyes. The game was over, and I should have run into the clubhouse. But I didn't. I just stood out there and watched Hartnett circle the bases, and take the lousy pennant with him."*

As the crowd spilled onto the field, Paul wondered if Hartnett could actually make it around the bases to home plate. Maybe he would fail to touch one of the bases. No such luck.

Phil Cavaretta: *"Gabby hit the ball, a line drive. It didn't look like it was going to get into the bleachers. It looked like it was going to hit the bottom of the bleachers, two bases ... the umpire at third ran out there, and he made the right call. It did go into the bleachers."*

Lloyd Waner: *"It went right over my head. I saw it in my sleep for a long time. I know I didn't move—I looked around disgusted. I knew it was gone."*

The Chicago crowd went absolutely mad, and fans mobbed Hartnett and the rest of the Cubs. Photos of that game show a disheveled Hartnett trying to find each base through a wild, loving throng of fans.

Hartnett's twilight shot was immediately written up as the "Homer in the Gloamin'."

Billy Herman was playing second base for the Cubs that day.

Billy Herman: *"I don't know why he [Brown] didn't waste one; maybe he figured it was so dark Hartnett couldn't see it anyway. But Gabby swung and rode it right out of there.... He had to fight his way through to touch third and then fight his way through to touch home plate."*

In the Pirates clubhouse, the mood was black. Even the 1927 World Series defeat to the Yankees hadn't made Paul and Lloyd feel so bad—then, at least they had gotten to the Series and enjoyed the satisfaction of knowing they were the league's best team that year. This loss hurt in deeper ways, as if the pennant had been yanked right of out their hands.

Though Hartnett's homer was the clutch shot, the Pirates didn't help themselves by committing four errors that game. At the plate, the Poison brothers tried to do their part as Lloyd collected two hits, including a double, and a walk in five trips to the plate, and Paul singled twice in five at bats.

Paul Waner: *"It was terrible. Mace Brown was sitting in front of his locker, crying like a baby. I stayed with him all that night. I was so afraid he was going to commit suicide."*

Still, this was not the end, and the Pirates could have charged back, mathematically speaking. After the "Gloamin'" game, they were a half game behind the Cubs with three more games to play. They couldn't shake off the defeat, though.

The next day the heartbroken Pirates lost, 10–1, to the Cubs. Now, Chicago basked in a 10-game winning streak, and on October 1 the Cubs swept a doubleheader in St. Louis to clinch the pennant.

It was over for Pittsburgh.

Phil Cavaretta: *"To this day I feel that home run in the gloaming demoralized those Pittsburgh players so badly. We had two more games to play against them, and we swept the series. They came out and played, but they weren't the Pirates team we saw earlier. From that home run."*

Billy Herman: *"Well, that broke Pittsburgh's back. We went out the next day, and we could've beaten nine Babe Ruths.... If they'd won that last game, they would have left town a half game ahead.... That sort of thing can happen to a team, any team, big league or not. What it does, most of the time, is upset you badly for two or three days, and when it happens late in the season, you just don't have the time to recover."*

Years later in the 1960s Paul Waner would still see Brown, who was by then scouting for the Boston Red Sox. Time had numbed some, not all, of the pain.

Paul Waner: *"He can laugh about it now, practically 30 years later. Well, he can almost laugh about it, anyway. When he stops laughing, he kind of shudders a bit, you know, like it's a bad dream that he can't quite get out of his mind."*

Paul felt just as bad and years later waxed philosophical. "All of us 1938 Pirates are sensitive about that season. I was certain I'd get to play in my second World Series, and against the club that licked us in 1927, the Yankees. We all felt pretty sick. But after seeing Brooklyn blow a 13 and one-half game lead (in 1951), I don't feel as bad about it."

The sting of Hartnett's swat remained for long afterward. Elbie Fletcher, a slick-fielding first baseman, was traded to the Pirates the next year, in 1939.

Elbie Fletcher: *"And you know, it was sad, because that's all they talked about on that Pirates club that year: Hartnett's home run. I knew we weren't going to win it. That home run was still on everybody's mind, haunting them like a ghost. Management knew it, and that's why they were trying to shake up the club. But it didn't help. They talked about Hartnett's shot all year and finished sixth."*

Yet all the heat of midsummer could not overcome the chill of September. Enos Slaughter remembered the heartache among the Pirates.

Enos Slaughter: *"Well, I was just a rookie that year, and everything on other clubs was a blur. But I remember Mace Brown pitched that game. It took them a long time to get over it. Maybe some of them didn't."*

Beyond that one dramatic game in Chicago, what really happened to the 1938 Pittsburgh Pirates? To begin, Pittsburgh had begun to collapse well before Gabby Hartnett stood at the plate that fateful evening. Going into September, Pittsburgh had a reasonably safe five-game lead. Yet they wound up losing the pennant by two games, finishing 86–64 to Chicago's 89–63. The Pirates, 62–35 on August 9, went 24–29 down the stretch.

Baseball insiders predictably blamed the Pirates starting pitchers. The 1938 *Spalding Guide* said the starting pitchers had collapsed, displaying a tendency to weaken in the late innings. It's true the Pirates finished last in complete games with 57, and in the 1930s not being able to finish a game was viewed as unmanly. Brown led the team in wins, the first time in baseball history that a relief specialist had topped his squad in wins.

Pie Traynor: *"And what would we have done without Mace Brown? He's been in almost 50 games almost all in relief."*

It wasn't the pitching. It was the hitting. As Bill James points out, Traynor got all he could out of an undistinguished starting rotation by giving his bullpen a chance to help out. Maybe he was ahead of his time in this regard. His downfall was—like Leo Durocher in 1969 and Don Zimmer in 1977—riding his position players too hard.

In a revealing statistic, every Pirates regular that season except for the catcher had 600-plus plate appearances. And the catcher, Al Todd, caught 132 games to lead the majors in his position. The position players were tired going down the stretch into September. As a result, Pittsburgh's offense slumped badly in the closing weeks while the team's ERA actually improved.

The only Pirates regular who dazzled come September was Lloyd. He hit safely in 22 games from September 5 to September 29.

But the offense was lukewarm otherwise. That season Paul Waner fell to .280, his lowest batting average of his career. Still, the Pirates had three .300 hitters that season—Lloyd Waner at .313, Johnny Rizzo at .301 and Arky Vaughan at .322. Rizzo was the big bat, driving in 111 RBIs on his 23 home runs, thereby giving the Pirates a power dimension they had lacked before.

Lloyd had the rare occasion of putting up some better numbers than brother Paul. Little Poison's 194 hits and 79 runs were higher than Paul's totals (175 and 77), and he tied his career high in home runs with five. And he whiffed just 11 times in 619 at bats.

Paul's production had declined noticeably, especially in his once mighty doubles (31) and triples (6) categories. This was the last season that Paul and Lloyd would record more than 600 at bats each, and they gradually found their playing time reduced from here on out.

As Hartnett's homer exploded the Waners' pennant dreams, the 1938 season marked the closing of a chapter in Pittsburgh baseball, one dominated by the Waner brothers and Pie Traynor and Arky Vaughan. The world was changing fast, and so was baseball and America. The season was the closest the Pirates had come to the World Series again after 1927, and there was a bitter feeling brewing in some quarters. It would be a long 22 years of baseball in the Steel City before the Pirates would make the postseason.

18

Requiem for a Lost Season

> You can't see a blind spot, Kierkegaard says, but in there now, between when the ball leaves the bleacher background and I can hear it plop all fat and satisfied in the catcher's mitt, there's somehow just nothing, where there used to be a lot, everything in fact, because they're not keeping me around for my fielding, and I already see the afternoon tabloid has me down for trade bait.
>
> —*John Updike, from "The Slump"*

In Pittsburgh that winter, fans and the sporting press hotly debated the sorrowful 1938 season, and come spring the winds of change started to blow. Nothing makes heads roll like an unexpected collapse.

Including the Waner brothers. Including Pie Traynor. Including half the team. If it wasn't any one player or manager's fault, concern was widespread about this "team" as a whole. Something was amiss.

If the Pirates were still reeling, so were many people worldwide as war struck. In the year ahead Germany attacked Poland and Great Britain declared war on Germany. Peace and war, and violence and compassion, were the themes of the year. John Steinbeck's Pulitzer Prize–winning novel, *The Grapes of Wrath*, published this year, touched on the plight of a family in Dust Bowl Oklahoma who lost their farm to greedy bankers and had to move to California to work as migrant laborers.

If that did not hit home close enough for Paul and Lloyd Waner, they were challenged in the 1939 season for their starting jobs. In almost a decade and a half, this was an unknown position for the Poisons to be in. But Paul was 36 and Lloyd, 33. Toward the middle of the season, the Pirates

Lloyd Waner in the late 1930s (courtesy of Jim Knight).

brought up outfielders Bob Elliott and Maurice Van Robays from their Toronto minor league club, and they were young and spry contenders for playing time.

Change was in the air. During the winter meetings, team president Bill Benswanger had done considerable wheeling and dealing, trading catcher Al Todd—the over-worked backstopper was blamed in part for last September's collapse—and outfielder Johnny Dickshot to Boston for catcher Ray Mueller, an Iron Man in the mold of Gus Suhr. As Suhr showed signs of slowing down in the season ahead, Benswanger acquired Elbie Fletcher, a solid-fielding first sacker who demonstrated a knack for getting on base.

Before the season started, Paul Waner actually picked Chicago and New York to contend for the pennant, with his own Pirates "a third place team at best." As for his own chance of rebounding from his worst season to date, Paul sounded more sure of himself than of his teammates. He predicted he would hit .350 and lead the league in batting.

Paul Waner: *"I've never had a better chance to lead the league in hitting. I feel fine and I'm in good shape. There's no reason I shouldn't do as well as I've ever done."*

As for Lloyd, he uncharacteristically returned his 1939 contract not once, but three times, before signing. It was a winter of discontent.

"I figure I'm worth more money," Lloyd said.

On the Pirates pitching staff that year was a sandy-haired Alabaman named Truett "Rip" Sewell. He got to know the Waners and talked about them years later.

Rip Sewell: *"You know, they came from back on the farm in Oklahoma.*

18. Requiem for a Lost Season

Paul and Lloyd Waner kicking up dust against the Phillies. Why are they sliding into the same base? (courtesy of the Pittsburgh Pirates).

They used to raise corn there, and they always used to have a great big stack of corncobs after shelling the corn and getting rid of it for the grain feed. Lloyd told me that's where he and Paul learned how to be good batters. They'd throw wet corncobs all day and try to hit them. You take a wet corncob and break it in half and throw it, and it'll go like a rocket. He said that was their pastime out there when they were kids growing up. For a bat they'd use an old pick handle or anything else they could come by."

Sewell's claim to fame was his blooper or "eephus ball." The etymology of the word, according to author Michael Seidel, comes from the crap-shooting phrase for the high roll of the dice—"eephus-eiphus-ophus." Sewell learned it the hard way. A couple years later on December 7, 1941, the day the Japanese attacked Pearl Harbor, Sewell was out deer hunting when another hunter accidentally shot him. His big toe, which he pitched off of, was all smashed up.

Rip Sewell: *"I had to learn to walk all over again, keeping that big toe up when I moved. Naturally my whole pitching motion had to be changed.*

I had to pitch just like I walked, like I was taking a step forward while keeping that big toe up. That's how the blooper ball came about, from having to learn to pitch with that motion. I was the only pitcher to pitch off the tip of his toes, and that's the only way you can throw the blooper. It's got to be thrown straight overhand. I was able to get terrific backspin on the ball by holding onto the seam and flipping it off of three fingers. The backspin held it on its line of flight to the plate. So that ball was going slow but spinning fast. Fun to watch, easy to catch, but tough to hit. It helped me win 21 games in '43 and again in '44."

But in 1939 the eephus pitch was a long way away, and no trick pitches could save the Pirates that season. While Paul Waner got off to a hot start, hitting safely in 27 of 29 games in May, the team went into a tailspin after Opening Day, suffering a 12-game losing streak at one point. The pitching staff was so weak that by season's end only one pitcher, Bob Klinger, had started more than 30 games.

By the end of May, manager Pie Traynor was desperately tinkering with his lineup. He benched Lloyd, who was hitting poorly, and inserted Paul into his brother's customary lead-off spot. Traynor then dropped long-time clean-up hitter Arky Vaughan into the second spot, and moved Fern Bell into the four spot. And while Paul was hitting the ball well enough, he started getting more days off.

Traynor pinned his hopes on Bell, but that would prove unfruitful. The outfielder from Ada, Oklahoma, near the Waners' hometown, would play only two years in the majors, seeing action in 89 games and hitting only two home runs. Yet in early 1939, Bell was a consistent clutch hitter, and that impressed Traynor.

There were brief explosions of the old Pirates hitting attack. In one game that spring, Pittsburgh collected 17 hits in a victory against Chicago. Paul went 4 for 5 and was creeping toward the .300 mark for the first time in two years. Beating the Cubs was no small feat, considering the psychological aftermath of the Hartnett homer and the fact Chicago had won 10 of the last 11 encounters between the teams.

Paul's resurgence was attributed to an extra 10 pounds on his frame and a steady diet of milk instead of coffee at breakfast. Maybe so, but the extra rest may have helped, too.

The lack of power on the Pirates was noticeable. One anonymous Pirates hurler was quoted as saying, "Well, I see (Brooklyn's Dolph) Camilli has eight homers already, which is as many as our whole club has made to date."

The pennant seemed a distant dream for Pie Traynor's Bucs. By mid-

18. Requiem for a Lost Season

June, they were under .500 and slipping into the second division. The manager sometimes resorted to pinch-hitting for Paul and some of the other veterans. Around the league Pittsburgh was given little respect, and the sharks circled their prey with no mercy. One *New York World Telegram* headline read: "Giants Glad to See Bucs: Pittsburgh Seen As a Surefire Remedy for Slump of Terrymen."

In Boston, the Pirates dropped three games in June, with two of them running into extra innings. During this East Coast trip the team batted only .211, winning two and losing six. It could have been worse. Some of the beat writers observed Pirates players so demoralized they could not eat after the games. This seems hard to believe, but everywhere the image persisted of a team not coping well with blowing the pennant the year before. The pitchers, meanwhile, showed inklings of life. A young Russ Bauers tossed a one-hitter in Boston, only to lose 1–0.

No matter how difficult the circumstances, the Waners demonstrated brotherly concern for each other. Wisconsin-born Ray Berres was a second-string catcher for the Pirates from 1937 to 1940. He recalled the special bond between the Waners.

Ray Berres: *"I enjoyed the fondness or love they had for one another, and how they referred to each other as 'Little Brother' and 'Big Brother.' I remember a game in which Lloyd got drilled or hit with a pitch, and Paul asked him if it hurt. 'You dang right it hurts,' said Lloyd. Paul then said, 'I'll get even with him for you,' and wouldn't you know it, Paul got the pitch he could handle and hit the ball right back at the pitcher, and struck him on the knee."*

The Waners, Berres said, were not fazed by the pressure of playing baseball. "Stardom never affected them. And they were very solicitous when anyone of us were struggling."

Even when they were struggling just seeing the ball. Though he had amazing powers of eye-hand coordination, Paul still needed glasses, and this became evident in the late 1930s. He first started wearing them on the field in 1940. Before that he used them for reading and other activities.

Les Biederman, a writer for the *Pittsburgh Post-Gazette*, once spotted Paul wearing glasses while playing cards with a few other Bucs on the train. Biederman asked him about it.

Paul Waner: *"I'm nearsighted. I have a difficult time reading the scoreboard in left field when I'm playing in right field. Sometimes a player will yell at me from a distance, and I wouldn't know who it was until I recognized a mannerism. But at the plate, when the pitcher started throwing, the baseball looks as big as a grapefruit."*

In his writing, Biederman gave great currency to the "looks as big as a grapefruit" phrase, and it stuck with Paul, becoming one of his trademark sayings.

Back then, eyesight issues were considered almost fatal for a ballplaying career, and few players wore glasses, especially infielders. The first bespectacled player in the modern era was pitcher Lee Meadows, a right-hander with the Cardinals, Phillies and Pirates from 1915 to 1929. He twice led the National League in losses but fared much better after he was traded to Pittsburgh in 1923. He was a 20-game winner in 1926 and pitched the opener of the 1925 and 1927 World Series. A sore arm—not bad eyes—ended his career in 1928.

Pittsburgh pitcher Carmen Hill, another rookie in 1915, also wore glasses. Infielder George "Specs" Toporcer was the first position player to wear glasses, when he joined the St. Louis Cardinals in 1921. By 1940 several other players had worn them regularly, including Mel Ott, Dom DiMaggio, Chick Hafey, Danny MacFayden, Walter "Boom Boom" Beck, Bill Dietrich, Dizzy Trout.

Paul knew he needed them, but had mixed feelings.

Paul Waner: *"I don't know. That ball looked big as a pumpkin when it came up to the plate. Just seem I couldn't miss it if I tried. And when I did miss it or foul tip it, or send up a weak little pop, I don't understand how it happened.*

"I'm not proud, but I can't hit wearing those glasses. Sure, I see the ball better with glasses. The ball seems sharper and more distinct but the trouble is it's smaller too. Without glasses, the ball seems like a big white blur, and all I have to do is hit that blur in the middle."

The Pirates had an assortment of characters that season, from retreads to freaks of nature.

Pirates nemesis Chuck Klein donned a Pirates uniform that season. Though only 34, the slugger had been unconditionally released by Philadelphia on June 7. He signed the same day with the Pirates, and on July 17 returned to Philadelphia to smack two homers against his old team in a 7–4 Pittsburgh victory.

Klein was raised on an Indiana farm. As a young man, he worked on a state road crew and then took a job in a steel mill where he tossed 200-pound, white-hot ingots into blast furnaces and toiled in eight-hour shifts without any time for lunch. When he wasn't muscling around in steel mills, he played ball for several semipro teams. After breaking a leg in the minors, he eventually won a try-out spot with the woeful Phillies in the middle of the 1928 season. Thereafter Klein posted five spectacular seasons, and a

18. Requiem for a Lost Season

long-running joke in Philadelphia was that the city's newspapers kept a headline set in type reading: "Klein Hits Two As Phillies Lose."

Early on, Klein ranked up there with Jimmie Foxx, Lou Gehrig and Mel Ott as one of the most productive players of the period. In his first five years of full-time duty he led the league in homers four times, RBIs twice, runs scored three times, and had over 200 hits each year. But after the Phillies traded Klein to the Cubs in 1933 after winning the Triple Crown, his prodigious ball smacking declined. Whether it was due to leaving the hitter-friendly Baker Bowl as home turf, or the onslaught of injuries the next few years, Klein's best days were quickly behind him.

After exiting baseball, Klein ran a bar in the Philadelphia neighborhood of Kensington until 1947. A heavy drinker, Klein neglected his diet and began suffering from malnutrition. He ended up with a severely damaged nervous system and one leg partially paralyzed. In 1958 he died of a cerebral hemorrhage. Once among the game's most feared sluggers in the early 1930s, Chuck Klein today seems, fairly or unfairly, a ready example of ballpark effects on players' statistics. But he was more than that. His career was front-loaded to the ultimate extreme and spread out over the 17 years he played—300 homers, .320 lifetime average, and .543 slugging average—looked good enough for the Veterans Committee to induct him into the Hall of Fame in 1980.

Another fading star that joined the Pirates that season was Heinie Manush. Soon to become a drinking buddy of Paul's, Manush batted .330 in his 17-year career that would land him in the Hall of Fame. In approach, the left-handed Manush was similar to the Waners—lots of doubles and triples, little power, and a solid grasp of hitting technique. As a young player on the Detroit Tigers, he was advised by Ty Cobb to "slash-and-poke" the ball instead of swinging for the fences. Probably the funniest incident of his playing days involved the 1933 World Series between Washington and the New York Giants. After a close call on a ground ball that ruled him out at first base, an enraged Manush suddenly grabbed umpire Charlie Moran's bow tie, stretched it back as far as the elastic band would go, and let it snap back. Manush tried to take his place in the outfield the next inning, but was tossed out of the game. He initially refused to go, but after awhile his teammates managed to escort him off. Commissioner Landis, who was at the game, disagreed with the umpire's decision to kick Manush out, and ruled from then on that no player in the World Series could be thrown out without first getting the commissioner's almighty permission.

One of the tallest players of all time played for the 1939 Pirates. Before the season Pittsburgh purchased Johnny Gee, a 6-foot 10-inch pitcher in the International League, from the Cincinnati Reds for $75,000 and four players. This was the biggest deal made in the IL since Baltimore peddled Lefty Grove to the Philadelphia Athletics. And it would turn out to be one of the biggest busts in Pirates history. When Gee made his rookie debut with Pittsburgh on September 17, his teammates committed eight errors, and he lost the game, 7–3. He won his next game, but soon thereafter suffered arm trouble and pitched sporadically. When Gee finally retired after the 1946 season he had a lifetime mark of 7–12.

All the personalities didn't matter. That season the pitching-plagued Pirates finished in sixth. Dethroned Chicago also suffered a collapse of their hurlers and wound up in fourth place. It was the ex–Pirates manager Bill McKechnie's Cincinnati Reds squad that won the NL pennant, four and one-half games ahead of St. Louis.

Whether Paul wore glasses or not, it didn't matter to see how the Pirates were beginning to view him. That season he appeared in just 125 games, his all-time low thus far. Though his batting average perked up to a healthy .328, he tallied only three homers and 45 RBIs. The season highlight came on September 16 when he stroked a perfect five hits in five at bats with a double and triple. It was a busy month for Big Poison, and he generated a 20-game hitting streak as well.

For the year, Lloyd got into only 112 games but made the most of it hitting a respectable .285. His lighter bat grew even softer, as he managed only 18 extra base hits—none of them homers—and 24 RBIs in 379 at bats.

The younger players like Fern Bell, Bob Elliott and Maurice Van Robays were seeing more playing time in the outfield that usually would have gone to the Waners.

The season sounded the death knell for Pie Traynor. In nearly six years of managing, he compiled a winning percentage of .530, but this also included being at the helm of the team's 1939 flop and for Hartnett's homer the year before. In keeping with franchise tradition, Traynor "resigned" after the season.

In firing the easygoing Traynor, the Pirates swung the pendulum the other way and hired the intense Frankie Frisch in 1940. He had been replaced as the Cardinals manager in late 1938, working the 1939 season as a broadcaster. "I didn't know how much I could miss the game until I began broadcasting in Boston," Frisch later said.

Local sportswriters blasted Pittsburgh ownership, charging that Traynor was made a scapegoat for inept front-office management.

The whole experience was rough on Traynor. After the 1938 debacle, he had lost 20 pounds to worry and anxiety. After being let go, Traynor slipped into semi-obscurity, except for his induction into the Hall of Fame in 1948. Out of the national limelight, he worked as a sports director for the Pittsburgh radio station KOV, coached at Duquesne University, and served as a Pirates scout. Each spring Traynor could be seen tutoring young players on how to play third—and he was always willing to chat about the game. Old-timers recalled Traynor talking baseball with anyone he met on the street.

Another Pirates player who was turned loose after 1939 was Johnny Rizzo, the homer-happy rookie of only two years ago. He slumped to six homers and a .261 average in 94 games. It turned out his personality didn't hold up well under the pressure of major league play. Enos Slaughter, who played with Rizzo in the Cardinals' minor league system, recalled Johnny's rise and fall.

Enos Slaughter: *"I tell you what happened to Rizzo. He couldn't control his temper. He'd fight the fans, and you can't do that. He hit 23 home runs his first year—and they got all over the Cardinals for letting him go to the Pirates and keeping me—but then Rizzo went down after that. He finally wound up going to the Dodgers and Cincinnati, where Bill McKechnie [the manager] said he had to let him go. He just had a temper. He and I battled neck-and-neck at Columbus [St. Louis' minor league team], and I wound up hitting .382, and he finished at .354. That's what made me, playing at Columbus. I had 245 hits in a short season there. After Rizzo left ball, I kept up with him a little. I know he went back home to Houston, though I don't know what he did there."*

The Pirates were fast becoming a revolving door of major league proportions.

Go Gently Into the Night

Two stars keep not their motion in one sphere.
— *William Shakespeare, from* Henry IV

In 1940, America prepared for war and approved the first peacetime draft, Germany occupied France, and the Battle of Britain began. By now, 30 million Americans had radio sets to hear such news from around the world. This year Ernest Hemingway published *For Whom the Bell Tolls*, the first successful helicopter flight was conducted in the U.S., and prehistoric cave paintings were discovered in France. In Pennsylvania, the state opened the original Pennsylvania Turnpike, the nation's longest toll road, and President Roosevelt visited Pittsburgh and inspected its flood-control program, steel mills, armament plants, and new public housing projects.

Meanwhile, the Waner brothers prepared for the coming of Frankie Frisch. Like his one-time mentor, John McGraw, Frisch was a take-no-prisoners personality with a track record of winning in St. Louis. Though he would never win a pennant after 1934, Frisch was expected to rejuvenate the franchise in Pittsburgh with a more aggressive style of play. This had its toll—Frisch had a knack for rubbing people the wrong way.

Still, the Waners were good troupers and at the outset sounded positive notes about the changing of the guard. Shortly after Frisch was hired, a writer asked Paul about his new manager.

Paul Waner: *"I believe Frank Frisch is going to be a big help to the Pirates as manager. All of the players on the squad have admired Frisch for his ability as a player, his fighting spirit and intelligence as a manager."*

19. Go Gently Into the Night

In other words, "we know he'll drive us hard."

Paul reported to spring training in 1940 weighing 145 pounds — light even by his pencil-thin standards. Frisch eyed him suspiciously when Paul told him he had burned up a ton of calories playing golf over the winter. The manager wondered how much he could use Paul at age 37. The same held true for Lloyd, now 34.

To the public, Frisch disputed any intention of getting rid of the great Paul Waner. Or Arky Vaughan, as another rumor had it. But the facts spoke otherwise. Clearly, the Pirates were marching forward with a youth movement. From the start, the Waners had to win back their starting jobs, and they never did. They had lots of competition.

Lloyd, left, and Paul, right, in either 1940 or 1941 when the Pirates donned this particular mustachioed logo (courtesy of Jim Knight).

One promising outfielder was Bob Elliott, who cracked the 1940 lineup with a .292 average in 148 games. That performance and the arrival of Vince DiMaggio — another member of baseball's most famous three-brother set — and Maurice Van Robays relegated the Waners to the bench for most of the year. Based on the numbers, it's easy to see why. Van Robays's first full season in the majors was 1940, and he lit up the scoreboard for 116 RBIs and a .273 average. DiMaggio, who came over in a trade from Cincinnati, smacked 19 home runs and etched a .289 average. All three outfielders were solid players — if not on the level of the Waners career-wise — and would start regularly for the Pirates through the war years. Still, the best Pittsburgh would finish during this span was in second place in 1944.

The 1940 season was the last full year that Paul and Lloyd played together for Pittsburgh. It was Paul's 15th season and Lloyd's 14th.

Paul Waner was a proud veteran up in years, and he knew he could be jettisoned from the team at practically any time. So he had his inevitable

Forbes Field after the introduction of night baseball. Notice the huge expanse in center field (courtesy of Jim Knight).

run-in with Frisch—it came early, at the first clubhouse meeting. At that meeting, Frisch was in the middle of establishing ground rules on drinking when, ironically, Paul wandered in, 10 minutes late. Frisch wanted to cut down on the Pirates' drinking tendencies, and here was a chance to lay down the law.

"Mr. Waner," said Frisch, "you are 10 minutes late."

"Don't mention it, Frank, I was glad to get here," replied Paul.

"You're fined $50, Mr. Waner," Frisch said, and then turned away to continue the meeting.

That incident got Paul and Frisch off on the wrong foot.

As the season began, both Waners found their usage limited to pinch-hitting and defensive substitutions. There were few high points that season. Lloyd started his first game on April 25 and promptly banged out four hits and scored three runs. He earned himself more playing time over the next week, but after that saw little action in May and June.

On April 23, Paul came to the plate as a pinch hitter in the ninth inning of a game against the Chicago Cubs. The bases were loaded and the score was 2–2. He singled to drive in the winning run. But like Lloyd he didn't start his first game in the outfield until two days later. On May 18, he homered and doubled with two RBIs for his best showing the first half of that season.

One historic occasion for the Pirates came on June 4. In the first night game at Forbes Field, Pittsburgh beat the visiting Boston Bees, 14–2. Baseball was ushering in night baseball, giving the working man the chance to see games on their free time.

The well-lighted Pirates were joined that year by Sportsman's Park in St. Louis and the Polo Grounds in New York. Cincinnati had been using lights for night games since 1935 when Reds owner Larry MacPhail turned them on. Since 1937, lighting systems had popped up in Shibe Park in Philadelphia, Municipal Stadium in Cleveland, and Comiskey Park in Chicago. Griffith Stadium in Washington would begin night games in 1941; by the end of the 40s, Fenway Park in Boston, Yankee Stadium in New York, Braves Field in Boston, and Briggs Stadium in Detroit would all be using lights. Wrigley Field in Chicago waited until 1988 to install a lighting system.

Amid all the lights, Pittsburgh's new luminary was outfielder Bob Elliott. He became the main offensive force on the Pirates over the course of the next few years. In 1947 Elliott would win the National League Most Valuable Player award, though in a Boston Braves uniform. Trading Elliott was one of the worst swaps in Pittsburgh's history. He was so valuable to his team the other Braves nicknamed him "Mr. Team."

In 1942, manager Frisch moved the awkward-fielding Elliott to third base and told him to just get in front of the ball. As St. Louis' manager in the '30s, Frisch had told Pepper Martin, also an outfielder, the same thing when he switched him to third.

Frankie Frisch: *"It's an easy position to play, Bob. All you need is a strong arm and a strong chest, I even played it myself. Whatever I couldn't* stop with my glove I stopped with my chest. Playing the outfield wears out your legs. You can play third base on a dime, no running or nothing. It will add five years to your playing career."

So Frisch tirelessly hit grounders to Elliott during practice. One day he hit Elliott squarely between the eyes with a ball, knocking him out cold. When he regained consciousness, Elliott was said to mutter, "Hey, Frank, remember what you told me about third base adding five years to my career? Well, I think I lost three of those extra five years."

Frisch was a tough customer. But he got results—most of the time.

Elbie Fletcher: *"He was aggressive and fiery and, God, teed off all the time. He'd fine you as quick as look at you. He fined me $250 once. That was during spring training one year, in San Bernardino. I was watching the floor show at a nightclub and sort of let the night slip by. I don't know what time it was when I got back to the hotel, but when I looked into the lobby, there was Frisch, Honus Wagner—he was one of our coaches—and Mr. Benswanger, the owner of the club. I walked around the block a couple of times, but each time I came back they were still there. Hell, I thought they must be waiting for me. So I figured why make bad enough worse, and walked in.*

"I marched right by them, said, 'Good evening, gentlemen,' and went upstairs. When I got to my room, Debs Garms, my roomie, said, 'They've been looking for you.' 'I know,' I said. 'I found them.'"

The next morning when Fletcher went downstairs to check his mail, he found a letter waiting for him. It read, "Dear Mr. Fletcher: Due to the fact you broke training rules you are hereby fined the sum of—" and it started with $50, but that was crossed out, and so was $100, $150, and $200.

The final number was $250.

Fletcher, to preempt any trouble, called his wife and told her what had happened. She said she'd take out $250 from the bank and that "we won't say anything more about it."

Elbie Fletcher: *"Later I got a bill for $28 for the phone call. So that episode cost me $278. To see a floor show. I went into the service not long after that, for two years. When I got out and returned to the ball club, there was Frisch, welcoming me back with a big smile on his face. 'Elbie,' he said, 'do you know what we're going to do for you? We're going to give you back the two fifty we fined you a couple of years ago.' That was Frisch. Always unpredictable."*

Fletcher saw the frustration in Frisch, however. The best the Pirates

19. Go Gently Into the Night

would do during Frisch's reign from 1940 to 1946 was second place in 1944. And that was wartime baseball, 4-Fers and all.

Elbie Fletcher: *"He always said he was never taught how to lose, and when he was with those great Gashouse Gang teams in St. Louis, he didn't lose very often. Then all of a sudden he gets with a ball club that's giving him an education in losing. It was a pity we didn't do better in those years because we had some good ball players. We had Arky Vaughan, Johnny Rizzo, Bob Elliott, and of course, the Waners.*

"Paul was kind of along in years when I joined the club, but he could still hit. He was a master. You know how some players have their favorite bat, how they rub it and hone it and baby it along? Well, Paul maintained that the bat had nothing to do with it. One day, just to prove his point, he told us to pick out any bat we wanted and he'd use it on the game. Each time he went up to the plate we'd toss him a different bat. Well, he went four for five. 'It's not the bat that counts,' he said after the game. 'It's the guy who's wheeling it.'"

Paul had fewer and fewer chances of wheeling it. On July 1, he played in his 2,000th major league game and wondered how many more would be in a Pirates uniform. In that game he didn't get a swing, though. Big Poison was pinch-hitting with the bases loaded in the 10th inning of a game against Philadelphia. The Phillies' pitcher, Hugh Mulcahy, threw a wild pitch that gave the Bucs a 5–4 win.

By the All-Star break, Paul had only 120 at bats, but was hitting .291. Lloyd was way back of him with 58 at bats and a .276 average. He had gone one six-week stretch in June and July without a hit, though lots of those appearances were solitary pinch-hitting occasions. While the Waners' offensive numbers were in decline, so were the rest of the league's.

Reading through box scores in 1940 one sees plenty of 2–1, 1–0, and 3–1 games. Runs and averages were down that season. After a decade of intoxicated offensive numbers, the stark realism of the 1940s was beginning to set in on baseball.

Symbolic of this, the Pirates that season would boast yet another batting champion. But it was none of the usual suspects like Paul Waner or Arky Vaughan, and he remains one of the most forgettable batting champs ever. Before the season the Pirates had picked up journeyman outfielder Debs Garms from the Boston Bees. In 1938 Garms had hit .298 with two homers. With the Pirates in 1940 Garms hit a career-high .355, and won the National League batting title, despite having played in just 103 games and collected just 358 at bats. On the last day of the season, Garms got five hits against the Reds to serve as an exclamation point on his out-of-the-blue season.

Under today's rules, Stan Hack of Chicago would have won the title at .317. All signs pointed to baseball heading for lighter-hitting years ahead, especially as the government pondered rationing manufacturing items for the building war effort. In the near future this would have the effect of changing the composition of the ball, thus influencing offensive production.

In 1940, Cincinnati's sparkling pitching—a league-leading 3.05 ERA—led them to their second NL pennant in a row. And for the first time since the Black Sox Scandal of 1919, the Red Legs won the World Series, defeating Detroit in seven games. Ex–Pirates manager and Cincinnati pilot Bill McKechnie was the toast of the league.

While the pitchers dominated in the majors that season, ball clubs wondered how to improve their punch at the plate or on the mound. One intriguing possibility arose that summer in Pittsburgh. Whatever the motivations it was an insightful illustration of race relations at that point in American baseball, and it followed on the heels of the 1938 episode wherein some of black baseball's best players were offered up to the Pittsburgh Pirates. The capital of black baseball in the 1930s, Pittsburgh had perennial Negro League powerhouses in the Homestead Grays and Pittsburgh Crawfords. And Pittsburgh boasted the cultural vibrant Hill District, akin to Harlem west of the Hudson. Not only did the African-American citizens turn out for black baseball, but the whites did as well. When Josh Gibson, Satchel Paige and Buck Leonard took to the field, black baseball in Pittsburgh was arguably superior to its local white equivalent.

Only the year before, as Jules Tygiel explained in *Baseball's Great Experiment*, Wendell Smith of the black-owned *Pittsburgh Courier* reported that Pirates owner William Benswanger had promised a try-out for Gibson and Leonard. Then, almost as soon as this invitation arose, the offer mysteriously vanished. Then it all came to a head in 1940, and Benswanger was pressed by the media to explain his position.

"If it came to an issue, I'd vote for Negro players," Benswanger declared. "There's no reason why they should be denied the same chance Negro fighters and musicians are given."

Those were revolutionary words, but they needed to be backed up by deed. And the Pirates never signed the black stars. Benswanger had changed his mind, and he spun his own alibi. He said Cum Posey, the Homestead owner and rival to the Pittsburgh Crawfords on which Gibson was playing, had asked him not to sign Gibson or the Negro National League would be ruined, bereft of its major star. It gave him cover for his retreat.

Benswanger was ambivalent, not fancying himself as a revolutionary baseball owner, though he may have sincerely admired the caliber of Negro League baseball in Pittsburgh. It was hard not to notice, and to envy. If only for utilitarian purposes, the Pittsburgh club would benefit from recruiting the best of the Negro Leagues—right in their own backyard.

The Pirates wavered almost annually on this issue. In 1942, the *Daily Worker*, a New York–based Communist newspaper, put more pressure on the Pirates. Roy Campanella, the Dodgers great, said in his autobiography that he was approached by a man from the *Daily Worker* who said he had arranged for a Pirates try-out for Campanella and a few other Negro League stars. Indeed, some time after that encounter, Campanella did receive a letter from Benswanger inviting him to a try-out. It never materialized.

Roy Campanella: *"I got a letter from Mr. Benswanger of the Pirates. He told me he would contact me later. He also said I would have to come up through their farm system just like any other player. I wrote him right back and said I'd be more than willing to, but I never heard from him again."*

The *Daily Worker* later quoted Leo Durocher as blaming the baseball commissioner's office for the freeze-out. Commissioner Kenesaw Mountain Landis angrily responded.

Commissioner Landis: *"Negroes are not barred from organized baseball by the commissioner and never have been during the 21 years I have served. There is no rule in organized baseball prohibiting their participation and never has been to my knowledge."*

Another time Landis observed, "The colored ballplayers have their own league. Let them stay in their own league."

In any event, Pittsburghers would have been glad to know of the birth that year of one African-American baby back in Paul and Lloyd Waners' Oklahoma. On March 6, Wilver Dornel Stargell was born in Earlsboro, Oklahoma. One day Stargell would set the Pittsburgh career record for home runs and grace the city of Pittsburgh and his teammates with his leadership, class and decency.

How would have the Waners reacted to black players on the Pirates? They probably would have welcomed them if it meant winning more ball games.

Negro League All-Stars who played against the Waners in exhibitions said they were gracious and accepting in attitude, not aloof and cold like some of the other white players. They never protested playing against the black players—like some white players—and never criticized the possibility one day of African-Americans in the major leagues. From all accounts, the Waners were not inclined to put down other players, whether white or black. And as they grew older, they reached out to the younger players on the Pirates.

Frank Gustine, a former Pittsburgh infielder, saw the Waners in their twilight days.

Frank Gustine: *"In 1940, three of us, Bob Elliott, Maurice Van Robays and I, broke into the lineup and they benched the Waners. Both of them could still play, but there was kind of a youth movement. But nobody ever heard Lloyd or Paul complain. In fact, they helped Bob and Maurice learn the outfield.*

"They were still very capable. But there's an erosion of your greatness if you don't play. It's hard to be a part-time player."

On the bench or in the field, the Waners still had fun. Gustine remembered a prank that Lloyd pulled on him.

Frank Gustine: *"Lloyd introduced me to chewing tobacco in spring training. I was a gum-chewing rookie. He said I had to chew tobacco to be a big leaguer. So I tried it, but got so sick I never touched it again."*

Gustine recalled Paul's ability to wield a lethal stick, even then.

Frank Gustine: *"He could wait until the last second, and snap those wrists. He never got fooled."*

Once on a spring training trip to Los Angeles, Gustine drew Paul as a roommate. For five days while they played at the Cubs' West Coast version of Wrigley Field, Gustine and Paul roomed together.

Frank Gustine: *"I never saw him. I roomed with his bags for five days. He showed up at the ball park and hit tons of line drives. That's all I know."*

Paul in the twilight of his career in the late 1930s (courtesy of Jim Knight).

That season Paul's line drives settled in for a .290 average. Now a part-timer, he got into 89 games and came to bat 238 times. He had one homer and 16 doubles and one triple. Lloyd played in 72 games for a .259 average. He managed only three extra-base hits, all doubles, in 166 at bats.

That season Frankie Frisch moved the Pirates up to fifth place in the rankings, an improvement over the year before. But the Bucs could have used a lot more help in their lineup and rotation.

Paul was becoming better known for his drinking than his hitting. Ray Berres was a teammate of Waner's from 1937 to 1940. He considered Waner a considerate man who had become the butt of too many drinking stories.

Ray Berres: *"Regardless of what has been said or written adversely about him, I always found him to be a gentleman, ready to lend a word of encouragement or a helping hand. Words fail me in expressing my affection for Paul as a player and as a man. He had his moments of fun, but let's not condemn him for it."*

Paul Waner did admit to sometimes playing hung over. He thought relaxed players performed better than uptight ones. And, he added in jest or not, it was easier to see the ball once it looked blurry.

Paul Waner: *"More of it to hit."*

Lloyd, in defense of his brother, once said, "How could Paul be drunk and play all those games every year? He never over did it. He thought a few beers after a ball game did you good. He would spend time with the gang and have a few beers and talk baseball. But I never saw my brother drunk. I never saw him unable to play because of drink."

Paul reportedly once swore at his manager for suggesting that he would be dumb enough to leave a half-filled bottle of liquor around the clubhouse—no good drinker did that.

Paul was not the only heavy drinker among baseball's greats. Jimmie Foxx once refused to slide into second base because he didn't want to break the whiskey flask in his pocket. Babe Ruth, Hack Wilson, Hoss Radbourn, King Kelly, John Clarkson, Rube Waddell, Pete Alexander—patrons of the flowing bowl, one and all.

For decades, the Pittsburgh Pirates featured colorful drinking types, whether it was Rabbit Maranville or Paul Waner. Pittsburgh was a blue-collar city with a hard-hat tradition, and that often translated into cooling down at the end of the day with a few beers at the neighborhood bar. In those days, players were much more likely to mingle with the regular public than today. Francis Stann of the *Pittsburgh Post Gazette* remarked that the Pittsburgh Pirates of the 1920s and 1930s always won in the "liquid diet league."

Hank Greenberg noticed the hard-drinking Pirates tradition when he signed on with Pittsburgh in 1947 after starring for years for the Detroit Tigers. In the final year of his Hall of Fame career, Greenberg helped mentor Ralph Kiner, the next big star in Pittsburgh after the Waners, Vaughan and Traynor. Not much of a drinker, Greenberg preferred coffee and muffins to beer.

Hank Greenberg: *"Sitting on bar stools was a hallowed rite at Pittsburgh, like sitting on the fence at Yale."*

Bill Veeck—no stranger to tall tales—once swore he saw Waner playing drunk in a game. Incredibly, Waner banged a double off the wall and crashed the game-winning home run. Yet his sobriety was questionable, Veeck claimed.

Bill Veeck: *"[I saw him] take a wide turn at second base and go sliding into the bullpen mound in the left-field foul ground ... more than 60 feet away from his destination."*

While Veeck never let the facts get in the way of a good story, there's the case of Giants pitcher Roy Parmalee. Before playing against Waner he would talk to the outfielder to see if he had been drinking. It was common knowledge that a drunk Paul Waner tended to pull the ball to right field, and a sober one hit it to left.

Roy Parmalee: *"So we'd pitch him just the opposite, depending on whether or not he had a drink. Not that it made a great deal of difference."*

When a player gets more ink for his drinking stories than his line drives, one begins to wonder what is around the corner.

Farewell Steel City

When I had (Paul Waner), he used to take a drink or ten but he could hit. I told my players to listen to him whether he was drinking or not and he could teach you how to hit a line drive.

— *Casey Stengel*

The year 1941 was one to forever live in the annals of history. In perhaps the most pivotal year in the 20th century, Japan attacked Pearl Harbor and Germany invaded the Soviet Union, setting a world on fire as never before, and all else paled alongside this monumental conflict. At least the baseball season wrapped up before the bombs began dropping on Pearl Harbor.

And what a season 1941 was. The top highlights included Ted Williams batting .406, and Joe DiMaggio hitting safely in 56 straight games. Below those headlines old Lefty Grove struggled to win his 300th game, young Bob Feller won 25 games and then enlisted in the Navy, Dodgers rookie Pete Reiser captured the batting championship, and the press hounded MVP Hank Greenberg about his draft status before he became the second big leaguer to join the U.S. Army.

The world was spinning fast, and things were coming loose—including the Waner brothers.

In the winter between the seasons, Pirates manager Frankie Frisch had attempted to convince the Pittsburgh front office to depose of the Waner brothers either by trade or release. Frisch thought Big and Little Poison didn't fit in with the youth movement—a youth movement that would, in fact, create a worse-off team the next several years, but that's another story. Besides, the cocksure veteran Paul had just caused Frisch too many headaches.

Pirates president Bill Benswanger agreed. To make the whole affair more cordial, the team initially allowed Paul, the more marketable of the pair, to try to engineer his own trade and work something out for Lloyd. But no suitors were found for the 38-year-old outfielder or his kid brother. So the Pirates took the next step themselves.

On December 10, 1940, Pittsburgh granted Paul Waner his unconditional release.

In breaking up the Waner act, the Pirates had terminated the longest running brother combination in baseball history. The next closest mark is that of Joe and Luke Sewell, who played together 10 years on the Cleveland Indians from 1921 to 1930. Wes and Rick Ferrell played for about four and one-half years for Boston and Washington. Dizzy and Paul Dean had a four-year hitch in St. Louis. Back in the 19th century, George and Harry Wright were with the original Cincinnati Red Stockings in 1869 and 1870, moving to Boston in 1871. They parted company in 1878 when George left Boston to manage Providence and Harry continued on as Boston's manager.

Paul was given an unconditional release because, as Dan Daniel of the *New York World Telegram* wrote, no team was willing to pay the waiver price for a veteran like Waner on the downside of his career. When he was let go, Paul Waner had a .340 lifetime average. But he was now a part-timer.

Gone golfing. Lloyd, foreground, and Paul, background (courtesy of Jim Knight).

Bill Benswanger: *"We didn't like to let him go because he has been an institution in Pittsburgh. It's different when a player spends his whole career with one club than when he sticks in the majors a long time but bounces around from one team to another. We parted friendly. Paul came here from* his home in Florida and we told him to try to make a deal for himself. He wasn't able to do this, so we had to give him a release. He realized we didn't have any choice, that youngsters were coming up to take his job just like he came in fresh to take somebody else's spot."

When released, Paul automatically became a free agent. This meant he could sign with any team of his choice, though certainly at a severe cut in pay. It took until February but Paul finally landed a spot with the Brooklyn Dodgers after selling himself to manager Leo Durocher, a golfing buddy.

Back in Pittsburgh, it seemed impossible to see Paul Waner wearing a rival's uniform come Opening Day. That winter the Pirates also sought to trade another Hall of Famer, Arky Vaughan. Though Frisch had soured on Vaughan, the shortstop had just notched another .300-plus year and scored a league-leading 113 runs. But the Vaughan trade didn't happen until 1942. By then Frisch's abrasive style and tart tongue had so alienated Vaughan that Frisch lobbied hard to send the shortstop to Brooklyn in exchange for Pete Coscarat, Jimmy Wasdell, Babe Phelps, and Luke Hamlin. Frisch was getting rid of the veterans on the club and looking for younger talent.

One of Paul's supporters in the press, Les Biederman of the *Pittsburgh Post-Gazette*, summed up the awkward situation between Waner and the Pirates. Unfinished business remained on a couple fronts.

Les Biederman: *"Paul had only two regrets when he left the Pirates at the end of the 1940 season. One was that he had slumped so badly in 1938 that he felt responsible for the collapse of the pennant dreams. The other was that he failed to record his 3,000th hit at Forbes Field. Waner fell below .300 for the first time in 1938 when the Pirates desperately needed his bat. The year before he had hit .354 but in 1938 he lost 74 points and finished at .280."*

When the Bucs released him two years later, Waner needed just 132 hits to reach 3,000. As a role player he might have achieved that in a season or two of play. But expensive bench players are unwelcomed on most clubs.

Sometimes veterans were the victims of their own success in the baseball business. After years of glory in St. Louis, the front office traded Enos Slaughter to the Yankees in 1954.

Enos Slaughter: *"I know exactly how he felt. When Augie Busch bought the Cardinals on December 28, 1953, I was the first ballplayer he signed to a contract. And he says, 'You'll always be with the Cardinals, Enos.' Two months later I was traded to the Yankees. That's when I found out it was a* *cold-hearted game. You could be loyal to a team, but they would turn you loose if they thought you weren't in their plans. But I went to New York, and helped them win three more pennants and two more World Series. I was the first 40-year-old, I believe, to hit a home run in the World Series. I did it off Roger Craig in '56.*

"But we're talking about the Waners, now. In those days, the ballplayers were more loyal to the club they played for. I was loyal to the Cardinals, and then when I went to the Yankees, I was loyal to them. I know the Waners felt the same way about Pittsburgh. They'd been there their whole careers, and played with some great ballplayers. When you leave the group you've been playing with, and go to another group, it's not the same. Sure, if somebody is having a bad time with the club and not doing well, sometimes it can help him to leave the club. The Waners had a good environment in Pittsburgh, and I think they kind of resented having to leave there. Besides, they'd never been apart in the big leagues, having always played in the same outfield.

"I remember them quite well. Good fielders, though maybe Lloyd was a little better than Paul with the glove. At the plate, you couldn't play Paul any certain way. He didn't hit many home runs, but he could sting that ball down third base, but if you played him that way, he'd jack up on the bat and drill it down the first base line. Never saw a guy place hits like Paul Waner. Everybody knew he could hit anything."

Paul had other options besides major league baseball that winter.

In February, the Seattle Rainiers in the Pacific Coast League asked Paul to manage the club the upcoming season. If he wanted, they would allow him to be a player/manager, all for $10,000. It was a tempting offer. The Rainiers were just coming off a PCL championship season, and the idea of bringing on an old PCL star like Paul was exciting for their fan base.

Paul mulled it over. The money sounded good but the Pacific Northwest seemed faraway. He declined. His heart—if not body—was still in major league baseball. And he wanted his 3,000th hit.

One key to Paul's signing on with Brooklyn was how much time he spent golfing in the off-season with manager Leo Durocher, outfielder Joe Medwick and scout Ted McGrew. Somebody suggested the Dodgers had better sign Paul, "or it would be a shame to break up the foursome."

Others, however, cautioned that signing the old right fielder would have a bad effect on the young Pete Reiser, the team's rising star right fielder.

In his first year away from the Pirates, Paul had a change of spring training scenery from the Pirates' traditional West Coast digs. The Dodgers trained in the exotic locale of Havana, Cuba, home to a multitude of gambling, drinking and eating establishments.

Durocher thought Paul might reclaim some of his past glory. The manager observed that late the season before Paul had begun to pull the ball down the right field line, even against the league's fastest pitchers. Durocher hoped Paul would continue to do so in the season ahead. In lefty-friendly Ebbets Field, Waner stood a decent chance of being productive for his age. Still, no one thought he would return to full-time duty.

Leo Durocher: *"Paul will play some outfield for me, I guess. But mostly we will carry him for base hits. He'll hit when the other boys slump off, and all told his hitting should do us some good. You can't tell me that a guy who hit around .330 in 1939 is all through at the plate."*

Paul seconded Leo's confidence. "I feel I'm in better shape today than I have been in several years at this time. My legs are stronger and I'm even surprised at myself with the way I can run with little effort. It must have been the hot weather in Havana."

His exhibition season record was encouraging. On March 21, Paul slapped a double and two singles as the Dodgers beat Detroit 3–1. A day later, Paul went 2 for 2 in a 7–0 Dodger triumph over the Yankees. His pre-season average stood at .333, for what spring training averages are worth. Only Pete Reiser and Joe Medwick had higher averages on the team.

But Paul opened the season sluggishly. He just couldn't produce those hits, and multiple-hit games were rare. In May, after just 11 games, the Brooklyn Dodgers gave him his unconditional release. He had managed six hits in 35 at bats for a woeful .171 average.

Lloyd, too, had his difficulties. After seeing action in only three games—two of them as a pinch-runner—and getting one hit in four at bats, Lloyd was traded by the Pirates to the Boston Braves for Nick Strincevich, a 25-year-old right-hander who went 4–8 for the Braves the year before.

Lloyd was crushed. His best days in baseball seemed past. His frail body had finally caught up to him; insiders whispered around the league. He wasn't as fast as before, and his average fell as he could not leg out ground balls for hits—something he had always done when he was younger. The season before Lloyd had posted his lowest average in the majors, and his game and at-bat totals had dwindled in recent years.

Lloyd Waner: *"I can tell you the saddest day of my career. It was the day in 1941 when the Pirates traded me to Boston for pitcher Nick Strincevich. I never thought I'd get over it."*

When the Boston Braves released the aging Earl Averill that spring, it touched off a flurry of unconditional releases of older ballplayers, including Wes Ferrell, Dick Bartell and now Waner. Next year, however, many older players found themselves welcomed back—including the Waners—as the younger players marched off to the war.

Some of the tilt toward age wasn't popular at first. New York critics charged the Dodgers bumbled in picking up Paul—the hometown favorite was Dixie Walker. Dodgers fans even sent Walker a telegram, signed by more than five thousand people, Bill James reports, threatening a mass boycott of Ebbets Field if Waner was given the job. According to Lee Allen, the Brooklyn front office was "baffled by the adulation of Walker." It was this groundswell of popular support that gave Walker, 32, his Brooklynese nickname, "People's Cherce."

In the press, Dan Daniel wrote, "It looks as if the great Waner experiment on the Brooklyn club had worn itself out. All through the training season Leo Durocher played up Paul, the Pittsburgh reject and snided Dixie Walker. Now Paul sits on the bench, and wonders at the vagaries of baseball and the shortness of spring."

Two weeks after Brooklyn released Paul, the Boston Braves picked him up, reuniting him with his brother Lloyd. In Boston, Paul would have his last hurrah under a kindred spirit in manager Casey Stengel. Stengel, who once called Paul the greatest National League right fielder, said Big Poison "probably (had) been hitting from memory the past couple of years."

Waner was good copy for the yarn-spinning Stengel. Another time Casey said, "Waner had to be a very graceful player, because he could slide without breaking the bottle on his hip."

On a more serious note, Stengel once said that the only ballplayer he ever saw who seemed immune to the effects of heavy drinking was the amazing Babe Ruth. Others, Paul Waner among them, inevitably paid a price in the loss of their physical powers.

In Boston, with Big and Little Poison in the same outfield again, the Braves hoped to catch lightning in the bottle. They didn't.

In their first game back together, Lloyd, coming off an injured shoulder from the week before, had to leave the game after the first inning. Paul himself went hitless and then failed in four more attempts the next day. Lloyd, with all his aches and pains, seemed questionable every day thereafter.

Stengel put a positive spin on it. "There's plenty of good baseball left in both of them. They'll do all right."

Paul's fashion angle—loud—was also intriguing to Stengel. One day Paul showed up at the ballpark wearing a brightly checkered suit.

20. Farewell Steel City

"What did you do, borrow that from Lew Dockstader?" asked the horrified Stengel.

"No," replied Paul, "I bought these draperies down in Cuba and they chucked in a banjo and a pair of extra pants."

Another time when Paul and the Braves were staying at the Edgewater Beach Hotel in Chicago, a waitress spied Paul and deduced he was a new member of the team.

"You're a new boy on the team, ain't you?" she said.

"Yes, sister," Paul said. "Those wrinkles you see on my map are hereditary."

The reunion was short-lived. A month later, the Waners were split up—and for good. After 51 at bats and a .412 average, Lloyd was traded yet again, this time to Cincinnati for pitcher John Hutchings, a 24-year-old right-hander more acquainted with Pensacola in the Southwestern League than the major leagues. Paul stayed with Boston through the remainder of the season.

Buddy Hassett roomed with Paul on the Boston Braves in 1941 and 1942. A first baseman in the Yankee minor system during the reign of Lou Gehrig, Hassett broke in with the Brooklyn Dodgers in 1936 and put together a .292 lifetime average over seven seasons. He went into the Navy after 1942 and never played in the big leagues after the war ended.

Buddy Hassett: *"You know, I roomed with Paul Waner for a while. He could drink pretty good. That's no secret. But he could also sober himself up in a hurry. He would do back flips. He had a remarkable ability, like an acrobat. Fifteen or twenty minutes of back flips and he was cold sober, ready to go out to the ball park and get his three hits.*

"We were playing a game of pepper one time and right out of the blue I hear Paul saying to me, 'You know, they say money talks. But the only thing it says to me is, 'Goodbye!'"

Jimmie Wilson, a catcher from 1923 to 1940 for several National League teams, once told Hassett a story about playing against Waner. When Waner came to the plate, he asked Wilson where he wanted the ball hit.

"I called the right and left-field lines four times," said Wilson, "and he hit four doubles right where I said, and of course we're pitching him exactly opposite."

At Cincinnati, Lloyd was a teammate of Bill Werber's. Years later, in *Memories of a Ballplayer*, the third baseman described Paul as wild and Lloyd as mild.

Lloyd Waner with the Cincinnati Reds in 1941 (courtesy of Jim Knight).

Bill Werber: "The Schenley Hotel was only a block or two from Forbes Field, and it had a cool and comfortable bar where visiting players could sip a beer. Paul was frequently among the visitors with a glass of whiskey in front of him. It never seemed to affect his play, but may eventually have done him in.

"Lloyd, on the other hand, was never seen in the bar and lived to age seventy-six, passing away in 1982. He was my teammate with Cincinnati in 1941, and sitting beside him in the dugout I never smelled anything but shaving lotion. One afternoon, I asked Lloyd how come Paul and he could run so fast. He said it was a matter of life and death.

"Lloyd said, 'There's a big Indian living outside of Harrah who owned a small farm and grew cantaloupe, watermelon, eating corn, and tomatoes. We used to walk a mile or so to that farm and steal whatever was in season, and the Indian got sick and tired of our shenanigans. He learned our habits and would lurk in the woods to cut us off, and when he was sure he had us he'd pounce. We'd scatter like a covey of quail with hearts in our mouths. He was a big mean Indian and would have killed us.'"

On three different teams, Lloyd finished the season with a .292 average in 77 games. Incredibly, he did not strike out once in 219 at bats that season.

Paul closed out 1941 with a .267 average in 106 games and 329 at bats. He was only 46 hits from the magic 3,000th hit—and that would move Big Poison into some heavyweight company.

At that point in baseball history, only five players had reached the 3,000-hit pinnacle. They included Ty Cobb (4,190), Tris Speaker (3,514), Honus Wagner (3,415), Eddie Collins (3,315), and Nap Lajoie (3,242). Revisionists have since adjusted Cap Anson's hit total to 2,995, but Anson was widely acknowledged as a member of the group. In the days when there were fewer games per season and players did not have the benefit of today's conditioning methods or the designated hitter rule to prolong careers, acquiring 3,000 hits was arguably more difficult than doing so today.

Beyond his personal highlights, Paul was still seeking a championship. He had no luck. As it turned out, his original team that season, Brooklyn, won the National League pennant. And they did it at Braves Field in Boston. After beating the Braves in the pennant-clinching game, Dodgers manager Leo Durocher and his players held a noisy celebration in the clubhouse. A reporter leaving the scene encountered Paul Waner, dressed and showered by then, waiting outside the clubhouse.

"Do you think it's all right to go in?" Paul asked the reporter. "I'd like to congratulate Leo and the boys."

His former Dodgers teammates welcomed Waner into the clubhouse, for he was a greatly respected player even after his brief tenure. Paul congratulated everyone and talked about the season and all the things ballplayers talk about at that special moment.

As Paul was preparing to leave, Durocher, who was feeling plenty cocky after steering Brooklyn to its first championship in 21 years, took time out to nod in the direction of the departing Big Poison.

"Now, there goes a fellow with class," Durocher was heard to say. One scribe wryly noted that this was one of Leo's rare comments that didn't lead to an argument or fistfight.

Fighting was in the air late that year. But the Waners took time for some light-hearted moments, too. After the end of the 1941 season with war brewing in the Pacific, Paul and Lloyd attended a sportswriters' banquet in Pittsburgh. Even if the team no longer wanted them, the writers liked having them around for good copy, and the brothers were still immensely popular in Pittsburgh.

At the banquet Paul and Lloyd broke out their famous saxophones, and it was a sight reminiscent of their vaudeville tour after the pennant-winning 1927 season. Instead of licking their wounds over a World Series defeat, however, this time the Waners sounded melancholic on their Pittsburgh estrangement.

Sportswriter Chilly Doyle was on hand for a night of surprising emotion.

Chilly Doyle: "*Both had finished their Pirates careers and were special guests of the writers, the banquet hall being packed, with the audience acclaiming the brothers as few Pittsburghers have been acclaimed. Those of us on stage saw the tears well up in Lloyd's eyes, and his usually carefree brother* *choked up for a moment, too, while he fingered the stops on his sax. But like another famous Oklahoman, Will Rogers, Paul was ready with a quip and in a jiffy the touching scene was turned into one of merrymaking.*

"When it was all over the brothers both realized they had been the big figures of a dramatic moment, an incident based on the sincere appreciation of Pittsburghers, who had come to love them."

A Hallowed Hitsmith

> To while away the time I play my solitaire card baseball game Lionel and I invented in 1942 when we visited Lowell and the pipes froze for Christmas—the game is between the Pittsburgh Plymouths (my oldest team, and now barely on top of the second division) and the New York Chevvies rising from the cellar ignominiously since they were world champions last year—I shuffle my deck, write out the lineups, and lay out the teams. For hundreds of miles around, black night, the lamps of Desolation are lit, to a childish sport, but the Void is a child too.
>
> — *Jack Kerouac, in his novel* Desolation Angels

All winter long Paul focused on the upcoming 1942 season. His hits total had given his lagging career new meaning, and that was solace enough for outside the world of baseball the news was grim. In the Pacific, the Japanese took Manila, thousands of American soldiers died on the Bataan "Death March," General Doolittle led the first air raid over Tokyo, and the U.S. won big battles in Midway and the Coral Sea. Back home the American government started rationing gasoline, sugar and coffee, and people saw Casablanca at the theater and listened to Bing Crosby croon "White Christmas."

World War II spawned a musical tradition in baseball. Before the war the "Star Spangled Banner" was only heard on special occasions at the ballpark. Now the national anthem would be heard before the start of every game.

Serious debate existed about whether to curtail major league baseball during the war. Among the top officials, however, baseball had support.

"What does baseball do for America? It provides an opportunity for hundreds of thousands of war workers to relax in the fresh air and sunshine—and to continue to enjoy something that has been a significant part of American life for almost 100 years."—Congressman La Vern Dilweg, from a speech delivered in the U.S. House of Representatives, 1942

"It would be best for the country to keep baseball going."—Franklin D. Roosevelt

With the green light from FDR, major league baseball swung into action that spring of 1942. As teams headed south for spring training, 39-year-old Paul Waner signed on with the Boston Braves again and declared himself in fighting shape at 144 pounds. His regimen consisted of only two meals a day and no more than seven hours of sleep a night.

Paul Waner: *"I think I'm in better condition this year than I've been for several years. I don't get tired. The only thing that bothers me is that my muscles are always a little stiff when I start a game. I have to be careful not to pull a muscle. But as soon as I run and get warmed up, they loosen up and don't give me any trouble. Otherwise, I eat only breakfast and supper, and seldom heavily. When the weather gets real hot, I don't eat meats. In the hottest weather, I eat salads. I think steaks are too heavy to digest properly in hot weather. Sometimes I'll go a week or longer without eating a steak."*

The Sporting News noted, "For one month every summer, he eschews meat, living on salads and milk and, if he feels like it—and he often does—beer for breakfast, or even a touch of stronger stuff. 'Been doing it for years,' he says, 'and it's helped me keep my weight down and stay up here.'"

Making his tour of National League clubs, Lloyd Waner hooked on with the Philadelphia Phillies that season.

While the Waners made the rounds, some of their peers watched how they played to see if they had lost much. The second baseman Billy Herman said Paul had enough left to justify continuing to play.

Billy Herman: *"He could still hit. He couldn't run so well anymore, and his eyes went bad on him. But he could still swing the bat."*

Paul's march to 3,000 hits was one of the first times that the baseball press covered that particular milestone. As Bill James pointed out, the recent opening of the National Baseball Hall of Fame gave the press impetus to start paying attention to lifetime distinctions.

Paul started the season off well enough, picking up three hits, including a triple, on April 14 and 15 against the Phillies. Then he went four straight games without a safety.

21. A Hallowed Hitsmith

Lloyd had one four-hit game in April, but that was about it. Incidentally, when 36-year-old Lloyd had begun the 1942 season, he had 2,370 hits.

On May 5, Paul had his best day of the season, going 4 for 5 against the Pirates. No doubt Big Poison turned it up an extra notch against his former team.

On May 13, though, Paul was overshadowed by Braves pitcher Jim Tobin in one of the most spectacular two-sided performances in baseball of all time. At the plate, Tobin launched three home runs, and on the mound he pitched a five-hitter to beat the Cubs 6–5 at Braves Field. The only modern-era pitcher with three home runs in a game, Tobin set the record for total bases by a pitcher in a game with 12—solo round-trippers in the fifth and seventh innings and a two-run shot in the eighth to win the game. Ironically, he had homered the day before as a pinch hitter.

In late May, Paul got two hits each in three straight games. On May 28, Paul collected two hits off Brooklyn's Whit Wyatt to draw within 10 hits of 3,000. In the same game he also made a stupendous catch against the right field wall to rob former teammate Arky Vaughan of a home run.

Bill Corum, the *New York Journal American* sportswriter, chuckled in print at the idea of the hard-partying Waner becoming one of baseball's elite. It seemed almost vindication against the sport's blue noses and disciplinarians. Besides, he wrote, "Every man's life is his private life, and that privacy should be respected."

Bill Corum: *"It would be a fine thing if we could truthfully say to the All-American boy that Big Poison achieved this feat because all his life he ate up his breakfast food and spinach, refused to read fine type newspapers, and went to bed at 10 o'clock on the dot. Oh, let's be honest. Paul has played all the wheels, and his favorite time for going home to bed has been whenever they locked the doors of the particular spot in which he chanced to be pleasuring himself."*

After a series in Chicago, where Paul picked up three hits, the Braves traveled to Cincinnati for a series opening June 17 with a doubleheader. Only two hits separated Paul and the big number. It seemed a safe bet he would do it in Cincinnati.

What happened was revealing of Paul Waner's sportsmanship and character. In a sense, the anecdote pays tribute to the image in baseball of the truly great ballplayers earning their way to fame and playing the game squarely—sometimes a novel concept in the early years of baseball. At the turn of the century, baseball sought to associate itself with ideals of virtue and fair play and distance itself from rowdyism and cheating. Players like Christy Mathewson exemplified this ideal. When such distinctions actually occurred on the diamond, a fluttering of typewriters duly followed suit as baseball history and mythology intertwined.

In the first game of the doubleheader in Cincinnati, Paul collected his 2,999th hit. In the second game, he lined a sharp grounder to Reds shortstop, Eddie Joost. As Joost raced in at the crack of the bat, he made a backhanded stab, and knocked the ball down. He was unable to throw to first in time to get Waner. The play could have been scored a hit or error.

The official scorer, Gerry Moore, ruled it a hit. But Paul, standing on first, waved at Moore. He did not want a tarnished 3,000th hit. He'd rather have it clean and square, than not at all. Fair play.

Paul motioned to umpire Beans Reardon, who had already obtained the ball from Joost and was ready to give it to Paul. But Paul made it clear he thought it should be judged an error. Moore agreed to rule it an error, upholding the virtue of Paul Waner's imminent stroke to greatness and all the ideals associated with the image of the honest and humble American athlete.

Joost could have been unhappy with getting an error on the play. Paul realized this. Later he approached Joost. "I'm sorry to see you get the error, kid, but I wanted the hit to be one that I could be proud of."

Unlike many baseball myths or stories, this one was true. Paul would have to wait for his big hit. After the game, the Braves headed to—where else—Pittsburgh. The delay merely heightened the suspense.

On June 19, Paul stepped up to the plate against his former Pirates teammate Rip Sewell—one hit shy. And so, in Paul's greatest irony, he connected for his historic 3,000th hit against the Pittsburgh Pirates. He lashed a single up the middle in Forbes Field, his home of many years.

The umpire-in-chief Tom Dunn retrieved the ball for Paul, who said he'd hold on to it for his 13-year-old son Paul Jr. Frank Frisch, managing the Pirates, and Casey Stengel, the boss of the Braves, ambled out of their respective dugouts to pose for a photograph with Waner and Sewell, both of whom were standing together at first base. The Pirates went on to win the game 7–6 in 11 innings on Bob Elliott's two home runs.

Paul Waner: *"I haven't collected many trophies, but I'm really proud of that ball. I've saved a dozen balls or so for one reason or another."*

Back in 1927 some Pirates boosters had given the free-spending Waner a wooden chest for winning the National League Most Valuable Player award. "But what was inside it is long gone," he said. Asked what that was, he replied, "A thousand dollars in gold."

On June 22, the Boston Braves held a formal dinner party to honor

21. A Hallowed Hitsmith

Paul at the Sheraton Hotel in downtown Boston. Paul received tribute from, among others, Ford Frick, the National League president, Eddie Collins, general manager of the Boston Red Sox and peer in the 3,000-hit club, Boston Braves president Bob Quinn, Braves manager Casey Stengel, Braves coach George Kelly and sportswriter Joe Cashman, head of the Boston chapter of the Baseball Writers' Association of America.

Cashman gave Paul a shiny watch with inscriptions from Boston sportswriters. In return, Paul expressed his gratefulness to the Braves for hiring him, thus making it possible to reach the milestone.

The party was vintage Paul Waner, the writer Bob Broeg observed.

Bob Broeg: *"Afterward, Waner collared a Boston writer and he said he would like to throw a party for the players, for the Braves' front office, and for the press. He asked the BBWAA [Baseball Writers Association of America] chapter to handle the arrangements. 'Do you think $1,000 will be enough?' said the three-time batting champion who never received more than $18,500 a season. A grand then was like $3,000 now. Even though the Braves were suffering the financial shorts, the club's president, Bob Quinn, wouldn't let Waner pick up the tab. Party-loving Paul had grabbed enough checks in his time."*

Now the writers had to figure out how to handle Paul Waner, recently elevated among the game's greatest players. Baseball is mighty conscious of its heroes and images, and sometimes the writers help out.

There seemed an inclination to portray him in distinguished terms, avoiding some of the rural flackery attached to him in past years. No longer the boyish-faced Oklahoman, Paul was the senior batsman among many juniors, the thinking man's ballplayer that represents the fusion of brain and body into a perfect player of eminence. Paul Waner was a "smart" baseball player, the type who could aim his line drives to all fields when he wanted. Such players, like Cobb and Speaker, were not just dumb brutes with a bat in their hands, slugging vacantly at the skies. They won by outsmarting the competition, at the plate and in the field.

Howell Stevens of the *Boston Post* contrasted Paul with the average "heathen ballplayer."

Howell Stevens: *"Unlike many ballplayers, Waner likes to read serious literature. He is extremely fond of philosophy. He is presently reading* The Morals of Seneca.*"*

It was an odd choice in philosophy, an exceptionally musty one to be sure, but maybe fitting in light of his Midwestern upbringing and career path. Seneca was a Roman philosopher from 3 B.C. to 65 A.D. who advocated Stoicism—generally defined as the ability to not be affected by emotions or feelings, pain or pleasure. Practicality was a virtue.

"While we are postponing, life speeds by," Seneca once uttered. Top athletes master performance under pressure. Paul certainly had the relaxed composure to elicit Stoic images.

Despite the flattering press, Paul's personal habits were not lost on the more skeptical public, especially in New York and Brooklyn. Later that season Paul was playing right field for the Braves against the Dodgers in Ebbets Field. Brooklyn's Dixie Walker rocketed a ball past Paul and through a small knothole in the wall. As no ground rule existed on the hole, Paul knew the ball was still in play, so he dropped to his knees—as Walker was circling the bases—and stuck his hand through the hole, clutching vainly for the ball.

One loud fan yelled, "What are you looking for, Waner, a beer bottle?"

Paul could laugh at himself.

Paul Waner: *"I remember one day when I was with the Boston Braves in 1942. Casey Stengel was the manager. I was supposed to be just a pinch hitter, but in the middle of the summer, with a whole string of doubleheaders coming up, all the extra outfielders got hurt and I had to go in and play center field every day. Oh, was that ever rough! One doubleheader after the other."*

During a doubleheader against, of all teams, Pittsburgh, an opposing player hit a long triple to right center, and a tired Paul Waner chased it down. The next guy hit another triple, this time to left-center, and sent the exhausted Waner scurrying. Then the next guy blooped one over second base into short center field, and a weary Waner charged in toward the ball.

Paul Waner: *"In I went, as fast as my legs would carry me. Which wasn't very fast, I'll tell you. At the last minute I dove for the ball, but I didn't quite make it, and the ball landed about two feet in front of me and just stuck there in the ground. And do you know, I just lay there. I couldn't get up to reach that ball to save my life! Finally, one of the other outfielders came over and threw it in."*

Beyond the easy caricatures, what do we know about the inner life of ballplayers?

We do know that at some point in their careers Paul and Lloyd Waner joined the Freemasons fraternal organization. Other ballplayers such as Earle Combs, Ty Cobb, Rogers Hornsby, Branch Rickey, and Honus

21. A Hallowed Hitsmith

Wagner were Masons. What this means is unclear—Masons are lively in charity activities and represent a harmless "old boys club" to many. On the other hand, conspiracy theorists would say that Masons harbor a "secret fraternity" that helps professionals and workers alike advance through the ranks into positions of power. The truth is probably somewhere in the middle.

Paul did enjoy reading, we know that, with a definite baseball spin. His favorite sportswriter was Ring Lardner. He even corresponded with Lardner, and treasured the letters he received from the *You Know Me, Al* creator.

Lardner was one of the few sportswriters who graduated to higher callings in the literary world. Using the fictional rookie Jack Keefe, Lardner was able to turn a spotlight on the baseball world in a way unrivaled until the appearance of *Ball Four* decades later. Keefe starred in a series of vignettes that were combined into book form as *You Know Me, Al*. Much of the humor was derived from the difference between what Jack said and what Lardner implied. *The Chicago Tribune* ran the stories in comic strip form for years. Lardner also wrote gothic, non-baseball stories like "Haircut," and many of his writings became standard reading in college English courses.

Most significant, Lardner immediately had suspected the Chicago White Sox of throwing the 1919 World Series to Cincinnati. While others turned a blind eye, he walked through the team's railroad car during the ride back from Cincinnati to Chicago parodying, "I'm Forever Blowing Bubbles," a popular song of the day, by singing instead, "I'm Forever Blowing Ballgames." Disillusioned with the game in the wake of the Black Sox scandal, Larder quit covering baseball and turned his talents elsewhere. He died at age 48 in 1933—during the peak of Paul Waner's career.

Lardner and his baseball passion wasn't always taken seriously by the snobby literary types. Novelist F. Scott Fitzgerald said of Lardner upon the old sportswriter's death, "Ring moved in the company of a few dozen illiterates playing a boy's game. A boy's game with no more possibilities than a boy could master, a game bounded by walls which kept out danger, change or adventure."

Paul would have gladly been a boy playing the game in 1942. But his skills and body were of a 39-year-old who refused to call it quits before squeezing out every last drop of game.

He had some big hits, though, and helped the Braves play the role of spoiler that season. As late as mid–August, the Dodgers had what seemed to be an insurmountable 10½-game lead. On August 4, however, the Cardinals swept a doubleheader from Brooklyn and suddenly caught fire.

With Dodgers phenom Pete Reiser suffering from a head injury, Brooklyn stumbled the rest of the way.

In one critical September game, Paul smacked a hit to win a game against Brooklyn. It drove a stake through the heart of the Dodgers and their pennant chances. A few days later Paul was asked how it felt to knock off the gasping Dodgers. He guessed right on the pitch, Big Poison replied, not taking the bait to kick the Bums when they were down.

Paul Waner: *"I do a lot of guessing with certain pitchers. That particular hurler had two strikes and no balls on me and he generally tries to fool me with a hook when he has me in the hole. So I relaxed with the idea of making him believe I would look at the pitch. Up it came, and right on the inside corner. All I had to do was swing hard."*

Paul finished that season with a .258 average in 333 at bats. So many intangibles exist in older players—besides bringing a decent bat off the bench, Paul's veteran presence helped calm the younger players, and he had an encyclopedic knowledge of the league, its pitchers and players.

Paul thought through his at bats carefully, especially as he got older and did not have the whip-like swing of his youth. Sometimes the drama between Paul and a pitcher played out over the course of an entire season.

Paul Waner: *"Look, a smart pitcher always is trying to build up a batter to a letdown. A smart hitter should do the same thing. For example, when I was playing with the Braves against the Dodgers, Whit Wyatt [a Dodgers pitcher] went to work on me one day in Brooklyn. When he got two runs ahead, he threw me fast balls as well as curves outside if there was nobody on base. He was trying to find out if I had the power to pull his high, hard one. If I showed I could by hitting one over the fence, he'd still be a run ahead, and he'd know what not to throw me in the clutch. I was thinking right with him, and I knew one run wouldn't help us. So I backed away and fouled that inside pitch to left field, giving him the impression that he was too fast for me to pull. All the time I was telling myself the time would come in the game when I could win it by unloading on that pitch.*

"I was right, too, but sound strategy robbed me of that chance. I came up in the eighth with men on first and second, and none out. A home run would win the game, and I knew I'd get Whit's fast one inside again. I got it, too, and I'm confident I could have hit it out of the park but I had to sacrifice. I couldn't take a chance on popping up. The percentage called for a bunt."

But playing on the moribund Boston club had its drawbacks. This team faced even greater odds than Pittsburgh in ever winning a pennant. So the players had to demonstrate their competitive natures somehow.

21. A Hallowed Hitsmith

Paul Waner: *"When I was in Boston we were in last place late in the season. The Phillies, too, were near the cellar. Neither team wanted to finish last, of course. So the Phillies and Braves would fight like heck when they played. We wanted to beat each other to keep from being in the cellar. We'd save up our best pitchers and get everybody in tip-top shape for those games."*

While Paul made headlines in 1942, Lloyd was tucked away in the box scores. In 101 games for the war-depleted Phillies, Lloyd hit .261 with 10 extra base hits. He appeared in 26 of those games as a pinch hitter or runner.

When the Phillies would play the Boston Braves, the Waners were united again—on opposing sides. With Lloyd three years Paul's junior, he could rub it in a little at this point in their waning careers.

Paul Waner: *"Lloyd seldom misses a chance to get a dig in. Last time we played the Phils, he said, 'Why don't you quit and give us young fellows a chance? You're all washed up, anyhow.'"*

Some of Lloyd's fly-catching ability rubbed off on fellow Phillies Danny Litwhiler. The left-fielder was a bright spot on a dismal 42–109 Phillies team. Litwhiler played 151 games that season without making an error, setting a record for major league outfielders. Tutored by Lloyd on how to play the outfield, Litwhiler had 308 put outs and nine assists in his errorless year.

Both Little and Big Poison were aging gracefully, not showing the bitterness that sometimes accompanies a veteran on the way down. They would continue to display this attitude well after their playing days. Later in the 1950s, when Paul reflected on which era of ballplayers was the best, his opinion was unselfish and realistic. He also admitted to not knowing everything about baseball and learning more about the game at the tail end of his career.

Paul Waner: *"See that man over there? He was trying to make me feel good by telling me that the present day ballplayer isn't near as good as the old-timer, or even fellows who were playing with me. I surprised him by telling him that players are better today than ever. They're bigger, faster and smarter. They're taught more today. Managers and coaches pay more attention to them. After I'd been in the National League for 15 years I was learning things somebody should have told me when I was breaking in. For example, there's the pitch with the infield in. You know it's going to be a low pitch because they want you to hit the ball on the ground. But nobody ever told me that when I was a kid. It wasn't until I got with the Braves [in 1941] that Casey Stengel taught me to move up in the box when bunting. That way I had more fair territory to aim at."*

Stengel himself expressed mild astonishment at Paul's lack of formal training—and beginner's mind when it came to seeking out knowledge.

Casey Stengel: *"It's hard to believe that he didn't know how to drag a bunt. But he didn't. I showed him early this year, and he watched very carefully. Twice he's tried it, and both times he's beat out hits. But I'll tell what I like about Waner. He still wears the same hat. I mean, he's been a great player in this game, but as the manager you would never know it. He never squawks, or kicks about anything. Whatever you want him to do is all right with him. He never comes up with alibis or complains about things not breaking right for him. I'd like to have a whole ball club with everybody on like him."*

Amid the baseball, there was a war going on. After the season in November 1942, Paul joined Paul Derringer of Cincinnati and Butch Henline of the Boston Braves in setting up a physical conditioning program at Drew Field, a military base outside of Tampa, Florida.

Speaking for the trio, Derringer said, "We want to do something to help in the war effort and believe we can do a great deal in the conditioning program of the soldiers."

After the season Stengel visited Paul in Florida, and he would come back North with new respect for Paul's drinking durability. According to Stengel, Paul would wake up at dawn to go fishing with his teenaged son, Paul Jr. He'd come in, eat breakfast, practice baseball until past noon, eat lunch, and then go golfing. After dinner, he'd go out drinking, and then repeat the whole process the next day.

Same old Big Poison.

Wearying War Years

You never had time to learn. They threw you in and told you the rules and the first time they caught you off base they killed you.
— *Ernest Hemingway, in* A Farewell to Arms

Hemingway could well have been writing about wartime baseball. World War II gave the Waners a chance to play a little longer as most of the draft-age men went overseas. By 1943, big league teams had come to relish veterans and physically deferred "4-Fers"—players with some chronic condition, such as allergies, color blindness, ulcers, subpar hearing, or minor heart problems. Three outstanding American League players fit the 4-F bill—Lou Boudreau, Cleveland's player/manager who at age 24 was bothered by heel spurs; Vern Stephens, the St. Louis Browns' slugging young shortstop who suffered from extreme allergies; and Hal Newhouser, a pitcher for Detroit who despite a heart murmur was the best hurler in the majors in 1944–1945. An extreme example of a 4-Fer was the one-armed outfielder, Pete Gray, of the Browns.

Both the Waners knew their services were more valuable in this type of player market. Besides, it gave Paul a chance to add to his career-hits total—3,042 and still climbing.

Paul Waner: *"I knew I wasn't going to last forever. I played as long as my legs could carry me. It just happened to be during the war years that I was useful to some clubs. If it hadn't been so, if there were more younger fellows around, I wouldn't have been able to play because I wouldn't have been good enough. I mean, I was mostly a pinch-hitter anyway."*

The Waners were joined in their prolonged careers by, most notably, 38-year-old Luke Appling of the White Sox, 37-year-old fellow Oklahoman Bob Johnson of the Red Sox, 37-year-old Jimmie Foxx who managed some at bats for the Cubs and Phillies, and Babe Herman, who at 37 had not appeared in a game since 1937. Several underage players also made debuts—15-year-old Joe Nuxhall of the Reds was the extreme example.

In January, 1943, both Waner brothers were in New York City for another sports banquet. The writer Chilly Doyle noted how relaxed Paul was in the glow of a golden career winding down.

Chilly Doyle: "At 40, brother Paul has a good chance to be a topflight Dodger in the coming baseball race, and he's still a totally relaxed athlete who might be coaxed into taking a sip of beer or a high ball on top of a hot day on the diamond, whereas brother Lloyd, if he lives up to his known habits, will be in bed and up with the chickens, daylight time to the contrary notwithstanding."

While their personalities were different, Doyle said he never saw any problems between the two—"not even the hint of a snide trick or anything showing a lack of sportsmanship."

Sometimes the late-rising Paul would arrive to the ballpark just in time for batting practice, Doyle said. Lloyd would be there already. But no matter how early Lloyd got there and how late Paul rolled in, it was Paul who got the better of the pitchers over the long run. He seemed more robust than his younger brother, Doyle wrote.

"Lloyd was also a worry to the pitchers, but he did not enjoy the glow of health always felt by Paul, despite Lloyd's careful manner of living," the writer observed.

In an example of how newspaper writers sometimes protected the players in that day and age, Doyle defended Paul against charges of excessive drinking. "Those folks who put down Paul as a heavy drinker were as wrong as a left-handed shortstop. Actually Paul was a light eater and light drinker and could relax without effort."

On January 19, Paul could hardly relax. That day he learned the Boston Braves had unconditionally released him.

He quickly signed on with the Dodgers for his second round of duty with them.

Not long thereafter Lloyd surprised everyone by refusing to sign with the Phillies and retiring to Oklahoma City. He must have looked askance at another season of 100 or so losses with one of the worst clubs in the majors.

It made the Phillies unhappy. Manager Hans Lobert said, "We'll miss him. He was a big help to our outfielders. I signed him two years ago as insurance, and he showed (outfielders) Dan Litwhiler, Ron Northey, and Earl Naylor a lot of things about outfield play."

Now an "Average Joe" in the war effort, Lloyd went to work for Douglass Aircraft where he played on the company's baseball team. *The Sporting News* observed, "Like the fighter who sees his punch fading, he prefers his slippers and an easy chair to taking a licking from fellows he used to laugh at."

Back in Oklahoma, Lloyd said he was content in his retirement and wouldn't report to the Phillies unless "my feet begin to itch." They never did that season.

In June, Lloyd attended a banquet in Oklahoma City honoring fellow Oklahoman Carl Hubbell. Though the Waners and Hubbell had grown up only 16 miles apart, they first got to know each other in high school when their schools played against each other. The 1943 season was Hubbell's last one in a career spanning 16 years and 253 victories.

At the dinner, Hubbell surprised everyone, perhaps good-naturedly, that he'd wish he had known the Waners earlier on than high school. He secretly harbored a desire to be a hitter.

Carl Hubbell: *"I've always wanted to be a hitter. When I take my bat, stroll to the plate, and get set for the pitch, I always look at my shadow. To me, it looked just as good as Ruth's, Hornsby's, the Waners' or any of the other great hitters. But when the ball came sailing up there and I take a cut at it, something always goes wrong. Those Waner cobs might have made a hitter out of me."*

The 1943 season was a point of departure for the two brothers. Paul couldn't get baseball out of his system, and Lloyd wanted some relief from it, at least for awhile. Big Poison was turning 40 that spring, and Lloyd was 37.

Ted McGrew, chief scout for Brooklyn, predicted a big season for Paul, almost likening him to an ageless wonder. It was a bit of a stretch.

"I wouldn't be surprised if he hit .350. He hits inside balls solidly and makes line drives on them all because of that wrist snap and perfect control of his bat," McGrew told the beat writers.

Dodgers general manager Branch Rickey hoped that Paul and the other motley mix of youngsters and oldsters in Brooklyn's lineup could pull off some magic. "We'll be all right. With kids and over-age men, and 4-fs, we'll get along."

Actually, Brooklyn didn't have many outfield options that season.

When Paul reported to spring training with the Dodgers, he came along with friend and new Dodgers recruit Johnny Cooney. At 42, Cooney was in his 19th season, having just been released from the Boston Braves like Paul. Both of them worked out in Sarasota for 10 days before the Dodgers opened their camp in West Point, New York. They were described as the "slimmest, trimmest, and most tanned outfielders" that manager Leo Durocher had on his roster sheet.

Rickey had signed Waner and Cooney to replace one of the best players in the game, Pete Reiser, who was now in the Army. Clearly, these were desperate times for baseball clubs. Worried about first baseman Dolph Camilli's availability, Rickey even signed his old favorite, George Sisler to what was ostensibly described as a scouting contract but what was really an insurance pick-up just in case. At 50, Sisler had not played in the majors for the past 13 years since 1930. Nor, as it turned out, would he that season. But so went the back-up plans hatching around the player-depleted major leagues.

There was a lot of scrambling to put bodies on the field. After Lloyd rejected the Phillies early that spring, Brooklyn was able to list him as "voluntary retired" in case he decided to return. Asked about his brother Lloyd's silence on whether he'd play in the upcoming season, Paul said he had not heard a word, even after writing Lloyd twice and his parents once.

But that didn't matter, he said. "Oh, he'll be here after awhile," replied Big Poison.

Cooney, overhearing the question, said, "Yeah, all of us think we're going to quit, but it's pretty hard to leave the game."

Sometimes it was just hard to "see" the game for the older players.

Paul Waner: *"For the last couple of years, the ball looked bigger and blurrier than it used to and I had trouble in locating it after it left the pitcher's hand until it was almost on top of me. Since using these glasses in a game, the ball looks smaller and clearer and I can follow it all the way."*

One of Paul's competitors for playing time was Luis Olmo, a young outfielder from Puerto Rico. The 24-year-old was called up to the Dodgers from the minors in July and took the right field spot in a game against Cincinnati. Olmo, a lithe and speedy sort, was discovered by the scout McGrew. He could hit for power and had a strong arm. And, as Tim Cohane of the *New York World Telegram* observed, "He runs like a Southeastern Conference halfback."

Olmo would hit .303 in 57 games that season. The next two years he started full-time in Brooklyn's outfield, hitting .258 in '44 and .313 in '45 when he also led the league with 13 triples. However, his big league career

22. Wearying War Years

was short-lived, as he missed the next two years and only saw limited action from 1949 to 1951.

According to *Total Baseball*, the first known Puerto Rican to play in the major leagues was Hiram Bithorn, who joined the Chicago Cubs in 1942 and preceded Olmo by one year. The Santurce native won 18 games for the Cubs in 1943. A few years before Jackie Robinson, this showed some willingness to recruit players of color.

The 1943 season opened amid complaints about the new official ball introduced by the A. G. Spalding company to meet war rationing requirements. With an interior made of reclaimed cork and balata instead of rubber and cork, the new ball was for all intents and purposes a Dead Ball. About 25 percent less resilient than the balls used the season before, the 1943 ball resulted in 11 shutouts in the first 29 games that season. The manufacturer quickly reintroduced another version, and run production picked up gradually.

Controversy followed the Dodgers that season. One of the low points came when Dodgers second baseman Billy Herman, after lining out, threw a ball into the dugout and hit Leo Durocher between the eyes. Herman was angered because Durocher gave him two take signs with the count at 2-0. In another wacky incident, umpire George Barr called a balk on Dodgers pitcher Johnny Allen. The pitcher went berserk, and nearly choked Barr with his own tie—leading to the end of tie-wearing among umpires.

When the Dodgers played their cross-town rivals, the Giants, Carl Hubbell was asked what made Paul Waner a great hitter. It was question he heard often during his career.

Carl Hubbell: *"You can shift around your infield and outfield on most strong hitters to play to their power, and they seldom cross you up. But you couldn't do that with Paul. He is the greatest I have ever seen at hitting any pitch wherever there was a hole—in the infield or outfield. Say you threw him an inside pitch, as I have done, and figured he would have to pull it. Waner would still smash it to left if the hole was there. You just had to play Paul straightaway and take your chances. The secret, of course, was that Waner gave absolutely no tip-off on his intention by change of stance or grip. The whole of his hitting, as far as direction was involved, was in his wrists."*

Writer Fred Lieb said Paul Waner "rarely hit a bad pitch and had strong, sinewy wrists, forearms, and shoulders, intuitive timing, and split-second reactions." Another writer, Harry Keck, described Paul as a "late hitter with great wrist action and could hit to all fields, and was a master at playing drives off the right field stand."

All these were skills that Paul utilized as he settled into his role as a pinch hitter—one of the best around, too.

When Paul had the rare starting assignment, he could show glimmers of glory. On May 5, he started a game in right field for the first time that season, slamming two doubles and two singles—all vicious line drives—as the Dodgers routed the hapless Phillies 18–6. On June 14, he punched out two doubles in four at bats, and on June 30, he homered and doubled, going 3 for 5. But as the season wore on, Paul infrequently started in the outfield. In August and September, he only started four games total and was used as a pinch hitter on most occasions.

In 54 pinch-hit at bats for Brooklyn that season, Paul compiled a .519 on base average with 14 hits and 13 walks. As he grew older, Paul seemed more willing to take a walk, and his eagle-eye pitch selection benefited him.

Big Poison drank at the fountain of youth that season. Overall, he hit .311 in 225 at bats and played in just over half of his team's games, 82. He had 16 doubles and one home run.

It opened his eyes to another season. Heck, if he could hit over .300 in part-time duty, he wasn't ready just yet to hang up the cleats.

◆ ◆ ◆

So confident of his success in 1943, Paul was able to convince his brother Lloyd to give baseball another try. Lloyd loved baseball as much as his brother, though he felt that even at three years his junior his time had already passed him. Still, the idea of playing again on the same team intrigued Little Poison.

Having dropped out of baseball the prior year, Lloyd, 38, received permission from Commissioner Kenesaw Mountain Landis for reinstatement. It wasn't an easy decision for Lloyd, who had told many friends he had planned to keep his job at the aircraft plant in Oklahoma City and continue to serve as a volunteer fireman at the nearby Will Rogers Air Base. Paul persuaded him to come back, and now Lloyd was slated to share Brooklyn's center field duties with the veteran Dixie Walker.

In February 1944, Lloyd and Paul were headed to the Dodgers spring training camp. They expected to play another full season together—the first time since 1940.

Branch Rickey, general manager of the Dodgers, also hinted that his 39-year-old manager, Leo Durocher, might have to play infield in light of the shortage of available players.

Branch Rickey: *"I think that Durocher will have to give serious consideration to conditioning himself to play ball."*

22. Wearying War Years

It did not turn out that way for Durocher. The manager made the wise move of benching himself.

Neither did Lloyd make much of an impression that spring. By June, Brooklyn had given him his unconditional release. At 38, Lloyd Waner was one of five players that Rickey and Durocher agreed to release on the last day they were allowed to trim their rosters down to 25 men. It was brief duty for pinch-hitting Lloyd—in 15 games he came to bat 14 times and managed 4 hits, all singles. He played in the field four times.

After his release, Lloyd was picked up by the Pittsburgh Pirates, no doubt, as both a fan favorite and practical necessity during the wartime conditions. With Pittsburgh in 1944, Lloyd had 5 hits in 14 at bats for a .357 average. He played in the outfield seven times.

From the start in 1944, the Waners were quizzed by sportswriters as to the state of the game in these war-weary times. Paul tried to sound upbeat. It was obvious that the war had taken a toll on the caliber of talent in the majors.

Paul Waner: *"It will be a big year for good hitters. I'll tell you why. The armed forces have taken the bulk of the superstars. As a result, play in general won't be up to prewar par. That's no secret to anyone. Hitting, pitching, fielding all figure to fall off. But the good hitter will get the principal break. He won't be facing many good pitchers and he will be less frequently robbed of a hit by sensational fielding. Pitchers will turn in lower earned run averages, but will find it harder to win. The answer to that, of course, will be inferior fielding. Runs will be cheaper. There will be a lot of one run innings in which only one hit is made."*

Paul got some good ink during the war-weary season. Tim Cohane of the *New York World-Telegram* wrote that Paul Waner was "still a threat" as a pinch hitter, and penned poems about him:

> Paul Waner, still at 41
> a wizard with the wand
> came up again to have his fun
> with ducks on the pond
> three thousand hits and more he made
> incredible sums
> what was another, more or less
> to save the Brooklyn Bums?

The wizard managed some key hits early on in 1943. In April, Paul delivered a pinch hit against the Phillies' Curt Davis to drive in the winning run for Brooklyn. On June 1, Brooklyn lost a game to Pittsburgh 2–1, but Big Poison connected in the eighth inning for a hard-hit single in his 12th pinch-hit appearance of the year. The shot caromed off the first-base bag and eluded the Pirates' Babe Dahlgren. Though the Dodgers rally eventually died, it seemed Waner had some hard hits still in him.

Still, aging pinch hitters are not high priorities for teams not headed to the postseason like Brooklyn. In September, the Dodgers placed him on waivers. He was hitting .287 at the time.

Acting as a free agent after the Dodgers had placed him on waivers, Paul fielded inquiries from the Yankees, Browns, Tigers, and Red Sox—interestingly, all American League clubs. The Yankees picked up Paul right away.

A bit of confusion existed about the episode. In releasing the popular Paul Waner, the Dodgers' Branch Rickey sought to look magnanimous, but it backfired. Initially Rickey told reporters he was releasing Paul with complete pay for the season (which proved true) but early enough before the deadline for players to join another team and still receive World Series benefits. As it was revealed, the Dodgers did not release Paul until just after the deadline passed, and so when he joined the Yankees in late '44, (which the Dodgers knew he would), he was not eligible for championship pay. It would have meant $7,500 for Paul. As it turned out, New York gave Paul a $500 signing bonus and assured him a slice of the World Series pie if the Yankees made it. Though New York had made the Series the previous three years, they would miss the mark this time around.

On September 1, 1944, in Paul's first game ever in the American League, the Yankees lost, 10–7, to the Washington Senators. New York melted down in the eighth inning when they coughed up five runs. Paul, in his first plate appearance, singled home a run in the sixth inning. He was pinch-hitting for pitcher Steve Roser. It would be his only hit in the American League and the last hit of his 20-year career. It came off Washington rookie Arnold Thesenga.

After the game, New York was in third place, two games behind the surprising league-leading St. Louis Browns and the surging Detroit Tigers.

At the time, much speculation focused on the possibly sudden return of Joe DiMaggio to the Yankees. Amazingly, Ed Barrow, the New York general manager, was quoted as saying that if DiMaggio was released from the Army, New York would not make the roster cut to allow Joltin' Joe back on the club. It proved a moot point, for DiMaggio did not return to the Yankees until 1946.

Paul found himself in a jam once he joined the Yankees. He spouted off opinions like a veteran, but he was no longer on his home turf, and it

22. Wearying War Years

showed. In the last few hectic days of the pennant race, he told Dan Daniel of the *New York World Telegram* that the Detroit Tigers would win the AL pennant—because they had the league's best pitching. In the National League, Big Poison said the St. Louis Cardinals "hasn't the fierceness of the Gas House Gang." Losing Enos Slaughter and Terry Moore to the war deprived the Cardinals of some key bats as well as their field leadership. Worst of all, he was quoted as saying the National League plays "smarter ball" than the American.

An upset manager Joe McCarthy called Paul into his office to explain himself. Waner denied the story, saying he had never given such an interview or said anything to that effect. Rumor had it that Waner was on the brink of getting an unconditional release if the interview had been traced back to him. McCarthy relented, allowing both Paul and the Yankees to both save face.

Sometimes that season Paul felt simply like he was in the wrong place. Once while he was playing the outfield at Yankee Stadium a fan in the bleachers yelled out, "Hey, Paul, how come you're in the outfield for the Yankees?"

"Because," Waner replied, "Joe DiMaggio's in the army."

The Yankees finished in third place, behind the Tigers in second and the Browns in first. The Cardinals went on to win the World Series in '44, beating the cross-town St. Louis Browns—the Brownies' one and only pennant. The Cardinals still had a guy named Stan Musial.

One of the most poignant recollections of that season came from Ellis Clary and Don Gutteridge of the St. Louis Browns. They were on the field against Waner in his next-to-the-last major league plate appearance. At the time, the Browns were battling the Yankees to win the pennant in the closing days of the season.

Waner almost spoiled it for St. Louis.

Ellis Clary: *"They put up Paul Waner to pinch hit with the bases loaded. Paul Waner was my all-time, all-time, all-time hero when I was a young'un. In my book no one else played the game like Paul Waner. I said to myself, 'Jesus Crist Almighty, here's my all-time man walking up there to pinch hit. He's gonna knock me out of the World Series. This is terrible.' It was the only time in my life I've ever pulled against him. And he hit a line drive at Don Gutteridge that ended it. He hit that ball, and Gutteridge jumped up and caught it."*

Don Gutteridge: *"Paul Waner pinch-hit, and there was a man on second base, and he hit it over my head, kind of a looper. I went back and caught* *the ball backhanded with my back to the infield. I made one hell of a play, if I say that myself. And that was the third out of the inning.*

"*Two or three years later, I was in Florida, and Paul Waner said, 'Don, I'll tell you something. You caught the last ball I ever hit in the major leagues.'*

"*Isn't that something?*"

End of Encores

> Annie and I were in Cooperstown once. We looked at Shoeless Joe Jackson's shoes reposing under glass. "How come a guy named Shoeless Joe had shoes?" Annie wanted to know.
> — *W. P. Kinsella, in his book,* Shoeless Joe

Nineteen forty-five was a monumental year, the end of an era and the beginning of a new one. That year Adolf Hitler killed himself in a Berlin bunker and the war ended in Europe, President Roosevelt died and Vice President Harry S. Truman was inaugurated as president, atomic bombs were dropped on a soon-to-be-defeated Japan, and George Orwell published *Animal Farm*, a powerful metaphorical novel about repression. Almost overnight around the world, the phrase "Kilroy was here" appeared, at least wherever American GIs set foot, on streets, billboards, latrines, walls and other available surfaces. Kilroy represented a kind of abstract conglomerate of all GIs.

It was a year of changes in baseball as well. A new baseball commissioner, Albert B. "Happy" Chandler, was selected in the wake of Kenesaw Mountain Landis's death, both the Dodgers and Yankees were sold to new owners, and Abbott and Costello introduced the "Who's On First?" classic baseball comedy routine. In late October, Dodgers general manager Branch Rickey stunned the baseball world by signing a black, Jack Roosevelt Robinson, to play in Brooklyn's minor league system the next season. It was the beginning of the end of the color ban.

The year 1945 was also the end of the Waners.

Lloyd signed on again with the Pittsburgh Pirates that season, coming full circle on his sentimental journey. *The Sporting News* in early 1945 noted the return of Lloyd to the Pirates.

"Little Poison did not get much of a chance to work last year, but he was, and is, a swell insurance policy to have around. One of baseball's most beloved veterans, especially in Pirates circles, where he played for more than 14 years after first coming up to the big show, and a very popular chord was struck when the Pittsburgh club brought him back to Forbes Field on June 18 last year, following his release by Brooklyn, which made him a free agent. No better liked player ever wore Buccaneer flannels."

One of Lloyd Waner's fellow Pirates that 1945 season was Rip Sewell, the "eephus" ball pitcher. While he had pitched for the Pirates since 1938, it wasn't until the war years that Sewell introduced his blooper ball. When Sewell first started throwing the pitch, he had more trouble from the umpires than hitters. It could reach an arc of 25 feet and would baffle the hitters, who often swung and missed. Few if any could hit it for a home run.

Rip Sewell: *"Some of the umpires said they wouldn't call it a strike, no way. I heard about that and told Frisch. He became concerned because that damned pitch was becoming a drawing card. We had people coming in from West Virginia and Ohio and everywhere else just to see it."*

The Pirates management had Bill Klem, the National League supervisor of umpires, check out whether the eephus ball could be thrown as a strike. He had Sewell throw a few to a catcher, and gave it his blessing—"Okay. It's a strike, and I'll see that they all hit," he said.

That season Lloyd Waner appeared in 23 games for the Pirates, mostly as a pinch hitter, and played three games on his old outfield turf of Forbes Field. In 19 at bats, he had five hits for a .263 average. He struck out three times in those 19 at bats, unusual for a guy who took on average almost 45 at bats before striking out.

After his last game on September 25, Lloyd hung a sweaty uniform up in the clubhouse and talked with reporters. He told them he had asked the Pirates to give him his unconditional release. But the hard part, the misty-eyed Little Poison said, was suddenly realizing he would not wear a major league uniform again.

Lloyd Waner: *"I'll probably never wear one again. But I won't be out of baseball. I'll be around next year. I have some business to take care of, or I'd stay the rest of the season."*

As he dressed, Lloyd said he planned to catch a train southwest to

23. End of Encores

Oklahoma where his farm and family awaited him. He made certain not to close the door on opportunities with the Pirates. The organization might hire him next spring, as manager Frankie Frisch indicated.

Frankie Frisch: *"He'll be connected with the club next year. You can count on that."*

When he retired, the diminutive Lloyd Waner was one of the finest ballplayers of his era. His lifetime .316 average and 2,459 hits put him in a rare class of center fielders and lead-off hitters. His greatest asset—speed—is not as quantifiable as other yardsticks of excellence, but it helped him achieve superlatively on both offense and defense.

Fielding prowess is difficult to express statistically, but there are a few numbers worth mentioning about Lloyd. Range can be measured by total chances per game, and in this category Lloyd ranks 10th among all major leaguers ever with 2.81 chances per game. Taylor Douthit, who played for the Cardinals in the 1930s, is first with 3.16 per game, and Richie Ashburn of the Philadelphia Phillies is second at 3.04 per game. Lloyd's 2.68 put outs per game is 9th best all-time. He could get to fly balls like a cat on a bird.

Bill James, in his *Historical Baseball Abstract*, posthumously credits Lloyd with eight gold glove awards from 1927 to 1937.

The uniform Lloyd wore in the final game of his career ended up with Art Bissell who lived near Pittsburgh. Apparently, Lloyd had given the uniform and glove to Bissell, an avid memorabilia collector and professional clothier, sometime in the late '50s or early '60s. News reports indicate that Bissell had an amazing assortment of objects, including an unrivaled Honus Wagner collection and a ball signed by pitchers Leon Cadore and Joe Oeschler who battled in a record-setting 26-inning game between Brooklyn and Boston in 1920.

When Lloyd was inducted into the Hall of Fame in 1967, Lloyd requested that Bissell send it to the hallowed corridors of Cooperstown. Bissell did so.

◆ ◆ ◆

Before the 1945 season, 42-year-old Paul Waner told reporters he expected to play another two or three years. That was a bit optimistic. But the hits lured him on and on.

"When I look at the records and see how many hits fellows like Cobb and Speaker made, I get the notion I'm only a beginner," he said.

It's no secret Paul Waner faced self-induced obstacles to keeping in shape at that age. Some whispered that his heavy drinking had contributed to the numerous shifts in employment in his twilight years. He was not as reliable.

Paul saw it more as a physical decline problem.

Paul Waner: *"The game demands a lot more of a man these days. A player has to have everything now. He has to have speed of foot and a good throwing arm, and he has to be a finished fielder in addition to being a good batter if he hopes to stick in the major leagues. One bad fault now, and a player is mostly out of luck. Of course, I'm speaking of baseball before and after the war."*

The Yankees cast Paul Waner exclusively as a pinch hitter for the season ahead. Manager Joe McCarthy made Paul's role clear to writers when training camp in Florida opened. In return, Paul sounded notes of gratitude, though deep inside he wanted more playing time, like any competitively minded player.

"I'm satisfied with one hit a day now, so long as it helps win the game," the old Poison said.

Paul was a realist on retirement. The major leagues were a food chain of evolving player talent, with younger ones pushing in and older ones falling out. The natural course of events was to be expected.

Paul Waner: *"An old ballplayer is just like an old piece of furniture. Everyone's just wondering how much wear is left. When a young fellow comes along, somebody has to move over, and now it's me. I have no regrets."*

In the dying light of his professional baseball career, Paul Waner found ample time to share his thoughts on the subject of baseball.

Paul Waner: *"I'll tell you where I learned a lot of baseball. When I was with the Yankees, at the end of the line. I used to sit beside [manager] Joe McCarthy on the bench, and he taught me plenty. I wish I could have listened to somebody like Joe 20 years ago. As for home runs, it's a funny thing, but the home run took a lot of hits away from me. If I happened to hit a home run on Tuesday, I didn't hit much the rest of the week. Suddenly I thought I was a slugger, and of course I wasn't. But I did make three thousand hits. You have to steal a flock to get that high. I could run in those days. Still can. But not for very long.*

"The man who could run was my brother Lloyd. I've never seen anything like him. And his legs weren't any bigger 'round than this [holding his hands narrowly apart]. His step was as light as a feather. He could run through sand almost without leaving a print. Lloyd was so fast he'd even fool

23. End of Encores

the umpires. They'd see the ball coming and see Lloyd coming, and think he couldn't beat the throw. But he did, many times. He lost a lot of base hits that way. Nobody was as fast as he was."

Paul seemed content with pinch-hitting. But even that role eluded him.

He only got into one game in the 1945 season before the Yankees released him.

Paul's last major league appearance came in Philadelphia's Shibe Park when he pinch-hit for pitcher Al Gettel, drawing a walk. He was let go the next day, May 4, 1945.

At 42 and slowing down fast, Waner was "not exactly up to Yankee standards" as James Dawson of the *New York Times* put it.

The Yankees were trying to make room on their roster for the slugging outfielder Jeff Heath of the Cleveland Indians. Heath was embroiled in a bitter contract holdout early that season. The Indians were seeking offers on Heath from other teams. As it happened, Heath stayed with Cleveland that season.

Paul elicited some interest from Cleveland, depending on the outcome of Heath's holdout, and the Chicago White Sox.

But nothing materialized.

Finally, after 20 years and 2,549 games, it was the end of the road for Paul Waner. Only five players in the history of the game at that point had played in more games than Big Poison—Ty Cobb, Eddie Collins, Honus Wagner, Tris Speaker, and Rabbit Maranville.

Paul stood tall with 3,152 hits and a lifetime .333 average. The other numbers are spectacular as well—609 doubles, 191 triples, 1,627 runs scored, and 1,309 RBIs. And, not least of all, three batting titles and one Most Valuable Player award.

While one of the best contact hitters ever, Paul Waner was no "Punch and Judy" hitter. He banged out more than 900 extra-base hits and only struck out 376 times in 9,459 at bats. His .404 lifetime on-base average demonstrated a mastery of the strike zone.

Fleeing New York for Pittsburgh, Paul immediately signed on with a semi-pro baseball team in Dormont, a neighborhood just outside Pittsburgh. Dormont competed in the Greater Pittsburgh League. No statistics are available for how Paul did, but he just wanted to keep playing more ball.

After the season, Paul put some distance between him and the game when he joined a USO Tour of the China-Burma-India zone to help out with the war effort. Ironically, he was accompanied by fellow major leaguers

Luke Sewell (brother of Joe Sewell, the only player tougher than Lloyd to strike out) and Dixie Walker (brother of Harry Walker). The Walkers are the only two brothers to each win a batting title. Paul won three but Lloyd never won one.

One day the players were in a large mess hall when a bat—the flying kind—flew in through the window and zoomed about the room. Everyone ducked under the tables while the Indian staff raced to retrieve tennis racquets. Those were the only objects wide enough to hit the creature and bring him down.

Paul coolly rolled up a newspaper. As the bat whirled toward him, he stood poised as if at the plate. And then he swung, swatting down the bat.

Red Patterson, one of the trip's organizers, said to Waner, "Why Paul, think of your reputation as a great hitter. Suppose you had missed."

"So what?" Paul said. "I still would have had two strikes."

In the spring of 1946, Paul signed on as a player/manager/part-owner with the Miami team in the International League. While he hit .325, it didn't go well in other aspects. For once in his career, Paul verbally castigated the umpires. Maybe he was venting frustration at playing below the major league level for the first time in 20 years.

Paul Waner: *"I managed in Miami in '46. We had some terrible umpiring. One time I protested a game, and swore at the umpire. Called him everything in the book. And he says, 'Now, Paul, you've never been thrown out of a game. I don't want to put you out.'*

"And I says, 'Why, you son-of-a-bitch, you can have the honor of it. Just go ahead and have the honor of being the first one.'

"But he says, 'Yeah, you get away from here now or I'll throw you out.'"

Paul, who owned 20 percent of Miami's stock, was fired after the season. Four of the five club directors voted not to renew his contract. The lone dissenting vote came from Waner himself. The Class C team had lost money at the gate, and the other owners scrapped around for $26,000 to make up the difference.

Paul did not enjoy managing. The free-spirited Big Poison knew his strengths and weaknesses.

Paul Waner: *"I don't ask too much of the game. I have no ambition to be a manager. I tried it awhile in Miami after finishing in the big leagues, but it's not my kind of business. It isn't my nature to be tough, especially with kids who make fielding mistakes. I feel sorry for them."*

Years later Maury Allen weighed in on Paul's habits and preferences.

Maury Allen: *"One of the game's most notorious drunks, Paul Waner*

23. End of Encores

was always being annoyed by managers, preachers, and wives—he had a pair of them—to stop drinking.... [But] Waner had one of the smoothest, easiest strokes in the game. He held the bat loosely and could wait on a pitch before swinging until it was almost in the catcher's glove. He had eight seasons with 200 or more hits, won three batting titles, hit over .350 six times, and hit .325 at the age of 43 in his final professional season in the minors at Miami in 1946. There he served as a player-manager, but found dishing out discipline contrary to his style—he had too much of a soft spot for young ball players. So he quit."

Paul simply had a reputation for breaking rules. How could he enforce them? The same was said about another ballplayer of freakish talent, Babe Ruth. Despite being baseball's biggest drawing card during his career, the Babe was never asked to manage a major league club. In those days, owners were not about to turn over the club to someone who failed to dish out discipline.

Paul was feeling his time slipping by. At an age when other men are enjoying the peaks of their careers, Paul was getting the message that he was a "has-been" and an "over-the-hill" old man. Such is the arc of life for a baseball player. The whole career seems to flash by most noticeably in the very final moments, Paul said.

Paul Waner: *"Those 24 years that I played baseball—from 1923 to 1946—somehow, it doesn't seem like I played even a month. It went so fast. The first four or five years, I felt like I'd been in baseball a long time. Then, suddenly, I'd been in the Big Leagues for ten years. And then, all at once, it was twenty.... Somehow ... I don't know ... it seems like it all happened only yesterday."*

Speculation revolved around Paul's ability to keep in shape. Fred Lieb saw—and wrote—a lot about the Waners, especially Paul.

Fred Lieb: *"Frequent imbibing was a problem with Paul and it accounted in part for his numerous shifts in his twilight years. It has frequently been said that Waner could have been an even greater player had he led a more temperate life."*

Paul, according to Lieb, would have none of that.

Paul Waner: *"I'll admit I did my share of drinking. But I was a sociable type and stories of my drinking were exaggerated. I'm proud of the record I left in the baseball books, and I do not think any player who was a real lush could have remained in the majors for 20 years, batted out 3,152 hits and hit .333."*

Now, what would the Waner brothers do in extra-innings life beyond baseball?

The Professor of Batting

> Francis remembered the color and shape of his glove, its odor of oil and sweat and leather, and he wondered if Annie had kept it. Apart from his memory and a couple of clippings, it would be all that remained of a spent career that had blossomed and then peaked in the big leagues far too long after the best years were gone, but which brought with the peaking the promise that some belated glory was possible, that somewhere there was hosannah to be cried in the name of Francis Phelan, one of the best sonsabitches to ever kick a toe into third base.
> — *William Kennedy, from* Ironweed

Today it's easier for a major league ballplayer to retire knowing they have a baseball pension and money in the bank to look forward to. In the mid–1940s when players like the Waners retired, they had none of this financial security. Salaries, of course, were more modest in pre-free agent days; baseball pensions were non-existent. Both Paul and Lloyd would never collect a baseball pension, having retired a year too early to be eligible. Ironically, Pittsburgh was ground zero for the player's budding union movement that would produce such benefits as pensions.

After the upheaval of the war years, the history textbooks say, America sought a return to normalcy in 1946. Yet at the same time the post-war years issued forth some of the greatest changes in American society, from race relations to the rise of the middle class and powerful labor unions. To be sure, these were not normal times.

By 1946, the war industry had greatly strengthened the power and appeal of union labor. Pittsburgh, home of the steel industry, was a strong union town. That year an attorney named Robert Murphy organized the American Baseball Guild among Pirates players. In June his call for a strike vote carried by only 20–16, falling short of the required two-thirds needed for major league baseball to formally certify the union. While the guild died, the warning it sent the owners was clear—they had to appease the players somehow.

Still, many players did not immediately feel comfortable about endorsing unionism. The case had not yet been made for their self-interest in organizing on a labor front. For many, unions smacked of Communism and everything un–American.

Oddly enough, Paul Waner did not support the rise of unionism in baseball, even after years of wrangling with owners over every penny in his contract. At the time of the Pittsburgh crisis—it was for the owners—Paul was playing and coaching at Miami in the International League. When asked by writers he made clear his stance on unions.

Paul Waner: *"Guilds have no place in baseball. I was in the big leagues 20 years and never once figured I was being underpaid or mistreated. Baseball is very generous and has kept quite a number of fellows from pushing plows for a living."*

So baseball patriotic were Paul's comments—and off the mark, considering how many times he held out for higher pay—one might think major league baseball's public relations machine penned them. With retired greats talking like this and exposing the rear flank, player unionists had no chance to shift public and player attitudes.

Still, the owners were businessmen by and large, and they could sense danger on the labor front when they saw and heard it. To defuse the situation, they created a modest pension plan, the first of its kind in the major leagues. A player had to be in the majors five full years to be eligible. After the age of 50, a five-year player would get $50 a month for life, a 10-year player, $100, and so on.

Paul later changed his tune. After his induction to the Hall of Fame, Paul told writers that Hall members who played before the pension plan was adopted should be entitled to receive benefits. It was, he believed, yet another example of the owners overlooking the players who had made the game great.

Paul Waner: *"I don't say it should be full benefits—but in some way. I know quite a few Hall of Fame players where a few hundred a month would be very, very nice for them and I believe they really deserve it. I think it's kind of a slur on baseball that they're not in it."*

With such a modest start on the pension plan, the players finally got the owners to upgrade the pension plan in 1954, but those who retired before 1946 never got included. While the pensions stayed at the same level, the pension fund would get guaranteed funding from All-Star game receipts and 60 percent of the World Series radio-television money. This was the year that the Major League Baseball Players Association attained formal existence.

So Paul began a second career—as a hitting coach. He would be one of the first such specialists in major league baseball. His credentials of 3,152 hits and a lifetime .333 average were at the top of his resume and on the tip of his tongue when he sought work.

Paul had a missionary zeal about the role of batting instruction in the majors. As late as the 1950s, teams usually did not employ full-time hitting coaches. That began to change with the spreading of the gospel by Paul Waner and others. During the 1950s he published a 34-page pamphlet on hitting, *Paul Waner's Batting Secrets*, that sold for 50 cents. It appears Waner actually wrote the text, with illustrations provided by Martin Filchock. Nick Robertson, sports editor of the *Sarasota Herald-Tribune* and a friend of Waner's in his adopted hometown of Sarasota, wrote the introduction. The first thing Robertson points out is the physical underdog nature of Paul Waner.

Nick Robertson: *"How many records would Paul "Big Poison" Waner have shattered if he'd weighed 180–190 and stood six feet or more?"*

In his booklet, Waner summarized the gospel of hitting according to Big Poison:

> The most important of these illustrations, are developing a fast bat, keeping the head steady in order to see the ball clearly, rolling your wrists instead of breaking them. Hitting from the back toe by reaching with the front foot, instead of stepping forward, getting the hips around fast by opening front toe with stride.
>
> To eliminate the sliced pop-ups, keep the barrel over your hands by swinging out from your body with long arms with the back elbow coming over the front elbow. This creates a faster bat. Please don't guide bat to ball with your hands, pull through it.
>
> Good judgment is very important in hitting. The strike zone illustrations will give you some clues. A hitter has the advantage of three strikes, and the better hitters are ready for the first good one. Join this select group, the membership is free, and the salaries are much better.
>
> Be relaxed, don't wave the bat, don't clench it. Be ready to hit down with the barrel of the bat. Just swing it and let the weight drive the ball.

Let the pitcher move first. Then, as he draws his arm back, you draw the bat back and you are ready. If a pitcher sees you fiddling with the bat, he'll stall until your arms are tired before you even get a chance to hit.

While Paul preached a relaxed approach at the plate, he had no patience for hitters who wiggled their bats while waiting for the pitch. He did not advocate any particular stance, just the one that came most naturally to the hitter.

What he did advocate was more hitting instructors.

Paul Waner: *"Why doesn't baseball have professional batting instructors? They have professional instructors in golf, tennis, swimming, track. So, why not baseball? Rogers Hornsby, the new manager of the Browns, is one of the few men who specialized in teaching batting before he returned to managing. Rogers is one of best—he knows all the fundamentals.*

"Clubs employ coaches, but most of them are employed to help out the manager, get the pitchers ready, relay signs, check on the players and keep up team morale. But few, even those who were good hitters, are competent to teach batting. Now, as a batting instructor, I think I can help anyone. I wouldn't necessarily have to spend all my time with one club, but if a crack hitter went into a slump, they might call me in as a batting consultant."

Paul advocated the use of pitching machines. He went so far as to suggest the machines taught hitting as well as live pitching. Well, he had a financial incentive most of the time. In the early 1950s he showed up in major league spring training camps selling the contraptions. His batting cages operated in Harmarville, Pennsylvania, near Pittsburgh, from April to October and from October to April in Sarasota.

In 1951, Paul Waner missed induction into the National Baseball Hall of Fame by a mere eight votes. The writers elected Mel Ott and Jimmie Foxx that year. But it was a good sign the deed would be done soon.

The next year, Cooperstown came calling.

In 1952, the Baseball Writers Association of America chose Paul along with Harry Heilmannn of the Detroit Tigers for induction into baseball's hallowed temple. Paul received 195 out of 234 votes. He and Heilmann were the 61st and 62nd players elected to the Hall. Falling short that year—to give some idea of the respect accorded Waner and Heilmann—were Bill Terry (short by 21 votes), Dizzy Dean (24), Al Simmons (35), and Bill Dickey (37).

At the time, Paul owned a batting cage and golf driving range in Sarasota. He also owned a batting cage in Pittsburgh. The one in Florida became a hang-out for players—active and retired—during spring training and in the winter. In Florida, Paul, 49, hung around former major leaguers Heinie Manush and Paul Derringer, playing golf as much as possible.

Heinie Manush: *"Pound for pound, Paul was the greatest. We had been friends since 1927, and what a guy he was. Day in and day out, Waner could beat me anytime he wanted to. He was a real good putter. I called him 'One Putt' and that's all he ever took. He still had that beautiful swing. But he couldn't hit the ball more than about 150 yards. I usually saw him about once a week."*

Where was Paul when he got the call from the Hall informing him of his selection to baseball's hallowed grounds? Why, hitting, of course. His lifetime average of .333 still pulsed through his veins.

Paul Waner: *"You know what I was doing when Heinie [Manush] told me about the election? Hitting. Hitting away at my pitching machine. I must have hit 200 or 300 balls that day. Just for fun. Almost made me feel like making a comeback. I weigh 142 [pounds], five pounds under my playing weight. Can I still hit? I can hit as good as ever. Maybe better. Those pitching machines are great practice. They never get tired throwing. Wouldn't I like a chance to do it all over again? Next time I'd do things a little different. That's what I say now. But I'd probably do just the same all over again. They get more extra base hits now. But the pitchers are wilder. More bases on balls. You don't get so many stolen bases because it's a different game."*

When he heard about the Hall, Paul was overjoyed. "I have realized my life's ambition. This is what I have been looking for a long time. Thank God I have lived to see the day."

The writer Fred Lieb visited Paul in Florida shortly after the Hall announcement.

Fred Lieb: *"Traveling southward on busy U.S. Highway 41, shortly after passing the Manatee-Sarasota county line, one's eye is attracted by a green sign with the familiar baseball name— "Paul Waner." Looking in from the road, one sees a group of young men hitting at batted balls served up by robot pitchers, while nearby other men and women of assorted ages are being coached on how to get more power and direction into their golf swings. The place is Paul Waner's batting practice and golf driving range. And Professor Paul, dressed in a sports shirt and brown slacks, is the busy bee about the establishment."*

Paul couldn't get enough of hitting—golf balls or baseballs. Once the writer Tommy Holmes dropped in on him, and when he went to shake Paul's hand, Big Poison winced. His hands were badly blistered.

Holmes quoted an anonymous friend of Paul's on what had happened. "Paul won't tell you what happened, but I will. We were up around Clearwater yesterday and we found what used to be a driving range with a couple of those pitching machines. You know—nine pitched balls for a quarter. Well, Paul grabbed a bat, and hit for almost three hours steady."

While batting instruction was Paul's second career, it paled in comparison to his induction to the Hall of Fame on July 21 in 1952. That day in Cooperstown, New York, a large crowd of friends, fans and baseball insiders turned out to witness firsthand the glorifying of two stars from the '20s and '30s, Paul Waner and Harry Heilmannn.

Warren Giles, the National League president, presented his opening remarks. His subject was a curious one. As Waner and Heilmannn sat at his side, Giles lashed out at increasing salaries and bonus payments for rookies.

Warren Giles: *"We must recruit boys who play ball because of their burning desire to excel, not because of an extravagant influence. If we cannot get enough by those means, I believe it would be better to operate with fewer clubs, and fewer players than to compromise in any way with the traditions of the game. We must maintain baseball as a vigorous and competitive game, one that captures the imagination and excites the fans. And, we must continue to be alert and very critical of ourselves."*

After Giles introduced Waner, he spoke up for the little guy, but he wasn't making union talk.

Paul Waner: *"I always enjoyed baseball very much. I've made many fine contacts through it. Boys and their fathers come to my batting range now and worry if the boy is going to be big enough to play ball. I tell them they don't have to weigh 190 or 200 pounds. A little man can do it all right, too."*

On the day of his induction Paul's only son, Paul Jr., was studying aeronautics at Georgia Tech. He already held a mechanical engineering degree from Duke University. Paul Jr. had so little interest in baseball—and he was just as distant from his father—that he didn't realize his father had been chosen until one of his professors told him about it. When he was in the 10th grade, Paul Jr. suffered an arthritic condition that kept him from playing most sports, although later on in college he lettered in gymnastics.

Paul Jr. was the spitting image of his father—blond, blue-eyed, same height and weight, with chiseled features. Rather than baseball, he preferred classical music, opera, and airplanes. The columnist Furman Bisher interviewed Paul Jr. in his room at college.

Paul Waner Jr.: *"It's not that I don't like sports. It's just that I don't care much for watching sports events. I guess I saw every home game Pittsburgh played when I was young. Maybe that's what happened. Maybe I got fed up on it. I can't remember any of the ball layers, but I have a vague recollection of old Honus Wagner, who was coaching then, I believe. I never did take much interest in baseball as I grew up, and dad never did try to force it on me. You know, he wasn't shoving a glove and ball in my hand and trying to make me play. Sure, we played some catch together, but that was about all. When I was in 10th grade I developed an arthritic condition in my back that just about eliminated me from athletics. I've still got it. I can't run or swing a bat very well.*

"Airplanes are my sin. I've been interested in them ever since I could remember."

Most of Paul Jr.'s childhood was spent in Sarasota, Florida, away from the harsh winters of the Oklahoma range. He received his pilot's license at age 16. Flying and music motivated him. "I like music in general. I lay these on the machine. I hear all the popular stuff I want to on the radio. No sense in buying popular records."

As for his dad's election to the Hall, Paul Jr. was reserved about it. "I'm happy about it because I know it made dad happy."

Paul would go on to work as an aeronautical engineer in Virginia and Texas. He was employed at various times by NASA and General Dynamics. His whole life was focused on designing and building airplanes. His grandson, Derrick Waner, is left-handed, loves to golf, and is the spitting image of Paul the senior.

And while Paul Jr. turned away from baseball, he sadly fell prey to drinking. Paul Jr. was married to and divorced from Lillian Porter of Fort Worth, Texas. Like his father's failed marriage, the major reason behind the break-up seems to have been alcohol. Paul Jr. died in the early 1990s.

Lillian Porter: *"Paul and his wife, Corinne, were divorced when I met Paul Jr. I thought Paul Sr. had rehabbed from drinking before he died, but according to his last wife, he hadn't. He just couldn't shake that alcohol."*

Paul Jr. associated baseball with bad times and drunks. For him, it seemed as if all his dad's friends drank too much. It turned him away from the game.

Lillian Porter: *"Paul Jr. really didn't like any sports. It was like he was hostile, which is a shame. He never even golfed. All he did was gymnastics at Duke."*

24. The Professor of Batting

His relationship with his father was rocky. Paul Jr. became a difficult man.

Lillian Porter: *"I think the alcohol really interfered. I remember him telling me before we married that his dad had a drinking problem. Paul Sr. was supposed to be the best man at our wedding, but he never made it. He had to go into the hospital for something or another. They covered all this up pretty well back then, but nowadays, I guess, it wouldn't be. They—both Lloyd and Paul—were nice, country boys for the most part. But alcohol will do anyone damage. The couple of times I was around Paul, he was a loving, kind, more outgoing person than the son I married. That's why Paul Jr. and I divorced. He eventually died from alcoholism. I've talked to my children about it, and I think and hope we've broken the cycle of drinking."*

Porter's daughter, Beth Noe, remembered a grandfatherly Paul Waner.

Beth Noe: *"I was seven when he passed away. I remember going to his home in Sarasota. He was very ill at the time, and was hooked up to an oxygen tank from emphysema. I have vivid images of his home, a small home just filled to the gills with baseball memorabilia. It's a shame we didn't take pictures of all that. Years later, someone auctioned all the memorabilia off. But when my granddad got his three thousandth hit, he gave the ball to my dad. And today I have that ball."*

Paul used his new Hall of Fame credentials to sell his batting machines and tutelage. Late in 1952, he wrote to Pittsburgh general manager Branch Rickey offering his batting complex to the Pirates for the upcoming spring training. The letter shows Waner's cerebral approach to the art of hitting and he talks about his concept of "finger hitting." The stationary and text appear as:

Paul Waner
Baseball Batting Ranges
distributor of
The Paul Waner Special Rapid Robot Pitcher
FAMOUS HOFRAN BALLS / SPECIAL LIGHTING SYSTEM
DESIGNED NETS / BATTING CAGES

Dear Mr. Rickey:

I had hoped to see you in Pittsburgh before I came South—there were several things I wished to talk to you about for the coming season. One was I had a definite desire to take charge of the young hitters during training and also an invitation to a few of the players of your selection to come here a week in advance as my range here has all the facilities to do this at small expense—I would be glad to take responsibility for their improvement and well-being.

I am in fine condition and expect to stay that way because I have an ambition and great desire to help bring together a strong Pirates hitting club to Pittsburgh. To me it is a reality, because finger hitting instead of palms—plus one minute of explaining and showing how to perfectly time any pitcher's delivery—three simple but important things to do at bat. First, finger lock for snapping wrists. Second, timing pitcher. Third, eliminating a large majority of double plays by being out front of low pitches—low curves with the infield in—low fastballs or low fast curves, infield back—the advantage of finger hitting is that the wrists are much quicker getting the bat in front both on low pitches and inside ones.

You may be somewhat pessimistic regarding the scope of improvements obtained by such instructions, and though I'm soon 50, I can demonstrate the difference between incorrect and correct hitting. Dick Groat was quick to line up the problem after a few rounds of swinging. Also Billy Goodman, Walt Dropo, Duke Snider, Bobby DelGreco, and (Tony) Bartirome improved, but forgot after going on a road trip. I was disappointed in (Dick) Hall and (Frank) Thomas when they played at the close of the season. Both boys can be greatly improved and I have every confidence that Thomas can become another "Chick" Hafey.

My range has available a trailer, pitching machine completely equipped and can be set up by one person in a few minutes—if you desire to use one in Havana (Cuba) I could drive it to Miami or Key West and go to Havana by boat. This letter seems to have turned into a treatise on hitting. Nevertheless it has been an interesting study and an important one. Should you consider this letter as something new to add to the field of baseball—"Special Instruction"—I would appreciate your views in reply.

Sincerely,
Paul Waner

This letter shows Paul's aggressiveness to establish the role of the batting coach and simulated pitching at the major league level. Who better to lobby on this issue than baseball's greatest revolutionary, Branch Rickey? It was Rickey who had introduced the minor league farm system and broken major league baseball's color ban. While we do not know Rickey's reply, Paul Waner's dream would eventually be realized, and credit should be given to him for evolving baseball toward more specialization.

A couple of years later, in 1955, Paul would see a new face on the Pirates' spring training roster—that of Roberto Clemente. His speed, rifle arm and line-drive swing would take him into a Hall of Fame career and

24. The Professor of Batting

3,000 hits—the only other Pirates player besides Paul Waner and Honus Wagner in that elite club. Paul was gracious watching the youngster develop.

"I'm happy to see right field in such good hands," Big Poison would tell reporters.

Les Biederman of the *Pittsburgh Post Gazette* observed the first encounter between the two great Pirates right fielders. Later, Clemente, who had grown up in Puerto Rico and did not have the advantage of knowing all the American All-Stars of years bygone, took Biederman aside and asked, "You mean to tell me that little fellow had 3,000 hits?"

"Yes," Biederman said, "and all of them were line drives."

Line drives epitomized Paul Waner.

Paul Waner: *"I've always been a student of batting. I know how to take a man's swing apart, tell him what he does wrong, and teach him how to get his own power, and the power of his bat into his swing. I think I can teach the average hitter."*

Paul used to say when a hitter's hips are so quick, he "belly buttons" the ball as he throws his hips toward the pitcher.

Ted Williams, in *My Turn at Bat,* pays some credit to Paul Waner on batting tips. Their approaches differed greatly, however. Williams preferred majestic power to Waner's slashing shots.

Ted Williams: *"Paul Waner tried to help me, and from him I got the germ of the answer. 'Gee, it's easy,' he said the following spring. 'Just move away from the plate and chop down on the ball.'*

"It was easy all right, but it wasn't chopping down on the ball that made the difference. It was moving away from the plate. My normal stance was so close that, since they were pitching me tight to force me to pull into all that congestion in right field, I could do little else. All I had to do was stand a bit farther away from the plate, so that I would have room and time to push the ball a little more. Waner said swing down on the ball, but as long as I was snug up to the plate like that I couldn't swing down on those inside pitches. I know this. I beat that damn shift a lot more than people realize."

Echoing Ty Cobb's famous comment, Paul Waner once said the left-handed Williams would have hit for a higher average if he'd hit to the opposite field. Maybe, but Williams once said history is made on the inside corner of the plate where the batter is able to pull the ball with great power.

Everyone has a hitting philosophy—it's called, "what works for me."

Dick Groat, the Pirates' shortstop on the 1960 World Series championship club, was a rookie in 1952 when he visited Paul Waner's batting range in Florida during spring training. "I went there often. He was a real gentleman and very helpful to me."

Every year Paul made the rounds to spring training camps. Once at the Dodgers' site in Vero Beach, he demonstrated a pitching machine and gave some impromptu hitting lessons to Duke Snider, Gil Hodges and some of the Dodgers rookies. Apart from his tutoring, writer Bill Roeder depicted Waner as the rumpled "genius" with a .333 lifetime average who didn't know how to take care of himself but knew about hitting.

Bill Roeder: *"Waner has lived hard. He is only 48, but he looked like an old man as he sat in the press room, drinking beer out of a can and discussing his theories on hitting. He was all dressed in blue—blue shirt, blue slacks, blue suede shoes, a blue baseball cap."*

Wizened or not, Waner relished his professorial image, discoursing on the hitting game like an Ivy League lecturer.

Paul Waner: *"Those hands must be held high, so you're always swinging down at the ball instead of upper cutting it. Ruth looked like he was golfing the ball. But that was only his finish. He always held his hands way up high to get the start. You watch Musial do it sometime. I watched Joe DiMaggio last year. You know why he's not the hitter he was? His hands were dropping. The bat gets heavy for you as you get old ... I never understood these things when I was hitting. I just went up there and hit."*

Bats were different in Waner's era and in the 1950s. In the old days, they were heavier, and now they are much lighter. The key is bat speed, though Waner and other coaches didn't exactly use that term back then.

Paul Waner: *"Sometimes they're fighting the bat trying to uppercut, and have to use less wood. In my time, you didn't see many bats under 36 ounces, and many were much heavier. Now they use 32, 33, 34-ounce bats. Yet I never weighed more than 148 pounds, but used a 42-ounce bat, for example, in the 1927 World Series. I had the bat working for me, though."*

Ty Cobb and Paul discussed hitting. Paul was especially interested in the Georgia Peach's long-ball exploits.

Paul Waner: *"How was it that you [Ty], the greatest left-handed hitter, and Honus Wagner, the greatest right-handed hitter, held your hands apart about six inches?"*

Ty Cobb: *"I could control the bat better that way."*

Paul Waner: *"Yes, but you sacrificed some power by not holding them closer together and locking them. So did Wagner. I hit more home runs in 15* *years than Wagner did in 23. All right, maybe the ball was livelier when I was playing, but Wagner was twice as big as I was and should have hit more home runs, even with a Dead Ball."*

Cobb laughed, and then told Paul something he should have realized—they didn't try to hit home runs back then. But when a good hitter wanted to, it was possible.

Ty Cobb: *"When I was going for the long hit, I slid my left hand up the bat right together with my right hand."*

◆ ◆ ◆

Outside of pitching machines and the Hall of Fame, life was not all that easy for Paul, and his self-inflicted lifestyle took its toll. He and Paul Jr. grew even more distant after the father remarried on June 12, 1953, to Mildred Carroll. The relationship between the two wives was frosty. Porter recalled, "When my children were little and we would go to Florida, Corinne would threaten us and say we were not to go see Millie."

Paul and Mildred had a cocker spaniel named Soapy and a parakeet. They would have no children.

To some, it seemed Paul never quite got his proper recognition, even after induction into the Hall. In 1953, the writer Frank Graham penned an article on this subject with the headline "Whoever Speaks of Paul Waner?"

Frank Graham: *"Matter of fact, they never talked much about him [Paul], even when he was putting together his remarkable record [of 3,000 hits]. He was in there every day, beating the brains out of enemy pitchers, yet he never got much of a tumble outside Pittsburgh where he had his great years."*

Still, for those who respected and understood the game, Paul Waner boasted two outstanding credentials—3,000-plus hits and a bronze Hall of Fame plaque—and now could really lay claim to being baseball's top hitting instructor.

In 1954, the Milwaukee Braves hired Paul. For the next six years, he was the hitting instructor for Milwaukee's major league club and its 14 minor league teams. While he would work periodically for other teams, Milwaukee was the team he worked most closely with.

Paul Waner: *"When the big league club was at home, I'd usually be there. Then, when they went on the road, I'd start flying—California, New York, hitting all of the different teams. I'd talk with the Braves' major league* club, get their instructions and then spend four or five days with a particular minor league club and the hitters there."

Among those hitters were a young Hank Aaron and Eddie Mathews.

Aaron was thought by many to be a "wrist" hitter. But Paul discounted the perception that the future home run king's strength was in his wrists alone.

Paul Waner: *"He doesn't use his wrists at all. He uses his hips and when he uses his hips properly, they automatically control his wrists. When he starts using his wrists instead of his hips, that's when they send for me."*

He was right. The hips generate power. Aaron's powerful wrists just looked like they were his big weapon—at least to the unseasoned eye.

One time Paul took aside a slumping Aaron and worked with him on his technique. The problem stemmed from the media's focus on Aaron's wrists—photographs of him rolling his wrists filled the sports page one day. It got the young hitter off track.

Paul Waner: *"We were in spring training, and he was a little upset. He went for about a week in exhibition games, and he couldn't hit a ball to save his life. He wasn't getting it to the outfield. So I came down and sat next to him, and I said, 'Hank, those pictures in the paper about your wrists have made you use them more than you should. You do not need to focus on your wrists. Those writers don't know what they're talking about. Look, you're rolling your wrists and now you think that's the way to hit. It's an optical illusion. Now, you do just like I've been telling you, and your wrists just roll.'*

"So in his next batting practice Hank started knocking the ball against the fence and over the fence. I said, 'Hank, you didn't have to use your wrists, did you?' He said, 'I don't think I did, though it felt like it. But I didn't.'"

Waner also helped refine the raw slugger Eddie Mathews.

Eddie Mathews: *"He was standing there one day with a bat resting on his shoulder. I said to him, 'Show me how you stood at the plate.' Paul didn't move. 'I can't do anything' til they throw that ball,' he said. That taught me something. He was as relaxed as anybody could be until the pitcher threw. Me, I would be all tensed up, getting set, squeezing the bat, waiting for the pitch like a lot of guys do. But after that I stayed relaxed until the pitcher threw the ball and I was a better hitter for it."*

Even with sluggers like Aaron and Mathews, Waner espoused hitting to all fields, including the opposite one.

Paul Waner: *"Mathews, and no other big hitter, is going to be a great* hitter for his team until he learns to hit to all fields, and beat the shift. The genuine home run hitter will always have his place, but it's come to the point where some guys are desperately upper cutting the ball trying to hit 20 home runs a year. But to really help the team, they should give up this foolishness and hit to all fields.

"I used to pay no attention to the pitcher while he did all that winding up and messing around. I acted like he wasn't there. It's all in the timing. He can't pitch until he pulls his arm back. When he does, you just get that bat ready up there and be ready to go. Don't waste your time glaring at the pitcher."

Like all achievers, Paul turned an apparent weakness into a strength.

Paul Waner: "My being small has helped me more than anything. When you're big, you see, it's expected you'll bust some balls a long way just on natural strength. Now, because I'm small these young hitters look at me, and say, 'Gee, he must know something about hitting.' You see, I can't do it on strength alone—I've got to be like a good boxer, I've got to know how to hit."

In his approach, Waner reflected his own physical characteristics, the writer Fred Lieb noted.

Fred Lieb: "Waner knew that batting was not a matter of great physical strength. He proved that a comparatively small man, by mastering timing and leverage, could out-hit stronger and bigger athletes. He was not a singles hitter. Paul hit with considerable power and had the knack of placing hits between the outfielders."

To Paul, bat speed was the one thing all great hitters had in common. "If you have a fast bat, you can wait longer on the ball. You can hit the curve easier, and you can pull back just in time on the bad ones. When you see your pitch, you're quick through the zone with your bat."

Paul Waner: [Swinging a bat] "Now, do you hear it whistle like that? You can't make it whistle any way but that way. I don't care how strong you are, you can't make a bat hum until you have bat speed. That's the secret to this thing. You hit with your weight, and get that belly-button around fast."

Paul credited his father, Ora, for his hitting style. One piece of fatherly advice always stuck with him. As a child, Paul had a hard time lifting his dad's heavy bat. But his dad said, "Don't take a big swing, just put the bat on your shoulder, and drop it on the ball."

Paul Waner: "It's quicker and easier to swing down on the ball than up," Paul said. "Take a man chopping a tree with an axe—it's the same *theory. He swings down, and that's the secret of hitting. Keep your weight above the ball at all times. DiMaggio would hold the bat high, but he would still kill a low pitch."*

If it wasn't hitting, the graying Big Poison offered his thoughts on the current state of the game. It's easy for retired players to believe the era in which they played was the "Golden Age" and that the game was better back then. Sometimes Paul fell into this knee-jerk reflex. Once he remarked that baseball in the 1950s was a "gentleman's game."

Sometimes Paul Waner served as an advance scout for Milwaukee, analyzing hitters on other teams. He liked to get in on the action, too. Paul hurt his arm once throwing when he was working with one of Milwaukee's minor league clubs. Years later he described the twinge he felt.

Paul Waner: *"I was up at Waycross where the minor league club was practicing, and they had these batting cages. I grabbed a couple of those rubber balls, you know, the kind that the pitching machines use. I went to throw them back over the netting, and when I wound up and heaved it, something pulled in my arm. And now I can't throw worth a whip."*

Toward the end of the 1956 season when the Braves were in a pennant race with Brooklyn, Paul and former big leaguer Billy Southworth scouted the New York Yankees, the likely winners of the American League pennant. They found a squad under manager Casey Stengel that was solidly drilled in the fundamentals of the game and had plenty of depth in pitching and on the bench.

While Brooklyn would end up facing New York in the fall classic, the scouting report was a forerunner for 1957 when the Braves would square off against the Bronx Bombers in the World Series. But Paul would miss the Series due to illness.

The past year had been tough on his health. On January 4, 1957, Paul found himself in a Sarasota hospital confined to an oxygen tent, suffering from pneumonia, a 105 degree temperature, and lung congestion. He would stay in the hospital for two weeks. Through much of the year he was sick and in and out of the hospital.

In May 1957, the Milwaukee Braves sent Paul down to Atlanta on an emergency hitting mission. The Braves' minor league team, the Atlanta Crackers, had just gone through a span of 40 scoreless innings. Paul worked almost day and night with the players and declared after a few sessions, "They'll start hitting soon."

Later that summer, Paul spent three and a half months in Tampa State Hospital for tuberculosis. A series of respiratory problems had affected him during the past winter, and he had recently come down with pneumonia.

While in the hospital, Paul ate plenty of food and put seven pounds on his wiry frame. He also spent time reflecting on his life. He even penned an article for the Sarasota County Tuberculosis Association and had it published on their behalf. It's one of the few occasions of Paul writing directly, almost vulnerably, about his own life, as if he were fashioning his own obituary. A sister of his had died from the disease.

Paul Waner: *"Now that necessity has provided me with plenty of time to relax and think, it has gradually dawned on me why I am the unwilling landlord to a case of tuberculosis. Looking back over the 54 years I have lived to a fullness which sometimes amazes even me, I have finally realized that it is entirely logical that I should be benched by tuberculosis. It is about the only thing that hasn't previously happened to me."*

During his lifetime, Paul wrote, he had won batting titles, excelled in college basketball back in Oklahoma, performed capably in amateur boxing, received awards in golfing, and back in his elementary school days, even won an oratory contest. Those were some of the high points of his life, but there were some low points as well.

Paul Waner: *"Twice pneumonia almost removed me from the land of the living, once a Chicago hoodlum named Little Augie tried to erase me, I fell from horses while appearing in Honest Bill Newton's Wild West Show and Circus, I've been attacked by a barracuda, on various occasions I have survived airplane mishaps, and back in my younger days of saxophone playing, I escaped unscathed by unwilling listeners and music lovers. I've had many angry pitchers throw at my head with malice in their hearts, I toured angry and active war zones during World War II, I hit a home run off Grover Cleveland Alexander, and I've even been married twice [chuckle]."*

Paul recalled the day Dots Miller, the manager of the San Francisco Seals who stuck up for him when the front office wanted him cut, walked into the Seals clubhouse and told the team he had tuberculosis. Miller died three months later, and Paul was greatly disturbed by his death. "I wrote Dots some cheerful letters—I hope they were cheerful. Now I'm having my chance to learn how much letters can mean. Dots was filled with despair when he left his home and his ball club to make that one-way trip to the sanitarium. 'So long, skipper, God bless you.'"

Paul compared that to when he had to tell his Milwaukee Braves players that he had tuberculosis and would have to leave. In '57 Milwaukee went on to win the World Series, and Paul was not on hand for it.

Paul Waner: "I had waited four years to see the lads I nursed through the Braves farm system play in a World Series, and it was a blow to miss being part of that final stretch drive for the pennant. Watching the World Series on the television in my hospital room was not the same as watching from the bench of the dugout."

He had time now to contemplate the big picture. "Enforced idleness provides an opportunity to think and reflect," he wrote.

Paul Waner: "When I entered this hospital, I had all sorts of visions. I could see myself being probed and picked at and poked like a guinea pig. I suspected I would be permanently relieved of my cigarettes [he was not], and I'd have to lie flat on my back, and so feared the long hours of doing nothing. That's not how it worked out."

Paul said he was given "wonder pills" to speed up the healing process. He kept his cigarettes, indulged in the meals, and wrote at the typewriter. He'd watch TV until the banality of the "moronic commercials" was too much for him. As a famous ballplayer, he knew life had given him some good breaks. Maybe he was thinking back to Oklahoma where many of his neighbors while growing up ended up living and working on farms and leading rather meager existences.

Paul Waner: "I'm more fortunate than most in that I'm not faced with economic disaster. Milwaukee pays me on a six-month basis and I drew full salary for this season. So I'm in a much better position than the head of a family who must rely on receiving a weekly paycheck 52 weeks a year."

Paul praised the advances in medical science that made for better treatment of tuberculosis. Paul noted the irony of receiving direct mail fundraising from the local TB society during the Christmas season every year. He said he would write a small donation to the group, never realizing that one day he, too, would be among the sufferers.

"'I hope this helps some poor fellow,'" he recalled as he would mail his donation.

On December 11, he was released from the hospital. Sounding optimistic to the press, the doctors said he was "completely cured." Waner was in such a rush to leave the hospital that he dropped his discharge papers and a nurse had to chase him down as he hurried to his car to drive home.

The next spring, in 1958, Paul served as a hitting advisor for the Cardinals. The writer Joe Reichler observed how Waner's 55-year-old body was deceptive in its coordination.

24. The Professor of Batting

Joe Reichler: *"The thin, frail-looking, little fellow appeared old and almost feeble until he swung a bat. Then he became a picture of grace and beauty. The rhythmic stroke, the perfectly coordinated body control, the smooth flow through, all suggested a great hitter."*

That year *Sport* magazine selected Paul for their all-time National League team:

> 1B Bill Terry
> 2B Rogers Hornsby
> SS Honus Wagner
> 3B Pie Traynor
> OF Paul Waner
> OF Stan Musial
> OF Mel Ott
> C Gabby Hartnett
> P Christy Mathewson
> P Carl Hubbell

Accolades, however, are no antidote for declining health.

In August 1959, Paul had a heart attack in Omaha, Nebraska, where he was serving as a hitting coach for the St. Louis Cardinals' Omaha farm team in the American Association. He suffered the episode in his hotel room after a game. Paul was taken to the Lutheran Hospital, and a few days later his wife came up from Florida to see him. Omaha general manager Bill Bergesch said Paul had complained of a bad cold when he had arrived in Omaha a few days before the heart attack.

Waner thought it was a misdiagnosis. The hard-living Big Poison was not one to admit anything but minor health problems.

Paul Waner: *"I suffer from a certain amount of lung congestion. Fluid gathers in my upper lungs, and I become short of breath. So they think it's a heart attack. But when they give me some oxygen, I recover fast."*

After the Omaha attack, the doctors told him to give up drinking and tobacco—smoking and chewing—two of Waner's chief pleasures. He tried with moderate success, but when doctors also told him to quit golf, he balked. Next to swinging a bat, golf was his greatest passion.

Paul Waner: *"The doctors said I was to give up everything and rest. I don't know of any quicker way to die than just sit on my tail feathers and rest. I guess I'm just not the restful kind. I still do what I want to do. When I feel like golfing, which is usually three or four times a week, I play golf. I pull my own golfing cart around. I do that intentionally. It exercises and builds up* *chest and shoulder muscles. Riding in one of those golf carts is not for me. I still have baseball jobs as batting instructor to consider. My legs aren't what they used to be, but I keep them in as good a shape as possible."*

His health was unusually fragile for his age. He was only 56 in 1959 but looked 10 or 15 years older. Clearly, drinking and smoking did not help matters. For a young man with boundless energy who needed little sleep at night, he now had a broken-down body.

Paul ultimately believed his drinking wasn't a public nuisance. More of the friendly drunk type, he did not have an arrest record for absurd drinking exploits and did not become loud or angry when partying. While other players and managers knew about his indulgences, the fans and public were kept in the dark from it, and it was just as well, he thought.

Paul Waner: *"They knew I showed up at the ball park every day, and always gave them my best. I always could handle the stuff pretty well. But that's all in the past, and I've forgotten the drinks and the things that went with it. At this stage of my career, I especially wish to avoid giving a wrong impression to the kids. Sure, there have been drinking stars, but their after-hour diversions never helped them, or their careers. We all learn from experience, and if I had my life to live over, I would do some things differently. For one, I would dedicate myself to helping young players."*

♦ ♦ ♦

In 1958, Stan Musial joined Waner—and would soon pass him—as one of the National League's 3,000-hit club members. Paul was gracious in his appraisal of Stan the Man, as well as Ted Williams, another contemporary that Paul rubbed elbows with in Boston while coaching for the Braves.

Paul Waner: *"Stan's one of the finest players and gentlemen. I don't even mind if he beats me out. I've talked with Stan about that possibility. He can easily do it with two good seasons [Musial ended up with 3,630 hits lifetime]. Ted Williams, too, is a great hitter. He displays wonderful finesse. A student of the game quickly realizes his skill with the bat. The same person might think Musial was 'lucky' if he saw him go 4 for 4 in a game. But watch Stan do that for two or three games in a row, and it dawns on you this is a really great hitter—the best all-around ball player I've ever seen."*

Musial was likewise a big fan of Paul's, according to St. Louis sportswriter Bob Broeg. "Stan's idol, in case you hadn't heard, was Paul Waner." Waner ranked Musial as the "greatest team hitter" he ever saw. Musial was unselfish about hitting for power and would readily slap a single to the opposite field if it helped his team. The Giants' Mel Ott and Bill Terry were also comparable "team hitters," he added. Like Waner, Ott was short in stature though stockier in build. A dead pull-hitter, the left-handed Ott exploited the 290-foot right field wall at the Polo Grounds, hitting an extraordinary high percentage of his career home runs at his home park. As such, Waner noted the importance of ballpark effects.

Paul Waner: *"If Ott had played in Pittsburgh, he would have hit half as many homers, but I bet he would have won some batting championships. Ott didn't need the homer, he just took advantage of it in his park. But give him a little room on his off-side with a winning run on second, and you could be sure he'd patter the ball into left field."*

As for his choice of baseball's greatest hitter, Waner picked the Splendid Splinter.

Paul Waner: *"There's no telling what Williams would have hit if he'd gone to left when they were using the shift. He's the greatest, in my opinion. But he has his slumps. They all do when they don't roll those wrists."*

Life was rolling on for the Waners.

Little Poison Goes Home

I guess I never stopped being a farm boy.
— Lloyd Waner

While Paul crossed the country as a hitting coach in his later years and grabbed an occasional headline, Lloyd moved back to Oklahoma and settled down far from the limelight. He scouted for the Pirates from 1946 to 1949 and the Baltimore Orioles in 1955. Tired of the travel involved in scouting, homespun Lloyd Waner got a job working for the Oklahoma City streets department as an accountant and foreman. He worked there uneventfully for the next couple of decades before retiring.

Quiet or not, Lloyd was still a legend in Oklahoma. One young man who came into contact with a recently retired Lloyd Waner was Joe Bauman, then just 18. Bauman would wallop 72 home runs in 1954 for the Roswell Rockets in the Longhorn League. Until Barry Bonds' 73 in 2001, Bauman's mark still stood as an all-time record for organized baseball in the minors and majors. He is an interesting footnote to the legend of the home run.

Bauman, who lives in Roswell today, never made the majors, preferring to play in the Southwest and make a living from the ongoing oil boom. Years before his own summer of glory, Bauman was just a kid working at a gas station when he got to know Lloyd Waner a little. At the time Lloyd was scouting part-time.

Joe Bauman: "I knew Lloyd Waner back in '46 or '47 after he had retired and was living in Oklahoma City, doing some scouting. He was one of the nicest guys you ever saw. He was real quiet, and chewed tobacco, lots of it.

25. Little Poison Goes Home

Never talked much at all. Paul was more outgoing, from what I understand, and Lloyd quite the opposite. You see, I worked at a service station during the off season. It was kind of a hangout for ex-ballplayers. Lloyd would go down there like the others to trade. He'd come down in the morning, and sit around and spit tobacco juice. He would just listen, you know. Listen to what the other ballplayers had to say.

"One thing that sticks out is how difficult it was, Lloyd said, to make decent money playing ball. Every year they had a showdown with management, or it was at least enough to make your stomach grind. Owners were really cheap back in those days, but I think the Waners thought all right of the Pirates. They sure loved playing up in Pittsburgh.

"Lloyd was more of a conservative sort. From what I knew, he kept his money in property and didn't spend much. He was a slight little fellow, no fat, no nothing. He could run like a deer. Paul—I didn't know him or ever met him—was supposed to be more of an extrovert, and took his chances on things."

◆ ◆ ◆

Paul and Lloyd experienced some ill fortune in the early years of their retirements.

In December 1948, their father died after suffering a bad fall at the farm. He had been in the Oklahoma City hospital for a couple weeks recovering from a ruptured blood vessel, but then pneumonia set in. Paul rushed back from Florida, and Ralph, the older brother, from Kansas City. Lloyd, then scouting for the Pirates, was in Oklahoma. All three were at Ora's bedside as he passed on.

Ora Waner loved baseball like his sons and kept active in it. He pitched his last sandlot game when he was 55. It was a "town game" between McLoud and Luther on the Fourth of July. Ora won the game, 6–1, and then called it quits.

Like his sons, Ora loved

Ora Waner golfing (courtesy of Jim Knight).

Ora Waner tees off (courtesy of Jim Knight).

golf. For the last 10 years or so of his life he was a constant presence on Oklahoma City golf courses, often playing 36 holes a day and shooting in the low 80s. Vernon B. Snell of *The Sporting News* recalled Ora's passion for the sport.

Vernon B. Snell: *"About the time Pop [Ora] was 60, Paul and Lloyd were home for an off-season visit. They had their golf clubs along, as usual. They were practicing a few shots at the side of the big two-story country home. The balls would land in the closely mowed alfalfa field north of the house. Ora Waner walked out one morning while the boys were practicing. He looked the situation over and said, 'That looks easy. Let me hit one.' He borrowed one of Lloyd's right-hand irons and took a vicious swing at the ball. He missed it completely. The boys chuckled. Twice more he swished the air before he connected. But when he did hit the little sphere, a golfer was born. Said Ora, 'And to think I wasted 40 years of my life on that farm before I heard of this game.'"*

There were other rough times for the Waners.

On March 31, 1950, Ralph Waner was sitting in a restaurant in Kansas City, Missouri. He was enjoying a steak dinner with a girlfriend, Ethel Wilmouth.

Suddenly, Ralph's divorced wife, Marie Waner, walked up to him and started arguing with him. Both were angry, and they jumped up and headed outside. As they did so, Marie pulled out a pistol and shot Ralph. She plugged him twice in front of 40 startled people. Ralph tried to reach for the gun, and it went off another time, wounding her once. Ralph Waner, 53, died shortly thereafter. He and Marie, 54, had been divorced for two years.

Ralph Waner operated the Standard Maintenance Supplies Company, a surplus firm in Kansas City. A decent ballplayer in his youth, he was a director of a boys' baseball league in Kansas City. Wilmouth and Ralph had known each other six years. She later described the shooting to newspaper reporters.

Ethel Wilmouth: *"The next thing I knew Marie Waner was standing by the booth. She told Waner, 'I finally caught up with you.' Waner got up from the booth and walked to the front of the restaurant with her. Then I heard some gunshots."*

Marie Waner was a grade school teacher. After the shooting, she was reported in fair condition. She accused Ralph and Wilmouth of breaking up the Waner home and threatening her. She ended up spending years in jail.

◆ ◆ ◆

Baseball strategy continued to evolve in those years. After World War II and the end of the Waner era, the Pittsburgh Pirates finally boasted a home run champ in Ralph Kiner. Mentored by Hank Greenberg in 1947, the prodigious Kiner astonished baseball with a seven-year streak of home run titles. No one in Pittsburgh had ever seen anything like Kiner.

Carl J. Vitti grew up on Larimar Avenue in a blue-collar Pittsburgh neighborhood known as East Liberty. A tough place, as Vitti put it—"when people asked you where you lived, you would say Larimar Avenue, and they would know a little about you." Decades later he recalled his formative days as a Pirate, and Kiner, fan.

Carl J. Vitti: *"We used to take the streetcar to Forbes Field. They played day games then, back in the '40s and '50s. I went to a Christian Brothers High School four blocks from Forbes Field. On days the Pirates had a home game, especially Opening Day, we'd try to get early dismissals. I can remember an Opening Day in the early '50s where Bob Friend had to pitch in a snow storm.*

"The Pirates had a Knot Hole Gang where on Saturdays kids under 12 got into games free. They sat us in the upper deck in the right-field stands. If you had 50 cents, you could get a ticket and sit in the left-field bleachers and watch our hero, Ralph Kiner. They opened the bleacher gates after six innings, and you got in free. That's where the owners are missing the boat today. Get these kids into the games, and show them how to love the game. That's how you encourage fans for the future. When they're young.

"God I loved baseball! I'd go to Forbes Field every chance I could. Every

summer day, we'd play ball on the sandlots from morning until supper. We had to walk two miles to get to that field. I remember going to the Army and Navy store and buying a Bob Feller baseball that had stamped on it, 'Not for batting.' We pounded it until the cover came off, and then we wrapped it in a sticky, black friction tape. The best day of my life, my dad came home from work one day with a catcher's mitt he had bought at Sears and Roebuck. He bought it so he could play catch with me. Man, I loved him.

"*Ralph Kiner was our hero, our Babe Ruth. We sat in the left-field stands so we were close to him. He was the Pirates' only drawing card back then. Even with Kiner, Pittsburgh lost 90 or so games a year. In June 1953, when Pittsburgh traded Kiner along with Garagiola, Pollet and Metkovich to the Cubs for six mediocre players, I was devastated. All of Pittsburgh was brokenhearted. Years later, when I ran into Kiner at the Pittsburgh airport—he was a Mets broadcaster by then—I thanked him for all the thrills he had given me as a youngster.*"

Kiner was so unlike the great Pirates players who had preceded him. He was the embodiment of a home run king, Hollywood-style, an exotic creature for Pittsburgh baseball fans. He was not, however, an all around talent. Though he hit balls a long way, and lumbered around the base paths, Kiner couldn't be accused of turning heads with defensive gems. He was a far different player than the Waners. The Waners were symbolic of ballplayers in the first half of the 20th century, and Kiner epitomizes today's ballplayer.

Baseball brothers—great brothers, that is—are rare in baseball. Especially ones boasting .333 and .316 lifetime averages like Paul and Lloyd Waner. From 1876 until 2001, 356 brother sets in baseball have existed. Among the best are the Waners, DiMaggios, Ferrells, Alous, Meusels, and the Delahantys. Interestingly, biology tells us that brothers have 80 percent or more DNA factors in common while fathers and sons only have 50 percent in common.

What, then, could we expect of the Waners' prodigy?

Lloyd Waner Jr., a retired geologist in Edmond, Oklahoma, lived under the shadow of a famous father with a drinking problem. Lloyd Sr. was in his seventh major league season when his namesake son was born in 1933.

For one, Lloyd Jr. made sure he was his own man. Resisting the pull of baseball from early on, Lloyd Jr. went to Oklahoma University and became a geologist. He was 12 when his father retired from baseball. As a bat boy for the Pirates in the late '30s and '40s, Little Poison junior brushed his tiny elbows with some of baseball's all-time greats. Some of the memories were good, some were not.

25. Little Poison Goes Home

Lloyd Waner Jr.: "I wasn't very old when my dad Lloyd was playing ball. I remember the war years, traveling with mom and dad, and remember being a mascot for the Pirates. Dad would take me to batting practice, and I got a chance to work with some great players, like Honus Wagner [a coach then] who taught me how to play shortstop [chuckle]. Honus was so good to me. I have a ball signed by him. It reads, 'To Little Poison.'

"I remember when some of the old Pirates would come by our farm. My dad and them would sit up all night talking baseball. You know, my dad and uncle played for the love of the game, and just thought of themselves as common people. What I saw was a team spirit in Pittsburgh. I got to work out with the players, and shag flies and practice with them. I'm sure you can't do today what I did back then. It's sometimes hard for me to realize how specially gifted my dad and uncle were. After all, not many people who are 145 pounds play any sport well. I think a lot of their skills go back to my grandfather, who raised them so well in the sport."

Lloyd Waner Jr. recalled his grandfather Ora Waner, the family patriarch. "Great big fellow. He loved to play any game in the world, whether it was golf or baseball or anything. It was my grandmother who was a little wisp of a thing."

Lloyd Waner Jr.: "My dad's eye-hand coordination was unbelievable. He was a great golfer. You'd go hunting with my father, and he'd see things before you ever would. And then the way he could shoot. It seemed like one easy motion to bring the rifle up to his shoulder, and then fire. Both of them would go squirrel hunting, with a .22, and you have to be quick to shoot something so small that way.

"Hey, heard about the corncob stories? Well, they were true, all right. We'd dip them in a bucket of water. I used to try to hit them myself too. And I couldn't. Once they're in the air, the corncobs take all kinds of crazy angles. They move funny. Guess that's how my dad and Paul got so good at hitting."

According to Lloyd, the famous Waner farm was sold after Ora Waner died. The grandfather had even built a three-hole golf course for his stick-wielding sons and grandchildren.

Lloyd Waner Jr.: "When I was a little kid, they did work with me. I even coached Little League when I lived in Houston. Dad would come out and teach the kids the science of throwing the baseball in one smooth motion. He got a real kick out of working with young people. How much could you ask for if you were a Little Leaguer—tutelage by a Hall-of-Famer?"

Beyond baseball, Lloyd simply loved Oklahoma's sweeping ranges and wide open skies. There he felt at home, his son said.

Lloyd Waner Jr.: *"It was his dream to be a farmer. He was much happier out on the farm than he was in the city. Dad loved the farm so much, and he just wanted to be a farmer. If he was away from the farm, he wasn't much of a happy camper. As a bookkeeper for the city, he did pretty good, and he liked the people there. It was about a 20–25 mile ride from the farm into the city. He liked scouting, he just didn't like the traveling."*

Was it difficult for Paul and Lloyd living so far apart after their playing days? After all, these two were synonymous together.

Lloyd Waner Jr.: *"I don't think it was hard on them being apart after their playing days. They saw each other several times during the year, and my father would go to Bradenton for the Pirates' spring training for awhile. He worked with some of the young players there."*

Paul was a fun-loving uncle—too much, for his own good.

Lloyd Waner Jr.: *"I couldn't wait to see him come. He was a barrel of fun, and good with all the kids. He'd go out in the yard and play baseball with us. He had such good patience. That's the shame of it all. He could've been a YMCA director or worked with children in sports somewhere. He was truly good with people. Extremely good with children."*

Neither Lloyd nor Paul had big egos, Lloyd Jr. said.

Lloyd Waner Jr.: *"I never saw them act that way ever. They were humble. They never carried themselves any different than the guy walking down the street. I don't have much interest in baseball players today 'cause they think they're so great. My father and uncle never thought that.*

"They played for the love of the game, and thought of themselves as common people. They didn't make any money in those days, there were things they could have done to make more money, but they didn't. Geez, these guys today. Talk about loyalty, the Waners were enormously loyal to the Pittsburgh Pirates. I don't hear that from today's players. It's 'where's the money?' Not with dad and my uncle. They'd go out and play catch with the kids when they were home. That came through to all the kids in the neighborhood when I was growing up.

"They taught us that you learn something from every game you lose. The game isn't all just about winning. I haven't heard that since my dad has passed on."

Did Lloyd Jr. ever think of taking up baseball? No. Though his dad taught him about the game, and Lloyd Jr. played one summer in the YMCA League, he was "good field, no hit," as they say.

25. Little Poison Goes Home

"Like his dad he could shag those flies," wrote Vernon B. Snell of *The Sporting News*. But that was it. Lloyd Jr. did, however, beat his grandfather in golf when he was 12. He could never get Ora to play him again after that.

The dark side was the alcohol.

Lloyd Waner Jr.: *"They did have alcohol problems. Had it not been for that, they would have been better known, and enjoyed post-baseball careers that would have raised their profiles. But they were limited by their drinking, even after their baseball careers. That one article about giving Paul a drink so he could hit, well, that was true. It was a blooming shame. Dad tried to be protective of me, though. If there was any drinking around, he tried to keep it away from me.*

"I got really tired of it all. Sometimes it seemed the only guys who came by the house were drunks. Drunks. I went to the University of Oklahoma to protect my mother, as my father didn't have much money because of the drinking. I wanted to go to an Ivy League school back East, but it didn't happen, and it all worked out though. I had to buy a car so I could drive home and make sure my dad was OK after he passed out in the front lawn. I got so I couldn't even drink in college—it would make me vomit. The other guys would apologize if they had a drink in front of me."

Lloyd Jr. learned how to drink—very sparingly—only after college. He noted that his father gave up drinking for the last four or five years of his life. And that's when they finally had a chance to be father and son and enjoy a meaningful relationship.

Lloyd Waner Jr.: *"It was like having a real father around. I could talk to him, and it was the beginning of something special, right there toward the end of his life. At least we had a chance there, and I'll always treasure that period."*

In July 2001, Bob Hersom of the *Daily Oklahoman* interviewed Lloyd Waner Jr. and Lydia Freeman about their father. His piece revealed different perceptions among the brother and sister.

"I guess I've got to forgive him for a lot of the things," said Lloyd Waner Jr. "Keep this in mind: I guess he was OK as baseball players and professional athletes go. But, although I'm a scratch golfer, I couldn't hit a baseball if my life depended upon it."

Lydia, 62, was born six years before her father retired from baseball. Today she is a receptionist for her husband, dentist Wes Freeman of Oklahoma City.

"He was real sweet. Actually, daddy was pretty shy. But he was there for me."

She added, "Brother being five years older than me, he remembers better what was going on."

As Hersom put it, Lloyd Jr. grew up convinced his dad was "embarrassed to have a '120-pound weakling son' who was good at golf and tennis but not any so-called man's games," like baseball.

"Because you get these professional athletes, they want their boys to be husky and all that kind of stuff," Lloyd Jr. said. "Tennis to him was a sissy game. He wouldn't even watch it. My dad probably was the best baseball player pound-for-pound. He was very good, and he was not only good at that, but pretty nearly everything. I mean, his eye and hand coordination was superb."

Despite his dad's flaws, Lloyd Jr. is proud to be named after the Hall of Famer.

"Oh, sure, of course I am," he said. "Everybody has faults. He was a helluva guy. He ought to be an inspiration for this poor little kid out here who's like me, who's 140 pounds and wants to go do something. Well, here's a guy that did it. It's really neat to find some little frail guy who can compete against the top people."

According to Lloyd Jr. his father starting drinking more heavily after retiring from the game. "Mainly it was afterwards (after retiring) for dad, though he did drink when he was playing ball. Paul drank like a fish when he was playing ball," he said.

Lydia said, "They were characters, they really were. There was a lot of drinking, and I think that's what really took down Paul and daddy. But it seemed like back in those days that it was just a real fact of life, it really was."

Asked to describe his father as a person, Lloyd Jr. said, "Except for the alcohol, extremely good. You didn't lie about anything, even if it hurt. He had an awful lot of those traits that you really want to see in parents."

Today, in an ironic twist of fate, Lloyd Jr.'s son, Andy Waner, runs a drug and alcohol rehabilitation program in Oklahoma City.

Lloyd Waner Jr.: *"He doesn't look anything like us Waners—he's all-American, blond, blue-eyed, and big. Worked out, wrestled in school, and kept himself in shape all the way through his early 30s."*

So effective is Andy Waner in his rehab program that Oklahoma's politicians routinely call upon him, and CNN has tapped him for on-air interviews.

Lloyd Jr. hardly knew his counterpart, Paul Jr. To begin, the two grew up in different states—Florida and Oklahoma—and Paul's divorce made family relations that much more difficult. The first time Lloyd Jr. saw Paul Jr. was in his early teen years in Oklahoma.

"I didn't have a driver's license, but he did, and we went to a hamburger joint," Lloyd Jr. said. "I remember him as extremely good-looking and well-built."

Jim Cook is Lloyd and Paul Waner's nephew—the son of Lloyd's oldest sister. At 76, he has retired from working as an accountant and now resides in Dallas, Texas. He shared some memories of the Waners sticking together during the Great Depression in the 1930s.

Jim Cook: *"My parents, myself and two sisters moved in with our grandparents at the farm in Harrah. We lived with them for a couple of years during the Depression. The dust had not hurt that farm, so they were fortunate."*

Cook recalled his thrill as a young kid when his famous uncles returned to Oklahoma.

Jim Cook: *"Every spring the Pirates and my uncles would come through Oklahoma every spring training. You see, the Pirates then trained in Arizona with three other teams. They would play their way across the country toward the East Coast, taking the train. When they got to Oklahoma, the Pirates put on a big show 'cause they knew the Waners were a big draw in these parts. They always played in Oklahoma City and Shawnee. Before the game I'd get to go out on the field and play catch. I was six years old."*

Like Lloyd Jr., Cook's not a fan of today's baseball.

Jim Cook: *"I refuse to go to a baseball game. If they can pay those guys that much money, they expect us to pay for it. But I don't think they're worth that kind of money. I like the old days. When I went to the first game at the Astrodome, I paid a dollar and a half to sit in the bleachers. That was fun. It was a family thing then. But how can a family these days afford it?"*

Once his uncle Lloyd mailed a young Jim Cook his baseball glove. "Man, I was the hottest kid in town."

Without My Spikes

> When the One Great Scorer comes to write against your name—
> He marks—not that you won or lost—but how you played the Game.
> — *Grantland Rice, sportswriter*

    As the decade of the 1960s dawned, the world looked far different than it did in the 1920s when the Waner brothers broke into baseball. The enemy of the Free World was the Soviet Union and not Nazi Germany, the United States elected a Catholic president for the first time ever in John Fitzgerald Kennedy, the country was exploring manned space flights, and among the books published in 1960 was *To Kill a Mockingbird*, a gripping novel of prejudice in the South at a time when the Civil Rights movement was changing minds and hearts across the country.

    In major league baseball in 1960, just 8 percent of ballplayers were black. But in the decade of the 1950s that recently ended, 8 of the 10 NL Most Valuable Player awards were won by black players.

    Beyond the continued influx of black talent, the decade would witness the introduction of the 162-game schedule, expansion ball clubs, the rise of other spectator sports like football, the breaking of Babe Ruth's 60-home-run record and the fall of the New York Yankee dynasty, and the return of the pitcher in baseball's eternal struggle between the plate and the mound.

    In the spring of 1960, Paul Waner left the Braves to serve as a hitting coach with the cross-state Philadelphia Phillies. Ironically, his old team the Pirates would defeat the Yankees in that year's World Series in glorious underdog fashion to win their first World Series since 1925. Both Paul

26. Without My Spikes

> WIDE WORLD PHOTO : PLEASE WATCH CREDIT
> 925387
> TWO HEADS ARE BETTER THAN ONE.
> ST. PETERSBURG, FLA. --- THAT IS THE OPINION OF PAUL AND LLOYD WANER, SLUGGING MEMBERS OF THE PITTSBURGH PIRATES BASEBALL TEAM AS THEY TAKE UNDER ADVISEMENT THE BEST WAY TO PLAY A GOLF SHOT WHILE VACATIONING HERE.
> c-1/26/40 s

The Waners made golfing headlines (courtesy of Jim Knight).

and Lloyd must have rejoiced in Pittsburgh's obvious revenge of their 1927 Series defeat at the hands of New York. But now they were outsiders looking in—neither one was working for the club then as a scout or instructor.

Paul Waner on the Phillies—it seemed an odd fit, literally. At the Phils' spring training in Florida, everything looked too big on the 57-year-old Waner—cap, glasses, uniform, even the bat he used for instruction. He wore the number "32" on his Phillies uniform, and it stretched around to the front of his wispy body. Yet the venerable Big Poison could still swing, as Al Cartwright of the *Wilmington Journal* observed.

Al Cartwright: *"The years have been hard on Paul Waner, and vice versa, for he was one of those lost weekend pros who could show up at the ball park in the nick of time and slash his way to two or three hits. A welterweight Babe Ruth. But his name remains magic, and when he talks, the kids and the major leaguers pay attention. And Paul goes about his duties with intelligence and wit and an animal ability to stroke a baseball, even at his age. He jumped into the batting cage the other day, and peering from beneath and incongruous helmet, stroked a couple of line drives off Robin Roberts."*

In his vintage years, Paul's aptitude for stick games was still sensational. For years he was among the leading scorers in the Annual Baseball Players Golfing Tournaments held in Miami and St. Petersburg. He once won the national championship for left-handed golfers. In 1960 he was the runner-up in the National Association of Left-Handed Golfers Tournament at Sarasota's DeSota Lakes course. The association even named its top award the "Paul Waner Trophy," presented only to professional ballplayers who golfed.

Golfing aside, Paul had a duty that spring to teach the young Phillies hitters. His 3,152 hits spoke louder than his delicate appearance, though.

One of the Phillies beat writers, Wirt Gammon, said of Paul, "he doesn't look strong, a little leathery, wizened, gnome-like man."

Waner knew baseball was changing—pitchers, for example, threw harder than ever before. So he spoke out in favor of full-sized batting helmets. He recalled seeing one of his hitting students get beaned in a minor league game in North Carolina.

Paul Waner: *"My last game there Gerald Griffin went 5 for 5, and then he was hit in the back of the head. I almost cried. I was afraid he would die. They carried him off the field. It turned out to be a slight skull fracture. He ducked his head right, but his helmet flew off. Me, I'm for helmets covering more of the head, and strapped around the neck to stay on. Little League helmets cover the head well, that's what I'm for."*

Paul's head contained more than just baseball. There was a poetic streak in the lifetime .333 hitter. At an old-timers' dinner in Cooperstown in the early 1960s, Paul was asked to say a few words. He asked in return if he could read a short poem, and of course, those present agreed. Though we do not have a copy of this poem, it was described as "rather delicate" and touching on some of the vagaries of life. Not quite what one might expect from a former ballplayer. When Paul finished, the applause that greeted his recitation was tremendous. One of the other old-timers in the room applauded louder than the rest. It was his brother Lloyd.

On January 29, 1964, the writer Lawrence Ritter visited a 61-year-old Paul Waner at his home in Sarasota. Waner shared with Ritter his memories about playing ball. He would become a chapter in perhaps the most compelling baseball book ever published, *The Glory of their Times*.

After arriving at the Waners' house around 8 P.M., Ritter and his 15-year-old son, Stephen, were treated to hot chocolate and cookies by Paul and his wife Mildred. With the youngster present, the Waners served no alcoholic beverages, and Paul avoided the subject of drinking during the course of the interview. The five hours of conversation lasted until well after midnight, and Ritter and Waner talked on for an hour or two after the tape had run out.

"He was immensely polite," Ritter remembered. "He was gracious and solicitous to both of us, and was one of the most accommodating ballplayers I interviewed. Very well-spoken, too."

While some ballplayers' wives would interrupt Ritter in the course of the interviews, Mildred Waner did not. She let Paul do the talking. Though quiet and polite, Mildred wasn't very good-looking, Ritter said. "I don't know why that sticks out in my mind now, but it does," the writer said.

26. Without My Spikes

The Florida ranch-style cottage where the Waners lived was clean and cozy, Ritter recalled. Around Sarasota, Paul was known by people inside and outside of baseball, even some of the literati. Ritter recalled a book by the mystery author John D. McDonald that was signed by the author acknowledging his friendship with Paul Waner.

In talking to Ritter, Paul reflected on the ballplaying life. What he said is significant to the role of oral history in understanding baseball players.

Paul Waner coaching for the Phillies in 1964 not long before he died (courtesy of the Pittsburgh Pirates).

Paul Waner: *"You know why old ballplayers love to reminisce? It's because each of us has so many memories stored away in the old noggin', memories that are just begging to pour out. Think about it. We used to play 154 games a season, each one with at least 18 players on the field. I bet that after each game every one of those 18 could have told a story or two about the game, something that struck him as especially interesting. It might have been something technical about the way the game was played, or something mainly of human interest, or maybe something funny, or whatever. You can figure it out: 18 times 154, and that's just for a single season."*

Years later, Ritter gave the original tape—including portions not published in the *Glory of Their Times*—to the National Baseball Hall of Fame. After Paul died, Ritter asked Mildred if she would agree to include Paul's interview on a record version planned for release a couple of years after the book publication. Mildred declined, saying "his voice shouldn't be heard now that he's dead." It's too bad, for Paul's voice on the original tapes reveals the country twang of Oklahoma, and he talks in a high-pitched homespun voice.

◆ ◆ ◆

An effort to recognize Paul Waner existed in the twilight of his life. Back in Pittsburgh, the Pennsylvania Sports Hall of Fame inducted him as a member. The tributes started pouring out, as seems inevitable when great stars are fading. In 1963, in St. Petersburg, the Little League Boosters Club presented a plaque to Paul that mildly annoyed him. It read, "To the Oldest Ballplayer."

"I'm only 60," Paul replied, "I'm only a boy compared to Heine Groh and Tommy Leach."

To the end, Paul kept visible in the hitting-instruction circles. On June 24, 1964, Waner was in California helping young Phillies hitters. After watching Bakersfield lose, 7–6, to Fresno, he lamented the demise of contact hitting, the style that so epitomized Paul and Lloyd Waner in their glory days.

Paul Waner: *"The big trouble with young hitters today is that most of them want to hit the ball out of the park. If they would just meet the ball, they would get more hits and home runs would come by accident."*

The last time Paul would appear in Forbes Field was in late July 1964. That's when the Phillies called on him as a batting instructor for help with their flailing hitters. With the Phils in Pittsburgh, the wistful Waner was introduced to the fans, and he received a roaring, standing ovation.

Over the winter Paul didn't feel so good. On March 3, 1965, he was hospitalized at Sarasota Memorial Hospital for pulmonary emphysema and pneumonia. For two weeks he was in serious condition, and the doctors performed surgery. Gradually, he improved and was released.

Paul spared no time in getting back to baseball. In June, the Philadelphia Phillies rehired him as a batting instructor. He traveled some with the major league club, managed by Gene Mauch at the time, and then toured the team's farm clubs as a roving instructor.

In early August, Paul checked into a Sarasota hospital. There he wrote a revealing poem—the only one by Paul Waner in print. Focused on his own feeling of mortality, the untitled piece also paid homage to Big Poison's fellow brethren in the Hall of Fame:

> I sometimes pause for just a minute
> To think of this world with me not in it
> I can't think of another day
> Without me here alert some way
> I cannot think of another spring
> Without my spikes and a bat to swing
> These precious years will come and go

26. Without My Spikes

> With faster pace, but this I know—
> I have no fear or do I dread
> Of the marked day that lies ahead.
> My body will turn to ash and clay,
> But I'll be there somehow, some way.

About two weeks later, on August 29, 1965, Paul Waner died of pulmonary emphysema and pneumonia in his home. He was 62.

Paul was buried at Manasota Memorial Park in Bradenton—where every spring the Pirates hold their training camp, and baseball is in the air. Pirates manager Bill McKechnie is buried in the same cemetery.

The Sporting News intoned that Waner played in a day and age when a 150-pound man had the chance to make a ball club: "(It) makes one wonder whether a Paul Waner today would get the same opportunity in baseball which Paul himself got in 1923. With the accent on muscle and the home run swing, would a modern scout devote any attention to a 140-pound or 150-pound prospect? Probably not—unless the prospect swung the bat like Paul Waner."

Paul's second wife, Mildred, continued to live in the Sarasota area until the 1990s when her family relocated her to a nursing home in Winchester, Kentucky. Always proud of her Paul, she lived until 1997. In her room hung a glossy photograph of a young, smiling Paul Waner in a clean Pittsburgh Pirates uniform, his hands gripping a bat.

Paul Waner left behind a lasting legacy worthy of any ballplayer. Yet there were some that felt Paul could have been even better. Bob Broeg was one of them.

Bob Broeg: *"Paul Glee Waner undoubtedly would have lived longer and more comfortably if he had been willing to give up his heavy cigarette habit and forego those occasional extra-inning battles with John Barleycorn, who has a way of coming on stronger the older and weaker the foe. But in all seriousness, would the pleasant little man have hit better if he'd spent more time in the arms of Morpheus than out bending the elbow with Bacchus?"*

Make no mistake—Big Poison led a swashbuckling life.

From Corncobs to Cooperstown

> I've become convinced that every player who plays the game at the major league level for any length of time leaves an image lingering behind him, that if you really understood the history of baseball, that if one could see baseball, so to speak, with the eyes of God, one could see in each and every baseball game the image of every good and great player who has ever played.
>
> —*Bill James*

The year 1967 reflected a widespread disillusionment and loss of innocence in America. The Vietnam War escalated and thousands of protesters demonstrated across America against U.S. military action in southeast Asia, Newark and Detroit erupted in race riots, three astronauts died in a launching pad fire at Cape Kennedy, and Simon and Garfunkel's song "Mrs. Robinson" from the hit movie *The Graduate* provided its famous Joe DiMaggio catchphrase.

In the late 1960s while America was exploding, politically and psychedically, baseball was contracting into a horse-and-buggy relic. A year from now in 1968 baseball's 23.1 million gate would be 1.2 million off the total for 1967 and 2 million off for 1966. In that decade attendance-hungry baseball kept on playing through the Martin Luther King and John F. Kennedy assassinations, and caught hell for doing so. The game's profound slump was further exacerbated by the dreadful season of 1968—at least for hitters. The season seem to confirm everything critics had been saying about

27. From Corncobs to Cooperstown

baseball vis-à-vis football—boring. Batters in the National League hit a collective .243, and in the American League, .230. This didn't put fans in the seats.

Baseball, in the worst of times, always does well to focus on the great players in the game. That was the big reason behind establishing the Hall of Fame in another tumultuous decade, the 1930s. Now, with many of those players from the 1920s and 1930s growing older and more frail, baseball saw fit to honor them in the grandest of ways. This could only help stir interest in the sport in these heady days of competition.

In January 1967 Lloyd Waner was visiting friends and family in Pittsburgh when the phone rang for him. It was the National Baseball Hall of Fame. They had called to welcome the 61-year-old Lloyd Waner as its newest member. Granted, Lloyd had been tipped off that he would get the call, but for the press and public it didn't matter. With Paul having died recently and having squawked for years about his brother's deserving his own place in the Hall, it seemed a just way to recognize the Waner brothers, if not Lloyd solely, as baseball's best-hitting brother combination.

Unlike brother Paul, the Veterans Committee had selected Lloyd instead of the Baseball Writers Association of America (BBWAA). That year, Red Ruffing and Branch Rickey were also selected for the Hall—Ruffing by the BBWAA, and Rickey by the Committee.

♦ ♦ ♦

For years it was clear Lloyd would not get into the Hall of Fame through the more rigorous route of the BBWAA's writers. One problem was the galaxy of great slugging stars of his era. Against these luminaries a player like Lloyd known for defense, singles and speed did not always measure up well. In 1950, the writer Frank Graham predicted Lloyd would never join Paul in the Hall of Fame, and "for the rest of his life will walk in Paul's shadow, as he did through all his playing days."

Another issue is Lloyd's qualifications as a member—though the Hall has no criteria on admission. For context, it's important to note that the number of selections by the Veterans Committee skyrocketed in the 1960s—altogether, 30 players were chosen for the Hall of Fame during the decade, 22 of them by the Veterans Committee. When Lloyd was selected the committee included Frankie Frisch (or at least he joined the committee in '67) and the writers Fred Lieb, Dan Daniel, and J. Roy Stockton. Bill James has described the period from 1967 to 1973 along with 1945–46 as one of the "two most reckless periods" in Hall of Fame selections. James has quipped that when the Veterans Committee voted Lloyd into the Hall its members had mistakenly been studying the statistics of Lloyd's brother, Paul. If so, he noted, "it would be the only time the Veterans Committee paid any attention to the statistical evidence."

This may be harsh, but he has a point. But instead of asking whether Lloyd Waner belongs in the Hall of Fame, perhaps the better question is how does one measure "fame"? While James may be right, and the Hall of Fame selection process has demonstrated favoritism on a number of occasions, never has the Hall of Fame set forth a strict statistical yardstick with which to define "fame." And it would never do so. It is, after all, a Hall of "Fame," not a Hall of Statistics, though admittedly statistics are central to understanding baseball.

This raises the issue of intangibles—qualities not adequately reflected in statistics. To his credit, Lloyd was a defensive wizard in center field, one of the best of his era, and his speed reemphasized the importance of fleet-footed players in the game. Lead-off guys like Little Poison—a singles-hitting machine in a game that glorifies the long ball—are frequently overlooked despite succeeding in their specific roles. This time Lloyd did receive his due accolades. It wasn't his job to drive in runs or hit home runs. He also played the game with gentlemanly class. Alone, none of these so-called intangibles merit Hall selection, but together the total is greater than the sum of its parts.

Besides, the Hall of Fame should honor more than players who made a career of batting in the three, four or five spots. The game is more than just home runs and RBIs. This was illustrated in the 2001 Hall selection of the great defensive second baseman, Bill Mazeroski.

◆ ◆ ◆

On January 29, 1967, Lloyd Waner was honored for his selection to the Hall of Fame at the annual Dapper Dan sports banquet in Pittsburgh. On that cold winter day, a crowd of a couple thousand well-wishers gathered at the Hilton Hotel. The big ticket item was not Lloyd Waner—it was Pirates right fielder Roberto Clemente, who was to be recognized for winning the National League Most Valuable Player award for the 1966 season.

Lloyd was photographed alongside Hall of Famer Pie Traynor, Pirates owner Bill Benswanger, and Socko McCarey, the Forbes Field clubhouse manager, always an important figure. The paper noted the "eternally-baby-faced" Lloyd weighed but 150 pounds—five more than in his playing days—and didn't have a single gray hair.

Lloyd was asked about his feelings and thoughts upon learning of his selection. Surprise—Paul was foremost on his mind.

Lloyd Waner: *"The first thought I had was of my brother Paul. I just wish Paul were alive to share this moment with me. He always said I should be in the Hall of Fame. I'm simply overwhelmed because I didn't even know I was being considered. Another big thing that makes this such a big day is that it happened here in Pittsburgh. This is really my home because this is where I broke into the majors with the Pirates in 1927 and played for almost 15 years. This is where my friends are and this is where my fans were. And my wife is a former Pittsburgher."*

Another question elicited his views on the game, then and now.

Lloyd Waner: *"It's a real fast game today. The outfield is like a pool table and the infield like a carpet. When I was playing the outfields were so rough you didn't dare charge a ball. Also, today's gloves have improved the defensive side of the game. I caught a ball in the palm of my hand. Today they snag balls with these big webbings. I couldn't catch with one of today's gloves."*

The playing conditions were rougher back then, too. During the Waner era, Forbes Field would host college and professional football games in the Fall—while baseball season was still underway—and this would tear up the turf. Unlike today, there was never any attempt to clean up the field or do any grounds keeping after the games. "Lots of times I'd go out early in the morning and get me a rake and try to smooth up the outfield."

As a new inductee, Lloyd was getting all kinds of attention. He accepted an invitation from the New York Mets to attend an Old-Timers reunion at Shea Stadium on July 8. The sixth annual event honored George Weiss, president of the Mets and former Yankee executive. The game pitted Weiss's last Yankee team (1960) against his first Mets team (1962). It is not known whether Lloyd actually put on a uniform and played, or just milled about with the players.

A few weeks before journeying to Cooperstown for the midsummer induction, Lloyd was asked what kind of speech he would give.

Lloyd Waner: *"It won't be long. Everybody says I'll choke up and cry before it's over. I don't know, maybe I will. I know one thing. It's going to be one of my greatest thrills ever."*

He grinned and dug into his pocket for a handkerchief and wiped his glasses clean.

"I wish ol' Paul was living. We'd have a picnic," he said softly.

On July 24, light rain showers fell on the small New York town of Cooperstown as thousands of fans and insiders gathered at the Hall of Fame for the annual induction ceremony.

Lloyd went to the podium, without notes, to make his acceptance speech. At first, emotion seemed to nearly overcome him as he talked briefly, thanking his brother Paul, his parents, his teammates, and the Pirates. Eyewitnesses were not sure if rain drops or tears the streaked his cheeks.

A few hours later Roy McHugh of the Pittsburgh Press reached Lloyd by telephone. Little Poison seemed a bit uncomfortable with all the attention and adoration by fans.

Lloyd Waner: *"I don't know, it's just funny. They go wild sometimes, you know. They went wild today. Certainly was a mess of 'em here. I was kind of thrilled, though, going into the Hall of Fame with all these big stars."*

McHugh described Lloyd as "plainspoken," and probably thought more of himself as the man who does the record-keeping in Oklahoma City's street maintenance department than as one of the newest members of the Hall of Fame. Back in Oklahoma, Little Poison admitted, most of the boys had not even heard of him. Now they would, and that was a good thing, for Lloyd, like Paul, enjoyed being around kids. And while he expressed a yearning to get involved in recreation work with the City of Oklahoma, Lloyd continued working in the street maintenance department until his retirement there in 1970.

In grandiose fashion, fellow Hall member Pie Traynor weighed in on Lloyd's new club status.

Pie Traynor: *"How good a center fielder was he? I'd say this—better than Willie Mays in center field because Mays plays too deep. Willie gives you all those balls in back of second base. Lloyd played a natural center and he could go in and grab those balls."*

Traynor described Lloyd as the perfect team player, a gentleman on the diamond. "I never heard him squawk on an umpire's decision. No manager ever rebuked him. He played for Donie Bush and Jewel Ens and George Gibson and myself, and one of us ever had to say a word."

Every year it seemed Paul held out on his contract, Traynor said. Lloyd only did it once, and only briefly. In later years, Pirates owner Bill Benswanger said he allowed Lloyd to fill in the dollar amount on the bottom of his contract. Benswanger said he permitted only three other players ever to do that—Honus Wagner, Pie Traynor, and Guy Bush.

27. From Corncobs to Cooperstown

Left: This 1999 issue of "Oklahoma" featured the Waner brothers (courtesy of the Oklahoma Sports Museum). *Right:* This 1988 issue of *Oklahoma Today* recalled the exploits of the brothers from Harrah, Oklahoma (courtesy of the Oklahoma Sports Museum).

Said Lloyd, "I wanted to play ball. I'd play for nothing, I suppose. All I thought about was playing ball."

Parade magazine rhapsodized about the twin-like brothers in the Hall, noting the bittersweet emotion of Paul not being around for Lloyd's long-awaited entrance. "The two brothers always were exceptionally proud of each other's accomplishments. Lloyd went around beaming for days when Paul was voted into Baseball's Hall of Fame 15 years ago. So you can imagine how Paul would have felt had he still been alive when Lloyd was also voted in last Sunday."

Frank Boggs, the sports editor of the *Daily Oklahoman*, paid Lloyd a visit once Little Poison returned to Oklahoma. He discovered Lloyd had a houseful of memorabilia, from photos to balls and autographs. The room was covered on all four walls by signed photos like the one of Honus Wagner, Walter Johnson, Tris Speaker, George Sisler, Babe Ruth, Connie Mack, Cy Young, and a couple of unidentified players. Boggs asked Lloyd about it.

Lloyd Waner: "I get kind of a kick out of looking at it. I think one of them is Christy Mathewson. But I'm not sure. Ol' Honus gave me that years ago. That picture is priceless among the old-timers."

Enclosed in a glass case was one of Lloyd's longest hits ever. He launched it into the second tier of the right field bleachers in Braves Field when Pittsburgh played there in September 1929. On one side of the ball Paul scribbled a note to his brother—"This ball was well hit."

Another of Lloyd's favorites was a photo of the 1927 Pittsburgh Pirates who had the misfortune of crossing paths with the Ruth–Gehrig New York Yankees.

Lloyd Waner: "Babe Ruth hit only one home run the whole series, but the guy we couldn't get out was [Mark] Koenig, their second baseman. Paul and I had a good series. I hit .400 and he hit .333."

Waner told Boggs he received plenty of fan mail and autograph requests, some of it from young soldiers in Vietnam. The summer before he had managed the American Legion club in Missoula, Montana. As for golf, he was slowing down a bit, mostly due to a slipped disc in his back.

"I have to ride in a cart when I play golf. After I had some trouble with my back, my doctor told me not to lift anything heavier than my pipe."

One of his favorite hunting and fishing companions was Joe Milem, his old college coach at East Central in Ada. He also followed the Oklahoma City's 89ers baseball team as well as the Little League squads in his neighborhood.

Looking back on his career, Lloyd always paid tribute to his brother. He might never have had a major league try-out if it hadn't been for Paul.

Lloyd Waner: "It was Paul who got me the trial with the Pirates. If it hadn't been for him, I never would have had the opportunity, and if it hadn't been for his encouragement, I never would have lasted. He taught me a great deal."

When he returned to Oklahoma after the Hall of Fame festivities, Lloyd took the time to pen a gracious letter to Lee Allen, the Hall's historian, and enclosed a local news clipping with it.

Dear Lee:

My family and I were happy to make your acquaintance while in Cooperstown. We had a wonderful time. Hope I can come back again in the near future. I told you I would send Cy Blanton's wife's address. It is Mrs. Marie Blanton, 316 Davis Circle, Oklahoma City, Oklahoma. She is working for a bank here in the city. They had, I believe, four children, so she has had it pretty rough. She has not remarried. Frank Boggs, sports editor of our *Daily Oklahoman*, who you met with me in your office, had this article about you. Thought you might like to read it. He got quite a kick out of talking to you. He had several write ups about me, and the pretty scenery around Cooperstown. Just thought you would like to have this information.

Sincerely,
Your friend,
Lloyd Waner

The baseball world celebrated Lloyd Waner the next several months. Come spring 1968, however, Little Poison found himself in the hospital. He stayed there five weeks, and the doctors diagnosed him with diabetes.

A few years later in the 1970s, Donald Honig had an opportunity to sit down with Lloyd and interview him for his book, *The October Heroes*. He remembered the details behind the interview and Lloyd's demeanor.

Donald Honig: *"I was up in Cooperstown, and his wife, Fran, asked me to interview him. He couldn't have been nicer. Very sweet, unassuming people. We sat for an hour and a half in their hotel room, and talked. He was a lovable guy. Anybody who ever spoke with him noticed the absolute pride he had in Paul. This came through in every other sentence. It was a nice thing to see a lifetime's worth of love between brothers who had grown up together and played together and were roommates. You would think after all those years there would be some erosion. But there wasn't."*

Baseball opened a whole new world to the Waners. Lloyd told Honig that day, "It did seem like a miracle. We were the beneficiaries of it, and sometimes we'd forget there was a real world out there."

Donald Honig: *"They grew up in hard times, these guys. They accepted things like the Dust Bowl, and the fact they survived such a thing they felt was not so remarkable. In fact, I had to squeeze that information out of Lloyd. That's what life was like, and they accepted it. I remember them saying how stores were closed and farms were abandoned, and here they were making decent money as ballplayers. The Waners, I mean, here are these two little guys coming out of nowhere.*

"I remember Lawrence Ritter telling me one time that Paul told him he was an alcoholic as a young teenager on. The writer Tommy Holmes told me in Baseball Between the Lines *that he and Paul were going somewhere and Holmes kidded him about wanting a drink. Paul pulled out a fountain pen, and had a drink in it."*

In 1978, the town of Meeker in Oklahoma honored one of its legends, Carl Hubbell. Lloyd, who was just getting over a case of bronchitis, made the trip from Oklahoma City. Back in the early 1920s, Hubbell had played baseball at Meeker High School at the same time Lloyd was on the McCloud High School squad.

Lloyd Waner: *"I remember Carl when he just had a fastball. When he and I played against each other in high school and semipro, I don't think either of us realized we'd be up there some day."*

Somebody asked if they were friends in the majors.

Lloyd Waner: *"No, I never went out to dinner with Hubbell when we were in the big leagues. We weren't allowed to talk to the opposition in those days. The game's still the same. There's still a round ball and bat, but the times are different."*

Lloyd said Hubbell didn't give him too much trouble. "Hubbell's screwball gave the right-handed hitters more trouble. Paul and I were left-handed, and his pitches would come in on us."

Lloyd was asked to compare salaries, then and now. Remember, 1978 was a few years into free agency, which would usher in unbelievable salaries in baseball.

Lloyd Waner: *"We had to be hungry players, because the salaries weren't that high then. My highest in the big leagues was between $13,500 and $14,000. Oh, yes, I got a $1,000 raise after that first year in 1927."*

In July 1981, Lloyd fell in his back yard and broke his hip. The 75-year-old Little Poison was taken to the Oklahoma City Hospital for surgery to mend the fracture.

In May 1982, Lloyd suffered a bout of emphysema and bronchitis and spent three weeks at the Presbyterian Hospital in Oklahoma City. He had been living at the Four Seasons Nursing Center. His wife Fay summed up how he felt.

Fay Waner: *"He's weak as a kitten. He's feeling pretty bad."*

With so many fan requests for autographs, Fay had turned to using a stamp to autograph programs, pictures, programs and other memorabilia. She said one person complained about using a stamp for autographs. "It's the worst thing for the hobby of collecting autographs. If you can't sign anymore, it's better not to sign than to stamp," the fan wrote.

But Fay replied that Lloyd could no longer sign.

On June 14, Lloyd returned to the nursing home. On July 22, he died in Presbyterian Hospital of complications relating to emphysema. He was 76 years of age.

Waner was survived by his wife, the former Francis Mae Snyder; a daughter, Lydia Freeman of Oklahoma City; a son, Lloyd Waner Jr. of Oklahoma City; and five grandchildren.

Funeral services were held at 11 A.M. at the Hahn-Cook-Street and Draper Funeral Chapel in Oklahoma City. Lloyd was buried in Rose Hill Cemetery.

Fellow players credited Waner's speed with changing the game in the '20s and '30s. One of them was Al Lopez, former major league catcher, and manager Al Lopez. He roomed with Lloyd in 1941 as a Pirate.

Al Lopez: *"When he first came up, they tell me the infielders would play back like they normally did, and when Lloyd would beat the ball on the ground like he always did, he'd beat the throw to first. He had unbelievable speed for those days, and infielders would have to play him differently. I don't know if he was the reason why, but soon after he came up, you started hearing about teams looking for fast ballplayers."*

Frank Gustine, the Pirates infielder in the late '30s and early '40s, remembered Waner as a kind, quiet man.

Frank Gustine: *"I never heard anybody say anything bad about him, and if we all could go out of this world and not have anybody say anything bad about us, then I guess we had a pretty good stay."*

The 75-year-old Woody Jensen came down from Wichita, Kansas, for Lloyd's funeral. The fellow Pirates remembered Lloyd warmly.

Woody Jensen: *"There are a lot of guys in there [Hall of Fame] who don't deserve it, and there are some guys playing in the big leagues now who couldn't play high school ball back then. A lot of it is politics. Rabbit Maranville ... why that little shortstop was a good fielder and a funny guy, but he couldn't hit [lifetime .258 average] and doesn't deserve to be in there. A lot of it is luck, timing, I guess. Freddie Lindstrom [who hit .311 for 13 major league seasons] played with us for a couple of years [1933–34] and he's in there. But I remember whenever somebody who threw hard like [Dizzy] Dean or [Carl] Hubbell was going to pitch, Freddie'd get sick and I'd go in. But those Waner boys, now they deserve to be in there. They were great ballplayers. Paul was an extrovert and Lloyd wouldn't say much and stayed away from the cameras. But they stayed together and pulled for each other."*

The former pitcher, Allie Reynolds, now an Oklahoma City oil executive, also attended funeral services. He had memories to share of pitching against Lloyd Waner during spring training while breaking in with Cleveland in the early 1940s. Waner was in the twilight of his career then.

Allie Reynolds: *"Lloyd was a quiet, unassuming fellow. And in those days, I walked everybody because I couldn't find the plate, and I walked him, too. That was one thing I didn't want to do because he was such a terrific base runner. He could really fly. I guess he kind of created a revolution in baseball with his speed, but you don't get into the Hall of Fame if you can't do it all."*

So quiet and unassuming was Lloyd that a little-known fact is that he played all of his 1,992 career games without once being ejected.

Howard Talbot, director of the National Baseball Hall of Fame, arrived from Cooperstown, N.Y., for the funeral services. He said the Waners were to be remembered as the greatest brother combination in the history of the game.

Howard Talbot: *"They stayed together for so long and that was unusual. Paul hit the ball a little harder, and Lloyd always had that hustle. In those days, a lot of guys hustled, but he hustled even more."*

◆ ◆ ◆

In 1989, Lloyd's wife, Fay, passed away at the age of 80. The brothers were inducted into the Oklahoma Sports Hall of Fame in 1991. The duo are also represented in the recently opened Oklahoma Sports Museum in Guthrie. The museum has prominent displays of these National Baseball Hall of Famers. The front window of the west gallery exhibits a traveling trunk donated from the Waners' careers. Paintings of the brothers, donated by Lloyd Waner Jr., hang above their personal-model bats in a display of the bats of the eight Oklahomans in the National Baseball Hall of Fame. The Waner family has lobbied the Pirates—unsuccessfully so far—to retire Lloyd's and Paul's uniform numbers.

Somehow you know the Waner brothers are still playing together. Somewhere in a field bigger than a thousand Forbes Fields, somewhere in the breezy fields of a celestial Oklahoma, where brothers toss corncobs and swing broomstick bats, forever.

Appendix: Career Statistics

Paul Waner

Year	Team	G	AB	R	H	2B	3B	HR	RBI	AVG
1926	Pittsburgh	144	536	101	180	35	*22	8	79	.336
1927	Pittsburgh	155	623	114	*237	42	*18	9	*131	*.380
1928	Pittsburgh	152	602	*142	223	*50	19	6	86	.370
1929	Pittsburgh	151	596	131	200	43	15	15	100	.336
1930	Pittsburgh	145	589	117	217	32	18	8	77	.368
1931	Pittsburgh	150	559	88	180	35	10	6	70	.322
1932	Pittsburgh	154	630	107	215	*62	10	8	82	.341
1933	Pittsburgh	154	618	101	191	38	16	7	70	.309
1934	Pittsburgh	146	599	*122	*217	32	16	14	90	*.362
1935	Pittsburgh	139	549	98	176	29	12	11	78	.321
1936	Pittsburgh	148	585	107	218	53	9	5	94	*.373
1937	Pittsburgh	154	619	94	219	30	9	2	74	.354
1938	Pittsburgh	148	625	77	175	31	6	6	69	.280
1939	Pittsburgh	125	461	62	151	30	6	3	45	.328
1940	Pittsburgh	89	238	32	69	16	1	1	32	.290
1941	Brooklyn	11	35	5	6	0	0	0	4	.171
1941	Boston NL	95	294	40	82	10	2	2	46	.279
1942	Boston NL	114	333	43	86	17	1	1	39	.258
1943	Brooklyn	82	225	29	70	16	0	1	26	.311

*Led League

1944	Brooklyn	83	136	16	39	4	1	0	16	.287
1944	NY Yankees	9	7	1	1	0	0	0	1	.143
1945	NY Yankees	1	0	0	0	0	0	0	0	—
M.L. Totals		2,549	9,459	1,627	3,152	605	191	113	1,309	.333

Lloyd Waner

Year	Team	G	AB	R	H	2B	3B	HR	RBI	AVG
1927	Pittsburgh	150	629	*133	233	17	6	2	27	.355
1928	Pittsburgh	152	*659	121	221	22	14	5	61	.335
1929	Pittsburgh	151	*662	134	234	28	*20	5	74	.353
1930	Pittsburgh	68	260	32	94	8	3	1	36	.362
1931	Pittsburgh	154	*681	90	*214	25	13	4	57	.314
1932	Pittsburgh	134	565	90	188	27	11	2	38	.333
1933	Pittsburgh	121	500	59	138	14	5	0	26	.276
1934	Pittsburgh	140	611	95	173	27	6	1	48	.283
1935	Pittsburgh	122	537	83	166	22	14	0	46	.309
1936	Pittsburgh	106	414	67	133	13	8	1	31	.321
1937	Pittsburgh	129	537	80	177	23	4	1	45	.330
1938	Pittsburgh	147	619	79	194	25	7	5	57	.313
1939	Pittsburgh	112	379	49	108	15	3	0	24	.285
1940	Pittsburgh	72	166	30	43	3	0	0	3	.259
1941	Pittsburgh	3	4	2	1	0	0	0	1	.250
1941	Boston NL	19	51	7	21	1	0	0	4	.412
1941	Cincinnati	55	164	17	42	4	1	0	6	.256
1942	Phila. NL	101	287	23	75	7	3	0	10	.261
1944	Brooklyn	15	14	3	4	0	0	0	1	.286
1944	Pittsburgh	19	14	2	5	0	0	0	2	.357
1945	Pittsburgh	23	19	5	5	0	0	0	1	.263
M.L. Totals		1,993	7,772	1,201	2,459	281	118	27	598	.316

Sources

Chapter 1

Glory Days of Summer: The History of Baseball in Oklahoma, by Royse Parr, Bob Burke and K.A. Franks.
The October Heroes, by Donald Honig.
The Glory of Their Times, by Lawrence S. Ritter.
Dollar Sign on the Muscle, by Kevin Kerrane.
Associated Press story, September 14, 1967.
The Sporting News, March 29, 1961.
Undated *Pittsburgh Press* article by Kaspar Monahan found in Sporting News Waner file.
Christian Science Monitor, August 21, 1967.
Frank Graham, *Baseball Magazine,* March 10, 1961.
Old-timers Album, by Abby Mendelson.
Daily Oklahoman, July 23, 1982.
The October Heroes, by Donald Honig.
Letter from the Baseball Hall of Fame Waner clippings file.
Oklahoma Heritage.

Chapter 2

Unpublished portions of Lawrence S. Ritter's interview with Paul Waner from *The Glory of Their Times* archives at the National Baseball Hall of Fame.
The Glory of Their Times, by Lawrence S. Ritter.
Los Angeles Examiner, December 30, 1932.
Unidentified article from the Baseball Hall of Fame Waner file.
Article titled "Waner Meets Poor Fellow Whose Life TB $$$ Spared," *The Sporting News* Waner file.

Chapter 3

The Pacific Coast League: 1903–1988, by Bill O'Neal
Pacific Coast League Stars, Vol. II, by John Spalding.
The Grand Minor League, Dick Dobbins.
The Glory of Their Times, by Lawrence S. Ritter.
San Francisco Examiner article from February 1957.
Undated *Pittsburgh Press* article by Kaspar Monahan found in *The Sporting News* Waner file.
Unpublished portions of Lawrence S. Ritter's interview with Paul Waner from *The Glory of Their Times* archives at the National Baseball Hall of Fame.

Pittsburgh Gazette Times article reprinted in the Pittsburgh and Western Pennsylvania Sports Hall of Fame's *The Story of the Men and Women Who Made Us a Great Sports Area*, 1969.
Legends of Baseball: An Oral History of the Game's Golden Age, by Walter M. Langford.
Unidentified article from the Baseball Hall of Fame Waner file.

Chapter 4

The Pittsburgh Pirates, by Fred Lieb, 1948.
Fenway: From Frazee to Fisk, by Martin F. Nolan.
Baseball's Greatest Teams, by Tom Meany, 1949.
The Glory of Their Times, by Lawrence S. Ritter.
New York Sun Telegram, January 28, 1943.
Unidentified article by Havey Boyle from the Baseball Hall of Fame Waner file.
Unpublished portions of Lawrence S. Ritter's interview with Paul Waner from *The Glory of Their Times* archives at the National Baseball Hall of Fame.
The Glory of Their Times, by Lawrence S. Ritter.
The October Heroes, by Donald Honig.
Biographical Dictionary of American Sports, by David Porter.
Unidentified article by Frank Graham from the Baseball Hall of Fame Waner file.
Boston Post, Howell Stevens article, June 1942.
Undated *Pittsburgh Press* article by Kaspar Monahan found in *The Sporting News* Waner file.
Associated Press story, August 30, 1965.
Unpublished portions of Lawrence S. Ritter's interview with Paul Waner from *The Glory of Their Times* archives at the National Baseball Hall of Fame.
Unidentified article by Joe Reichler in the Baseball Hall of Fame Waner file.
The Glory of Their Times, by Lawrence S. Ritter.
Unidentified article quoting Ossie Bluege in the Baseball Hall of Fame Waner file.
The Glory of Their Times, by Lawrence S. Ritter.
Sport Magazine's All-Time All-Stars, by Tom Meany.
The Pittsburgh Pirates, Fred Lieb, 1948.
Unpublished portions of Lawrence S. Ritter's interview with Paul Waner from *The Glory of Their Times* archives at the National Baseball Hall of Fame.
The Pittsburgh Pirates, Fred Lieb, 1948.
The Sporting News, March 29, 1961.

Chapter 5

Universal Baseball Association, by Robert Coover.
Unpublished portions of Lawrence S. Ritter's interview with Paul Waner from *The Glory of Their Times* archives at the National Baseball Hall of Fame.
The October Heroes, by Donald Honig.
Associated Press story, February 24, 1962.
Wrigleyville, by Peter Golenbock.
Interview with Donald Honig.
The Pittsburgh and Western Pennsylvania Sports Hall of Fame's *The Story of the Men and Women Who Made Us a Great Sports Area*, 1969.
Unidentified article from the Baseball Hall of Fame Waner file.
Interview with Corinne Waner.
Pittsburgh Post-Gazette article by Les Biederman, September 1965.
Baseball's Greatest Teams, by Tom Meany.
Wrigleyville, by Peter Golenbock.
Baseball Anecdotes, by Okrent and Wulf.
Wrigleyville, by Peter Golenbock.
Still Standing After All These Years, by Victor Debs.
The Pittsburgh Pirates, by Fred Lieb, 1948.
New York Herald Tribune article by Rud Rennie, August 21, 1927.
Cincinnati Post and Times Star, March 16, 1963.
The Sporting News, March 16, 1963.
Unidentified article from the Baseball Hall of Fame Waner file.

Sources

Pittsburgh Post-Gazette, July 28, 1954.
Associated Press, February 24, 1962.

Chapter 6

How Life Imitates the World Series, by Thomas Boswell.
New York Herald Tribune, October 1–10, 1927.
New York Times, October 1–10, 1927.
Pittsburgh Post-Gazette, October 1–10, 1927.
The October Heroes, by Donald Honig.
The Sporting News, February 27, 1952.
Baseball When the Grass Was Green, by Donald Honig.
The Sporting News, February 27, 1952.
The October Heroes, by Donald Honig.
Shawnee News-Star, 1998.
Baseball When the Grass Was Green, by Donald Honig.
Oldtimers Album, by Abby Mendelson.
The Glory of Their Times, by Lawrence S. Ritter.
The October Heroes, by Donald Honig.
Unidentified article from the Baseball Hall of Fame Waner file.

Chapter 7

Unidentified article by Tom Meany.
Baseball Magazine article by Clifford Bloodgood, January 1928.
New York World Telegram, August 15, 1938.
Article by Frank Graham, February 2, 1950.
The Man in the Dugout, by Donald Honig.
Baseball Chronicles, by Mike Blake.
Wrigleyville, by Peter Golenbock.
Boston Post, Howell Stevens article, June 1942.
Oldtimers Album, by Abby Mendelson.
Daily Oklahoman, July 23, 1982.
Insider's Baseball, by Richard L. Field, edited by L. Robert Davids.

Chapter 8

Associated Press story, March 7, 1929.
Green Pastures, by Marc Connelly, 1929.
New York Sun article by Joe Vila, February 2, 1929.
New York Herald Tribune, February 26, 1929.
Unidentified article dated March 7, 1929, from the Baseball Hall of Fame Waner file.
Pittsburgh Post-Gazette article by Ralph Davis, March 21, 1929.
Baseball's 100, by Maury Allen.
Associated Press story, March 22, 1929.
Baseball Magazine article by F. C. Lane, June 1929.
Baseball Digest article by Tom Meany, May 1965.
Pittsburgh Press article by Ralph Davis, 1929.
The Pittsburgh Pirates, by Fred Lieb, 1948.
The Sporting News, August 12, 1967.
Christian Science Monitor, August 21, 1967.
Beckett Baseball, April 1991.
Unidentified article by Joe Reichler in the Baseball Hall of Fame Waner file.
The Sporting News, May 21, 1958.
New York World Telegram, July 9, 1934.

Chapter 9

Literary Digest, 1930 issue.
Pittsburgh Sun Telegraph, March 13, 1930.
Unpublished portions of Lawrence S. Ritter's interview with Paul Waner from *The Glory of Their Times* archives at the National Baseball Hall of Fame.
Pittsburgh Post-Gazette, March 6, 1957.
Diz, by Robert Gregory.
Daily Oklahoman article by Jim Lassiter, July 23, 1982.
Big Sticks, by William Curran.

Chapter 10

Pittsburgh Press article by Fred Wertenbach, undated.
Baseball America, by Donald Honig.
New York Herald Tribune, July 9, 1931.
Unidentified article from the Baseball Hall of Fame Waner file.

Daily Oklahoman article by Tom Kensler, July 23, 1982.
Oldtimers Album, by Abby Mendelson.
Pittsburgh Press article by Kaspar Monahan, undated.
The Pittsburgh Pirates, by Fred Lieb, 1948.
You Gotta Have Wa, by Robert Whiting.

Chapter 11

The Pittsburgh Pirates, by Fred Lieb, 1948.
New York World Telegram, February 24, 1932.
The Sporting News, article by Bob Broeg, March 1970.
Boston Daily Globe, September 5, 1957.

Chapter 12

A Little Pretty Pocket-Book, by John Newberry, 1744.
The Glory of Their Times, by Lawrence S. Ritter.
The Sporting News, article by Bob Broeg, March 29, 1970.
Column by Waite Hoyt in the *Clermont Sun* and *Loveland Herald*, found in *The Sporting News* file on Waner.
Only the Ball Was White, Robert Peterson.

Chapter 13

The Gashouse Gang, by Robert E. Hood.
Big Sticks, by William Curran.
The Pittsburgh Pirates, by Fred Lieb, 1948.
Sport Magazine's All-Time All-Stars, by Tom Meany.
Baseball When the Grass Was Green, by Donald Honig.
St. Louis Post-Dispatch article, November 1, 1934.
Unpublished portions of Lawrence S. Ritter's interview with Paul Waner from *The Glory of Their Times* archives at the National Baseball Hall of Fame.

St. Louis Post-Dispatch article, November 1, 1934.
Daily Oklahoman article, July 3, 2001.

Chapter 14

The Dust Bowl Ballads, music album by Woody Guthrie.
Baseball America, by Donald Honig.
The October Heroes, by Donald Honig.
Baseball's Greatest Quotations, by Paul Dickson.
Brooklyn's Babe, by Tot Holmes.
The October Heroes, by Donald Honig.
Baseball When the Grass Was Real, by Donald Honig.
The Sporting News, 1951, undated article by Tommy Holmes.
Interview with Harry Eisenstat.
The Sporting News, June 27, 1940.

Chapter 15

Unidentified article from the Hall of Fame file on Waner.
New York Times, July 4, 1936.
New York World Telegram, July 16, 1936.

Chapter 16

New York World Telegram, March 5, 1937.
Wilmington Journal, April 6, 1960.
Interview with Peter Beagle.
Unidentified article by Joe Reichler in the Hall of Fame Waner file.
The Spirit of St. Louis, by Peter Golenbock.
Baseball Chronicles, by Mike Blake.
The Grand Minor League, by Dick Dobbins.

Chapter 17

The Green Fields of the Mind, by A. Bartlett Giamatti.

Sources

Unidentified article in the Hall of Fame Waner file.
New York World Telegram, January 10, 1938.
Baseball, a film by Ken Burns.
Only the Ball Was White, by Robert Peterson.
New York Times, February 19, 1938.
New York World Telegram, January 18, 1938.
The Sporting News, June 2, 1938.
International News Service article by Pat Robinson, February 1952.
Oldtimers Album, by Abby Mendelson
New York World Telegram, June 1, 1939.
The Sporting News, June 2, 1938.
Baseball When the Grass Was Green, by Donald Honig.
Interview with Enos Slaughter.
The Sporting News, article February 27, 1952.
Boston Post, article by Howell Stevens, 1942.
Wrigleyville, by Peter Golenbock.
Pennant Races, by Dave Anderson.
Philadelphia Inquirer, July 23, 1982.
The Glory of Their Times, by Lawrence S. Ritter.
The Bill James Guide to Baseball's Managers, by Bill James.

Chapter 18

The Slump, by John Updike.
Baseball When the Grass Was Real, by Donald Honig.
New York Times, January 15, 1939.
New York Sun Telegram, article by Charles Doyle, June 1, 1939.
Letter from Ray Berres found in the Baseball Hall of Fame Waner file.
Pittsburgh Post-Gazette, July 1957.
Undated *Pittsburgh Press* article by Kaspar Monahan found in *The Sporting News* Waner file.
The Sporting News, article by Tommy Holmes, 1951.
Interview with Enos Slaughter.

Chapter 19

Associated Press story, February 19, 1940.
Baseball Biographical Encyclopedia, Total Sports.
Baseball When the Grass Was Real, by Donald Honig.
Baseball's Great Experiment, by Jules Tygiel.
Only the Ball Was White, by Robert Peterson.
Sport Magazine's All-Time All-Stars, by Tom Meany.
Bums, by Peter Golenbock.
Beckett Baseball, April 1991.
Oldtimers Album, by Abby Mendelson.
Still Standing After All These Years, by Victor Debs.
Pittsburgh Post-Gazette, March 6, 1957.
Baseball Anecdotes, by Okrent and Wulf.
A Donald Honig Reader, by Donald Honig.

Chapter 20

Baseball's 100, by Maury Allen.
New York World Telegram article by Dan Daniel, December 1940.
Pittsburgh Post-Gazette article by Les Biederman, December 1940.
Associated Press story, December 6, 1940.
Interview with Enos Slaughter.
Unidentified article from the Baseball Hall of Fame Waner file.
New York Herald Tribune, January 23, 1943.
New York World Telegram, March 22, 1941.
The Sporting News, February 19, 1967.
New York World Telegram, April 29, 1941.
New York Herald Tribune, May 27, 1941.
Memories of a Ballplayer, by Bill Werber and C. Paul Rogers.
New York Sun Telegram, January 28, 1943.

Chapter 21

Desolation Angels, by Jack Kerouac.
Pittsburgh Post-Gazette, 1942

Boston Post, article by Howell Stevens, June 1942.
Oldtimers Album, by Abby Mendelson.
New York Journal American, article by Bill Corum, June 6, 1942.
The Sporting News, May 30, 1970.
The Sporting News, July 2, 1942.
New York Sun Telegram, Jan. 28, 1942.
Baseball Digest, undated.
Unpublished portions of Lawrence S. Ritter's interview with Paul Waner from *The Glory of Their Times* archives at the National Baseball Hall of Fame.
The Glory of Their Times, by Lawrence S. Ritter.
New York Times, Nov. 13, 1942.

Chapter 22

Unpublished portions of Lawrence S. Ritter's interview with Paul Waner from *The Glory of Their Times* archives at the National Baseball Hall of Fame.
New York Sun Telegram, article by Charles Doyle, January 1943.
New York Sun Telegram, January 28, 1943.
The Sporting News archives, undated.
New York World Telegram, January 25, 1943.
New York Herald Tribune, June 25, 1943.
New York Times, March 27, 1943.
New York Herald Tribune, February 16, 1943.
New York Times, March 19, 1945.
New York World Telegram, May 6, 1943.
New York World Telegram, July 30, 1943.
Total Baseball, fifth edition.
New York World Telegram, June 24, 1943.
The Spirit of St. Louis, by Peter Golenbock.

Chapter 23

Shoeless Joe, by W. P. Kinsella.
The Sporting News, February-March 1945.
The Donald Honig Reader, by Donald Honig.
Associated Press story, March 2, 1945.
Associated Press story, August 30, 1965.
Christian Science Monitor story by "Rumill," undated.
New York Times, May 5, 1945.
New York Times article by Arthur Daley, September 1965.
Unpublished portions of Lawrence S. Ritter's interview with Paul Waner from *The Glory of Their Times* archives at the National Baseball Hall of Fame.
The Sporting News, article, February 27, 1952.
Baseball's 100, by Maury Allen.
The Glory of Their Times, by Lawrence S. Ritter.
The Sporting News, article, September 11, 1965.

Chapter 24

Ironweed, by William Kennedy.
Unpublished portions of Lawrence S. Ritter's interview with Paul Waner from *The Glory of Their Times* archives at the National Baseball Hall of Fame.
New York Times, June 11, 1946.
Unidentified article dated March 3, 1963 from the Hall of Fame Waner file.
Paul Waner's Batting Secrets, by Paul Waner.
Baseball's Greatest Quotations, by Paul Dickson.
Letter from Paul Waner to Branch Rickey, 1952, Library of Congress.
Pittsburgh Post-Gazette article by Les Biederman, undated.
The Sporting News, February 27, 1952.
My Turn At Bat, by Ted Williams.
New York World Telegram article by Bill Roeder, March 1, 1952.
The Sporting News, article, July 7, 1954.
Undated article by Garry Schumacher from the Baseball Hall of Fame Waner file.
Undated article from the *Sarasota Herald Tribune*.
Associated Press story, August 30, 1965.
The Sporting News, article, February 27, 1952.

Article by Tommy Holmes, 1951, from *The Sporting News* Waner file.
Associated Press, article, July 22, 1952.
Atlanta Constitution, column by Furman Bisher, February 1952.
Interview with Lillian Porter.
Interview with Beth Noe.
Interview with Corinne Waner.
Unpublished portions of Lawrence S. Ritter's interview with Paul Waner from *The Glory of Their Times* archives at the National Baseball Hall of Fame.
Article by Frank Graham, 1953, from *The Sporting News* Waner file.
Pittsburgh Post-Gazette, March 12, 1958.
Unpublished portions of Lawrence S. Ritter's interview with Paul Waner from *The Glory of Their Times* archives at the National Baseball Hall of Fame.
Associated Press story, March 1, 1952.
The Sporting News, article, September 11, 1965.
Wilmington Journal, April 6, 1960.
Boston Daily Globe, September 5, 1957.
Unpublished portions of Lawrence S. Ritter's interview with Paul Waner from *The Glory of Their Times* archives at the National Baseball Hall of Fame.
Article titled, "Waner Meets Poor Fellow Whose Life TB $$$ Spared," *The Sporting News* Waner file.
Sport Magazine, undated article from 1958
The Sporting News, article, March 29, 1961.
The Sporting News, article, May 21, 1958.
Unidentified article dated July 7, 1954 from *The Sporting News* Waner file.
Pittsburgh Post-Gazette, May 1957.

Chapter 25

October Heroes, by Donald Honig.
Interview with Joe Bauman.
The Sporting News, article, December 1948.
Associated Press story, March 31, 1950.
Interview with Carl J. Vitti.
Interview with Lloyd Waner, Jr.
Daily Oklahoman, article, July 3, 2001.
Interview with Jim Cook.

Chapter 26

Baseball's Greatest Quotations, by Paul Dickson.
Wilmington Journal, article by Al Cartwright, April 6, 1960.
Unidentified articles found in *The Sporting News* Waner file.
Interview with Lawrence S. Ritter.
Unpublished portions of Lawrence S. Ritter's interview with Paul Waner from *The Glory of Their Times* archives at the National Baseball Hall of Fame.
The Glory of Their Times, by Lawrence S. Ritter.
Pittsburgh Post-Gazette, article by Les Biederman, September 1965.
Undated article containing Paul Waner's poem in the *Bradenton Herald*, 1968.
The Sporting News, September 18, 1965.
The Sporting News, article, March 28, 1970.

Chapter 27

1990 Baseball Analyst, by Bill James.
Article by Frank Graham, February 2, 1950.
The Sporting News, article, February 19, 1967.
Christian Science Monitor, August 21, 1967.
Daily Oklahoman, article by Frank Boggs, September 11, 1965.
Pittsburgh Press article by Roy McHugh, July 25, 1967.
The Sporting News, article, August 2, 1982.
Letter from Lloyd Waner to Lee Allen found in the Baseball Hall of Fame Waner file.
The October Heroes, by Donald Honig.
Interview with Donald Honig.
Unidentified articles found in *The Sporting News* Waner file.
Daily Oklahoman, article by Tom Kensler, July 23, 1982.

Index

Aaron, Tommie 80
Adams, Sparky 104, 117
Agnew Sam 27
Aldridge, Vic 47, 104
Alexander, Pete 48, 78
Allen, Maury 118, 262
Alou, Jesus 80
Alou, Matty 80
Anson, Cap 11, 104
Arbuckle, Fatty 24
Arlin, Harold 65
Averill, Earl 34

Bancroft, Dave 64, 77
Barnhart, Clyde 66, 83
Bartell, Dick 31, 100, 107
Barzun, Jacques 7
Baum, Spider 24
Bauman, Joe 284
Beagle, Peter 187
Beaumont, Ginger 61
Beckley 111
Bench, Johnny 8
Bengough, Ben 89
Bennett, Floyd 42
Benswanger, Bill 80, 143, 147, 162, 181, 186, 196, 208, 222, 228
Berres, Ray 211, 225
Biedermann, Les 211, 229
Bierbauer, Lou 39

Bigbee, Carson 46, 59, 66, 111
Bloodgood, Clifford 103
Bluege, Ossie 55
Boggs, Wade 81
Bonds, Barry 57
Boone, Ike 33
Boswell, Thomas 84
Boyle, Havey 40
Brazill, Frank 31, 32
Broeg, Bob 151, 241, 299
Brown, Mace 106, 203
Bush, Donie 66, 97, 110, 118, 122
Bush, Guy 49, 156, 171
Byrd, Richard 42

Capone, Al 29, 113
Carey, Max 46, 55, 59, 105, 111
Carlson, Hal 53
Cartwright, Alexander 23
Chapman, Ray 102
Chase, Hal 29
Clarke, Fred 39, 55, 58, 111
Clary, Ellis 255
Clemente, Roberto 44, 57, 112, 167
Clift, Harlond 7
Cobb, Ty 30, 35, 39, 51, 67, 102, 104, 274
Coffin, Tristram 37
Cohane, Tim 253
Collins, Eddie 104

321

Collins, Pat 89
Combs, Earle 89
Comorosky, Adam 104, 116
Conigliaro, Billy 80
Conigliaro, Tony 80
Conn, Billy 187
Coolidge, Calvin 75
Cooney, Johnny 69
Cooper, Wilbur 42
Coover, Robert 65
Corum, Bill 239
Cox, Dick 44
Creamer, Robert 77
Cronin, Joe 31, 55, 109
Crosetti, Frank 35
Cuccinello, Al 80
Cuccinello, Tony 80
Curran, William 162
Custer, George 8
Cuyler, Kiki 55, 57, 66, 71, 80, 93, 104, 121
Cvengros, Mike 90

Daniel, Dan 228, 232
Davis, Ralph 116, 122, 143
Day, Pea Ridge 139
Dean, Dizzy 7, 8, 134, 138, 161, 201
Dean, Paul 161
Delahanty, Ed 104
Dempsey, Jack 23
Derringer, Paul 246
Devine, Joe 30, 31
Dickey, Glenn 136
Dickshot, Johnny 190
Dillinger, John 161
DiMaggio, Dom 35
DiMaggio, Joe 31, 35, 181, 196
DiMaggio, Vince 217
Doyle, Chilly 46, 66, 235, 248
Dreyfuss, Barney 31, 35, 42, 51, 58, 78, 80, 107, 113, 137, 146, 162
Dreyfuss, Sam 60, 115, 145
Dugan, Joe 89
Durocher, Leo 40, 173, 231
Dykes, Jimmy 197

Einstein, Albert 161
Eisenstate, Harry 175
Elliott, Bob 100, 217
Ellison, Bert 27, 31, 32

English, Woody 72
Ens, Jewel 123, 143

Feller, Bob 181
Ferrell, Rick 80, 159
Ferrell, Wes 80, 159
Fitzgerald, Justin 25
Fletcher, Elbie 204, 220
Floyd, Pretty Boy 161
Forbes, John 44
Freeman, Lydia 292
Frisch, Frankie 64, 76, 102, 199, 214, 216, 227, 259
Froelich, Ed 76

Gee, Johnny 213
Gehrig, Lou 4, 76, 85, 109, 144
Gershwin, George 136
Giamatti, A. Bartlett 193
Giambi, Jason 80
Giambi, Jeremy 80
Gibson, George 143, 156, 163
Gibson, Josh 154, 167
Giles, Warren 269
Gomez, Lefty 35
Grabowski, Johnny 87
Graham, Charley 26
Graham, Eleanor 145
Graham, Frank 275
Grantham, George 58, 79, 106, 116
Greenberg, Hank 226
Greenlee, Gus 154
Griffith, Clark 196
Grimes, Burleigh 104, 120, 135
Grimes, Oscar 74
Grimm, Charlie 42, 56, 152
Groat, Dick 273
Gustine, Frank 224
Guthrie, Woody 168, 193
Gutteridge, Don 255

Hamilton, J.A. 17
Harris, Joe 82
Hartnett, Gabby 201
Hassett, Buddy 233
Heilmann, Harry 104
Hemingway, Ernest 216, 247
Hemsley, Rollie 178
Herman, Babe 105, 174
Herman, Billy 163, 173, 203, 238

Index

Hill, Carmen 83
Hitler, Adolph 29, 180
Honig, Don 5, 10, 73, 169, 307
Hood, Robert 150, 174
Hoover, Herbert 103, 113, 127, 146
Hornsby, Rogers 48, 64, 74, 102, 104, 109, 123
Hoyt, Waite 85, 157
Hubbell, Carl 7, 16, 108, 121, 166, 249, 251

Jackson, Travis 79
James, Bill 179, 300
Jensen, Woody 139, 177, 309
Johnson, Bob 7
Johnson, Roy 7, 34
Johnson, Walter 43, 90
Jolley, Smead 33
Jolson, Al 65
Joyce, James 128

Kamm, Willie 35
Keeler, Willie 35
Kemp, Abe 31
Kennedy, William 264
Kerouac, Jack 237
Kiner, Ralph 57, 287
Kinsella, W.P. 257
Klein, Chuck 159, 182, 212
Klem, Bill 52
Koenecke, Len 148
Koenig, Mark 97
Kremer, Rey 31, 83, 135

Landis, Kenesaw Mountain 23, 86, 190, 223
Lane, F.C. 119
Lanier, Max 199
Lardner, John 23, 132, 243
Lazzeri, Tony 34, 88
Leach, Tommy 111
Lieb, Fred 52, 58, 66, 78, 104, 159, 263, 268, 277
Lindbergh, Charles 65, 75
Lindstrom, Fred 74, 155
Long, James 128
Lopez, Al 106, 309
Luque, Dolf 79

Malone, Pat 152
Mantle, Mickey 8
Manush, Heinie 213, 268
Maranville, Rabbit 42, 52
Martin, Pepper 7, 8
Martin, Speed 28
Mathews, Eddie 276
Mathewson, Christy 53
McCarthy, Joe 123, 202
McCarthy, William 29
McGinnity, Joe 19
McGowen, Roscoe 132
McGraw, John 39, 53, 58, 77, 95, 102, 131, 147, 148, 155
McInnis, Stuffy 46
McKechnie, Bill 44, 48, 51, 57, 95
McManus, Marty 7
McWeeney, Buzz 44
Mead, Margaret 103
Meadows, Lee 83
Meaney, Tom 44, 76
Medwick, Joe 153
Mencken, H.L. 180
Meusel, Bob 87
Miljus, Johnny 95
Miller, Dots 25, 26, 27
Mitchell, Clarence 48
Monahan, Kaspar 140
Moore, Corinne 75, 116
Moore, Eddie 36
Moore, Wilcy 7, 52, 85
Mungo, Van Lingle 194
Musial, Stan 189

Nelson, Baby Face 161
Nettles, Graig 80
Nettles, Jim 80
Nin, Anaïs 185
Noe, Beth 271

O'Connell, Jimmy 31, 35
O'Doul, Lefty 31, 32, 131
Olmo, Luis 250
Ott, Mel 53, 147, 283

Paige, Satchel 42, 154, 167
Parmalee, Roy 226
Paschal, Ben 87
Pennock, Herb 89
Peterson, Robert 160

Pierce, Billy 28
Pipgras, George 90
Porter, Lillian 270
Putnam, George 31, 32

Rennie, Rud 78
Reynolds, Allie 7, 311
Rhem, Flint 47, 76
Rhyne, Hal 31, 35, 44
Rickey, Branch 199, 250, 252, 271
Ripken, Billy 80
Ripken, Cal 80
Ritter, Lawrence 10, 296
Rixey, Eppa 79
Rizzo, Johnny 199
Robertson, Nic 266
Robinson, Wilbert 69, 88
Roosevelt, Franklin 162, 176
Root, Charley 49
Ruether, Dutch 90
Ruth, Babe 21, 23, 39, 80, 85, 105, 109, 127, 170, 181
Rye, Gene 133

Sandberg, Carl 42
Saulsberry, Charles 19
Schacht, Al 87
Scopes, John 29
Sewell, Rip 172, 208, 258
Sheely, Earl 117
Shocker, Urban 89
Simmons, Al 109
Sisler, George 43, 104
Slaughter, Enos 112, 199, 215, 229
Smith, Al 103
Smith, Casey 29
Smith, Chet 66
Smith, Earl 64, 77, 93
Smith, Wendell 222
Snyder, Francis 118
Speaker, Tris 104
Stalin, Joseph 113
Stallings, George 34
Stargell, Willie 8, 57
Steinbeck, John 169, 207
Stengel, Casey 227, 246
Stennett, Rennie 61

Stevens, Howell 241
Street, Gabby 145
Suhr, Gus 31, 43, 100, 129, 191
Suzuki, Ichiro 2

Talbot, Howard 311
Terry, Bill 54, 72, 79, 135, 142, 147, 155
Thorpe, Jim 10
Tobin, Jack 81
Traynor, Pie 55, 66, 82, 94, 106, 111, 143, 163, 182, 190, 195, 205, 210, 304
Twain, Mark 18
Tygiel, Jules 222

Uhalt, Frenchie 191
Updike, John 207

Van Baek, Clifford 102
Vaughan, Arky 100, 112, 149, 153, 165, 171, 217
Vila, Joe 114
Vitti, Carl 287

Wagner, Honus 39, 44, 57, 76, 91, 112, 155
Waner, Alma 9, 11
Waner, Etta 9, 21
Waner, Lloyd, Jr. 288
Waner, Ora 9, 10, 11, 15, 21, 22, 93, 169, 285
Waner, Ralph 9, 286
Waner, Ruth 9
Waner, Travia 105
Washington, Chester 195
Werber, Bill 233
Wertenbach, Fred 137
Williams, Dick (Nick) 20, 21
Williams, Joe 35
Wilson, Hack 123, 135, 142
Wilson, Owen 111
Wright, Frank Lloyd 185
Wright, Harry 4
Wright, George 5
Wright, Glenn 39, 83, 100, 106

Yde, Emil 90
Young, Cy 10

www.ingramcontent.com/pod-product-compliance
Ingram Content Group UK Ltd.
Pitfield, Milton Keynes, MK11 3LW, UK
UKHW041923140426
5217IPUK00014B/285